Anne Ogden Boyce

Records of a Quaker Family

The Richardsons of Cleveland

Anne Ogden Boyce

Records of a Quaker Family
The Richardsons of Cleveland

ISBN/EAN: 9783337403287

Printed in Europe, USA, Canada, Australia, Japan

Cover: Foto ©Suzi / pixelio.de

More available books at **www.hansebooks.com**

RECORDS

OF A

QUAKER FAMILY:

The Richardsons of Cleveland.

WITH PORTRAITS OF ISABEL CASSON, JONATHAN PRIESTMAN,
AND JOHN RICHARDSON PROCTER;

ALSO

NINE GENEALOGICAL TABLES, AND AN INDEX TO THE MARRIAGES.

BY

ANNE OGDEN BOYCE.

LONDON:

SAMUEL HARRIS & CO., 5, BISHOPSGATE WITHOUT.

1889.

TO

The Memory

OF

JOHN RICHARDSON PROCTER

AND

HIS DAUGHTER MILDRED,

THIS BOOK

IS OFFERED AS A LOVING TRIBUTE.

PREFACE.

Nearly twenty years ago I was asked to write a short memoir of my aunts, the three sisters, Elizabeth, Mary, and Hannah Richardson. At that time I thought it improbable that the story of their lives could be so told as to interest many persons—impossible that I could so tell it. But these twenty years have brought many changes! The Present, as we see it in our children, strangely reminds us of the Past of which we have only heard from our parents; and as we ourselves grow old, we turn with interest to picture the youth of those whom we only knew in age, a youth which, although passed amid surroundings so different, was yet filled with the same thoughts, feelings, and aspirations as that of the young to-day.

I have therefore tried, however feebly, to tell the story of the lives of these three sisters, with these differences and these resemblances, to the daily lessening circle of those who knew them well, to the larger circle of those who dimly remember them, and even to a new generation to whom they are known only by family tradition.

Attempting to revive their memory, I have been led on to write of those amongst whom they lived, and thus it has happened that a book, originally intended to be a Biography of three maiden sisters, has developed into what may almost be called a Family History. It was at one time my ambition to add to it a Genealogical Chart, comprising all the descendants of William Richardson, who was married to Elizabeth Wilson at Lythe Church, Whitby, in 1684. This was found to be impossible, but by the ability and perseverance of Mary Northcroft, my relative by marriage, the end has been obtained by dividing the families into nine Tables.   To facilitate reference to these Tables, and to render the Record more complete, an Alphabetical List of the Marriages has been added.

In spite of much care and labour, I fear that errors and omissions may still be found.   For these and for the many defects of the book, more especially for its discursive character, I solicit the indulgence of my readers.

To those members of the family whose kindness has rendered the Record possible, to Thomas William Backhouse, of Sunderland, from whose Genealogy the idea of the Marriage Index has been taken; to Robert Foster, of Newcastle, who placed at my disposal the materials collected by the well-known genealogist, Joseph Foster, for a Richardson Pedigree; and to the friends who have contributed their recollections of the heroines of the book, my warmest thanks are due.

The chapter on Ackworth School is based upon the valuable 'History' of the Institution by Henry Thompson, and the notice of Dr. Fothergill is abridged from James Hack Tuke's charming 'Sketch' of the life of that distinguished Yorkshireman, in the book published at Ackworth Centenary, 1879.

I have received kind assistance in many ways, and must here especially thank my friends Ernest Hartley Coleridge and Alfred John Greenaway.

The work could never have been undertaken had it not been for the 'Annals of the Richardsons of Cleveland,' printed by George Richardson forty years ago; and it could never have been carried to completion had it not been for the store of family writings and traditions entrusted to me by my late dear relative John Richardson Procter.

A. O. B.

THE CEDARS, CHERTSEY,
        October 26th, 1889.

CONTENTS.

PAGE

CHAPTER I.—CLEVELAND (INTRODUCTORY).   1

CHAPTER II.—AYTON, 1684–1740.

Marriage of William Richardson, of Ayton, in Cleveland, to Elizabeth Wilson, at Lythe Church, Whitby, in 1684—Extracts from a letter from their eldest son, John Richardson, of Langbarugh, describing the character of his parents and incidents in their lives—The Malt Kiln—An oath refused—Distraints—Affirmation Bill passed, 1702—Numerous descendants of William Richardson and Elizabeth Wilson   4

CHAPTER III.—WHITBY, 1688–1780.

Importance of Friends in Whitby in the seventeenth century—Henry Vasie, of Whitby—John Richardson inherits Langbarugh, and marries Lydia Vasie—Langbarugh—Margery Vasie—Her dreams—Descendants of John Richardson, of Langbarugh, and of his brother, William Richardson, of Ayton—The Hesletons, Martins, and Sewells—Isaac, third son of William Richardson, settles at Whitby, and marries Isabel Vasie in 1732—Bog Hall—Character of Isaac and Isabel Richardson—Their travels in the Ministry—Illuminations—Tar-barrels—Descendants of Ingram Chapman, of Whitby, by his marriage with Elizabeth Richardson   11

CHAPTER IV.—WHITBY AND STOCKTON, 1740–1792.

The Priestmans, of Thornton—Henry, third son of Isaac Richardson, of Whitby, marries Hannah Priestman in 1768—He settles at Whitby—Birth and death of children—He removes to Stockton in 1779—Birth of younger children—Mary Galilee, of Whitby—Death of Hannah (Priestman) Richardson in 1791—Childhood of heroines   20

CHAPTER V.—SCHOOLS, 1784–1800.

Day Schools in England a hundred years ago—John Chipchase—Girls' School begun at York in 1785—Esther Tuke its first Superintendent—Poem addressed to the York School Girls by Thomas Wilkinson, of Yanwath—The Lothersdale Friends—James Montgomery—Friends' Meeting in York Castle—Isabel's needlework—Younger Sisters at Stockton—Visit to the family of John Chipchase, at Cotherstone, in after years   27

CHAPTER VI.—Books for the Young, 1785-1805.

Few Children's Books — Mrs. Trimmer — Thomas Bewick — Day's 'Sandford and Merton'—Dr. Aikin and Mrs. Barbauld—Miss Edgeworth—Enfield's 'Speaker'—Mrs. Hannah More—'Miseries of Human Life'—Pope's 'Homer'—Letters of Meta Klopstock, translated by Elizabeth Smith—Remarkable personality of the translator—Old English Ballads—The 'Bee'—Lyrical Ballads published at Bristol in 1797—Sir Walter Scott's 'Lay of the Last Minstrel' in 1805—Writers since that date 35

CHAPTER VII.—Travelling, 1792-1805.

Langbarugh — Richardsons and Maysons, of Hull, and Peases, of Darlington—Richardson, Overend, and Gurney—Gilbert Baker, of Kew—Malton — Thornton — Adventurous Moorland rides on "double horse"—Whitby—Isabel Richardson's first visit to the Yearly Meeting in 1795—Journeys to London in those days—A visit to Edinburgh in 1805—"Maister Leslie" 46

CHAPTER VIII.—Isabel Richardson, 1800-1826.

Isaac, second son of Isaac Richardson, of Whitby, settles in London, and marries Sarah Mayleigh, daughter of Samuel Barnes, of Clapton—He returns to York, and builds a house at Cherry Hill in 1780—He dies in 1791—Isabel goes to Cherry Hill to reside with his sons, Samuel and William Richardson, in 1800—Her life there—William Richardson marries Martha Mildred in 1810—Isabel is recorded a Minister in 1812, and goes to reside at Hull with her cousin, Thomas Priestman—He builds East Mount—He marries Esther Tuke in 1817—Isabel's varied life—She marries Henry Casson, of Hull, in 1824—He dies in 1826—Affection between Isabel Casson and her husband's children—Her travels in Ireland and in America 58

CHAPTER IX.—The Low Lights, 1758-1834.

John, eldest son of Isaac Richardson, of Whitby, comes into Northumberland in 1758—He meets Margaret Stead—Her dream—He takes a farm at Seghill, and marries Margaret Stead in 1760—He removes to Pew Dene, afterwards called the Low Lights, in 1766—Description of the place and the family—Death of Margaret (Stead) Richardson in 1781—Second marriage of John Richardson—His ministry and influence over his children—His death in 1800—His widow's death in 1801—His son Henry settles at the Low Lights—Mary Richardson goes to reside there in 1802—Her life there—The Procter Family—Joseph Procter and Joseph Unthank take Willington Mill, on the Tyne—Hospitality at the Low Lights 63

CHAPTER X.—Elizabeth and Hannah Richardson, 1800-1809.

No "Golden Age" in English History—Country life sometimes dull to the young—Thornton—The Home at Stockton—Intellectual energy of Elizabeth and Hannah Richardson—Elizabeth's taste for art disapproved by Friends—Ill-judged interference—The two sisters resign their membership in the Society—They go to live in Derby to manufacture hosiery—Their plan fails—Their life at Derby—Miss Bennett—Death of their father in 1808—The homes at Derby and Stockton are broken up, and the sisters go to live in Newcastle in 1809—Rachel White, of Ayton, and her sisters . . 75

CONTENTS

CHAPTER XI.—NEWCASTLE-UPON-TYNE, 1809–1811.

Northumbrian accent—Newcastle in 1809—Life and character of George Richardson—King George's Jubilee—The sisters leave Newcastle in 1811, and go to reside in North Shields 87

CHAPTER XII.—LETTERS, 1811–1813.

Hutchinson's Buildings in 1811—Letters from Elizabeth and Hannah Richardson to their cousin, Jonathan Priestman—Coleridge's 'Friend'—Anna Seward's Letters—William Richardson, of North Shields—His strict Quakerism—Marriage Laws of the Society of Friends—Elizabeth's letters from Leeds—Marriage of Jonathan Priestman to Rachel Bragg in 1814—Elizabeth Richardson opens a Drawing School in Hutchinson's Buildings . 95

CHAPTER XIII.—NORTH SHIELDS AND SUNDERLAND IN FORMER DAYS.

North Shields in the Thirteenth Century—Tynemouth Priory—The Monk's Stone—An interrupted funeral—Parish Church built and consecrated in 1668—Dockwray Square begun to be built in 1763—Social life in Shields a hundred years ago—Schools—The War with France—"Starboard, John!"—Resistance to change—"Nee leets!"—The Library—The Steam Ferry—The green bag—Shields forty years ago—Subsequent changes—Sunderland—Some old stories—The Ogden Family—Solomon and Jane Chapman—Dr. Brown—Tom Taylor—Edward Backhouse 112

CHAPTER XIV.—CHANGES, 1818–1839.

Elizabeth Richardson opens a school in North Shields in 1817—Its success—She conducts it until 1839—Mary Richardson's active life at the Low Lights—Affection between her and the descendants of John Richardson—Excursions by the sea-shore—Marriage of Mary Richardson, of Langbarugh, to Joshua Wilson, of Sunderland, in 1802, and, after his death, to William Brown, of North Shields, in 1807—Mary Brown's death in 1817—Her husband's marriage to Sarah Richardson in 1821—Change in Hannah Richardson—She leaves North Shields for York 120

CHAPTER XV.—LINDLEY MURRAY, 1745–1834.

Lindley Murray born in Pennsylvania in 1745—Early life—Remarkable incident in his boyhood—Called to the American Bar in 1766—Marriage—Illness—Lindley Murray and his wife leave America for England in 1784, and they settle at Holdgate, near York—Lindley Murray a confirmed invalid—His writings—His interest in the Girls' School at York—His 'English Grammar' published in 1795, and followed by other works—Visitors at Holdgate—Hannah Richardson goes to reside there in 1814—Her life there—Correspondence with America—John Murray, of New York, and his family—Death of Lindley Murray in 1826, and of his widow in 1834—Hannah Richardson goes to Ackworth School 138

CHAPTER XVI.—ACKWORTH SCHOOL, 1778–1846.

The Foundling Hospital—Branch established at Ackworth in 1759—Zeal of its promoters—The branch abandoned in 1773—Building bought by Dr. Fothergill for a Friends' Boarding School in 1779—Remarkable Career of Dr. Fothergill—His garden at Upton—His friendship with Franklin, and attempt to avert American War—Sarah Grubb's letter, describing Ackworth School—Extracts from William Howitt's 'Boy's Country Book'—Joseph John Gurney—Robert Whittaker, Superintendent from 1804 to 1831—Fevers—Luke Howard — Temporary Depression of the Boys' School — Thomas Pumphrey enters as Superintendent in 1834—Hannah Richardson takes the post of Governess in 1836—She remains for ten years—Popularity of Girls' School during that time—Letter from a Mistress—The pet mouse—General Meeting of 1846—John Bright—James Hack Tuke—Changes at Ackworth since 1846 155

CHAPTER XVII.—Origin of Flounders' College, 1658-1846.
(Communicated by J. R. Procter.)

Thomas Procter, of Clifford, near Tadcaster—His grandson, Emmanuel, settles at Yarm—Emmanuel's son, Joseph, marries Jane Flounders—Early history of her brother, John Flounders—His marriage to —. Bickerdyke—Their son, Benjamin, marries Mary Walker, of North Shields—Her early death, and that of her only child—Benjamin Flounders inherits the Bickerdyke property on condition of leaving part of it for the benefit of the Society of Friends 218

CHAPTER XVIII.—The Sisters in Age, 1839-1869.

Elizabeth's visits to Yorkshire and to the Lake Country—Her accident—Mary's later years at the Low Lights—Marriage of Hannah Procter to Isaac Sharp—Visitors at the Low Lights—John Bright's first visit to Northumberland in 1838—Gives notice of his marriage at North Shields in 1839—Marriage takes place at Newcastle in November, 1839—Affection between John Bright and the family of his first wife—Marriage of J. R. Procter in 1847—Mary Richardson and her sisters live in Dockwray Square—Letter from Miss Priestman—The five sisters—Isabel's friends in Ireland and in America—Catherine Morris, of Philadelphia—Stephen Grellet—Change in Friends' dress—The miniatures—Ministers of Shields Meeting—Dr. Thomas Hodgkin—Charles Brown—Deaths of the sisters—The descendants of William Richardson in our day—Position of the Society of Friends 217

APPENDICES.

Abridged copy of letter of John Richardson, of Langbarugh — Abstracts of Wills — Copy of Isabel Vasie's Sampler — Letters of Isaac and Isabel Richardson, of Whitby—The Chapman Family—The Priestmans, of Thornton, near Pickering — A Whitby Household — The Richardsons and Maysons, of Hull — The Peases, of Fishlake, Yorkshire — Richardson, Overend, and Gurney — John Richardson's Farm and the Low Lights — The Procters, of Clifford, near Tadcaster—Willington Mill—Dr. Collingwood Bruce on George Richardson — Coleridge's 'Friend' — Solomon Chapman, of Sunderland—Dr. Joseph Brown — Lindley Murray's Publications — Rhymes on Ackworth School— Dr. Thomas Hodgkin on Charles Brown — Newspaper articles, and the Rev. D. Tasker's Sermon on John Richardson Procter 247

RICHARDSON, DAVID, of the Gables, Elswick, Newcastle-on-Tyne; m. at Spiceland Meeting House, parish of Culmstock, Devon, July 3rd, 1861, Catherine Fry 6, 10

RICHARDSON, EDWIN, J.P., River Wear Commr., &c.; m. March 24, 1864, Emma Phillips, dau. of John Walker of Brixton and his wife Mary Lake . 6, 10

RICHARDSON, FREDERICK, of Sunderland, m. at Cockermouth, Jan. 8, 1861, Sarah Maria, dau. of Jonathan Harris and his wife Sarah Hall Mason . . 6, 10

RICHARDSON, JOHN WINN, m. Sept. 6th, 1860, Mary, dau. of James Green of Shillingford and his wife Ann Rutter 6, 10

RICHARDSON, PHILIP, b. at Newcastle, 1865, son of Wigham Richardson and his wife Marianne Henrietta Thoel: m. 1891, Rosa America Colorado . . 6, 10

ROWNTREE, WM., b. 1843, son of Wm. Rowntree and his wife Ann Cooke; m. at Winchmore Hill, 1874, Amelia, dau. of Joseph and Ellen Amelia Dell of Stoke Newington 4, 10

SAINSBURY, HARRINGTON, M.D., m. Maria, dau. of D. Hack Tuke, M.D., and his wife Esther Maria Stickney 4, 10

SEWELL, JOSEPH STICKNEY, m. (1st) 1843, Mary Ann Ellis of Thornton; (2ndly) 1876, Lucy Ellis, of Belgrave, Leicester 4, 10

SLINGSBY, WM. CECIL, eldest son of Wm. Slingsby of Carlton-in-Craven; m. 1882, Alizon, dau. of Wm. Farrer Ecroyd and his 1st wife Mary Backhouse . 4, 10

*STICKNEY, WALTER MENNELL, of Danthorpe Hall, Holderness, farmer, member for the Aldborough Division of the East Riding of Yorkshire County Council, b. at Ridgmont, Dec. 1846, son of Joseph Stickney and his wife Eliza Mennell; m. at Hull, Sophia Helena, dau. of Alfred West and his wife Sarah Ann Petchell 4, 10

TAYLOR, ALFRED HENRY, b. at Malton, 1858, son of Henry Taylor and his wife Elizabeth Rowntree; m. 1884, Helen Rowntree of Scarborough . . 4, 10

TAYLOR, FREDK., b. at Malton, 1861, son of Henry Taylor and his wife Elizabeth Rowntree; m. 1887, Annette J. Fry of Ipswich 4, 10

THORNE, JAS. C., of Wiveliscombe, Somerset, m. Alice Mary, dau. of Joseph Stickney Sewell and his 1st wife Mary Ann Ellis 4, 10

TUNSTILL, HARRY, eldest son of William Tunstill of Reedyford, near Burnley; m. Jan. 8, 1879, at Little Marsden, Margaret, dau. of Wm. Farrer Ecroyd of Lomeshaye and his 1st wife Mary Backhouse . . . 4, 10

VATTER, EMILE GEORGES, m. 1891, Alice Emily, dau. of William Metford and his 1st wife Margaret O'Callaghan 4, 10

WILSON, GEORGE EDWARD, b. Feb. 7, 1860, son of Wm. Edward Wilson of Kendal and his wife Catherine Stacey of Tottenham; m. at Darlington, Oct. 8, 1884, Henrietta Rachel, dau. of Henry Pease and his 2nd wife Mary Lloyd . 9, 10

WILSON, WM. JOHN, m. 1863, Adeline, dau. of Charles Binns and his 1st wife Elizabeth Walmsley 4, 10

* This entry is inserted to correct a mis-statement on page 213. " The Stickneys have long ceased to be farmers."

HOLMES, BENJAMIN, of Lancaster Gate, b. at Sunderland, Nov. 16, 1830, son of John Gilbert Holmes and his wife Margaret Richardson ; m. at St. George's, Hanover Square, Nov. 29, 1878, Alice, dau. of James Fred. Wulff of Tooting and his wife Mary Ann Claisse 6, 10

HOLMES, WM. HENRY, b. at Newcastle, March 29, 1824, son of Wm. Holmes and his wife Ann Smales ; m. at Manchester, May 15, 1851, Mary Jane, dau. of John Beeby Brockbank and his wife Eliz. White 7, 10

HUTCHINSON, ALFRED, m. at Mount Forest, Ontario, Harriet (not Margaret), dau. of Alexander Allen 2

HUTCHINSON, ERNEST, m. at Holloway Meeting (not Westminster), Louisa M., dau. of Frederick G. Cash and his wife Maria Bowly 2

JOHNSON, WM., of Leeds, m. 1872, Lucy, dau. of Joseph Stickney Sewell and his 1st wife Mary Ann Ellis 4, 10

KING, HENRY, m. 2ndly Feb. 1860, at Hull (not York), Sarah Casson . . 2

KING, WM. SEWELL, b. at Birkenhead (not York) 2

KITCHING, ALFRED EDWARD, of Ayton Firs, J.P., D.L., &c., b. at Darlington, Oct. 20, 1858, son of Alfred Kitching and his wife Mary Ianson Cudworth ; m. at Stockton-on-Tees, April 24, 1884, Anne Backhouse, dau. of Joseph Richardson and his wife Ann Eliza Backhouse 6, 10

LLOYD, HENRY JOHN, m. at York, June 3, 1891, Emily, dau. of Henry King and his 2nd wife Sarah Casson 2, 10

METFORD, WILLIAM, son of Joseph Metford of Whitney and his wife Esther Rowntree ; m. (1st) 1865, Margaret O'Callaghan ; (2ndly) 187—, Thérèse Flory . 4, 10

PEASE, ARTHUR FRANCIS, b. March 11, 1866, son of Arthur Pease and his wife Mary Lecky Pike ; m. Oct. 1, 1889, Laura Matilda Ethelwyn, dau. of Charles Peter Allix, of Swaffham House, Cambridge 9, 10

PEASE, EDWARD LLOYD, b. March 4, 1861, son of Henry Pease and his 2nd wife Mary Lloyd ; m. Jan. 15, 1890, Helen Blanche, 4th surviving dau. of Sir J. W. Pease, Baronet, and Lady Pease 9, 10

POHL, HEINRICH, m. 1864, Marion, dau. of Jonathan George Binns and his wife Fanny Harker 4

PORTSMOUTH, NEWTON, Earl of, son of Isaac Newton, 5th Earl of Portsmouth, and his wife Lady Eveline Herbert ; m. Feb. 17, 1885, Beatrice Mary, only child of Edward Pease of Darlington and his wife Sarah Lloyd . . 9, 11

PUMPHREY, ARTHUR, b. at Newcastle, 1862, son of George Richardson Pumphrey and his wife Hannah Maria Sewell ; m. 1889, Helen Swinburne Dixon of Ayton 4, 6, 10

PUMPHREY, THOS. WALTER, b. at Newcastle, son of Thos. Pumphrey and his wife Emma Richardson ; m. 1889, Emily Knight . . . 6, 10

RICHARDSON, ARTHUR, b. at Newcastle, 1865, son of David Richardson and his wife Catherine Fry ; m. in London, Nov. 6, 1890, Lydia Susan Russell . 6, 10

RECORDS OF A QUAKER FAMILY.

(The Richardsons of Cleveland.)

✦

CORRECTIONS AND ADDITIONS TO THE MARRIAGE INDEX.

TABLE

BAUMGARTNER, RICHARD JOHN, M.R.C.S., m. 1887, Augusta Maria, dau. of James Richardson and his wife, Augusta Ann Dixon 6, 10

BINKS, CHARLES, m. at York, June 4, 1890, Esther Richardson, dau. of Henry King and his 2nd wife, Sarah Casson 2, 10

BLAKENEY, W. R., m. 1889, Eliz. Adeline, dau. of Wm. John Wilson and his wife, Adeline Binns 4, 10

BURTT, THEODORE, son of Henry Burtt, of Fulbeck, Lincolnshire, and his 1st wife, — Keymer, m. at Wellingboro', Sept. 25, 1890, Jessie, dau. of Henry Hutchinson and his wife Eliz. Richardson 2, 10

BUXTON, GERALD, eldest son of Edward North Buxton, J.P., D.L., &c., of Knighton, Essex; m. at Guisboro', Dec. 3, 1890, Lucy Ethel, dau. of Sir J. W. Pease, Baronet, and Lady Pease 9, 10

CHAPMAN, FRANCIS ROBERT HENRY, Capt. Bombay Staff Corps, son of Major-General Ingram Francis Chapman and his 1st wife Louisa Aplin; m. Feb. 17th, 1890, Margaret Hamilton, dau. of Wm. Ritchie of Dunnottar House, Stonehaven 7, 10

FOX, REGINALD W., son of Charles H. Fox, Shute Leigh, Somerset; m. at the Chapel, Benwell Tower, by the Bishop of Newcastle, Mabel, youngest dau. of John Wm. Pease and his wife Helen Fox 9, 10

FRY, LEWIS, of Goldney House, Clifton, M.P. for Bristol; m. at Saffron Walden, Sept. 1859, Eliz. Pease, dau. of Francis Gibson and his wife Eliz. Pease 9, 10

FRY, LEWIS GEORGE, b. July 8, 1860, son of Lewis Fry and his wife Eliz. Pease Gibson; m. Oct. 6, 1888, Agnes Chauncey Salisbury, of Brookline, Mass., U.S.A. 9, 10

GAYNER, ROBERT HEYDON (not Haydon), b. at Fylton (not Felton), Gloucestershire, son of John Gayner and his wife Martha Sturge Builder; m. Dec. 27, 1866, Emily Richardson 6, 10

GRAVELY, ARTHUR F., of Wellingboro', son of Frederic Gravely and his wife Eliza Stansfield; m. 1884, Margaret Hutchinson 2, 10

HARTLEY, WM. HARRY, only son of Henry Waddington Hartley of Fence Gate, near Burnley; m. at Nelson, May 30, 1888, Gertrude, dau. of Wm. Farrer Ecroyd and his 1st wife, Mary Backhouse 4, 10

HARRIS, HENRY, b. 1866, son of Henry Harris of Tottenham and his wife Eliz. Sewell; m. Margaret Prideaux Naish of Birmingham . . . 4, 10

A DAUGHTER OF HENRY RICHARDSON OF STOCKTON.

PROBABLY SARAH, AFTERWARDS THE WIFE OF WILLIAM BROWN
OF NORTH SHIELDS.

RECORDS OF A QUAKER FAMILY.

CHAPTER I.

Cleveland.

"Life has broken the slumbrous spell,
And it is not all good,—but it is all well."

WALTER C. SMITH, D.D.

FIFTY years ago, probably few people in the southern counties of England, unless they happened to be lovers of fine horses, had heard of Cleveland, in North Yorkshire; and probably no part of England was more profoundly wrapped in rural seclusion.

Yet Cleveland had not always been so unimportant. Before the days of written history, its early inhabitants dug their pit-dwellings upon many a moor and hill-top, from Whitby to Roseberry Topping, and both wrought and wore the Whitby jet.

And when our English forefathers came, and the Kings of Northumbria were Over-lords of Britain, Oswi built for the noble Lady Hilda an Abbey upon the cliff looking far over the wild North Sea. Here kings and bishops came to seek her counsel; here saints were numbered amongst her scholars; here arose the first strains of English poetry; and here, at the Synod of Whitby, was the fate of English religion decided for eight hundred years.

But these great days passed with the fall of the Northumbrian Kingdom and the coming of the Danes, who wrecked St. Hilda's Abbey, and who left their names and their size and their strength as an inheritance to the people of North Yorkshire.

B

When this stubborn race was at length subdued by the Norman Conqueror, its devastated lands were given to his followers, the Percies and Bruces. William de Percy rebuilt Whitby Abbey; Robert de Bruce founded, in a valley in the heart of the Cleveland Hills, the Priory of Guisborough.

The lofty towers of Whitby Abbey, seen far over sea and land, were a constant mark for the spoiler, and the monks lived in peril of their lives. Pirates entered their little harbour from the sea; robbers, whose fastnesses were in the neighbouring moors, assailed them from the land. Very different was the fate of Guisborough Priory in its valley: equally protected by its surrounding hills, and by the powerful Barons of the North, who extended over it their fostering care, who loaded its shrine with their lavish gifts, and who chose its walls for their last resting-place. Here lie the bearers of chivalrous names, Nevilles, Talbots, Fauconbergs, Percies, and, above all, the de Bruces, ancestors of the Scottish Royal House and of our present Queen. The priory has long stood roofless; the beautiful east front alone remains to tell of its departed glories, and green grass covers the stone coffins of the mighty dead. Forty years ago there could not have been imagined a scene of deeper peace than those hills enshrined.

Now the stillness of centuries is broken in the valleys of Cleveland, but not by monkish chaunt nor by knightly clash of arms. The invading armies are those of Toil, their weapons are the pickaxe and the spade, and the name of Cleveland ironstone is known in lands of which the Bruces and the Percies had never heard.

But the beautiful hills look down on us as they did on them: Roseberry, high and bare, with its singular pointed top, known for many a mile around; Cliffridge, with its softly-rounded, wooded outline;* Easby, with its long, straight line only broken by the monument of Captain Cook, who was born beneath its shadow.

And beneath the shadow of those hills, two hundred years ago, lived the sober persons with whom my story opens. Little, indeed, had they in common with knights and barons and the mediæval glories of Cleveland; but they seem to have transmitted to their descendants a love for its hills

---

* Since the above was written, I have been told that the "outline" of Cliffridge is no longer "softly rounded," and that the streets of Leeds are paved with stones quarried from the sides of that once beautiful hill!

and valleys, for its "becks" and "thorpes," and even for its ruined abbeys and priories whose names were household words in the ears of their children; one of whom now writes the names of Roseberry and of Guisborough with pleasure once more.

Biographies of Friends are wont to begin with some mention of the members of the family who first joined the Society: our record must follow the time-honoured rule.

CHAPTER II.

Ayton.

1684—1740.

"Keep thou my feet; I do not ask to see
The distant scene; one step enough for me."

CARDINAL NEWMAN.

STANDING upon the West Pier at Whitby, and looking towards the north, the eye rests on a little church on a hill near the sea. At this church of Lythe, William Richardson, of Ayton in Cleveland, was married to Elizabeth Wilson on the 31st of July, 1684. These bare facts the Parish Register gives us, but our knowledge of the character and history of these persons is derived from a letter written by their eldest son, John Richardson and dated "Langbarugh, 1756." It is addressed to a nephew, and was written for the purpose of informing the grandchildren of William and Elizabeth Richardson what manner of people their grandparents had been.

In such a document, written by a man who lived all his life on a farm amongst the Cleveland Hills, and who endeavoured in age to recall the memories of his childhood, we can look for no graces of style. But through the long, intricate sentences, utterly guiltless of punctuation,* the intense truthfulness of the writer makes itself felt, and it is this truthfulness that gives his narrative interest to those who trace their descent from the simple persons whose lives it attempts to describe.

From this letter (an abridgment of which will be found in the appendix to this book) we learn that William Richardson and Elizabeth Wilson were both educated in the principles of the Church of England, associating with its more serious members, and continued in communion with that church

* The only change made in the sentences quoted has been the insertion of stops where the sense required it.

until the time of their marriage. They were afterwards led to see that, for them, outward rites had little meaning; and believing that they saw the way to a higher spirituality in the doctrines preached by George Fox, they thought it right to join the Society he had founded. We are told, and can well believe, that only the strongest conviction induced them to become members of so despised and persecuted a sect.

William Richardson was by trade a tanner, and esteemed by his neighbours for his uprightness and integrity. As if in apology for dwelling little upon his father's character, the son says, "I must say most on my mother's account, being the most under her care in the house; while my father was caring for us out of doors."

The portrait he draws of his mother is full of striking details. We see her, in calm dignity, moving about her well-ordered household; "never seen to be in haste, neither in words nor works"; "never heard to laugh, yet always remarkably cheerful"; "seldom leaving the house, except to visit and assist the sick and those in want, or on some religious account": so placid in temper that her son often wondered "what passions she was naturally inclinable to?" To her twelve children she seems to have been a most tender and watchful mother; teaching them all to read and write, and to take pleasure in their books, and training them to habits of industry, and of innocent employment.

She was a Minister in the Society she had joined, and much of the letter is devoted to recording how earnestly she strove to impress on the minds of her children and of others its distinguishing doctrines. Love to God and love to man has ever been the key-note of Quakerism. John Richardson says of his mother, "As her heart was filled with His love, she longed to have us all filled with the same love to Him and to one another. Now, as her mind was then longing for the good of all, the Established Church of England was in her view; and she would express, at times, her regard for them, and her hope for many of them, though they performed several ceremonies in a way she durst not." After enlarging on these points of difference, her son says, "But though she thus laboured to promote the spiritual worship, and to lay aside outward performances, which too many were in practice of, without ever coming to the life of true religion, yet she had a great regard to all in the way she had been brought up in, who were careful to walk agreeable to what they professed, and believed it their duty to take bread and wine in remembrance of Christ. She was very careful not to discourage any in what they believed was their duty; but would endeavour to persuade them to 'prove all things, and hold fast that which is good'; and be sure not to act, in matters of worship of the Almighty, without faith to believe that what was to be done was agreeable to his will."

She advised, "Not to perplex ourselves about a day of judgment, as many do, how it may please the Almighty who made us, to order us then, but to be content to wait to hear this Preacher (in the heart) who preaches to all, with a loud voice: though it is loud to the humble (only), the proud and covetous will not hear it. . . . . . Be content to follow its directions, it is the Lord who made and upholds us; and it is His right to reign and rule in us here, and to do with us as He thinks best hereafter. . . . . If we cast our care upon Him, He will take care of us, now and for ever."

As to their daily life, she reminded her children of the precept, "Whether ye eat or drink, or whatsoever ye do, do all to the glory of God"; and that "as we remember Him, when we have bread to break, morning, noon, or evening, for the nourishing of the outward man, He, at such times, strengtheneth our faith in Him, so that our hearts are thankful for His favours every day, although all silent as to the outward ear."

"Much endeavour was used that we might take delight in our books, and in doing any little turns, if but innocent, though of little service. When very young, to play a little was allowed, but not on the first day of the week, which Christians have set apart for worship. And to play for anything, were it but for a pin or a cherry-stone, is better let alone. Childer have pride enough in overdoing one another without playing for anything. . . . . 'I remember the time when I would have fought for a cherry-stone' adds the old man.

"Though she had such care over us, lest we should do wrong, yet she behaved to us, when we did amiss, as she advised us to do to one another and to all; not to give one bad word for another, but to endeavour to overcome evil with good. 'Railing did but add fuel to the fire,' she often said, but 'a soft word turneth away wrath.' If one said 'it is,' and another said 'it is not,' there was a fault, because one must be wrong. To say 'I will' or 'I will not' was not to be in practice, because of the uncertainty of all things."

Thinking of all his mother's care and instruction in his childhood, John Richardson says, "Where I have been amiss, it has been my own fault"; and, speaking of the example of her life, "I have often seen, as I may say, her footsteps: whenever I tread in them, I have been sure to step safe, but there is no hitting them without taking up this daily cross, which, for want of, I have, at times, missed my way."

In another place he says, "I may not forget how thankful my mother often was that we, all of us, had the use of all our members, and were in a likely way to work for our livings, which she regarded as the safest situation in this life; only to have something whereby we may be rather helpful than needful."

He also says, "I cannot understand that they (his parents) meddled much with each other's business, for they well knew that they need not bid one another do their best; though I know they used to advise one with another in things of moment."

A remarkable instance of this "advising one with another" is given by their son. "Before I can remember, my father had built a malt-kiln near to his little tan-house. There was a good pump, which supplied his lead cisterns for steeping his corn, as well as his cisterns for tanning, and all things to appearance went on with good success. Although he had no great stock, he could get what money he thought proper to venture in trade. Things looked as though the advance of the income might answer the outlies of an increasing family. But this malt trade was soon over-turned; for my mother (as it was her daily care to wait to know what to do, and what to leave undone), thought it her duty to advise to let go that profit, though it seemed considerable, and need of it to bring up so great a family. I can remember (although thy father and I were so young that we were not fit to go anywhere with a horse) her saying to our father, 'If these lads live, and this malt-kiln be kept on, they may likely be sent to ale-houses with malt, and if they should get a habit of drinking, what will all that we can get signify? Let us part with it. I have no fear but that Providence will provide for us and them if we do as we ought. Let us be content with the tanning-trade.' "

This led to some discussion. It appears that William Richardson's neighbours had thought his malt-making a wise and prudent move; and he naturally disliked to appear changeable, and even regardless of his family's welfare in their eyes. But Elizabeth thought the opinion of the world of no consequence, if they did what they thought to be right, and her advice prevailed with her husband. The son says:—" So as nothing less than making all things useless for malt-making would do, the drying-place for malt was put into a little dwelling-house; the chamber where the barley was, was made a bark-chamber; the lead cistern was taken to tan leather in; the malt-chamber to lay corn in. Chambers were not then so plentiful among the farmers as they now are (1756), and a very plentiful crop of wheat, and very cheap: the farmers pressed on my father to take their wheat, as they knew he had a large family, and good lying for it. He bought as much as his chambers would hold, at or near two shillings a bushel, exceeding good. This proved well, for, harvest coming on, the weather was so wet that much of the wheat was wasted, and what was got into the barns was so bad it was not fit to use: if better could be had, and, bad as it was, it was sold for seven shillings per bushel. This looked like a favour, for, had the chamber not been cleared, we should likely have been obliged to live upon very ordinary wheat, as our neighbours did, and pay very dear for it. As it was, we had as good, if not the best, I ever knew, and the cheapest; but I cannot understand that things looking like the world's favouring any more lifted up, than its seeming to frown cast down.

" Now things took a very sudden turn for the tanning-trade, the only visible means for a livelihood. A duty was laid upon leather, and an oath or affirmation obliged to the entering of all leather taken out of the pit to dry. At the request of some of our Friends, the Government had, some time before this, granted an affirmation, which my father took once or twice, but the more he considered it the less he liked it."

In the amended oath, called an affirmation, granted to the Friends in 1696, the name of God was still invoked. It need not surprise us that William Richardson, after "considering it," refused to take it, or that his wife supported him in his refusal, saying, "Dare we call the Almighty to be a witness on every worldly concern?" Yet we can also well imagine that, to the magistrates and their officials, it was somewhat provoking that this new form of words, granted by the Government, did not satisfy those for whom it was intended, and a time of great trial to the Friends followed. In William Richardson's case, a fine was imposed every time he refused to take the oath, and leather was taken away to pay the fine. The "high looks" and upbraiding words of an official person, who came for this purpose, were remembered by the son, and the calmness by which these reproaches were met by his parents. The trial was a heavy one. Repeated fines swallowed up a third of their little property. They had money borrowed at six per cent. interest, "which was as common then as three and a half per cent. is now," writes the son in 1756.

William Richardson, at one time, entertained the idea of giving up the tanning business, while he had enough money left to pay what he owed. But his steadfast wife still counselled patience and trust, and even the giving up of all, for what they believed to be right. The magistrates, before whom William Richardson was brought many times, became convinced that his scruples were not from conceit or obstinacy, and their officers testified that he was more careful not to "wrong the King" than many who swore readily. His case, and that of many other Friends, was represented to the Government of the day, and a measure was passed by which a simple affirmation was accepted in lieu of an oath from members of the Society of Friends.

This event occurred in 1702, when Queen Anne was on the throne, and the much-abused eighteenth century was beginning to run its tolerant, peaceful, and prosperous course in England. The family of which this history treats participated in its peace and prosperity. The son says, "This trial being over, ... in a few years they had more of the world's wealth than before; it looked as though there had been a confirming of what had often been said, that 'All things work together for good to those who love God.' ":

William Richardson was "esteemed by rich and poor," and his sons found the advantage of inheriting his honest and honourable name. He and his wife had their family-sorrows, three of their daughters dying in early life. One of these, Martha, an unusually intelligent and attractive child, died of small-pox in her ninth year. A description of her engaging qualities, and of the circumstances of her illness, may be read in her brother's letter, from which all these details are taken. It unfortunately contains no dates, except its initial one of 1756, but we know from other sources that Elizabeth Richardson, the devoted mother described in its pages, died in 1718 when some of her children were still very young. Her husband survived her until 1740, dying about the age of eighty. Of the twelve children of this couple, nine lived to be married; but the families of the four elder daughters, Mary, Rachel, Rebecca, and Sarah, appear to be extinct.*   The descendants of the remaining daughters—Hannah, who married Daniel Fossick, and Lydia, who married Richard Richardson, of Hull—and of the three sons, John, William, and Isaac, are sufficiently numerous. In 1839 they were said to be more than three hundred, and we may well shrink from the task of computing their numbers in the present day.

The majority of these descendants of William Richardson and Elizabeth Wilson continue attached to the Society of which their ancestors were such devoted adherents, and in that middle class of English life in which the strength of that Society has always lain. Many of them are well known within its borders, and some even beyond them. Such are the Rowntrees, of York, known as philanthropists, and as good "citizens of no mean city," one of whom was its first Quaker Lord Mayor; the Stickneys, of Ridgmont, marked by their individuality and strength of character, one of whom was the authoress, Mrs. Ellis; Thomas Richardson, founder in his youth of the great firm of Overend and Gurney, promoter in his old age of the Ayton Agricultural Schools; Gilbert Baker, of Kew, the botanist of world-wide reputation; and the Peases, of Darlington, whose energy has transformed the old home of their ancestors, and has carried the name of Cleveland over the world, and who, in 1832, gave the first Quaker member to Parliament.

But we must return from the nineteenth century, when Friends are Judges, High Sheriffs, and Lord Mayors, to those earlier times, when they were much more likely to be brought as culprits before those awful personages.

---

* See Table I., 'Richardsons of Cleveland.'

CHAPTER III.

𝔚𝔥𝔦𝔱𝔟𝔶.

1688—1789.

"She layeth her hands to the spindle, and her hands hold the distaff."
"She openeth her mouth with wisdom, and in her tongue is the law of kindness."

Proverbs.

SOME of the persons mentioned at the end of the last chapter are descended from the daughters of William Richardson, of Ayton. Turning to the records of his descendants in the male line, we meet again and again with a type of character which resembles his own. We find the Richardsons, as a rule, men diligent in their worldly callings, endowed with sound sense and with practical judgment, tall and stalwart in person, with good constitutions, with long lives, and with large families.

William Richardson had three sons, John, William, and Isaac. With the eldest and the youngest we are first concerned, and their marriages take us back to the town of Whitby.

At the end of the seventeenth century the Friends of Whitby appear to have been a numerous and important body. In their annals we meet with many names known afterwards in other towns than Whitby, and in denominations other than the Society of Friends. Such are Linskill, Chapman, Wakefield, and Lotherington. Another name is that of Henry Vasie, who was a ship-owner and ship-builder in the town, and of whom solid memorials descended to our own times in the shape of silver tankards presented to him upon the launching of different ships. A more frail memorial lies before me, being a sampler worked by the hands of his youngest daughter, Isabel, at the age of eleven, in the year, sadly famous in Northumbrian ears, of 1715. Isabel's sampler records the marriage of her parents, Henry Vasie and Mary Mackridge, in the still more famous year of 1688, and of the birth, to them, of many sons and daughters.

A copy of the will of Henry Vasie, made in 1726, "when sick and infirm of body," remains in the possession of one of his descendants. He divides his property equally amongst his eight children: two sons, two widowed daughters, and four unmarried girls. These last, Mary, Lydia, Margery, and Isabel, alone concern this history.

After Henry Vasie's death, his daughter Lydia was sought in marriage by John Richardson, to whom we owe the letter so largely quoted in the last chapter. He inherited the Langbarugh Estate from his father's brother, John; and to the house on that property, which is about a mile from the village of Ayton, he took his wife.

As I write the name of "Langbarugh," the memory rises before me of a long, low house, almost hidden to its red roof by climbing roses; of a large garden, bounded on two sides by low walls, overgrown by flowers and fruit-trees, and on a third side stretching away into an orchard carpeted in spring with snowdrops and daffodils. There were many seats and arbours in the garden; and, opening a door, you passed from it directly into a long, low parlour, known in those days as "the house," where there was a sort of sofa, which was called a "squab." This room had many doors besides the garden-door: one led to the cool, sweet-smelling dairy; a third opened into an inner room; a fourth (to the amazement of town-bred children) directly upon a staircase which led to the upper rooms, or chambers, as they were called, one of which, less old than the rest, was called "the new chamber," and one, where fruit was stored, "the apple chamber."

Old Langbarugh stood at the foot of a hill, as did most houses of its day. New Langbarugh stands above it, a handsome, well-planned house, built in 1833. I believe it is now called "Langbarugh Hall." But it is about the old rambling-place that the memories cluster. A paradise of beauty it appeared in the eyes of a child from the bleak banks of the Tyne, half-a-century ago. Did it look as fair, we may wonder, in the eyes of the bride from the banks of the Esk a century before, when George the First was King?

John Richardson invited his wife's three sisters to make their home at his house. While the proposal was under consideration, Margery—one of the three—had a dream. She dreamed that she saw her father distinctly, and heard his voice telling her that, should she and her sisters accept the invitation of their brother-in-law, each of them would meet her future husband at Langbarugh. It may be that the dream had some influence in deciding the question; it is certain that they agreed to go, and that the foretold events followed in due time.

"I tell the tale as 'tis told to me."

In these days of "Psychical Research," another family tradition of the same mystic Margery may have some interest. She had retired early to bed one evening, and was sleeping in the inner room, which, it has been said, opened out of the parlour at Langbarugh. A late visitor arrived suddenly from Whitby, bringing news of an event which, although only too frequent on that stormy coast, does not by frequency lose its terrors. The Vasie family had a cousin at sea, and the news brought by the visitor was that the ship he sailed in was lost, and that all on board had perished. Upon the ears of the excited group in the parlour came the voice of Margery, who had been awakened by the discussion. "My cousin is not drowned," she said. "He is saved! I can see him now in a boat full of water." Whether the rest of the party took any comfort from this assurance we do not hear; but the news arrived in due course that the cousin's life was indeed saved, and that he had been in a boat which at one time was full of water.

Mary Vasie met her husband at Langbarugh, as Margery's dream at Whitby had foretold. His name was George Myles. Of the dreamer herself I grieve to know no more, not even the name of her husband; and as the rules of the Society of Friends forbade the marriage of first cousins, we dare not hope that the rescued sailor was reserved for her.

In 1732, the youngest girl, Isabel, married Isaac, the youngest son of William and Elizabeth Richardson. All these marriages are supposed to have taken place from the hospitable home of Langbarugh, and to have been solemnised at the meeting-house in Ayton Village. On the marriage of Isaac Richardson, the small house at Ayton in which his parents had lived was settled upon his wife Isabel. To ensure the legality of the document, John Richardson, of Langbarugh, signed it as heir-at-law to his father.

Other members of the same family, Christopher and Nicholas Richardson, resided at Ayton. They were probably descended from an elder branch, as their estates were larger than that of Langbarugh. They were never connected in any way with the Society of Friends, and doubtless looked with little favour upon their relative's change of faith.

William's brother, remembered in village tradition as "Old Johnny of Langbarugh," may have also joined Friends, as the marriage of his only daughter, Ann, to Robert Shields in 1687 appears to have taken place at Broughton Meeting-house. Ann died early, leaving no child, and her father left his property to his brother's eldest son, because he bore his name.

This son, the John whose letter has been quoted, and who married Lydia Vasie, died in 1786, at the age of eighty-eight. He left a son, William, who resided at Langbarugh for ninety years, from his birth there in 1736 to his death in 1826.

William married Mary Muskett from the county of Norfolk. She was a lively, sociable woman, and, during her sway, great hospitality reigned in the old house at Langbarugh. She and her husband had five daughters, and, their elder sons all dying in early life, it seemed as though only girls would be left to inherit the land. The birth of a younger son, John, in 1795 was therefore a very important event, especially to William Richardson, and the child of his age ran great risk of being spoiled by over-indulgence. Fortunately, when about twelve years old, the boy himself begged to be allowed to go to a school in Darlington, kept by a Friend named Joseph Sams. It was with great difficulty that William Richardson (then seventy years old) was induced to part from his son, and his last words to the boy were, "Now, John, if thoo doesn't like it, just tak a chaise and come home." The boy had, happily, too much sense to take advantage of this suggestion, and, having fair abilities, he made good use of his time under Joseph Sams, and afterwards under Joseph Tatham at Leeds. Little trace of the Cleveland dialect could be observed in John Richardson's speech or reading, although he resumed the homely accent at will. His father, William Richardson, at the end of his long open-air life, could never resign himself to sitting in the chimney-corner, as old men do. One day, having been out in heavy rain, he would not be persuaded to put on dry clothing, saying, "I have gone out all my life without minding the weather, or thinking of changing my clothes, and I won't begin now." When, in consequence of this imprudence, he died from a chill, his death (at ninety) was considered to be decidedly premature.

His son, John, lived on the same estate, although not in the same house, for eighty-seven years, from 1795 to 1881. He married a relative, Jane Procter, of North Shields, in 1833, and it was for her that the new house on the hill was built. He and his wife had seven children, but none of them reside at Langbarugh. On John Richardson's death, in 1881, it passed from the family.*

Returning for a moment to the first William Richardson, and his wife, Elizabeth Wilson, it may here be stated that their second son, William, lived at Ayton, during his long life of ninety-four years, from his birth there in 1700 to his death in 1794. This second William, of Ayton, was twice married, and by his first wife, Mary Robinson, of Rounton, he left many descendants, some of whom were conspicuous figures in Ayton fifty years ago. The Hesletons were quiet country gentlemen, straying little from their native village, where the beck ripples between the red-roofed, grey stone houses, where "a cloud on Roseberry" gives warning of a coming storm to all Cleveland, and where life was so very peaceful and so very long! Some of William's descendants have strayed far out of sight of Roseberry. The Martins and Armstrongs have, long ago, settled in Western America; and another descendant, Joseph Stickney Sewell, has, in our own day, been a Missionary to Madagascar.†

Isaac Richardson took his wife, Isabel Vasie, back to her native town of Whitby. They lived at Bog Hall, a plain, grey stone house, still standing in a little hollow near the banks of the Esk, on the landward side of the town. A tablet above the door bears the inscription, "William and Ann Foster, 1719." These persons were probably the builders of the house, and its first inhabitants, but nothing is known of them. A stone's-throw off are the remains of the small tannery where Isaac Richardson carried on the same business as his father; and on the other side of the house, across a flagged pathway, is the garden, now neglected, but still showing the traces of former care. A pear-tree grows against the house. It is now let to poor families, but it retains an appearance of solidity and comfort. Isaac and Isabel Richardson lived for many years at Bog Hall. They must have had many relatives in Whitby. Of the Vasie family,—Isabel's brothers and sisters,—we have no information; but the children of Isaac's eldest sister, Mary, who married John Ward, of Whitby, and of Rebecca, who married Timothy Chadwick, certainly lived in that town.

* See Table II., 'Richardsons of Langbarugh.'
† See Tables III. & IV., 'Richardsons of Ayton.'

A man of delicate health, of keen affections and nervous and sensitive temperament, Isaac Richardson found a true helpmeet in Isabel Vasie. She has been described as "a most peaceable woman," and she seems to have possessed the strength and firmness which is sometimes found in persons of that type of character. She and her husband were both recorded ministers in the Society of Friends, and, in that capacity, visited many parts of England. The south-western counties, including the city of Bristol, and all the northern counties, Isabel visited on horseback and alone. A visit to the county of Norfolk, and another to London and the places near it, was made in company with her husband, riding with him "on double horse"* in the primitive fashion of the day. These journeys involved no small self-denial to the mother of a family, for let no one suppose that the grave Quaker women who thought it right to become preachers of the gospel, either in that generation or succeeding ones, were neglectful of their home affairs. Isabel Richardson's daughter, Mary Gallilee, herself noted for her housewifely qualities, described her mother as "of great energy, and very industrious habits; rising early to accomplish her domestic engagements, so as to prepare her family for the diligent attendance of meetings," held not only on Sundays, but on two week days at Whitby, in the zeal of those early times. "Her industry and management were such that much of their clothing was of home manufacture."† Her eldest son never had a coat of bought cloth until his marriage.

The Vasie family have been said to be of noble origin. Any solicitude upon such a point would ill become a Quaker biographer; but, if the belief be true, it proves that such kinship may consist with the homeliest virtues.

The middle of the eighteenth century, the date at which our history has now arrived, was a time of religious peace. The prevailing faults of the clergy of the Church of England were not those of zeal. The older Dissenting sects had somewhat cooled in fervour, and diminished in numbers. Methodism, from its rise in a tolerant age, had never suffered from the strong hand of the law as Quakerism had done a hundred years before; but both sects at times met in full force the

* "On double horse." This expression was made use of when a lady rode upon a cushion (called "a pillion seat") placed upon the horse's back behind the saddle. The horseman was supposed to wear a belt, by which his companion held; failing the belt, the large buttons of the day were made use of.

† 'Annals of the Richardsons,' page 29.

hatred which singularity in religion sometimes excites in the rougher classes of English people. Some of the minor peculiarities of the Friends brought them into collision with the populace in its moods of excitement. Dwellers on the coast know well that the mob of a seaport town, though rarely cruel or vindictive, is reckless and rough. Isaac Richardson has left it on record that the mob of Whitby three times broke his windows and destroyed his property, because he, like other Friends, refused to illuminate his house on occasions of public rejoicing. Of the first two of these calamities we only know that he suffered severe loss; of them he has left no details. They were probably days of rejoicing over victories gained by English troops; and, as the Friends objected to all war, their refusal to join was consistent. We can less understand their abstention from rejoicing on the coronation of the young King George the Third in 1761; but our business is to record, not to criticise. That day had been looked forward to with no pleasant feelings by Isaac Richardson, who feared a repetition of former losses, and even the occurrence of greater ones, as his third son, Henry, was engaged in the flax business, and his warehouses stored with that inflammable material, and his "heckling chamber" adjoined the street, "where the rude creatures used to run with squibs and burning tar-barrels." However, times had improved in Whitby. The narrative goes on to say:—"The rulers of the town took more care to keep the rabble in subjection than they had ever done before, and my neighbours, who aforetime had been ready to laugh at me, and to make light of my suffering, showed me kindness, and assisted in dispersing the rude people, so that through the mercy of Providence, I suffered little damage."*

We may rejoice that this gentle, sensitive man, who hardly seems to have been of so strong a nature as his father, fell upon milder times. Fifty years later, the French Revolution and the long war which followed it, lighted afresh in England the almost extinct fires of political and religious hatreds, and stirring scenes occurred in some northern seaport towns. In Sunderland, blazing tar-barrels were rolled along the streets to burn down the house of a Friend who would not illuminate on some occasion when popular feeling ran high. The work had begun when a

* 'Annals of the Richardsons,' page 85.

gentleman whose sympathies were with Friends, but who, not being a member of the Society, was not bound by its regulations, hurried to the barracks and appealed to the officer in command. The soldiers were soon on the spot, and the half-burned house was saved.

Isaac Richardson died in 1780 of a fever. His widow wrote a short account of his life, which is given in the appendix to this volume. In it, speaking of his daily life, she says, "I may truly say he was a man fearing God and hating covetousness."

Isabel Richardson survived her husband nine years, dying in 1789, at the age of eighty-four. Her grandson, George Richardson, says of her, in the 'Annals':—"She passed her declining years in much peace and tranquillity, frequently having one or other of her grandchildren residing with her. She was of a weighty and serious deportment, as I well remember, and at times endeavoured to sustain the office of peace-maker amongst her friends and relatives."* In such a town as Whitby, a hundred years ago, when the energy of people of strong character was pent up within somewhat narrow limits, such an office was sometimes required, even amongst the members of the Society of Friends.

Isaac and Isabel Richardson had eight children, five sons and three daughters. The eldest daughter, Elizabeth, was married to Ingram, eighth son of Solomon Chapman and his wife, Ann Linskill. The Chapmans were a very old Whitby family. Elizabeth Chapman died when on a visit to her father's house in 1773, at the age of thirty-eight. A touching letter is preserved, written by Isaac Richardson to his eldest son, giving details of the event. Another daughter, Mary, who married George Gallilee, will be again mentioned in these pages. She and her younger sister, Isabel, who married William Hudson, have left no descendants, but those of Ingram and Elizabeth Chapman are very numerous. Their eldest daughter, Ann, married Michael Watson, of Raby. The Watsons were an old Durham county family, in which there was a dormant baronetcy. Michael's brother was a physician in good practice at Staindrop, but he himself was always a poor man, distinguished by quaint wit and humour, but with little practical faculty. He and his wife lived in their old age at the meeting-house at North Shields, and their children— all more or less original and eccentric characters—were in comparatively

* 'Annals of the Richardsons,' page 29.

humble positions in life, some being makers and menders of umbrellas. Being Friends, Ann Watson and her descendants are recorded with due honour in the 'Annals,' but Ann's brother, Ingram, son of Ingram and Elizabeth Chapman, is somewhat curtly dismissed:—

"Their son, Ingram, was a seaman and ship-owner. On his marriage with a near relative, he left the Society of Friends. He died in London, whither he had gone for medical advice, leaving two children."*

The "near relative" whom this second Ingram Chapman married was Jane, daughter of John Chapman and his wife, Jane Mellor. The marriage at church of these two young people, both of them Friends, seems to have been an important event in the family, and to have been celebrated in verse by one of its ready rhymers.

Of the "two children" mentioned above, the son, Ingram, was married at Bombay in 1827 to a daughter of General Willis; and the only child of the marriage, Major-General Ingram Francis Chapman, of the Bombay Army, is now living at Weymouth, and has many sons and daughters.

Elizabeth, the daughter of Ingram and Jane Chapman, married David Vesey, of Huntingdon, and had three sons and a daughter. One of the sons, the Rev. Francis Gerald Vesey, is now Archdeacon of Huntingdon and Canon of Ely. Such are the vicissitudes of a Quaker family!

Hannah, younger daughter of Ingram Chapman and Elizabeth Richardson, married Gideon Smales, of Whitby. The grandchildren of this couple are very numerous in the present day. Some of the grandsons of Gideon Smales are still prominent persons in the old town of Whitby, and many of the granddaughters are married to clergymen of the Church of England. Other branches of the family continued to be Friends, and, of these, some have intermarried with the Chapmans and the Richardsons.†

Of the five sons of Isaac Richardson, the third son, Henry, must first be noticed. He was the father of our heroines.

---

* 'Annals of the Richardsons,' page 40.

† See Table VII., 'Chapmans of Whitby' It will be seen that Michael and Ann Watson had but two grandchildren, both of whom married and had children. One, now deceased, married a man of culture and ability, Walter Jenkinson Kaye, Principal of Ilkley College.

CHAPTER IV.

Whitby and Stockton.

1768—1792.

"Oh! blest with temper whose unclouded ray
Can make to-morrow cheerful as to-day."

POPE.

In the records of all families, the marriages are very important. Some have reconciled rival houses and ended cruel wars; others have affected the fate of kingdoms, and the course of history. By some brides, retainers have been added to the warrior's train, broad lands to his estate, fresh quarterings to his escutcheon. But humbler brides may bring precious dowries. Who can compute the value of the bright, cheerful companion to the harassed brain-worker? of the strong, steadfast spirit to the wayward genius? of the woman with constant sympathy to the man of many cares? Above all, in the records of a Quaker family, amongst whom women have always held so prominent a place, must the marriages be held important, and it must be evident to all who have read this simple history that, in the Richardson family, much has been inherited from the "spindle side." To the portrait of Elizabeth Wilson, drawn for us by her son, we need not add one word. To the sterling qualities of Isabel Vasie, her children and her grandchildren have done justice. These women had the gravity natural to the members of a persecuted sect, who had borne, without flinching, first the terrors of the law, and afterwards the unbridled fury of the mob. This firmness won for their descendants peace and respect, and is worthy of our reverence. But, with the next marriage we have to chronicle, it seems as if brighter threads crossed the web of our sober history.

The Priestmans have left the quiet homes of their ancestors, and have become dwellers in large towns,—energetic citizens,—makers of mighty machines. Yet doubtless they all look back lovingly upon the early homes of their race. To the old York house, in Mary-gate,—almost under the shadow of the venerable Abbey, and hardly more hallowed by such neighbourhood than by the holy lives spent within its own walls by the gentle men and women amongst whom John Woolman died in 1772,—to quaint old Malton by the Derwent; and to Thornton, the first known home of the family.

Many wooers came to that lovely valley in the early days of King George the Third. The "Priestman of Thornton" of that day had many sons, and one fair daughter. Tall, blooming, bright-eyed, smiling, cheerful, she stands before us in that peaceful place, in that long past time, as depicted for us by family and local tradition. More lasting portraits, alas! belong not to the Quaker biographer. The only daughter of the house, she was prized in her home. "Aye, there's many a one wants her," said the old nurse at Thornton, "but I am maist feared o't tow man." Henry Richardson was a flax-dresser.

The nurse's "fears" were realised. The "tow man" won the prize from all other wooers. He was married to Hannah Priestman at the meeting-house at Pickering on August 11th, 1768, and it was doubtless on a pillion seat behind him that he bore her away from her father's house at Thornton across the moors to Whitby. Heavy troubles awaited the bright young bride in her new home. Whether from some epidemic, or merely from the keen winds from the North Sea, we have no information, but her first five children died in early life, leaving her and her husband childless. We know only the bare facts, but they speak to the heart of every parent. Five more children, two sons and three daughters, were born to them at Whitby. Of these the youngest was our heroine, Elizabeth, born in 1778.

About this time, and continuing until the end of the century, there seems to have been an exodus from Whitby of many of its principal inhabitants. Some of them fixed their residence in Newcastle, and some in Sunderland. One of them, John Walker, was already settled in what was then a newly-built quarter of North Shields—Dockwray Square. Doubtless Whitby, shut in from the outer world by its moors, already began to be thought a stationary and old-world place in comparison with the towns on the Wear and the Tyne.

Henry Richardson left Whitby about the year 1779, but he did not travel so far north as did many of his fellow-townsmen. He settled at Stockton-upon-Tees. This ancient corporate town was, at that time, a rising river port, with Custom receipts of £6000 per annum, and a population of 3000 persons. Henry Richardson was now an iron merchant, as well as a flax merchant. He settled with his family in a large, red house in the main street of Stockton, near to the then newly-built bridge over the Tees. Here our other heroines were born, Mary in 1780, Hannah in 1783, and then some younger children, of whom a son and daughter survived to later life.

Very varied dispositions soon manifested themselves in this group. Elizabeth, Mary, and Hannah are the subjects of this book, but another sister must here be mentioned. Isabel, just older than Elizabeth, was a fair flaxen-haired child, mild and gentle; so nervous, that their tutor's "Child, where are thy wits?" entirely scattered those wandering particles; so timid, that she trembled at crossing the Ouse in the York ferry-boat, yet she lived to cross the Atlantic, and to traverse America as a preacher.

Very different from her was Elizabeth, fearless, bright, ready in speech and in action. When a visitor asked the difference in age between the two little girls, it was always the younger who answered, "A year, a month, and a day," before the meek elder sister could begin to falter a reply.

Mary, when about nine years of age, spent nearly a year at Whitby with her aunt, Mary Gallilee. Travelling was then too difficult for short visits, and it is probable that this lengthened stay influenced the child for life. Aunt Gallilee's name was one often upon the lips of her nieces. To the gentle Isabel it had been a "name of fear." But Mary was a child after her aunt's own heart, and she instilled into her little namesake her housewifely ways, and initiated her into many secrets of cookery and of needlework, which the child never forgot. It was Aunt Gallilee who, a rigid economist in her daily life, used to say, "There are three times when I never grudge money: the one is when I go from home, the second is when I entertain my friends, and the third is when there is sickness in my home or my family." It was Aunt Gallilee, too, who, when she paid a visit to a bride or any relative in a new house, was wont to pass her fingers lightly over the top of the door, and, if any dust adhered to them, to warn the lady that she had yet to learn the duties of a mistress.

In her youth she had, in Quaker phraseology, "married out of the Society," and was accordingly "disowned" by it. Her husband, however, afterwards became a "Friend," and she was "reinstated in membership." In later life, she was reproving a young Friend "who appeared inclinable to marry in a manner contrary to the rules of the Society." The retort was obvious. "But, Mary Gallilee, thou didst the same thyself." "I did, but my husband was one of a thousand," was Aunt Gallilee's reply. Yet an impression seems to have prevailed that this stalwart ship-owner was not so entirely master in his own house as every Englishman is supposed to be. When "Aunt Gallilee" was remonstrated with upon the subject, she attempted no denial of the charge, but would answer, "Well, and what matter does it make so long as he is managed for his own good?" It was said that in his later years, when he proposed to walk out for pleasure, she would say, "What dost thou want to go out for? mucking thy shoes." In her old age she had a grievance which was often cropping up. "Bury it, bury it," said a younger friend. "Aye, aye, bairn, but where will I find a sod big enough to cover it?" was Aunt Gallilee's reply. It is grievous to know that no descendant of this vigorously-minded woman survives in our day. Mary Richardson's memories of her were those of affection and respect, and her sayings were often quoted with approval, though sometimes with a smile.

Hannah, three years younger than Mary, was a lively, active child, disliking confinement to lessons and needlework, and loving the freedom of the open air. She grew up tall and vigorous. They were a happy group around their grave father and their cheerful, amiable mother. The differing dispositions of the elder children were receiving her careful guidance and sympathy, the younger ones were still the objects of her tender care, when, in 1791, the loving mother was taken from them. The elder girls, amidst their own grief, were awe-stricken by that of their father. He was a firm, reticent man, and they had never before seen him weep. He knew, far better than they could do, how irreparable to him and to them was the loss. Isabel long mourned the mother upon whose love and sympathy her timid nature was so dependent, while the younger children vaguely felt that some bright protecting presence had been withdrawn from their young lives.

The eldest daughter, Ann, naturally became the head of her father's household; but it was Mary, the child of eleven years, who soothed the little ones, and took them under her loving care. She it was who knitted the warm socks, and who, very soon, made and mended the little garments, and saw that the dresses were trim and neat. Visitors found her sitting at home, absorbed in these cares, while Elizabeth and Hannah were running about the woods and fields.

Another sorrow fell upon the household in the death of the eldest son, Henry, from consumption. He inherited the sweet disposition of his mother, and, though his illness was long, his sick chamber was never a place of gloom or despondency. Isabel often spoke in after years of her brother's constant cheerfulness, and described how, when they entered his room in a morning, after hearing his cough almost all night, he would still answer their enquiries with a bright smile and "Oh! I'm bravely." The youngest sister never forgot how he liked her to climb up to kiss him, and how he had always a packet of sweets hidden under his pillow to give an added pleasure to the visit. When Henry and his mother died, two sweet and loving influences were withdrawn from the home at Stockton.

Another sad event happened in the year 1791. Rachel, the third daughter of William and Elizabeth Richardson, of Ayton, had married Francis Husband in 1713. Francis and Rachel Husband lived at Stockton, and their youngest daughter, Catherine, married Jeremiah Henderson, and had an only son, Robert. This young man, the sole survivor of his branch of the family, was in a rowing-boat on the sea off the coast of Northumberland, near Alnemouth, when he was overtaken by a storm, during which he perished. The event made a great sensation in the family, and books which had belonged to Robert Henderson were treasured in memory of him and of his tragic fate.*

We have few details of the children's daily life. Isabel remembered the first umbrella possessed by the family,† and how they walked up and

---

* See Table I., 'Richardsons of Cleveland.'

† Henry Richardson was much more tolerant of the new invention than another Friend, Robert Foster, of Hebblethwaite Hall, a remarkable man who is described in one of Southey's letters. His daughter, Mary Spence, related that, as they were returning from meeting one Sunday morning in heavy rain, a neighbour offered her father an umbrella. The old naval officer's answer was civil, but emphatic: "I am obliged to thee, James, I despise them!"

down the back garden with it in fine weather, delighted with the new possession.

To a younger sister, who was passionately fond of music, the passing through the town of a military band was a memorable event; and she told of the miles they would walk to prolong the pleasure.

All of them loved wild flowers, and, as they grew older, long rambles were taken to spots where they grew. The immediate neighbourhood of Stockton was, at that time, somewhat denuded of wood. The local historian states that, for that reason, "a walk by the new bridge and an island in the river below the town were planted with trees by George Sutton, Esq." This gentleman was the great man of the little town, and was commonly called "Squire Sutton." He and his wife were, like others, attracted to the bright little children of their Quaker neighbour, and made overtures of friendship, inviting the little girls to tea. They were allowed to accept the invitation, and became frequent visitors, although much amusement was caused by the little creatures addressing their kind host and hostess as "George Sutton" and "Grace Sutton."

The leader in all their games and escapades was Elizabeth. When very young, she was once seen upon the top of a wall by an old legal gentleman of the town. He called angrily to her, "Come down, come down, you will kill yourself!" shaking his stick at her in a threatening manner. She undauntedly replied, "Neighbour Wright, it is not thy wall." The quaint answer disarmed the old lawyer, and he and the child became friends. It was in no daring adventure, but in a game of play in an empty warehouse belonging to her father, that Elizabeth seriously injured her knee. She hopped about, making light of the accident, and no one perceived its gravity. When it was too late, medical advice was taken, and many remedies tried, but she was lame for life. She was for some weeks under the care of persons who were called "the Whitworth Doctors," who had an establishment to which persons resorted who needed surgical aid, somewhat as invalids went to Ben Rhydding, in its early days, to be cured of their maladies, before hydropathic establishments became great pleasure resorts. But neither from authorized nor from empirical sources did Elizabeth obtain much help. At one time she used crutches, managing them with such dexterity, and moving with such swiftness, that a woman passing her in the street said, "Lame, she's none lame!" She soon discarded her crutches, nor did she even use a stick; but her free enjoyment of open-air life was over. Her indomitable energy had to seek other fields for its exercise.

CHAPTER V.

Schools.

1784—1800.

" In ancient York, by Clifford's hoary tower,
  I passed a portion of the musing hour;
  Creative fancy marshalled to my view
  The scenes which York, in long past ages, knew.
  Round Clifford's Tower, an army I beheld,
  Gloomy and fierce, impelling and repelled;
  But from my mind the dismal picture fades,
  As, near its base, passed on a troop of maids,
  Led forth in order, with religious care,
  To meet their Maker in the House of Prayer;
  To wait His presence, and in holy fear,
  Worship the One on High with hearts sincere."

T. WILKINSON.

IT has been said of Boston, not of course of the humble town in Lincolnshire, but of its far greater namesake, that "One half of its society had gone to school with the other half, and they knew each other's ages to a day." *

Something like this was true of the smaller English towns a hundred years ago; and, if it were any drawback in later life, that a native of Stockton or of North Shields could, like a Bostonian, "no more hide his age than a crowned head could," there was yet some compensation in the kindliness of feeling which endured between those who had sat side by side on the same benches, had read out of the same books, and had learned the use of the same globes. But, alas! the day schools of England, in those days, bore no resemblance to those of cultured Boston. The education imparted depended entirely upon the individual schoolmistress.

* 'The Bostonians,' by Henry James.

If a clever woman "set up a school" in a town, it was well for the inhabitants; otherwise, too frequently their children's education was in the hands of very incompetent persons.

The day school in Stockton attended by the children of Henry Richardson was kept by a married lady with a young family, whose energies were severely tried by her conflicting duties. Except the mere rudiments of learning, and proficiency in needlework, we imagine the girls owed little to her teaching. But at that time, and for many years afterwards, a boys' school was conducted at Stockton by a Friend, John Chipchase, whose attainments greatly exceeded those of the poor over-worked lady. It was arranged that he should occasionally come in the evenings to give the children an hour's lesson. The house in Stockton had, like most old houses, large kitchens, and the clean and well-warmed front kitchen was set apart for the evening's lesson. There the tutor used to walk up and down, imparting his instruction, and upon one occasion, as he was about suddenly to take a seat to inspect some writing, a scream of "Stop, John Chipchase, stop," hardly saved the good man from sitting down in a bowl of milk! The perturbed instructor resumed his walk, shaking his coat-tails to dry them, while as to the pupils, we fear "that day they read no more." But, although milk, even in a Friend's house, might for once be out of place, and children many times be merry out of season, the warmest esteem and respect subsisted between John Chipchase and his pupils, both then and in after years.

For the elder daughters of Henry Richardson, Ann and Isabel, the teaching of the day school, and of John Chipchase, was supplemented by their being sent to a boarding school at York, opened in 1785, under rather remarkable circumstances. It was thought that such a school was needed for girls who, from age or other circumstances, were not likely to be sent to the large school at Ackworth, which had been recently established for the education of the children of "Friends not in affluence," at the charge of eight guineas for the year of fifty-two weeks. Ackworth School has its own place in this history, which at present is concerned with the smaller establishment at York.

Nine "Women Friends" were the shareholders in the undertaking, and the first Superintendent was Esther Tuke. This lady, born Esther Maud, was the second wife of William Tuke, whose name is known to the

world as the Founder of the Retreat at York, the first Lunatic Asylum
begun in England upon the system of kindness with moral control, as
opposed to that of severity with mechanical restraint. Esther, the wife of
William Tuke, must have been almost as remarkable a person as her
husband. From the early days of the Society of Friends, the women of that
religious body have held their own meetings, monthly and quarterly, to
watch over the welfare of the individual members of their own sex, their
marriages, changes of residence, &c., and to answer the "Queries"
addressed to each meeting, as to the character and conduct of its
members. The answers to those "Queries" were sent up to a Yearly
Meeting, held regularly since 1678, "in the week called Whitsun week,"
at Devonshire House, in Bishopsgate, London, by "Men Friends" alone.
The journey to London was probably thought too formidable a one for
"Women Friends" to take every year, and we hear of no wish for a
"Women's Yearly Meeting" until the last quarter of the eighteenth century.
But that was a time of change. During one of the sittings of the
Yearly Meeting of 1784, it was announced that two "Women Friends"
were at the door, desiring admittance: one of these visitors was Esther Tuke.
The Clerk of the Yearly Meeting holds a position resembling that of
the "Speaker" in a more august assembly. Tradition says that as the
stately woman and her companion walked up the meeting, the clerk felt
inclined to address her in the words of Scripture, "What wilt thou, Queen
Esther, and what is thy request? It shall be even given thee to the half of
the kingdom." Her "request" was for a "Women's Yearly Meeting,"
and a document authorising its establishment was at once issued by the
assembly she addressed.

This queenly woman and her husband undertook the care of the new
school at York, which was opened on New Year's Day, 1785. They gave
their services gratuitously, furnished their own apartments, and paid a
handsome sum as their board for living in the family. Some of William
Tuke's daughters and other young Friends, also gave their services, so
that for some years the sewing mistress was the only paid official.
During the thirty years of the existence of this school, its fees were
raised from time to time, until they finally reached the sum of thirty
guineas. In 1799, "a native of France" was engaged to teach his own
language; but at first the education was a plain English one, and the fees

fourteen guineas for the year of fifty-two weeks.   There were no vacations.
The teaching was of a very thorough character, and especial attention was
given to the art of reading aloud.   On Sunday evenings, the elder girls
read the Scriptures to the assembled household, and to any visitors
who might be present.   One of these visitors has described the scene
in verse :—

> " On Sabbath evening, pleased, I saw you meet,
>   Beloved girls ! like forty sisters sweet,
>   All of one Parent; innocent and fair,
>   Alike in vestments, and alike in air ;
>   Round one mild maid, a still attention hung,
>   While Gospel truths fell gently from her tongue ;
>   Alternate three, His sacred precepts read,
>   And how His life the dear Messiah led."

The schoolroom on a week-day morning is thus described :—

> " With eyes attentive, bending o'er the page,
>   They gather wisdom for maturer age ;
>   Or trace, with hearts affectionate and kind,
>   The lines of love to parents left behind ;
>   O'er fingers bend the linen, white as snow,
>   That distant brothers may their kindness know ;
>   Or plant with steel, in purple, green, and white,
>   The alphabet with every thread aright ;
>   Or through the canvas lead the Tyrian twine,
>   Till colours rise that Joseph's coat outshine ;
>   That coat, recorded as a showy dress,
>   Led not to harmony or happiness,
>   But in my sex it sowed the seeds of ill
>   In brothers' bosoms, envy, and ill-will.
>   Oh ! gentler sex, let never gay attire
>   Such alien feelings in your breasts inspire."

It was after a visit to his niece, then a pupil at the school, that
Thomas Wilkinson, of Yanworth, wrote the 'Affectionate Address to those
who compose the Tower Street School at York ' from which these lines are
quoted.   The poem is not the author's best work, but it is a pleasure to
associate with this record of simple people, the name of a man who, tilling
his land with his own hands, was the chosen associate of such men as Lord

Lonsdale and of Edmund Burke, and the intimate friend of Thomas Clarkson and of Charles Lloyd. So strongly did the union, in Wilkinson's life, of refined taste with rustic toil appeal to Wordsworth, that he has immortalised in his verse the humble implement of that toil as a "tool of honour."* Many admirers of Wordsworth have wondered who was the "rare master" of the spade whom Wordsworth not only claims a "friend," but acknowledges as a "poet"; and it was a happy thought in a near relative of Thomas Wilkinson to revive his memory in a charmingly written biographical sketch.†

For the girls of the York School was written the famous Grammar of Lindley Murray: and for them were compiled the 'English Reader,' the 'French Reader,' and many other books by the same author.

Another noteworthy circumstance happened to these school girls. They were taken to a Friends' Meeting held in York Castle. In the year 1796, a number of Friends from Lothersdale were imprisoned in that fortress for refusing to pay tithes. They were allowed to hold meetings on Sunday in a large room, where some of the debtors joined them; and on one occasion the forty girls of the school were brought to the meeting by Ann Tuke. Their "modest and grave deportment" is recorded by one of the prisoners with pleasure, and their young faces must have brightened the gloomy place.‡ The poet, James Montgomery, was at that time also imprisoned in York Castle for a "Patriotic Song" published in his newspaper, the 'Sheffield Iris.' He wrote with much affection of his Quaker fellow-prisoners, and describes one of them, Henry Wormall, as "My principal and best companion, a very gay, shrewd, cheerful man, with a heart as honest and as tender as his face is clear and smiling." Montgomery's Hymn, beginning "Spirit, leave thine house of clay," was written on the death of another of the Lothersdale Friends.

The needlework executed by the York School girls merited the admiration of Thomas Wilkinson, and would be equally admired in the present day. While a pupil there, Isabel Richardson worked a map of England and Wales upon white silk, in which the shape of each county

* See Wordsworth's lines, 'To the Spade of a Friend,' beginning "Spade! with which Wilkinson hath tilled his land."

† 'Thomas Wilkinson,' by Mary Carr. Reprinted from 'Friends' Quarterly Examiner.'

‡ 'Historical Sketch of York School,' by Lydia Rous.

was defined with an exactness of outline equal to any work of the engraver. This was done in chenille, whilst the names of the counties and of the chief towns were worked in silk. Some liberty of action must have been allowed, for the names of Ayton and Guisborough were carefully inserted, while those of more important places less familiar to the worker might be sought for in vain.

As to dress, Isabel Richardson was wont to say :—" I was made into a little woman when I went to York School at fourteen. I wore very high-heeled shoes, and my hair was strained up very tight both before and behind, and done up on the top of my head." A little round cap was worn on the top of this erection by the elder girls. To the washing and doing-up of these caps, a morning was occasionally devoted by both teachers and scholars : a very great penance to the latter. In those days of muslin caps and handkerchiefs, clear-starching was almost raised to the dignity of a fine art. Membership in the Society of Friends seems to have been thought essential to the attainment of the highest standard of " clearness." Much labour was subsequently saved by the introduction of net as an article of wear amongst lady Friends. This change occurred about the reforming and utilitarian period of 1830. Caps and handkerchiefs of this material could be intrusted to the care of persons "not in membership," but the refined delicacy and beauty of the earlier dress was not equalled.

But, in spite of any little trials, there is no doubt that Isabel Richardson was influenced for life by the teaching and examples of the devoted women who took charge of the York School as a labour of love. It was probably through their mother's influence that Ann and Isabel were placed there : how long Isabel remained after her mother's death is not known, but none of the younger girls were sent to York. Often in later life did they regret this fact, and contrast their writing with that of their more favoured elder sisters; yet it is only doing justice to their instructors at Stockton to say that (if we except Mary, whose well and tersely-expressed letters were hastily scrawled in the brief pauses of her busy life) the sisters all wrote good, clear, legible hands; that they read aloud with taste and feeling; and that their spelling was faultless. So well known was Elizabeth's skill in fine-darning, that she had only too many opportunities to exercise that accomplishment. Embroidered muslin aprons were then fashionable, and the sisters used to say,

"Everybody brought their aprons to Bessy to darn, because she did them so beautifully."

The impress of Quakerism, much deepened in Isabel by the influences under which she was brought at York, was less strong upon the four younger sisters. Remaining longer at the day school, they formed more intimacies with their schoolfellows and neighbours, whose names were associated with the memories of their happy youthful days. The younger sisters, to their latest years, spoke with the greatest affection of ladies of the name of Beckwith, one of whom married a gentleman well known as Secretary to one of the great London Companies.

To us the most memorable figures amongst the Friends of Stockton are John Chipchase and his daughter, Hannah. For their old tutor, simple, kindly, and learned, if a little formal in speech, the sisters had the highest esteem and respect, and for his daughter they had the warmest affection. She corresponded with them to the end of her long life, and always met them with pleasure.

It must be quite fifty years ago that the writer of these pages, staying with her mother at the delightful old town of Barnard Castle, accompanied her on a visit to Cotherstone, where Hannah Chipchase then lived. Cotherstone is a beautifully-situated hamlet in the heart of the "Rokeby" country, and close to the junction of the Balder with the Tees. But personal incidents make more impression upon a child's mind than scenery, however beautiful; and the meeting of the rivers is less vividly remembered than an overturn from a carriage into a ditch, which resulted in sad consequences to the spotless white shawl of Hannah Chipchase. This misadventure occurred during a drive at Cotherstone, and, confidence in the driver having been somewhat rudely shaken, he and his horse and vehicle were sent back to the inn at Barnard Castle, from which they had been engaged. The return journey to Barnard Castle was made in a safer, if in a somewhat slower fashion. A Friend, of Cotherstone, who had a farm, drove the party in her cart. The effect of her rosy, sunburnt cheeks in the close silk bonnet then worn by Friends, her energetic management of her horse, and the greetings, full of kindly respect, which she received from the occupants of carriages which passed her cart with great difficulty in the narrow country lanes, were very striking.

F

The Friends of Cotherstone were a simple, homely community. One of them, Caleb Wilson, was at the time of this visit a very old man. Anecdotes were related about him, of which two may be given here, as characteristic of the time and of the place. At a Monthly Meeting held in a town where the Friends were more remarkable for their ability, energy, and force of character than for their complete unanimity of sentiment, the small numbers and "weakness" of Cotherstone Meeting formed the subject of discussion. At length Caleb Wilson rose in his place and said, "We know we are few, and we own we are weak, but we love one another." The other story was of some strong man in mortal sickness, and in anguish of body and mind, who said to those around him, "If Caleb Wilson were beside me, I think I could die in peace." A messenger was sent to the simple farmer, who was no preacher, and whose life alone had shown to his neighbours what Master he served. He came and laid down by the side of the dying man, and, cheered by this companionship, the perturbed spirit passed peacefully away.

CHAPTER VI.

Books for the Young.

1787—1808.

"My never-failing friends are they,
With whom I converse day by day."

SOUTHEY.

"My blessing on them,—one and all,—
Immortal Story-Tellers."

UNKNOWN.

"WHAT charming books children have now, as compared to those we had when we were young!" is an exclamation which we often hear. And with reason is this said to children to whose service have been devoted the artistic skill of Randolph Caldecott, and of Kate Greenaway; the rare literary genius of Robert Louis Stevenson, the weird fancy of George Macdonald, and the sweet pathos of Mrs. Ewing. Yet the same exclamation was often upon the lips of our parents with regard to what seemed to them *our* wealth of books fifty years ago. That wealth would appear poverty in the eyes of the children of to-day. What, then, would be thought of the still more scanty store of a hundred years ago?

But that scanty store was dearly prized in spite of—perhaps because of—its meagreness, and some of the treasures of our little heroines have reappeared in our own day. One of these, 'Goody Two Shoes,' has been reproduced in form and fashion much as they knew it in their childhood. The 'Looking Glass for the Mind,' with Bewick's woodcuts, a favourite then, is a precious possession now; and some who have preserved it, bind the well-worn book in costly and dainty raiment—unadvisedly, from the point of view of the book-collector.

Mrs. Trimmer's 'History of the Robins,' an especial favourite with the younger sister of our heroines, was out of print when she sought it in vain for her child in the "thirties" of this century. Her grandchild, living in its later decades, possessed illustrated copies of the work in scarlet and gold, but these external glories did not prevent her from thinking it a very dull book.

As to illustrations in the children's books of that day, they were coarse daubs indeed; but, on the other hand, it was an age of great engravers. Happy indeed must have been those little ones whose early taste was nurtured on the masterpieces of Boydell, and of Dawkins, Watson, and of Strange. Of these, our heroines may have had but brief glimpses; but the books of Thomas Bewick were to be found in nearly every Friend's house in the North of England. The 'Birds,' the 'Quadrupeds,' and, above all, the magnificent volume of 'Æsop's Fables,' with its curious "tail-pieces," played some part in the education of the children who were permitted to study them. Another work, perhaps more freely entrusted to the hands of children, was 'Cook's Voyages,' in the original large quarto volumes. Captain Cook was a hero indeed to all people of North Yorkshire birth or descent; for was he not born at Marton, amongst the Cleveland hills? and did he not go to school at Ayton? and were not his ships, one and all, built at Whitby, and manned by Whitby sailors? The pictures in his 'Voyages' of New Zealand chiefs, fearful with tattooing and feathered head-gear, and of soft-eyed island women, with necklaces of pierced shells, were a constant source of mingled terror and pleasure.

But when we come to books for children's reading, the store is indeed a scanty one. First on the list must stand those favourites of all time, the 'Pilgrim's Progress' and 'Robinson Crusoe.'

When Mr. Thomas Day decided not to print the long preface he had written to 'Sandford and Merton,'—"because it was possible no one might read the work itself,"—he could little have anticipated its immense celebrity, first as a book possessed by almost every child in England, and then as subject for burlesque. Recently its use as a Reading Book in Board Schools has been attacked in an evening paper, and defended in the 'Saturday Review.' The teaching of 'Sandford and Merton,' in accordance, as it was, with "plain living and high thinking," recommended it to Quaker parents, and to their children it was a welcome gift indeed.

But a still more favourite book, both with young and old, was the

'Evenings at Home' of Dr. Aikin and Mrs. Barbauld. This volume is happily not unknown to the children of the nineteenth century, who, if they have far outgrown the science of 'Evenings at Home,' may yet profit by its wisdom. If there be some formality in its language, there is no narrowness in its sympathies, which are bounded neither by class, nor creed, nor colour. Its lighter papers had a wonderful charm for the children of a Friend's family. 'Alfred' was generally the first drama they ever read, and 'Order and Disorder' one of the first fairy tales. It is right to say "one of the first," in speaking of the children of a hundred years ago, for fairy-land was not an utterly unknown country to them. Our little heroines had certainly heard, whether by tradition or reading, of Bluebeard and the Giant-Killer, of Ali Baba, and of Sinbad the Sailor. To us, whose childhood was passed in the "thirties" and "forties" of this century, when the atmosphere was, almost oppressively, laden with "Useful Knowledge," those personages had no existence. Our children live in the days of the romantic revival when fairy lore is again the fashion.

Dr. Aikin's valuable 'Biographical Dictionary,' although well known in Friends' houses, hardly comes within the scope of this chapter. Another work of his was the 'Woodland Companion,' a description of British trees. It contains excellent representations of the foliage and of the fruit of each tree. It was an especial favourite with the sisters, and Mary's well-worn copy is in the possession of the writer of these pages.

From the old house at Stockton, too, came the delightful volumes which contained 'Old Poz,' the 'Barring Out,' and 'Eton Montem.' The name of Edgeworth was held in high esteem by our heroines. The 'Essay on Practical Education,' by Richard Lovell Edgeworth, was a book highly valued by Elizabeth, and in after years she possessed nearly every work of his gifted daughter, some of which, like 'Castle Rackrent' and the 'Absentee,' deal with problems which the wisdom of our time has yet to solve.

Miss Edgeworth's moral standard is certainly of the highest. Her favourite characters are brave, generous, and true, and have a wholesome scorn of meanness and self-seeking. She had power to touch the finest minds. Sir Walter Scott is "said to have wiped his kind eyes as he put down 'Simple Susan.'"* Ivan Turgénieff said, "It is possible, nay probable, that if Maria Edgeworth had not written about the poor Irish of the County Longford, and of the squires and squireens, that it would not have occurred to me to give a literary form to my impressions about the classes parallel to them in Russia."† Sir Rowland Hill, as a boy, read and re-read her stories. They deeply impressed him, and he resolved to follow in the path she traced, and to do something before he died to benefit his fellow-men. Thus it may well be that we owe, not only touching pictures of peasant-life in Russia, but the Penny Postage in our own free England, to the influence of Miss Edgeworth, and that the 'Saturday Review' has reason in attributing many errors and follies of our day to the fact that few of those who are now men and women ever come under that influence.

With solid literature, every Friend's house was well supplied, and the sisters, especially Elizabeth, were ardent students. The names of the scientific writers whose works they read are forgotten; but there were the travels of Mungo Park, and of Bruce; the Memoirs of Sully, and of Mrs. Hutchinson; the histories of Rollin and of Robertson. Gibbon was excluded because of his anti-christian spirit, but the same objection was not enforced against Hume, whose many volumes were generally to be found in a Friend's library. Goldsmith's writings (his plays, of course, excepted) were there—his 'Animated Nature' and his 'Citizen of the World.' His Histories, of Greece, of Rome, and of England, if not models of research, are never dull; and they, with 'Plutarch's Lives,' were read with pleasure by children who, having few fictitious heroes, had more admiration to spare for real ones. Dr. Johnson's 'Lives of the Poets' and his 'Rasselas' were well known, and also those solid productions which that great writer pleased to call his 'Ramblers' and 'Idlers.' Addison's 'Spectator' was in every Friend's house, and stray volumes of the earlier periodicals, the 'Guardian' and the 'Tatler.'

There were some books written expressly for young people. The 'Tales and Reflections' addressed to his children, by Dr. Perceval, of Manchester, strikes us now as a somewhat dull book, and the 'Pleasing Instructor' as a particularly *uninstructive* one. A fashion prevailed for

* Miss Thackeray's 'Book of Sibyls,' page 55.
† Ibid. page 140.

'Eastern Apologues' and 'Oriental Tales,' and the results were not always edifying. A better collection was the 'Gleaner,' printed in Scotland; and Dr. Enfield's 'Speaker,' graced by a picture of Sterne's "Maria," and containing the fine speeches of Lord Chatham against the American War, was a book by no means despised in a later day. By the children now in question, it was eagerly read for its extracts from Shakespeare and other dramatists, known in no other way. There was also a 'Female Speaker,' with varied extracts of a somewhat milder character.

A well-known book of that day was called 'The Miseries of Human Life.' The writer was probably one to whom the real meaning of the word was unknown, for they are very minor "miseries" which are described in a series of vivid sketches; one being the scene of discomfort presented by your ordinary sitting-room if you happen to descend to it at an unwontedly early hour. Less widely read, perhaps less ably written, was a book published afterwards, and called 'Antidote to the Miseries of Human Life.' This was a narrative of a long journey by stage-coach. Amongst the passengers are two Friends, Deborah Placid and her daughter Rachel, whose appearance and language are very well described. That the girl's quiet manner hides a most sensitive disposition is shown by her distress on seeing an animal run over; and the calm courage with which both Friends bear the discomforts and perils of the journey, which include the furious driving of a drunken coachman, and the terribly profane language of some of the passengers, is depicted in a manner designed to prove that they possessed some "Antidote" to such "Miseries of Human Life."

The writings of that excellent woman, Hannah More, were of course read by all Friends. A copy of 'Cœlebs in search of a Wife' was presented to Isabel Richardson on its publication in 1805. About that time a Friend of York brought home a bride, the fame of whose sweet qualities preceded her from the southern county, where she had lived, to her new home in the North of England. Her name, "Priscilla," recalled that of Hannah More's heroine. "Surely another Lucilla is coming amongst us," said the young Friends of York. The alarm of the poor bride was great on finding herself identified with that pattern of propriety in whom Cœlebs found his happiness. Young readers, then as now, wearied over the record of her perfections, and longed for some more human and faulty heroine.

It will be seen from the foregoing list of books that, in the family described, the reason was more fed than the fancy. The door of a Friend's house was kept carefully closed against the entrance of prose fiction ; but, by a happy inadvertence, a window was left open which overlooked the fair garden of Poesy, full of delight for youth. In every generation of Friends known to the present writer, there have been minds to which the poet appealed. He met with keener sympathy beneath the closely-crimped cap of the young Quakeress than beneath the feathers and jewels of the votary of fashion ; and even the grave and reverend seniors of the Society were readers and admirers of the poets. Their chief favourites might be Milton, Goldsmith, and Young, but the poet after their own hearts was Cowper. His love of the country, and of quiet domestic life,—his hatred of oppression and of cruelty, whether to man, beast, or creeping thing,—were in unison with the whole spirit of Quakerism. His poems were a reading-book in every Friends' school, and a valued possession in every Friend's home. But, by the young, Cowper was chiefly read for his ballads. 'John Gilpin,' 'Alexander Selkirk,' and 'Boadicea,' appealed more to them than the 'Task' or 'Expostulation.'

Most young people have their memories "infested by tags of rhyme." Sir Walter Scott in his youth "shouted old Border ballads about the house." "Great words of Goethe, quip of Beranger," were ever on the lips of Matthew Arnold at Oxford. Strange as it may seem, the poetry most "on the lips" of little Friends a hundred years ago, whether they lived on the banks of the Tyne or on those of the Tees, was the 'Iliad' of Homer, in the version of Alexander Pope. Hector was the hero of their imagination, and his death an abiding grief. Many were the children then who could have said, with the gifted author of 'Eothen,' "I, too, loved Homer, but not with a scholar's love. The mesh of Pope's English cannot screen an earnest child from the fire of Homer's battles." Referring to the exalted praise of Homer, in the preface to Pope's translation, Mr. Kinglake says:—"I assented with all my soul. I read and re-read. I came to know Homer. A learned commentator knows something of the Greeks, as an oil-and-colourman can be said to know something of painting, but take an untamed child, and leave him alone for twelve months with any translation of Homer, and he will be nearer by twenty centuries to the spirit of old Greece. It was not the recollection of school or college learning, but the rapturous and earnest reading of my childhood, that made me bend forward so eagerly to the plains of Troy." And he afterwards speaks of his school-learning, as "small shreds and patches of Greek thrown like a pauper's pall over all your early lore."

In those days, there were few translations of the Greek tragedians, and to the children who delighted in Pope's Homer, Dryden's Virgil had an especial charm, for it told the fate of that wonderful city whose story had so enthralled them. Not only a hundred years ago, but fifty years ago, these two books seemed to stand out amongst all others. At that time the Greeks and Romans seemed much nearer to us than they do now. Nothing worth mentioning seemed to have happened in history between the fall of Rome and the signing of Magna Charta, no literature to be worth studying between the "Augustan age" of Rome and that of France and of England. But a glimpse into the ages of chivalry was given by Tasso's 'Jerusalem Delivered,' through the rugged translation of Hoole; and the 'Orlando Furioso' of Ariosto, and part of the great work of Dante were known to our heroines.

At that time the language and literature of Germany were known to few persons in England. Translations of the writings of Lavater, of Zimmerman, of Baron Haller, and of Sturm were esteemed in Friends' houses; and the poetical prose of Gessner's 'Idylls' was well known to the sisters. Klopstock was then esteemed the greatest poet of Germany, and what was called in those days an "elegant" translation of his 'Messiah' had been made by Mr. Sotheby. A translation of the letters between Klopstock and Meta, the first wife of the poet, excited great interest in Quaker circles, not only on account of the attractive character of Meta Klopstock, but of the still more remarkable personality of the translator, Elizabeth Smith. This young lady, who died at the age of twenty-nine, was one of those people whose acquirements fill the mind with amazement. With no instruction in any language but English and French, she acquired a literary knowledge of almost every European language, was able to translate Hebrew, and even attempted Arabic and Persian. The "Ossian" controversy made her attempt Erse, but here she failed for want of books. Her love of astronomy caused her to learn mathematics. She is said to have excelled in music, in sketching from nature, and to have been "absolute mistress of perspective." Living during her childhood in a beautiful home called "Piercefield," in the West of England, her family were reduced from affluence to poverty by the failure of a bank in 1793. Elizabeth lost her library, her harp, and her piano, and exchanged her refined home for a wandering life; but her mother, describing her buoyant cheerfulness and readiness of resource in new and forlorn surroundings, remarks, "I had to learn fortitude from my child."

Mr. Smith joined the army after his misfortunes, and his wife and daughters followed him to Ireland in 1796. In that country, during the four stormy years that followed, they passed through many privations and some perils, but they found many kind friends amongst its hospitable inhabitants. One of these was a Quakeress, Mary Leadbeater, of Ballitore, the friend and correspondent of Mrs. Trench. In this delightful woman, whose 'Cottage Dialogues' were introduced to the world by Maria Edgeworth, and whose 'Annals of Ballitore' pleased the old age of Carlyle, Captain Smith and his family found a congenial friend. By her or her husband they were introduced to our former acquaintance, Thomas Wilkinson (owner of the "Spade"), who found for them a home near his own, to which they withdrew from the troubles of Ireland in 1800. Mary Leadbeater laments the departure of "Juliet" (Mrs. Smith) and her daughters from Ballitore in a pleasing poem. During the remainder of Elizabeth Smith's short life she had intense pleasure in the scenery of the beautiful Lake country, and it was in the cottage at Coniston that the translations from Klopstock were made.

During the long walks over the mountains taken by Elizabeth Smith and her sister they often had the companionship of Thomas Wilkinson, of whom Mrs. Smith, writing after Elizabeth's death, says:—"He was one of the very few people who really knew my daughter, and he felt for her character that esteem which the wise and good ever entertain for each other." It is recorded of Elizabeth Smith that she made "a gown or a cap with as much skill as she displayed in explaining a problem in Euclid, or a difficult passage in Hebrew, and nothing which she thought it right to do was ever neglected." In these days, when women's claims are put prominently forward, such a character may well be remembered. By our young heroines it was regarded with the warmest interest and admiration. The 'Memoirs of Frederick and Meta Klopstock,' and the 'Life of Elizabeth Smith,' by Miss Bowdler, were favourite books of the writer's mother, and are still treasured for her sake.

We smile at the thought of Klopstock being called "the greatest poet of Germany," but his character may still claim our admiration. In the delightful letters of Samuel Taylor Coleridge, written from Germany in 1798, and soon to be given to the world by his grandson, a visit to Klopstock in his old age is described in a spirit of reverence, which is very noticeable in so much younger a man, and in so immeasurably greater a poet.

Returning to the childhood of our heroines, there were English ballads almost as dear to them as Pope's Homer. Dr. Percy's 'Reliques of English Poetry' was probably never in their hands; but a little volume called the 'Bee,' preserved by the sisters to their latest days, contained some of its treasures. Of these the 'Hermit of Warkworth,' 'Edwin and Emma,' and 'Edwin and Angelina' are with us still. 'Colin and Lucy,' and 'William and Margaret' are not entirely forgotten. But who now mourns over the sorrows of the parted lovers, 'Alcanzor and Zaida'?

> "Loveliest she of Moorish ladies,
> He a young and noble Moor."

Yet from some of those young sisters the story of their woes drew tears.

By some accident, a poem of a very different character, Anstey's clever, sarcastic, somewhat unpleasant 'Bath Guide,' was known to them; and "Captain Cormorant" a well-remembered character. It is almost superfluous to say how all the sisters admired the few masterpieces of Gray, and loved the sweet natural poetry of Goldsmith; how Elizabeth recited the impassioned 'Odes' of Collins; and how the pathetic ballads of Amelia Opie had a charm for the young members of the Society she joined.

Much of the poetry of the day was of an artificial character. It was the age of the Strephons and the Delias; of the Corydons and the Chloes; of the elegant ecstasies of Miss Seward, and of the sonorous couplets of Darwin. But not in this record of persons who, in their later life, held Dr. Darwin's character and talents in the highest honour, shall a word be written in disparagement of the 'Loves of the Plants' or of the 'Botanic Garden.' These relaxations of a busy and energetic life attract us more, in spite of their formality, than the affectations of Miss Seward. The sincerity of that lady's grief for the death of her friend Major André gives interest to her 'Monody' on that event, and we may agree with Elizabeth

Richardson, who wrote in later life of a writer she admired, "Judgment in Anna Seward was less conspicuous than strong imagination, and a highly cultivated poetic taste."

But the days of artificial poetry were numbered, and the standard of revolt against the accepted laws of the kingdom of poetical criticism was raised at Bristol, by the publication of the Lyrical Ballads in 1797. Of that band of young poets whose memory casts a glory over the old streets of that western city, the name of Southey was first known to the general public, and his ballads and poems became popular before those of his greater associates. We cannot claim for the heroines of this book that they were earnest devotees of Wordsworth, but their sympathies were on his side, when the strength of the 'Edinburgh Review,' in its great days, was put forth to crush him. In their age, they lived to read Lord Cockburn's 'Life of Lord Jeffrey,' and to recognise with surprise and pleasure the kindly and genial qualities of the man of whom they had only heard in their youth as the formidable critic.

Fragments of Burns's poetry clung to their memory in later years, but perhaps he was hardly so familiar a poet to them as to the dwellers on the banks of the Tyne, where the kindred tongue was well understood, and where, even in Friends' houses, some of Burns's verses were repeated by the old as well as by the young. But who may describe the delight brought to those young sisters by the song of the other "Border Minstrel?" Even in their old age, they never forgot the hour when a new world of romance opened to them with the words—

> "The way was long, the wind was cold."

As this chapter closes in 1805, while a brighter day dawns for English poetry, how many writers in the humbler walk of children's literature, whose books would have delighted our heroines' childhood, appear upon the scene! Maria Hack, a daughter of their own Society, with her delightful 'Winter Evenings,' and her 'Grecian' and 'English Stories'; Isaac and Jeffreys Taylor, with their 'Little Historians,' their 'Rural Scenes,' and their 'Scenes in Europe'; Ann and Jane Taylor, with their 'Nursery Rhymes,' their 'Original Poems,' and the still more interesting prose writings of the younger sister, whose 'Contributions of Q. Q.' have enlivened many a long Sunday afternoon to Quaker children; and, best loved of all, Sir Walter Scott, with his 'Tales of a Grandfather.' These writers and Miss Edgeworth, were unapproached until the close of this century, when imaginative literature has come in like a flood, bearing upon its topmost wave the old fairy tales in many disguises, the wild romances of Treasure Island and King Solomon's Mines; and bringing with the abundant American literature, the freshness and life of a young people back into the old land in the old tongue.

Happy are the millions of children all over the world, who, in that English mother tongue, hold the key that unlocks such a treasure-house!

CHAPTER VII.

Travelling.

1792—1805.

"Every Quakeress is a lily, and when they come up in bands to their Whitsun
conferences, whitening the easterly streets of the metropolis, from all parts of the United
Kingdom, they show like troops of the Shining Ones."

'A Quakers' Meeting.'—CHARLES LAMB.

THE sisters of our story had many interests beyond Stockton.   The line
of the Cleveland hills, visible from that town, was always a pleasant sight
to them.   An hour's drive brought them to Langbarugh, where their father's
cousin, William Richardson, lived with his cheerful wife, Mary Muskett,
from Norfolk.   This hospitable couple had, as has been said, no son in
1792, but they had five fair young daughters.   Of these, Mary, the eldest,
was afterwards married to Joshua Wilson, of Sunderland, and, after his
death, to William Brown, of North Shields.   In the latter town, her life was
closely linked with that of our heroines.

Another daughter, Elizabeth, escaped from the low kitchen window at
Langbarugh, early one morning, and was married at Edinburgh to the
village surgeon, Dr. Thomas Loy.   Not being a Friend, his suit had been
judged inadmissible by the heads of the family.   This runaway couple have
left descendants.   Both their sons were members of the medical profession,
and the early death of their grandson, Dr. Thomas Richardson Loy, of
Harrogate, was widely lamented as the premature closing of - a career of
unusual promise.

There were three other daughters at Langbarugh, Lydia, Ann, and
Henrietta, beautiful and gifted girls, not destined to long life.   But, in the
closing years of the last century, all five sisters were in the pleasant time of
childhood and of early youth, when marriage and death seem far away, and
in their companionship, their Stockton cousins, wandering at will through

the fields and orchard, climbing the hills, and fording the "becks," tasted
the purest enjoyments of country life.

In the village of Ayton, too, there were many relatives. At Darlington
there lived an aunt of their father, Lydia, the youngest daughter of
William and Elizabeth Richardson, of Ayton. She had married Richard
Richardson, of a family in Holderness, remotely, if at all, connected with
that in Cleveland.

Four Thomas Richardsons in succession seem to have lived in Hull, as
merchants and master mariners, during the sixteenth and seventeenth
centuries. The fourth Thomas, born in 1645, a man of some artistic skill in
wood-carving and painting, married, in 1682, at St. Mary's Church, Lowgate,
Mary, daughter of Richard Mayson, merchant of Hull, and his wife, Mary
Richardson.* The parentage of the latter is not known, but Richard Mayson
was the son of the Rev. Valentine Mayson, Rector of Driffield in the time of
King James the First. Richard Mayson was intended by his father for the
Church, but was so strongly impressed by the preaching of George Fox
during one of the latter's missionary journeys in Holderness, that, although
he did not join the Society which Fox founded, he declined to take orders.
His opinions probably influenced those of his family, for they all became
members, and some of them Ministers of the Society of Friends. The other
descendants of Valentine Mayson were mostly clergymen, and one of them,
the Rev. William Mason, born at Hull in 1724, was esteemed the first
English poet of his time.† Mary Mayson, whose marriage to Thomas
Richardson is recorded above, joined the Society of Friends with her husband
in 1695. He was excommunicated by the Church of England, prosecuted
by the Ecclesiastical Court, and imprisoned in York Castle, probably for
refusing to pay tithes. His wife became a Minister in the Society. Of their
many children, Richard alone need here be mentioned. Born at Hull in
1686, he was forty-nine years old when he married Lydia, the twelfth and
youngest child of the populous Ayton household, when she was but twenty-
five. The marriage took place at Whitby, where Lydia's brother Isaac had
recently settled with his wife, Isabel Vasie, and where other members of the
Ayton family resided.

* See Appendix, 'Richardson of Hull.' See also 'Smith of Doncaster, and other
Families,' by Henry Ecroyd Smith.

† See Appendix, 'Mayson of Hull.' See also 'Smith of Doncaster, and other
Families,' by H. E. Smith.

Richard and Lydia Richardson lived for some years at Whitby, and then removed to Darlington, where their daughter, Mary, was married, in 1763, to Joseph, son of Edward Pease, and his wife, Elizabeth Coates, of Casalee. Edward Pease came to Darlington in the year 1744, to join an uncle, Thomas Coldwell, in the wool-combing business. He was of a family of Pease, of Felkirk, near Pontefract, and had then recently joined the Society of Friends. For this act, he was discarded by his Yorkshire relatives, but his upright character and consistent life won him esteem amongst his new neighbours. One of these, not himself a Friend, remarked in his old age to his son, that a blessing must rest upon such a man, and that, though he himself might not live to see it, he was persuaded that " the family of Edward Pease would be one of the most flourishing trees ever planted in Darlington," and he desired his son to remember his words. The son lived to see the prediction fulfilled, and to repeat his father's words to James Backhouse, of York,* who has recorded them.

Joseph, the son of this first Edward Pease, of Darlington, was the husband of Mary Richardson. She became a Minister in the Society of Friends. Her father, Richard Richardson, died in the year 1764, at the age of seventy-seven. Tradition says he was of a somewhat milder type of character than his wife. She survived him nearly forty years, living into another century, and into more than another generation. To our heroines she was "old aunt Lydia," and they occasionally visited her at Darlington. But to her grandson, Edward Pease, living in the same town, his mother's mother was a very important and familiar figure, and at the close of his own long life he would dwell with humorous appreciation upon her strongly-marked and energetic personality. His stories are imperfectly remembered, but one is clearly of a long-past time. A tailor was employed in the house, and was at work upon some of the velvet waistcoats then worn. A vigilant supervision was exercised over his proceedings by the energetic Lydia, who feared that, if her oversight were but for a moment withdrawn, the costly material might be cut to waste. It happened that a visitor arrived to claim her attention, and she deputed one of the male sex, whether son or grandson is uncertain, to take her place in watching the tailor. That astute personage at once saw his opportunity, and, cutting one waistcoat double, carried off material to make another for himself. Other stories related by Edward

* 'Smith of Doncaster,' by H. E. Smith, p. 184.

Pease still more decidedly showed the firmness and determination of his grandmother, qualities which he thought had been transmitted to her descendants, and which had played no small part in their lives. The long labours of the younger brother, Joseph Pease, in the cause of the Negro race and of the then little-considered natives of British India have been too much forgotten in our day.* And Edward Pease and his sons needed all their inherited tenacity of purpose when they stood by the unlettered Northumbrian pitman, who, but for their aid, had nothing but his own genius to oppose to the territorial power of the few, and to the ignorance and prejudice of the many. But these days lay far in the distance. In 1792, Edward and Joseph Pease were youths at home, diligently building up their father's large manufacturing business, and George Stephenson was a boy at Killingworth Colliery. Thirty years were to elapse before the first English Passenger Railway, "the Quaker Line," was to connect the two towns of Darlington and Stockton, and to change the course of life in England.

Richard and Lydia Richardson had a son, Robert, who married Caroline Garth, and who lived first at Darlington and afterwards at Ayton. His son, Thomas Richardson, and his son-in-law, John Overend, founded, nearly a hundred years ago, the firm of Richardson, Overend, and Gurney. Thomas Richardson continued a partner in the firm until past middle life, residing at Stamford Hill. In his old age, he spent his summers at Ayton, and took an interest in educational matters, and enjoyed in his early home the consideration which waits upon the possessors of large means. His great-nephew, John Gilbert Baker, finds his happiness in paths of life where money has little power. Amongst all lovers of science his name is a household word. From every nook of the earth the plant-collector sends his treasures to Gilbert Baker, at the Kew Herbarium, to be named and classified ; and letters from the simple, unworldly man are prized as being, in Canon Kingsley's words, "from the hand of a master." His brother, Dr. Robert Baker, is the active and enlightened Medical Superintendent of the "Friends' Retreat" at York.

* See 'Life of W. E. Forster,' by T. Wemyss Reid, p. 153. Letter to Elizabeth Pease, now Mrs. Nichol, in which the "South Durham British India Society" is mentioned, of which she was Secretary. In that Society, and in Anti-Slavery work, Elizabeth Pease was her father's best helper.

H

Then there were more distant journeys for the girls. There were warm-hearted Priestman uncles, full of kindness for the children of their dead sister, delighting to drive them in their capacious "gigs" from York to Malton, or to take them up behind them on their sturdy horses for the moorland ride from Malton to Thornton, or from Thornton to Whitby. Sometimes a horse refused "to carry double." This happened to David Priestman and his niece, Elizabeth Richardson, and caused some excitement in the quiet streets of Malton. However, after a very determined rebellion, during which he twice kicked off his riders at street-corners, the horse resigned himself to his double load, and the uncle and niece proceeded on their journey.

No serious accident ever befel our heroines in riding, nor even so slight a one as happened some years later to one of their cousins. This young girl was paying a visit at Thornton, and wished to travel from thence to Whitby. The Priestmans, of Thornton, were millers, as well as tanners and farmers, and other Friends sent their sons to them that they might learn the art of these different businesses. One of these pupils was deputed to convey his master's niece to her destination, and they started upon their journey, she riding on a pillion-seat behind him. As they passed over those wide, wind-swept moors, they came to a gate, which the youth opened. He and his horse passed safely through it, but not so his companion. The wind, which was against them, blew the gate so violently against the girl's feet that she was pushed off the horse's back. Moorland bridle-paths are soft and sandy, and she was quite unhurt. After the momentary surprise of finding herself on the ground, she called to her conductor, but the wind, which had so roughly closed the gate, carried her voice away in the same direction, and he rode on unheeding. She walked after him until he passed over the brow of the next hill, and vanished from her sight. Then she sat down, forlornly enough, upon the heather. No one passed her on that lonely moor, and the time seemed very long until her careless cavalier, having at last missed his charge, rode back to seek her, and she resumed her seat behind him. Her story caused some amusement in her family, and her brother related it at Harrogate, many years afterwards, to the writer of these pages. The heroine of the narrative was present, a sweet, grave woman, rather past middle age. She quietly corroborated her brother's statements, mildly adding, " I never could tell why they laughed." The week after hearing this story, the writer visited the house of the neglectful horseman, then no longer a youth, but an old man,—all his life rather remarkable for his silence. She asked him if he remembered the incident in his early days which she had heard of the week before. He pondered long, and then said :—"Yes, I remember ; I thought she had been very quiet, and had said nothing for a long time, so I spoke to her, and she did not answer. Then I looked round, and I found she was gone. I turned my horse's head, and rode back a good way, and found her sitting by the road-side."

Another tale is of a youth and maiden riding together under similar circumstances, but who were less indifferent to each other than the hero and heroine of my last story. In this case the youth loved the girl, and put his fortune to the proof early in the day. Alas! the answer was adverse, and, as the journey was long, the day must have been a painful one.

Such were some of the incidents of travelling "on double horse." That mode of progression is still to be seen in the dales of Yorkshire and amongst the mountains of Wales, but even there it will probably soon become a thing of the past.

There seems to have been little travelling by public conveyances in the days of which I am now writing. The girls were driven to a town, where their friends met them, or an uncle or cousin came for a day or two's visit, for the purpose of taking them home with him. One memorable voyage was made from Stockton to Whitby by Hannah Richardson and her younger sister. The sea was rough, the miseries endured were great, and the description of them was vivid.

Their Whitby life was very different from that at Stockton. The back windows of "Aunt Gallilee's" house looked on to the harbour, and it was an amusement on the long Sunday afternoons to watch the proceedings on board the vessels, and to hear the singing of the foreign sailors. On other days, climbing the two hundred steps leading up to the grand old Abbey ; searching for the wonderful " snake-stones " in the cliff beneath ; rambling on the moors and over the rocks ; and, above all, hearing the stories about St. Hilda, which a young Edinburgh lawyer was so soon to weave into his charming verse, filled up the hours happily.

But Whitby had not the charm for them that it has for us. It was not all sunshine in the small houses in the narrow streets, when you lived with people whose mental powers were good, but whose education had been limited; whose prejudices, naturally strong, were intensified by such cramped surroundings; and whose subjects of interest were few, and those not always of a cheerful character. The Society of Friends was declining in Whitby. It had been early established in the neighbourhood, and its meeting-house, built in 1665, was the first Nonconformist place of worship in the town. For more than a hundred years Whitby was a stronghold of Quakerism. Then, as we have seen, many of its most energetic inhabitants deserted the banks of the Esk for those of the Wear and of the Tyne. Some of these left the Society of Friends, others were "disowned" by it for carrying guns on board their ships during the long war with France; and from the same cause, many Friends who remained in Whitby were lost to the Society.

For half a century Whitby seemed to be forgotten by the world. Encircled by its moors, hardly touched by railways, or by the changes which they bring, it preserved its primitive simplicity until what we may almost call its re-discovery in our own day. Now, the historian seeks it as the scene of early glories of our race, and the geologist for traces of a still earlier history; the lover of English poetry seeks the source of the stream which has grown into so mighty a river; the novelist—notably one bearing an old Whitby name—chooses it as a fit setting for the creations of her fancy; the artist loves it for its red-roofed houses climbing its purple cliffs, and for the glorious abbey which crowns them. May fashion never spoil the dear old place, nor corrupt its honest fishermen and fisherwomen!

Scarborough, too, was well known to our little heroines. Not, indeed, the Scarborough of our day, with its bands and its promenades, its "Cliff Bridges" and its "Grand Hotels." But the queen of English watering-places is not more loved by her subjects of to-day than she was in her uncrowned state, with her narrow streets, her miles of sand, Carnelian Bay with its treasures, Oliver's Mount with its pleasant climb, and the Castle with its dungeons, by those children ninety years ago. The journeys to Scarborough were often taken from Malton, where their uncle, David Priestman, lived. His house was a happy home to our little heroines, who found in his sweet-tempered sons and daughters, dear companions in youth, faithful friends to their latest days.

The "travelling" recorded in this chapter has been confined to South

Durham and North-east Yorkshire; but, when she was eighteen years old, a longer journey was taken by Isabel. We have seen in a former chapter that the Society of Friends is governed by Monthly, Quarterly and Yearly Meetings. One Sunday in every month, after the morning meeting, the "Men and Women Friends" separate into their respective meetings, to appoint persons to represent them at the ensuing Monthly Meeting. The Friends residing in three or four towns constitute these Monthly Meetings, which are held in each town in succession. They attend to the business of the Society, and watch over the welfare of its members, their marriages, changes of residence, &c., and in their turn send representatives to Quarterly Meetings, whose jurisdiction covers a wider area, consisting of three or four Monthly Meetings, and often extending over more than one English county. Each meeting, of course, increases in importance as its circle of representation widens, the Yearly Meeting, with its representatives from every Quarterly Meeting throughout the kingdom, being, as it were, the supreme council of the Society.

In the spring of 1795, Henry Richardson took his daughter, Isabel, with him to Durham Quarterly Meeting, supposed to have been held that year in the city of Durham. Isabel rode behind her father on a pillion. When the "Meeting for Worship" was over, and the "Women Friends" assembled in their own meeting-house, they proceeded to nominate persons to represent them at the Women's Yearly Meeting, which is held in London during the month of May. While different names were being mentioned, a Friend, of Newcastle, whose powerful intellect and strength of will gave her great influence in the meeting, pointed to Isabel Richardson, and said, "I do not know the name of that young Friend, but I should wish her to be one of our representatives to the Yearly Meeting." The timid girl sat in speechless terror, equally unable to raise her voice in refusal or to endure the thought of what was involved by acceptance. No sound came from her lips. The Friend who acted as Clerk to the Meeting, and who knew her name, though the Newcastle lady did not, wrote it down. There was little pleasure for poor Isabel that day in the remaining part of the meeting or in the social gathering afterwards. When again seated behind her father on their homeward journey, she sought in vain for words to tell him that she had, by her silence, agreed to go to London. To her great relief he began the subject by telling her the names of the "Men Friends" who had been appointed, adding, "And who have been appointed in your meeting, Isabel?" She told him the names of the three elder Friends, and then faltered out the words, "and me, father!" "What, *thee*, bairn!" was the astonished exclamation of the generally calm and reticent man; but, to Isabel's great surprise, he showed no displeasure. His cousin, Mary Pease, speedily arranged the matter. She was going to attend the Yearly Meeting with her daughter and her second son, Joseph, afterwards to be known as "Joseph Pease, of Feethams," the worker in the "Anti-Slavery" and "British India" Societies. Isabel completed the party, and they travelled to London in a post-chaise. They stayed in London at the house of another cousin, Samuel Fossick, whose mother was a daughter of William and Elizabeth Richardson, of Ayton, and whose descendants have intermarried both with the Peases and with the Richardsons.*

Isabel was, in after years, a frequent attender of the Yearly Meeting, of which she became one of the valued preachers; but to none did she look back with more pleasure than to this, her first Yearly Meeting, the attendance of which she had anticipated with so much fear. She always spoke of it as a time of especial spiritual benefit. She had also the enjoyment natural to her years in visiting some of the sights of London. It was long before the days of the Zoological Gardens, but the large lions, which were then kept at the Tower, were long remembered.

It was not many years before Isabel attended another Yearly Meeting. The journey was again performed in a post-chaise. This mode of travelling was preferred by Friends when a party of four could be formed to fill the vehicle. It was thought to be more private and less expensive than the same number of persons travelling by coach. On this occasion Isabel had a companion still younger than herself, Esther Tuke, of York, the grand-daughter of the Founder of the Retreat, and of "Queen Esther." The incidents of this journey were still dwelt upon with smiles after the lapse of half a century, when the two aged women who had been the girls of that party visited each other in Hull, whether in the little old parlours in "Cogan Street," or in the larger rooms of "East Mount." From their own account, they had found much to amuse them at the various halting-places of the journey, and the two elder Friends of the party (whose names have not been

---

* See , 'Table V., Fossick of Welbury.'

preserved) looked somewhat grave at their merriment.　It was feared that they felt they had the charge of two very giddy girls.*

These journeys to the Yearly Meeting were very important events. The few Friends who had carriages of their own sometimes travelled in them to London, and horses were engaged at the different posting-houses on the road.　The travellers slept at inns, but more often at private houses. Great hospitality was extended by Friends to each other, especially when there was any tie of kinship.　Friends who were dwellers near the sea-coast occasionally braved the discomforts and perils of the sea-voyage for the sake of attending the meeting.　A group of Lincolnshire farmers used to ride their strong horses as far as Tottenham, where a Friend who had fields and stabling took charge of the animals until they were again required for the return-journey.

Few persons had the leisure to convert the journeys to London into such pleasant tours throughout England as did our former acquaintance, Thomas Wilkinson, who, in 1791, performed the whole journey on foot, walking the distance of three hundred miles in eight days.　He passed from his beautiful Westmoreland home across the wilds of Stanmore, and the varied scenes of the Yorkshire dales, to the rich historical interests, and the cultured hospitalities of York; then visited the gardens of John Scott, of Amwell; and, in London, breakfasted with his friends, of whom he speaks as "Edmund and Jane Burke," and was taken by the great orator to see the trial of Warren Hastings.　On his way home, he visited Hagley Park, to see the groves where the poet Lord Lyttleton mourned with such long-drawn melody the loss of his beloved "Lucy."

On another journey to London, Wilkinson visited Hales Owen and the grave of Shenstone, and from the poet's walks at the Leasowes took the idea of the "pleasant walks by Eamont's side," which Wordsworth and the "spade" helped him to "shape."

On Wilkinson's first journey to London, in 1785, he chronicles that as he rode from the door of his home, "my mother shed tears, and my sisters looked as long as I was in sight."　This was the usual feeling of country people at that time, when their friends were setting out upon so long and perilous a journey.　The same feeling is exemplified in a story that is told of an excellent woman in a northern town during the present century.

---

* These girls were afterwards Isabel Casson and Esther Priestman, both of Hull.

Her strictly-performed duties had lain within a somewhat narrow circle, and she added something of scholastic precision to the ordinary formalities of speech peculiar to Friends. During the leisure of her later life, she made up her mind to attend the Yearly Meeting for the first time. An energetic man of business placed his services at her disposal, and every arrangement seemed to have been made to guard against any physical peril or mental perturbation to the traveller herself, when cause of anxiety arose for another. The name of the landlady of the inn from which the coach started was Joysey. "Thomas," said the quiet Friend to her kind helper, "hadst thou not better call upon Mary Joysey, a *little* to prepare her mind for my taking a seat in the coach which starts from her house for London? Might not the surprise of seeing me be too great for her?" It was the same estimable woman who was once handed into a public conveyance by a relative who was more anxious for her comfort than for the exact propriety of his language. "Put this lady out at the corner of Bridge Street," he called out to the driver in his cheery voice. The reproof given to him was public and instantaneous: "Oh! Cousin Caleb, thou shouldst have said, 'this Friend'!"

This somewhat discursive chapter on "Travelling" may be concluded by a notice of a first visit to Edinburgh, paid by the father of the present writer in 1805. The Friends of Edinburgh, if few in number, were hospitable and cultivated, and to them, as well as to some other persons, the youth had letters of introduction. Many things appeared strange, and struck him as very singular in the society to which he was admitted; for instance, a breakfast, where excellent fare was served upon a well-appointed table, and brightened by intellectual conversation, but where a literary Peer presented himself wearing odd boots (a top-boot and a black one), and the servant waited upon the guests barefooted. But one circumstance especially impressed the youth's mind, and made him feel that, though the accent he heard differed little from his native Northumbrian tongue, and the climate of the Forth closely resembled that of the Tyne, he was yet amongst a people altogether different from that he had left at home. One subject seemed to be of absorbing interest to the inhabitants of Edinburgh, alike to the man of literary leisure, to the busy citizen, and to the poorest artizan. The Professorship of Mathematics in the University was vacant, and a Mr. Leslie was a candidate for the office. When the young Northumbrian walked about the streets of Edinburgh, when he travelled in the public conveyances, above all, when he crossed the Forth in a boat crowded with working people, the same words rung in his ears:—"Maister Leslie." "Is he a fit man?" "Is he *soond* i' the faith?" At a supper party (not at a Friend's house) the prevailing topic was discussed with some warmth, and at great length, by persons holding opposite views on the matter. The host, who had listened to the arguments in silence, at last summed them up in these words:—"Weel, I dinna think Maister Leslie *can* be soond i' the faith. Some of you have spoken for him, and some against him, but you have one and a' allood that he traivels on the Sabbath-day!"

Note.—Mr. (afterwards Sir John) Leslie was appointed Professor of Mathematics in Edinburgh University in 1805, and elevated to the Chair of Natural Philosophy in 1819.

CHAPTER VIII.

Isabel Richardson.

1800—1826.

"Courteous and fair, and full of meekness,
  Cheerful and good and lowly."
                              CHAUCER.

"Always the same—serene of soul and eye."
                              UNKNOWN.

YEARS went on, and the heroines of our narrative passed from childhood into youth. The first breach in the group of sisters was made by the departure from home of Isabel. It happened that while Henry Richardson had many daughters, his brothers had many sons. His brother Isaac, the second son of Isaac Richardson, of Whitby, had settled in London, and married a young Friend, Sarah Mayleigh Barnes, daughter of Samuel Barnes, of Clapton. After some years, Isaac brought his wife to Yorkshire, and bought a cherry-orchard on a hill near the city of York. Upon this hill he built a house, and made a tan-yard. He died in 1791, while his sons, Samuel and William, were still young. A cousin managed the business for them until the year 1800, when they were of age and able to undertake it. Their mother having re-married, they were left without any female companionship, and they petitioned their uncle Henry to spare them one of his numerous daughters. Their request was granted, and, with the simplicity of Friends in those times, Isabel Richardson went to keep house for these two cousins of her own age. She used to describe, with a smile, in later life, her many difficulties and mistakes in her new position, for she was not by nature a good manager, like her sister Mary, of whom it was so often said that the name of Martha would have better suited her character. In spite of any little mishaps, the young cousins must have formed a cheerful household, and happy was the day to the girls at the school, where Isabel had so lately been a pupil, when they were invited to tea at "Cherry Hill." The young hosts and hostess would all join at a game of play in the garden, Isabel casting aside her housewifely cares, and becoming again the school-girl. One of those young visitors, who then bore the name of Bella Scarr, still remembered and spoke with pleasure of those merry evenings, in her sweet home at Staines, at the close of her long and honoured life. Many a group of school-girls played in after years in that pleasant garden!

When Isabel went to live there in 1800, Cherry Hill was comparatively a country residence. The garden abounded not only in cherry and other fruit trees, but in larches, sycamores, and purple beeches. On the one side it stretched nearly to the river, while on another it was overshadowed by the then ruinous walls of the city, which were afterwards restored. At their termination was the old "Baile Hill" (Vetus Balium), where formerly stood the fortress which corresponded with Clifford's Tower, on the opposite side of the river. Passing out of the garden, and over a stile, you came upon the remains of the foundations of St. Clement's Church and Nunnery. From these ruins, the neighbouring parish and hamlet took the name of Clementhorpe. This designation has been given, in our own day, to the abode of a descendant of the Richardson family in a northern town, for the sake of old memories.

It was only as a loved and honoured guest that Isabel Richardson ever returned to her father's house at Stockton. In 1808, she was called there to his death-bed. For ten years her home was at Cherry Hill. During this lengthened residence at York, she was again brought under the influence of the remarkable family of Tuke. The founder of the Retreat was still living, and, with his youngest daughter, Mabel ("very sweet, very wise," she has been called), was presiding over the girls' school. His son, Henry, was a minister in York Meeting, and, as such, highly esteemed by Isabel. With Henry Tuke's daughter, Esther, as well as with his sister, Mabel, she formed intimacies, which were destined to endure through life. It was in York Meeting, in 1810, that Isabel so far overcame her constitutional timidity as to open her lips as a minister, and it was by York Monthly Meeting, in 1812, that she was recorded as such. In 1810, her cousin, William Richardson, was married to Martha, daughter of Daniel Mildred, a well-known London banker. This was the well-remembered gentle Friend whose sweet face, musical voice, and most motherly kindness, gave for so many years its charm to the home at Cherry Hill.* Samuel, the elder brother, now left Yorkshire for the South of England. He finally married and settled at Fordingbridge, in Hampshire, where he lived until a great age, and left no descendants.

In 1804, Mabel Tuke had been married to John Hipsley, of Hull; and in 1812, Isabel followed her friend to that flourishing, if unpicturesque, town. Again she went to cheer a lonely household; this time that of her mother's nephew, Thomas Priestman, who had lost his wife. He then lived in Humber Street. During her residence there, Isabel laid the first stone of his new house at East Mount, about four miles out of Hull. Many were the walks she took to watch the progress of the building, generally wearing pattens, to keep her feet out of the water, so abundant in that locality. It was about the year 1814 that East Mount was ready for habitation. For three years it was Isabel's home, and then she had the pleasure of welcoming to it its new mistress: her friend, Esther Tuke, to whom Thomas Priestman was married in 1817.

After this date, Isabel had for some years a life full of varied experiences. One of her numerous cousins, Joseph Priestman, of Thornton, appealed to her for help in a time of need. He was suffering from a serious affection in the neck. She was his companion in a journey to London, and in his interviews with the skilled surgeons of that day. She used to describe their visits to the rough Abernethy, to the gentle and courteous Sir Astley Cooper, and to the fine old man, Mr. Cline, without whose sanction Sir Astley would not operate. The sanction was given, and the operation was successfully performed; but Isabel had need of all her placidity of temperament while nursing through the tedium of convalescence a most restless patient, accustomed to the open air life of the vale of Pickering. It was a singular experience for the once timid girl!

During this period of her life, Isabel was much engaged in ministerial work. She paid many visits in the neighbourhood of London, in company with Mary and Elizabeth Dudley, who were her intimate friends to the end

* This lady, and her twin sister, Mary, who married John Hustler, were both of them plain Friends, and the latter was a Minister in the Society. It is somewhat remarkable that eight of their nephews were beneficed clergymen of the Church of England, and that one of these, the Rev. Canon H. Mildred Birch, was for many years tutor to H.R.H. the Prince of Wales.

of their lives. They were sweet women, in whom the nameless charm
which comes with Irish birth softened the austerity of Quaker manners.
Another minister, Ann Jones, seems to have been made of sterner stuff.
Isabel was travelling in her company in 1821, when the marriage of Sarah,
the younger sister of our heroines, took place at North Shields. Isabel
naturally wished to leave her ministerial work to attend her sister's
marriage, but was sternly rebuked by her companion in the words, "Let
the dead bury their dead"!

Isabel had not been unsought in marriage in her youth, nor during
her early womanhood, but it was not until the year 1824, when she was
past middle life, that she consented to enter into the married state. Her
husband was Henry Casson, of Hull, brother of the first wife of her cousin,
Thomas Priestman. Isabel was married at the meeting-house at Pickering,
as her mother had been nearly half a century before. There are two
houses which stand by the clear stream, called "The Beck," at Thornton.
Isabel's marriage took place from the more modern house where her cousin,
Joshua Priestman, resided; but her wedding-dinner was given at the older
house, which had been her mother's home, and was now inhabited by
Joseph Priestman, whose companion she had been in London through such
painful scenes.

In 1826, two years after her marriage, Isabel accompanied her husband
to Harrogate, on account of his failing health. No improvement took place,
and he died on the return journey, while resting at her old home at Cherry
Hill. Very brief was the time during which Isabel Casson had been
permitted to enjoy the society of her husband; but her whole after-life was
enriched by the love of his children and his grandchildren. Between her
and her stepdaughter the tie of affection was so strong, that that of birth
could not have rivetted it more closely. They were inseparable companions
for more than thirty years.

Any account of the ministry of Isabel Casson lies outside of the scope
of this volume. In manner she had much of what has been called "the
beautiful recitative peculiar to the Quakers," and Gregorian chaunts have
often recalled her familiar tones. But her loving spirit, her large-heartedness bounded by no sectarian trammels, and her Christian wisdom, were
widely appreciated. Alike amongst the warm-hearted Friends of Ireland
and the cultured inhabitants of Philadelphia, she was most deeply beloved,
and formed life-long friendships.

It has seemed best to give here an outline sketch of the life of Isabel Richardson, after she left her father's house in 1800. Two years later, another of his daughters left home to fill a sphere of usefulness. To explain how this occurred, our history must once more return to the town of Whitby, and to the middle of the eighteenth century.

CHAPTER IX.

The Low Lights.

1788—1834.

"The outward shows of sky and earth,
  Of hill and valley, he has viewed;
And impulses of deeper birth
  Have come to him in solitude.
In common things that round us lie,
  Some hidden truths he can impart.
The harvest of a quiet eye
  That broods and sleeps on his own heart."

WORDSWORTH.

ISAAC and Isabel Richardson, of Whitby, had five sons, John, Isaac, Henry, William and Aaron. The changes of residence of the second son, Isaac, to London, and afterwards to York, and of the third son, Henry, to Stockton, have already been recorded. William, the fourth son, succeeded to his father's tan-yard, and married Mary Dale, of Scarborough. A man of remarkable personal beauty, he had little business-faculty, and the old place did not prosper in his hands. In his later years, he lived at Sheffield. His son, William, seems to have been a man of different tastes from the rest of his family. He resided in York, and took interest in sports not unknown in that city, but utterly condemned by the Society of Friends. His possession of different gold cups testified to his success in such reprehensible pursuits. In after years, he went out to the West Indies. His sister, Anne, married Isaac Spencer, of York, who was twice Lord Mayor of that city. A son of the marriage, the Rev. Isaac Spencer, M.A., was Vicar of Acomb, near York, and married an Irish lady, Harriet Phipps, at Clontarf Church, near Dublin. The marriage of his son, William Henry Spencer, an officer in the 6th West York Militia, took place in a more remote locality, the Cathedral of Graham's Town, South Africa. The name of Captain

Spencer's wife was Mary Lamont Lucas, and there are many children of the marriage.*

Aaron, the youngest son of the Whitby household, married and settled at Lynn, in Norfolk. He was highly esteemed by those who knew him in that distant part of England, and has left no descendants.

This history now follows the fortunes of the eldest son, John, born at Bog Hall in 1733. All the sons of Isaac Richardson, with the exception of Henry (who, it may be remembered, was a flax and iron merchant), followed the same occupation as their father and their grandfather. In 1757, three of them were employed in their father's tan-yard at Whitby. John was the first to leave home, in 1758, or the following year; and, like so many of his fellow-townsmen, he turned his face northwards. Arriving in Gateshead towards the close of a day, with his plans still unmatured, and not knowing where to look for a lodging, he enquired for the house of a Friend. He was directed to that of John Stead, a civil engineer. Making his way across a field to the house, the young Yorkshireman saw a girl standing in the doorway, and to her he addressed his enquiries. This was Margaret, the eldest daughter of John Stead. She timidly invited the stranger to come in and speak to her parents, who, with the hospitality of Friends of that day, at once made him welcome; and on hearing further of his parentage and of his plans, invited him to stay at their house.

Now it appears that, the night before this visit, Margaret Stead had had a dream. In this dream she saw a young man whose features were strange to her, but who, she seemed to know, would, one day, become her husband. The eldest daughter of a large family, Margaret had probably little time during the day for idle musings, but she did not forget her dream. As evening fell, and she stood at her father's door in the twilight, she saw a tall figure crossing the field, and approaching the house. The figure resolved itself into that of a young man, whose home-spun garments were of the strictest Quaker fashion, and, upon still nearer approach, his dark eyes and hair, and strong, well-marked features were those of the stranger in her dream. Need we wonder that, in the guarded language of the Quaker 'Annalist,' "when he accosted her, she felt some embarrassment"? †

John Richardson took a farm at Seghill, near Cramlington, about seven miles from Newcastle, and six from North Shields. The acquaintance

* Table VIII., 'Richardsons of Whitby.'
† 'Annals of the Richardsons,' page 45.

between him and Margaret Stead having ripened into affection, the two young people were married at the Friends' meeting-house in Newcastle, on January 4th, 1760. Their three eldest children, Isaac, Margaret, and John, were born at the farm. Seghill, lying midway between Backworth and Cramlington, is now the centre of a populous mining district, in which a great-grandson of John Richardson holds a very prominent position. The old farm is now grazing land, and upon it are raised the finest cattle in Northumberland, those of Sir Matthew White Ridley perhaps excepted. During John Richardson's occupation, some of it was arable land, and, as in those early days of King George the Third's reign, wheat sold for three shillings per bushel, it soon became evident that the farm would not support a family in comfort. Under these circumstances, John Richardson had recourse to the advice of his father, and old Whitby friendships became of use in time of need.

Readers of Captain Cook's Life may remember the names of John and Henry Walker, the good Quaker shipowners of Whitby, to whom young Cook, when released from his hated occupations on land, was apprenticed. These sensible and kindly men were the first to perceive the promise in the boy of the future fearless discoverer. They were his earliest friends and helpers, and he corresponded with them to the last year of his life. Isaac Richardson was the intimate friend of one of the brothers, John Walker, who had a son of the same name in North Shields. He lived in the largest house in Dockwray Square, then a new and aristocratic quarter of the town, and he possessed other property in the neighbourhood. From him, John Richardson took a piece of ground, near the mouth of the river Tyne, called the Pew Dene. The high banks of the dene afforded pasture for the horses and cattle, in the management of which John Richardson afterwards took so much pleasure, while on the level land below, he laid the foundations of his house, and planted his tan-yard. John Walker furnished the money for the purpose, on condition of rent being paid at the rate of six and a half per cent. on the outlay; and when, in 1766, the house and tan-yard were ready for occupation, he granted a lease for twenty-one years of the property (including the small farm), at the rent of £25 per annum. To this sum additions were made as the tanning business required increased accommodation, so that when John Walker died, in 1822, the rent amounted to £210 per annum.

When John Richardson brought his wife and three children from the farm at Seghill to their new home in the dene near Shields (a distance of about six miles), it is credibly reported that one horse carried the family! John Richardson had his eldest son Isaac on the horse before him; his wife Margaret on a pillion-seat behind him. His coat, probably still one of his mother's spinning, had long and capacious pockets. In one of these pockets was snugly ensconced a little John, and in another a little Margaret! Much has been said in this narrative of travelling upon "double horse," but what adjective can we apply to the animal which brought the first settlers to the Low Lights? We might be reading of an emigrant and his family coming to their new home in a clearing in the forest, and in truth the difficulties of John Richardson's undertaking must have needed as stout a heart to confront them as those which beset the path of a settler in a strange land. The house was well and strongly built, and its foundations made firm, but the land round it was a mere marsh. When the new owner took possession of the place, and plunged his walking-stick into the wet soil, the stick sank up to its very handle. In front of the house there stretched a tract of land which was called the "salt-grass," and was overflowed by the sea at spring-tides. So perfectly level was it, that the ships passing up and down the river could plainly be seen from the parlour-windows. At first the health of the family suffered from these surroundings, and a sweet child, Isabel, was lost to her parents by a fever; but as John Richardson gradually added to his tan-pits and buildings, drained his land, and laid out his garden, the place became more dry and healthy. The "salt-grass" was raised and made into a timber-yard. The house in the Pew Dene afterwards became known by the name of the Low Lights, from its proximity to the Lighthouse nearest to the mouth of the harbour, which was built in 1798, and was called the Low Light."*

A family of two daughters and seven stalwart sons grew up in this valley. The situation was a somewhat lonely one, and there was a considerable distance to travel to the other side of the town, before they could reach the meeting-house where the Friends assembled to worship.

---

* The higher Lighthouse, by Dockwray Square, was built in 1807.

They passed up a steep path through their own fields, until they reached the high land above the harbour. Going by Dockwray Square, which was then being built, they continued along the river-bank,—now Tyne Street, but called "the banks" for many a day,—and then past a colliery, on the site of which a theatre afterwards stood, and which has, in its turn, given place to shops and offices. They then went down the Church Stairs, and crossed by a "Wooden Bridge" over a little stream, which then ran where the lower part of Bedford Street stands now. From this point they pursued their way along a narrow street, parallel with the river, similar to that seen in so many sea-ports, but which was then the principal thoroughfare of Shields. They thus arrived at the Bull Ring, where bulls were baited in the early years of the nineteenth century. A little beyond the Bull Ring was the meeting-house, and near it was the burying-ground of those days. A new meeting-house was built in the high town in 1800, and the old one converted into a mill, which has now again become a place of worship.

Margaret, the wife of John Richardson, died in 1781. Her fourth son, George, became a well-known minister of the Society of Friends, and was the author of the 'Annals of the Cleveland Richardsons.' He was eight years old when his mother died, and thus speaks of her in that book:—"I remember her well; she was of a grave, circumspect demeanour, guiding her children and her domestic affairs with much discretion."* He also speaks of her very even temper, and says that he cannot remember to have ever heard an angry word pass between his parents. The eldest daughter, Margaret, was a kind care-taker to her brothers and to her little sister. Some years afterwards John Richardson married a second wife, who proved a good mother to his children, and a solace to him in the decline of life. She had two sons, Aaron and Joseph, who both died unmarried—the former of small-pox in early youth, the latter in age, having been for many years a ship's captain. The old sailor's genial smile and pleasant conversation are still remembered.

The descendants of John Richardson, of the Low Lights, by his marriage with Margaret Stead are so numerous that the minute details of this chapter will be pardoned, and some notice of John Stead, the father of Margaret, may be of interest.

* 'Annals of the Richardsons,' p. 48.

John Stead was born in 1710, at Ampleforth, in the North Riding of Yorkshire. He married, in 1738, Margaret, daughter of George Raper, of Stockton-upon-Tees, and settled in that town. By profession, John Stead was a civil engineer. George Richardson thus writes of his maternal grandfather:—"In 1742 or 3, John Stead is found to be residing at Washington Mill, in the county of Durham. Though possessed of very little school-learning, he became a clever and ingenious man; and whilst residing at Washington, it is said he invented the barley-mill, for taking the skin off barley to prepare it for the pot. In 1759 he is found to be a resident of Gateshead, where it was that my father, John Richardson, found him, and became acquainted with his daughter Margaret, as is before related. Whilst residing in Gateshead, he 'invented a machine for cutting timber and other purposes by the help of the fire-engine, and made application for royal letters patent that he might have the sole use and benefit of making and vending the said machine for the term of fourteen years.' He affirmed to the petition before W. G., a Master in Chancery, of Newcastle, on 'the seventh day of February, 1767.' He afterwards resided at Kenton, near Newcastle, was often professionally employed about collieries, and spent considerable portions of the latter part of his life in Scotland."*

In a letter from John Richardson to John Stead, dated "1st month 4th, 1779," the writer expresses the anxiety of himself and his wife lest her father's repeated journeys should be too much for his strength, and urges him to relinquish his profession, and to come and reside with his children. This anxiety was but too well founded, for John Stead died on the 12th of the same month, at Alloa, near Stirling. None of his family were present at his death, or at his funeral, which took place at Alloa, in the simple Scotch fashion, without any ceremony at the grave-side. Yet the English engineer did not go unhonoured, for Mr. Johnstone, by whom John Stead was then employed, and in whose house he died, acted as the chief mourner, and lowered the stranger's head into the grave, thus performing the duty of the nearest relative. As Mr. Johnstone rose from his solemn task, he said with emphasis, "Here lies an honest man," and added in a softer tone, "and I fully believe he was something more than that,"—doubtless referring to John Stead's christian character.

* 'Annals of the Cleveland Richardsons,' p. 47.

In the 'Annals,' George Richardson has naturally dwelt much upon the character of his father. He describes his anxieties during the early years at the Low Lights,—his great industry in the management of his tan-yard and farm,—his good judgment in only enlarging his business as capital increased,—and the honourable and upright course he pursued through life.* An anecdote which he gives may be quoted here, although the last paragraph is surely superfluous:—"Having at one time, during the latter period of his life, some hay to sell, an officer in the army came to buy it. On my father naming the price, the officer urged him to charge ten shillings per ton more, saying that it was very common in sales to the Government. My father steadily refused the proposal."† His care over his children was very great—to keep them closely in what he and his parents had seen to be the right way; and he would often take them aside into the garden, to converse with them tenderly and seriously. Some of them never forgot his words.

In 1785 he became a minister in Shields meeting. His son says, "He was of a deeply contemplative frame of mind, and frequently drew instruction from natural things, in a manner peculiarly impressive and appropriate." His accent was strongly provincial, being that of his native North Yorkshire moors, but his son dwells upon "the tenderness, humility, and simplicity of his manner." He remarks that, although his father's reading was limited, being chiefly confined to the Bible, Friends' religious books, and the weekly newspaper, he was yet a man of very general information, and well able to hold his own in argument with those whose reading was more extensive, including his own elder sons—his son William being somewhat given to controversy.

A remarkable type of character was developed in the seclusion of the Low Lights valley. While in towns the severity of manners of the earlier Friends had very much disappeared, and social intercourse with their neighbours had softened some of their more striking peculiarities, John Richardson had brought from the primitive society of Whitby and from the seclusion of his first farm to that of the Low Lights, the older form of Quakerism. His sons followed in his footsteps, reserving the warmth of their friendship for those within their own Society, and strongly holding

* 'Annals of the Cleveland Richardsons,' pp. 45—60.
† Ibid. p. 85.

its distinguishing doctrines. Isaac, the eldest son, was sent when a boy to reside for a time with his grandparents at Whitby, in order that he might have the advantage of attending a school in that town, conducted by a Friend. Of the school and its master we know nothing; but Isaac, who was thus favoured above his brothers, who attended the ordinary schools of Shields, is always spoken of as a man of superior abilities and attainments. He married and settled in Newcastle, where he died in middle life. Some of his grandsons are prominent figures amongst the busy communities on Tyneside. The descendants of the second son, John, who settled in Sunderland, are equally well known on the Wear, and one of his grandsons, Joseph Richardson, has recently filled the office of High Sheriff of the county of Durham. Others are far separated from the rest of their family, having taken up their residence in South Wales.

The third and fourth sons, William and George, have their own places in this history. Henry, the fifth son, a man of noble presence, and of a fine open-countenance, was much with his father during his later years. In the last letter written by John Richardson, he says, "Henry is very assisting to me, and demeans himself very kindly and well."

John Richardson died on March 29th, 1800. Two notices of his death —one from the 'Newcastle Advertiser,' the other a minute of the Newcastle Monthly Meeting—are to be found in an Appendix to this book; and also an extract from a letter written by the eldest son Isaac, during the following week. In the letter, Isaac speaks of his father's funeral as having been attended "by a large number of Friends and others. Uncle and cousin Henry from Stockton, and some of our cousin Peases from Darlington, with cousin Thomas Gallilee from Whitby, were there."* The Uncle Henry here mentioned was the father of our heroines. He was the only brother of John Richardson who followed him to the grave. Isaac (who built the house at Cherry Hill) was dead, and William and Aaron lived too far away to be present.

The biographers of Friends suffer not only from a dearth of painted portraits, but of verbal descriptions of the personal appearance of the subjects of their labours. Those who, in former days, wrote of departed worthies were too anxious to draw instruction from the example of their

* 'Annals of the Cleveland Richardsons,' p. 84, and Appendix to this book.

devoted lives, and to dwell upon their spiritual impressions, to waste many words upon outward things.   Yet a tradition has been handed down of the noticeable appearance of these five Whitby men, the sons of Isaac Richardson and Isabel Vasie.   The good looks of William (the father of the sporting man and of Mrs. Spencer, of York) have already been mentioned.   Our heroines' father was a man with the darkest of eyes and of hair, with an aquiline nose, a well-shaped mouth, and the ruddy complexion so often seen in North Yorkshire.   All were tall men.   George Richardson thus writes of his father and of his uncles:—" Some of them were a little above the usual average height of stature.   He [meaning his father] was six feet two inches without his shoes; and, in their prime, I remember that some of them were comely and somewhat portly persons."*

By his father's will, and the consent of all his brothers, Henry succeeded to the tanyard and to the house at the Low Lights.   In 1802 his stepmother died and he was left alone.   Again petition was made to the " Uncle Henry," of Stockton, for one of his many daughters, and now it was the housewifely, energetic Mary who was sent.   The loss to the household she left was a severe one, but the gain to the home she entered was proportionately great!   Under her auspices, the once desolate, marshy Dene became a place of beauty.   The back garden was tastefully laid out, and by slight alterations in arrangement that in the front of the house assumed somewhat of the character it bore in later days, when to some who loved to go there it appeared a true oasis in the desert of smoke and sand which surrounded it.   To children, a visit to the Low Lights seemed like going into the country.   The walk down the steep path through the fields leading to it, the warm welcome, the spotless cleanliness, the flowers, the fruit, and the home-made cakes, seemed rather to recall a house within sound of the beck at Ayton than one near to the busy harbour of Shields.   The front garden had a special charm for children, with its steep grassy slope on one side, down which they delighted to slide, while the white blossoms of a large Siberian crab-tree showered down upon them. On the flat, close-cropped plot of grass below, the prickly hollies flourished magnificently, and the lilies-of-the-valley grew in beds beyond as if in congenial soil.   In these days of smoke and machinery, it will hardly be credited that then, and for many years after, there grew on one side of the

* ' Annals of the Cleveland Richardsons,' p. 71.

door a vine, whose grapes formed, if they did not ripen, and on the other side a very productive jargonelle pear-tree, whilst over the porch there clustered a clematis, covered in spring with lovely flowers. The fruit-trees were numerous and productive, and twenty bushels of apples have been gathered from them in some seasons.

A hospitable home was that of the Low Lights for all Friends, but for those who had ever borne the name of Richardson a warm and special welcome was reserved, and for no one was the welcome warmer than for Elizabeth, the youngest daughter of John Richardson, when she brought her children to visit her old home. She had married Joseph Procter, who had recently come to North Shields, where he had settled in business as a draper. He came to the town from Yarm, but the Procter family came from a more central part of Yorkshire, where in the seventeenth century the name occurs frequently in the annals of one locality.* King Charles the First had a chaplain, George Procter, who in 1624 was a Prebend of Ripon Cathedral, and Master of St. John's Hospital in the same city. Hard by, at Studley, lived a more noted person of the same name, Sir Stephen Procter, who, in 1595, bought the estate of Fountains Abbey, and pulled down the Abbot's House, that he might build his own mansion from its ruins. The foundations of the Abbot's house are still shown to the visitor, and prove that it was a building of magnificent proportions, ingeniously built upon arches over the channel of the river Skell. Sir Stephen's mansion, Fountains Hall, and its chapel, are also to be seen. It would be little pleasure to trace the kinship between our friends and this despoiler, who had a chequered career, and the history passes to a direct and to an honourable ancestor.

The old Roman town of Tadcaster has witnessed some stormy scenes. Two miles off, on Towton Heath, was fought the fiercest battle in the wars of the Roses; on Clifford Moor the Northern Earls mustered the hapless "Pilgrims of Grace" under their woeful banner; and at Tadcaster itself, in the next century, Sir Thomas Fairfax, with nine hundred men, held four thousand Royalists in check for a day. The mansion of the Fairfaxes is still to be seen at Newton, a mile from Tadcaster, and in the adjoining village of Clifford was the house of another Parliamentary soldier, Thomas Procter. We may conjecture that he first went to the wars with Fairfax,

---

* See Appendix, "Procter of Clifford."

but we know that he served with distinction in the army of Oliver Cromwell. When that strange force, in whose camps "no oath was heard, no drunkenness or gambling was seen," was disbanded, it was observed that its scattered members were successful in every department of honest industry, and that if a man, in any walk of English life, "attracted notice by his diligence and sobriety, he was, in all probability, one of Oliver's old soldiers."* Such a man was the Yorkshire yeoman Thomas Procter. He seems to have left the army before it was disbanded, and held the office of constable at Clifford about the year 1658 or the following year. Trained to habits of military discipline, he was, no doubt, a terror to evil-doers, but when he was ordered to take a man to prison whose only offence was that he was a Quaker, the spirit of the old Ironside rose in revolt. "Nay, that I will not do," he said. Threatened with punishment for his contumacy, he did not quail. "I had rather be a sufferer than a persecutor," was his undaunted reply. Quaker and constable were marched off to prison together, and need we wonder that the constable came out a Quaker? In the year 1660, Thomas Procter was again in prison, this time in York Castle, for refusing to pay tithes. Of his son Stephen, we know little more than that he lived at Cowton and afterwards at Pallathorpe Hall, near Tadcaster, and that he married Sarah Whitton, of York. Stephen Procter died at Pallathorpe Hall in 1727. His son Emmanuel lived some time on his grandfather's estate at Clifford, and then went northwards and settled in the town of Yarm. By his second wife, Barbara Conyers, Emmanuel Procter had two daughters, who were both married to Priestmans of Thornton (uncles of our heroines), and a son Joseph, who married Jane, widow of Andrew Wheldon, and daughter of Benjamin and Barbara Flounders of Yarm.† Joseph Procter, who came to live at North Shields, was a son of this marriage.

Thomas Procter, the soldier-yeoman of Clifford, ancestor of these peaceful persons, was clearly a man who feared to offend against God and his own conscience, but who knew no other fear. The same calm unflinching courage, the same obedience to the call of duty, and the same hatred of oppression and of wrong, have been observed in our day in those who descend from "Oliver's old soldier." But amidst the strong fibres derived from that sturdy stock, softer threads have been intermingled. Strange

---

* Macaulay's 'History,' Chapter II.
† See Chapter XVI. The Flounders Institute.

as it may seem, the Procters of Yarm were of an imaginative and romantic temperament, and are supposed to have introduced a new element into what we must call the Low Lights branch of the Richardson family. Poems written by Joseph Procter, and by many of his relatives at Yarm, have been preserved by their descendants.

Elizabeth is said to have been as sweet in mind as in person, and Mary Richardson had much pleasure in her society during her early years at the Low Lights.

Margaret, the elder daughter of John Richardson, had married Joseph Unthank, of Whitby, in 1791. She did not take kindly to the Whitby life, and always pined for her old home. Prompted by a desire to gratify this feeling and to reunite the two sisters, Joseph Procter and Joseph Unthank took Willington Mill, on the banks of the Tyne; the father of the present writer, then a very young man, being for a time a member of the firm. This mill (whose fame has not been entirely confined to the excellence of the flour it manufactured) remained in the Unthank and Procter family for seventy years.*

During her residence at the Low Lights, Mary Richardson became more strongly imbued with the principles of Friends. A strong attachment existed between her and her cousin Henry Richardson, and it is probable that their submission to the rules of the Society, which forbade the marriage of first cousins, was the only hindrance to their union. Their self-sacrifice may seem strange in our eyes, but to them their duty was clear. It never occurred to them that their paths in life should be divided because they could not walk more closely hand in hand. No wife was ever more devoted than Mary Richardson, and no widow mourned more sincerely for a husband's death than she did for her cousin's in 1834.

Their lives were a source of happiness to many. When, in 1820, the six children of Joseph and Elizabeth Procter were left orphans, the three youngest, Hannah, Sarah, and John were adopted by their uncle Henry at the Low Lights. Thus the home was cheered by the presence of children, whose affection gladdened the after life of those who had stood to them in the place of parents.

We will now leave Mary Richardson in her happy and active life at the Low Lights, and return to the sisters left at home.

* See Appendix, Willington Mill.

CHAPTER X.

Elizabeth and Hannah Richardson.

1800—1809.

"The young heart hot and restless,
And the old subdued and slow."
LONGFELLOW.

Now that half a century of Reforms and Railroads has brought about such changes in English life and customs, a great wave of longing and of regret is sweeping over the land for the old order of things which is passing so quickly out of our sight. It is this feeling which lends such a charm to those Reminiscences and Recollections of their early days with which so many famous people have favoured the world; and it is this feeling, "to compare great things with small," which has caused the present humble volume to be written. But although it is written to preserve some memory of the past, it is not written to point to that past as to a Golden Age. The quiet life in the old homes, whether among the Cleveland Hills, or by the Thornton beck, satisfied our forefathers, and many of them returned with pleasure to its repose from a brief experience of the life of towns. "This is t' canniest place we have seen in all our travels," said the last owner of Langbarugh, using the homely Cleveland vernacular as if that alone could express his pleasure at coming within sight of his own dwelling after a short absence. And, then as now, the greatest pleasure was enjoyed by the country-bred man who returned during the intervals of his busy town life to his early home, with all his intimate knowledge of rural sights and sounds quickened and intensified by his long deprivation of them.

But, then as now, youth sometimes wearied in the Happy Valleys. Their quiet had no charm to those who had not known the din of towns;

their rest was no blessing to those who had not done their share in the work of the world. The younger sister of our heroines (the writer's mother) was, when a child, left for two or three days at Thornton, during the absence of her uncle and aunt, who were attending the Quarterly Meeting at York. The weather was wet. The stock of books (already well known to the little visitor) was soon exhausted. The servant, her only companion in the house, was busy with her work. Playfellows or neighbours there were none. Need we wonder that the child, parted from her many sisters, compared herself to Alexander Selkirk, and exclaimed with him :—

> "Better dwell in the midst of alarms,
> Than reign in this horrible place!"

In later life she felt more penitence for her sacrilegious thought of her mother's lovely home than did her active sister Mary, who confessed that she had also wearied during a visit to Thornton, "because she had nothing to do, and the beck always ran the same way!"

Stockton, a far less beautiful, was a less secluded abode than Thornton Dale; but the happiest days of the Stockton household were before Isabel and Mary left it; and although, in former chapters, the departure of Isabel for Cherry Hill, and of Mary for the Low Lights has been recorded, the narrative must yet return for a moment to those early days when the sisters were all at home, of which the writer inherits her mother's memories. Isabel's influence over her sisters was a peaceful one, "her face was so calm and placid, and she was always so very good." Yet she had a strong sense of humour, and would join in their little jokes, but would sometimes retire to the solitude of her own chamber if the mirth grew too loud, or the satire too keen. She was, like her sisters, fond of poetry, repeating Addison's hymns to her latest days, and confessing that, in her youth, she had wept over the sorrows of 'Alcanzor and Zaida'!

There was a spinning-wheel in one of the upper rooms of the house at Stockton, and all the sisters tried to make use of it, with varying success. Elizabeth, so persevering in the practice of other arts, failed to learn how to spin. Probably in her zeal for progress she despised the spinning-wheel as an implement which the world had outgrown (perhaps

as a sign of the subjection of women), and when, in her impatience,
she broke the threads she sang some refrain about, "Oh, the folly of
spinning!" Isabel, on the contrary, attained to some proficiency in the
art, and would refer to it while engaged upon the "fancy knitting" and
"wool-work" which were amongst the pleasures of her old age, and which
the lapse of time has rendered in their turn "old fashioned," though it has
not, as yet, dignified them with the charm of "quaintness."

And, if Isabel's gentle presence was missed by her sisters, how much
less smoothly ran the wheels of the domestic machine when Mary's
energetic guidance was withdrawn! She was the undisputed queen in
her own domain; her cakes were the best; her pastry was the lightest;
her task, whether of needle-work or household work was the most quickly
and deftly performed. Added to this housewifely activity, Mary possessed
vigorous mental powers and good taste in literature; but in matters
relating to the intellect, Elizabeth's supremacy was acknowledged. "We
all thought Bessy knew everything," said Isabel in later years. But no
one knew so well as "Bessy" herself how limited was her knowledge or
longed more ardently to increase it. An earnest student of the facts of
history and of science, she was in youth an enthusiastic lover of poetry, and
her impassioned recitations were long remembered by her sisters. Lessons
in elocution were given to the family, one instructor being John Thelwall,
famous for the prosecution in which, some years before, his name had
figured in company with that of John Horne Tooke. Some progress
was effected in French, and even an attempt made (probably at a later
period) to acquire the science of music. This was relinquished on
realising the number of years required to attain proficiency in playing
upon any instrument.

Then there were lectures and books on astronomy; and to watch the
stars in an evening and to learn their names, became a pleasure to all
the sisters, especially to Mary. Readers of Mrs. Somerville's 'Life' may
remember the difficulties which beset the path of that eminent woman,
in her early struggles towards scientific attainments. Mrs. Somervilles
are rare; our heroines were simply intelligent girls, with a thirst for
knowledge. They, too, had their censors, and in divers walks of life.
It was said that a neighbour, who may possibly have been the barber
of the little town, on being told that "the Miss Richardsons studied

astronomy," remarked, "I wish women would keep to their proper speers!" That worthy man has long been gathered to his fathers, but he is not without successors in the land! The girls had other and more formidable censors. Elizabeth, in addition to her taste for serious study, had a great passion for art. The fashionable pursuits of the day were painting on velvet and Japan* work. These arts were much practised by all the sisters. But for drawing, sketching from nature, and painting, Elizabeth had genuine taste, and her power of intense perseverance enabled her to attain a fair amount of success. This success was looked upon without favour in some quarters.

The well-stored minds and cultivated intellects of many Friends of former days have been a subject of comment, and a reason has been found for these peculiarities in the fact that the teaching of the fine arts was excluded from the curriculum of the schools of the Society, and the practice of these arts was discouraged in the homes of its stricter members. That young people who do not learn music have more time to spare for solid acquirements is a fact which it is quite impossible to deny; and that dancing should be neither taught nor encouraged will surprise no one; but it may be difficult for the many artistic young Friends of the present day to realise that Elizabeth Richardson's love for drawing and painting met with marked disapproval. Encouragement of art was thought to be a great departure from "plainness." One engraving alone then hung upon the walls of a Friend's house—that of Benjamin West's picture representing William Penn's treaty with the Indians. To the grief of biographers, family portraits were all but unknown† amongst Friends until the present century had entered upon its fifth decade. Then, some of the younger members of the Society began to entertain wider views of culture, and their opinion had more weight with their parents than the opinion of the young had been allowed to have with the elders of a former generation. "Surely Friends are more vain than they used to be, both of themselves and of their relations," said Edward Pease forty years ago, on being shown

---

* So important was the art of "japanning" considered to be, that a friend of the sisters, who was about to marry a gentleman with a limited income, said, "I will be so useful; I can japan my own chairs!"

† Not quite "unknown," for a portrait in oils of David Priestman, of Malton, the beloved "Uncle David" of our heroines, remains in the possession of his grandchildren.

a portrait in oils of the writer's father, which he had submitted to have
taken to gratify his sons.   The censure was half serious, half playful, and
but few years elapsed before the censor himself yielded to the wishes of his
family.   How many copies of Edward Pease's photographs were sold in
his native town of Darlington we should fear to estimate.   Elizabeth
Richardson lived to teach drawing to the children of some Friends who had
rebuked her for learning it.   But these changes in sentiment were far
distant in 1802.

The "dulness," and the "deadness," and the "low state" of religious
communities in England at that time, not excepting the Society of Friends,
has been, in the opinion of the present writer, quite sufficiently dwelt
upon; and, if it be not the purpose of this book to refer to that period as
to a Golden Age, it is still less its purpose to darken the shadows in which
it has been depicted.   Memory recalls the names of many Friends then
living whose quiet influence was a power for good in the localities where
they spent their active and useful lives, amidst homely surroundings.

> "Why? for this very reason that they felt
> And did acknowledge, wheresoe'er they moved,
> A spiritual presence, sometimes misconceived,
> But still a high dependence, a divine
> Bounty and government, that filled their hearts
> With joy and gratitude, and fear and love." *

Lives brightened by culture were spent in those plain dwellings, warm
human sympathies glowed beneath that austere garb, and pure worship
was offered in those colourless meeting-houses.   But in more bounded
circles, where there was no scope for youthful activities, no indulgence for
youthful aspirations, where the elders seemed as though they had never
been young, where "this is inconsistent with our principles," "that has
never been encouraged by Friends," were phrases constantly heard, it
seemed as though a petrifying process had passed over Quakerism, leaving
it little more than a formal protest against all forms.

A purely negative system was ill-fitted to retain the allegiance of such
ardent spirits as Elizabeth and Hannah Richardson.   These two sisters
were close companions after Mary's departure from home in 1802.   At that
time Elizabeth was twenty-four and Hannah nineteen years of age.

* Wordsworth, 'The Excursion,' 4th Book.

People who knew Hannah Richardson in her youth were wont to speak of her with a peculiar brightening of the eyes, as though they remembered looking upon a pleasant sight. Very lively and active in her childhood (Stockton neighbours said she was as likely to appear in the street by springing from the window of her father's house as by issuing decorously from the door), she grew up tall and of a vigorous constitution. Unusually warm-hearted, she was much more demonstrative of her affection for those she loved—and she loved many—than was usual in that formal age. Charles Lamb's verse might have been written of her—

> "Her parents held the Quaker rule,
> Which doth the human feelings cool,
> But she was formed in Nature's school;
> Nature had blessed her,"—

and, looking upon the world with "cheerful eyes," she brightened it for those around her. She may not have been handsome, but her fine figure, brilliant complexion, and countenance beaming with kindness, were full of attraction; and her unfailing vivacity completed the charm. We need not wonder that she had many friends and many lovers. Her after-life proved that she possessed the solid sense and good judgment which distinguish many members of the Richardson family; but her winning brightness and enthusiasm she inherited from her mother, Hannah Priestman, of Thornton, the tradition of whose pleasant looks and loveable character that of her daughter and namesake so forcibly recalls.

At nineteen, Hannah was naturally much under the influence of the powerful mind of her sister Elizabeth, who was five years her senior. The two sisters were full of dreams and aspirations—perhaps of ambitions. It is not only in our day that girls have longed "to have something to do," to break away from conventions, and to go out into the world to work as their brothers work, to make a career for themselves. We must remember how short was the time since it had seemed as though a new era of freedom and independence had dawned upon the world—when, as the grave Wordsworth wrote in after years :—

> "Bliss was it in those days to be alive,
> But to be *young* was very heaven!"

The dawn had been overcast, but the hopes it had excited were not dead in all hearts.

Henry Richardson, the father of our heroines, was thoroughly master of his own house as to things which he deemed of importance, but he interfered little with the pursuits of his daughters. He bore with equanimity the sight of the drawings and the paintings, the japanned chairs and the screens, with which, chiefly by the industry of Elizabeth, the rooms of his house were filled. Nor did he especially concern himself as to the manner in which Hannah's light brown hair was arranged under her cap, or as to the depth with which her train swept the ground. But there were persons, whose names have not reached posterity, who thought it their duty to direct Henry Richardson's attention to these outward signs of (what appeared to them) a love of dress, an absorption in frivolous pursuits, and a general "worldliness" of character unbecoming in the daughters of a Friend.

No perfection of character is claimed for the heroines of this volume. Elizabeth, high spirited and independent, had the defects of those qualities, and was, all her life, somewhat intolerant of dulness and narrow-mindedness. To Hannah, we have applied one verse of Charles Lamb's 'Hester,' and it may be that another verse of the same poem well described her at this period of her life :

> "A springy motion in her gait,
> A rising step, did indicate
> Of pride and joy no common rate
>   That flushed her spirit;
> I know not by what name beside
> I shall it call, if 'twas not pride
> It was joy to that allied
>   She did inherit."

The nameless Friends of Stockton, believing, it may be, that they were actuated by good motives, even in their interference between parent and children, tried to draw too closely the bonds of sectarian intolerance and found them break in their hands. The two sisters resigned their membership in the Society. No hint of any failure of love and respect towards their father has ever reached us, but there is no doubt that the step they took gave him pain. They asked him to give them the money which he intended to leave to them at his death, and to allow them to go into the world to maintain themselves. He acceded to their request, and the scheme they had formed was speedily carried into execution. It was with light hearts that they left the comfort and shelter of their father's house, and went "to seek their fortunes" like boys in the story books. "Some natural tears" might be shed in parting from their younger sister, to whom their departure was a grief, but there was no regret for their own decision. Behind them lay (or so it seemed) sectarian bigotry, old-world fears and restrictions, a narrow and a bounded life: before them, unfettered freedom of thought and of action, independent means of support, and unchecked intellectual advancement. Elizabeth, besides her artistic pursuits, was no stranger to those of literature, though none of her compositions, whether in prose or in poetry, have come down to us. But she was not so ambitious as to propose to support herself by either her pencil or her pen. Her mind seems to have grasped the idea that the future of England rested with the investigators and inventors who, in that time of fierce wars and political strife, were quietly maturing the forces which were to change the face of the world, and she wished to take her humble place in their army of workers.

Early in this century, the inventive genius and enlightened wisdom of Edward Strutt and of Richard Arkwright had made the town of Derby a centre of industrial activity, and the eyes of persons who looked to the future with hope, were turned to a town where such influences predominated. It is probable that Elizabeth and Hannah Richardson had already some friends in Derby when they took a house in that town, about the year 1805. Their intention was to engage in the manufacture of hosiery, by some newly invented process. What that process was, and by what agency it was to be worked, are matters entirely unknown to the writer of these pages. It would have been interesting to have traced the progress of the enterprise, and to have seen the bright hopes of success and independence with which it was begun, fade away in gradual discouragement, and end in failure and disappointment. The only financial result of the adventure was the diminution of the modest patrimony of the two sisters; but the years which they spent in Derby constituted a memorable epoch in their lives. There was much stirring of intellectual life in the town. Dr. Erasmus Darwin had just died within sight of its towers, his fame was at its height, and his sayings upon every tongue. And the town had had a painter of its own. "Wright of Derby" may not have been an artist of the first order, but his portraits of Dr. Darwin,

of Mr. Thomas Day, and of other famous men who lived in the Midland
Counties during the eighteenth century, lent an interest to the collection
of his paintings which was exhibited in London in our own day.

Although our heroines found their industrial occupation unremunerative, they were not disappointed in their hope of finding in Derby
means of intellectual improvement. In its Public Library, and in its
lectures on science, it was far in advance of quiet old Stockton. Life
in Derby was a time of great enjoyment to both the sisters. They were
introduced to a social circle, which contained many persons of liberal
minds and of extended culture, and others of considerable scientific
attainments. Amongst this group, as in the quieter circles of Quakerism,
both sisters, but especially Hannah, had many suitors, none of whom were
able to induce them to resign their dearly-prized independence. No hint
of such matters was ever dropped by the sisters in later years. Hannah
referred but little to the Derby episode in her life, but Elizabeth was less
reticent, especially as to the friendships formed. They lived on terms of
the closest intimacy with a young girl who, although bearing a French
name, came by her mother of a Cleveland family. She died in early life,
and the writer well remembers the passionate affection shown by Elizabeth
Richardson for her memory, and the intense interest with which, during
a visit to Guisborough, Elizabeth, then an old woman, gazed upon the
home of her lost friend. With another Derby family, intimacy continued
through life. Two ladies of the name of Bennett visited Elizabeth
repeatedly in North Shields and in the Lake District. They were clever,
cultivated gentlewomen, of the Unitarian persuasion, and with that vivacity
of manner, and wide social and literary interests which distinguished some
ladies of their day.

It was probably at Derby that the attempt to acquire the science
of music was made by our heroines; and in the same town, it may
be, were taken miniature portraits of the two sisters, once beheld for a
moment by some of their young relatives. On resigning their membership
in the Society of Friends, and removing to a town where they had no
association with members of that community, the sisters laid aside its
distinguishing garb. Elizabeth despised the habit of paying much attention to outward appearance, and dressed plainly and quietly. Hannah,
who had chafed under vexatious interference with her freedom in such

matters, indulged somewhat more in attire suited to her age and appearance. Great was the excitement amongst her north-country relatives when she appeared amongst them dressed in a fashionable pelisse which set off her striking figure, and in a stylish hat of the "gipsy" form, adorned with ostrich-feathers. Dancing was one of the accomplishments acquired at Derby, and Hannah was supposed to excel in the art.

But all these gaieties were interrupted by news which re-awakened home affections in the hearts of the two absent daughters. Their father's health was failing, and the sisters left at home began to suffer from their close attendance upon him. For more than a year, night-watching was necessary, and Hannah went home to take her share in the work. Their elder brother, then recently married to Deborah Procter of Selby, resided in Stockton, and proved an able assistant in nursing. All the family were gathered around their father before his death, which occurred in 1808.

Henry Richardson was a man highly esteemed by his friends and neighbours. Had his bright spirited wife lived longer, the intercourse between him and his children might have been closer and less restrained; but if somewhat grave and reticent towards them, he was eminently a just and a kind parent.

After his death, the youngest girl went for a long visit to her sisters in Derby. She became introduced to their friends, and entered into their social interests in the town, and shared in their intense enjoyment of the beauties of the surrounding country. In the memories of Matlock and Dovedale, of Haddon Hall, and of Chatsworth there was no alloy, and all the sisters referred to them with pleasure. Elizabeth painted Derby with all its towers and spires from many points of view. Cases of labelled specimens of Derbyshire spar, netting-weights and picture-frames of the same material were treasured by all the sisters, and remain in the writer's possession memorials of those long-past days.

And now it was decided to break up both the old home at Stockton and the newer home at Derby, and for the four sisters, Ann, Elizabeth, Hannah, and Sarah to reside together at Newcastle-upon-Tyne. After their life at Derby, it is probable that Stockton had few attractions for Elizabeth and Hannah, and Mary's warm affection was a magnet which attracted her sisters to the North. The family of their brother and of their old tutor John Chipchase were left with regret, and so doubtless were other Stockton friends whose names are less familiar.

With the final departure of our heroines from Stockton, they passed out of sight of the hills associated with the history of their family, and with their own earliest recollections. But Cleveland remained a district full of interest for all the sisters to the end of their lives, and the origin of one of the ties of affection which bound them to it may be here recorded.

A young Friend from Ayton, Rachel White, lived in Henry Richardson's family as nurse to his younger children. She afterwards passed into the service of a cousin and namesake of her former employer, who had a house in Stockton and another in Ayton, and generally resided at the last-named place. Rachel White, while still a young woman, was left in sole charge of the large house in Stockton, living in it alone for more than ten years, except for the brief visits of its owner. When in after years the writer of these pages was taken as a child to see her mother's old nurse, Rachel White lived with her sisters, first upon a farm at Little Ayton, and afterwards in a cottage upon Ayton Green. Both abodes are associated with memories of flagged passages of snowy whiteness, with a pervading sense and scent of exquisite cleanliness, with curd-cheese cakes never to be equalled, and with the kindest old faces in the world. Rachel's tall, strong figure was bent with age, but her smile had a grave sweetness, and her complexion a healthy tint. Another tall sister helped her brother with the farm ; a third, whose neat Friends' cap encircled a cheerful countenance and cheeks like rosy apples, presided at the tea-table. All the sisters attained to the ages usual at Ayton. But even at ninety-four, Rachel White never forgot the family she had loved so well and served so faithfully, nor wearied of speaking of their kindness to her during her long residence in Stockton. One fact was indelibly impressed upon her memory. Henry Richardson's daughters thought it unfitting, and even unsafe, that a young woman should be the sole occupant of their cousin's large house at night, and they resolved that the thing should not happen. " Who is going to sleep with Rachel to-night?" was a question which always met with a ready response from one of their number. Never once during all those years did that lonely woman look in vain at nightfall for the coming of one of those bright young girls to cheer her solitude. The boon to her was great, but the visitors had their reward, not only in Rachel's constant sympathy with their joys and sorrows, but in the benefit to their characters from constant association with so good a woman.

This chapter being entirely founded upon family traditions, certainty about dates is rendered difficult. A public event is here a landmark, and leads to the conclusion that the sisters left Stockton towards the end of the year 1809. When they settled in Newcastle, the inhabitants of that town, like other English people, were preparing to celebrate the Jubilee of the reign of King George the Third.

CHAPTER XI.

Newcastle.

1809—1811.

"He was one whose open face
Did his inmost heart reveal,
One who wore with meekest grace
On his forehead Heaven's broad seal :
Like a patriarchal sage,
Holy, humble, courteous, mild,
He could blend the awe of age
With the sweetness of a child."

JAMES MONTGOMERY.

A DELIGHTFUL writer, who if only for his intimate knowledge and love of Northumberland deserves to be held in honour by all its sons and daughters, has spoken of the "soft voices" and the "slow speech" of the Northumbrians.* These "soft voices" rise towards the end of each sentence in tones peculiar to the Border County. "How I do admire your recitative!" said a nobleman to a North Shields lady in a crowded London drawing-room sixty years ago. "Pardon me, Sir, but your voice sounded in my ears like old music!" said a Northumbrian exile to a perfect stranger whom he had heard speaking at a public table in the "sing-song" tones which had been familiar to him in his childhood. But all these pleasant sayings are perhaps more applicable to the country districts and smaller towns of Northumberland than to its metropolis, and we can well imagine that early in this century the rugged "burr" of Newcastle would sound somewhat harshly in the ears of strangers, even if like the heroines of our story, they had only travelled from the banks of the Tees to those of the Tyne. But these new-comers, although they had left behind them the country of the "ghylls" and the "becks," soon took

* Mr. Walter Besant, in 'Let Nothing You Dismay.'

kindly to the land of the "denes" and the "burns." Their house was in Pandon Street. Pandon, once a village, was joined to Newcastle in the charter of Edward the First. Pandon Gate, demolished in 1795, had been one of the towers of the Roman wall,* and Pandon Dene was, in 1810, still unspanned by a bridge. Not far from it was Jesmond Dene, as delightful to the sisters of our story in its primitive wildness as Jesmond Park in its cultivated beauty is to the inhabitants of Newcastle of our day.

To persons so fond of historical associations as our heroines were, their new home was full of interest. In 1790, less than twenty years before, Newcastle was still a fortified town, surrounded by its strong walls, with their twenty-four gates still standing. These, however, were now being demolished one by one, to make room for the rapid increase of population. The Close Gate and the Sand Gate, as well as Pandon Gate, had disappeared before the end of the century. In 1810, the Pilgrim's Gate had but just vanished from the street so well known to Friends; and "the West Gate, a mighty stronge thinge," with its gates of oak and its doors of iron, still gloomed over the thoroughfare that bears its name. Owls built their nests in the turrets of the massive structure, and their hootings accompanied the lonely evening walks of the few citizens of Newcastle whose homes were beyond its walls, in such remote localities as Summerhill. In those days the new streets of Newcastle were Dean Street and Mosley Street, which had been formed after the filling up of a deep "dene" near the town. Eldon Square was undreamed of: Grey Street and its surroundings are but of yesterday.

Our heroines had many relatives in Newcastle. One was of their mother's kindred, Jonathan Priestman, of Malton, who had recently come to the town in which he was to reside during the remainder of his long and honourable life. Feeling still a stranger in the place, he welcomed the coming of his cousins who knew his old home so well, and gladly spent his evenings at their house. He possessed a boat, which may

---

* "As auld as Pandon Yett" was a proverb in Newcastle, as the 'Monthly Chronicle of North Country Lore and Legend' (Walter Scott) reminded us in an article on "Pandon" in its June number. From this article we learn that Pandon was formerly a place of orchards and gardens, where, in early times, the Kings of Northumbria, in later years the Dukes of Northumberland, had their residences. Although these mansions had vanished, something of the rural character of the place seems to have remained in 1810.

have been used for some of the trips which were taken down the river
to the Low Lights, where Mary Richardson had a warm welcome for her
"own people."

   Two of the sons of John Richardson of the Low Lights had settled
in Newcastle.   Isaac, the eldest son, mentioned in a former chapter as
a man of unusual ability, died in the year 1810.   His four children,
early deprived of his care, found a second father in their uncle George
Richardson.   Of this remarkable man, so often referred to in these pages
as the author of the 'Annals' of his family, a 'Biographical Sketch' has
been written by his children and published, together with his own brief
'Early Autobiography,' and the 'Journal' of his travels in the ministry.
At the time of his death, in 1862, another sketch appeared in a Newcastle
newspaper.   This was from the pen of Dr. Collingwood Bruce, long George
Richardson's fellow-worker in the Bible Society, and happily still amongst
us to delight all true Northumbrians with his knowledge of their ancient
ballads and legends, and to be the highest authority upon such subjects
as the history of the Norman Keep of Newcastle, and the Roman Wall.
Dr. Bruce's Sketch is printed in the Appendix to this volume, and the
Life of George Richardson is accessible to all, but any work calling itself
"Records" of the Richardson family would be poor indeed if it contained
no attempt to portray the most noteworthy person who has borne the
name.

   George, the fourth son of John Richardson of the Low Lights, was
born at that place in 1773.   He came to reside in Newcastle in 1787, when
he was fourteen years of age.   In his 'Autobiography,' he speaks of the
great spiritual and mental conflicts through which he passed during those
early years.   One vivid mental impression, he remembered, flashed through
his mind when passing through one of the ancient gates of Newcastle,
through which so many generations of human creatures had passed before
him.   To other persons he appeared at that time as a "youth of sweet,
serious deportment, and one with whom the frivolities of youth had little
or no place."   He was but twenty years of age, and still under articles of
apprenticeship to his calling, which was that of a grocer and leather-
dealer, when his voice was first heard in Newcastle meeting-house as
a preacher, and only twenty-four when recorded by the Monthly Meeting
as one of its acknowledged ministers.   So strongly did his devotion of

N

character impress those around him, that his master, a Friend named Joshua Watson, used to remain at home to enable his apprentice to attend distant meetings.

A remarkable circumstance occurred during the early years of his ministry. One of the Whitby settlers in North Shields, a lively, energetic man, was so far carried away by the temporary prosperity brought to shipowners by the French war, as to begin to build what, in the eyes of his fellow-townsmen, appeared not so much a large house as a mansion. Nothing like it had been seen in North Shields before; there was much shaking of heads amongst friends and neighbours, with whom the impulsive man was a favourite. When the news of this wonderful building in quiet old Shields reached Newcastle, it was taken very seriously by George Richardson. This young man, under the strongest sense of duty, came down purposely to visit his former fellow-townsman in the height of his prosperity, and remonstrated with him upon the course he was pursuing, and solemnly warned him that if the enterprise was persisted in, few years would elapse before not one stone would remain upon another of the great house. We do not hear that any offence was taken by the elder man, but he did not heed the youth's warning. The house was finished and inhabited. In due time the crash came. Books and furniture were sold, but no purchaser came for the house. Dwellers in North Shields have generally been plain, unassuming people, and all feared to live in so great a mansion. It stood empty for years, and local tradition tells that a band of robbers took up their abode in its empty rooms, and sallied forth at night to make their depredations upon the peaceful inhabitants of Shields. It thus became a danger to the neighbourhood. One day, the two principal creditors were walking past the house, and discussing the question as to what purpose it could be made to serve. They were neither of them Friends, and knew nothing of what we must call the prophecy. At length one creditor said, "It will never be of any use as it stands; we had better pull it down, and sell the materials." This was done, the great house was pulled down to the very ground, "not one stone was left upon another." The row of houses forming the north side of what is called Northumberland Square stands upon its site, and is built from its ruins.

An inhabitant of Newcastle once said that when young he was

induced to take serious views of life by merely meeting George Richardson in the streets. Generally taking the middle of the road to avoid interruption, wrapt in solemn thought, and utterly unconscious of passers-by, the good man's reverent demeanour preached a voiceless sermon to his fellow-townsmen. But it preached no lesson of selfish seclusion, or of self-righteous isolation from his fellow-men. From his early years in Newcastle, when as a youth, he gathered men round him in an adult school, and had poor pensioners on his slender purse, until the days when, an old man of four-score, "he might still be seen," in the words of Dr. Bruce, "clambering the dark and dirty stairs leading to the tenements of the poor, he was a friend to those who had no helper." His was no indiscriminate charity, for every case was investigated and decided on its own merits, and no labour was spared to find out the deserving.

It was not only the poor of Newcastle who benefited by his thoughtful care. In his old age, he spent part of the summer at Cullercoats, now a prosperous sea-side resort, but then a mere fishing village. There was no church near it, and little means of either secular or religious instruction. George Richardson and his family, more especially his niece and his daughter, were real benefactors to the place, and much beloved by the hard-working fisher people, who then formed almost its sole population. With that practical wisdom so often found among members of the Society of Friends, the temporal as well as the spiritual wants of the "toilers of the sea" were thought of. A better supply of water was obtained for their houses; the foot-paths were mended, so that the women could carry their creels of fish more easily to the towns; a little pier was built for the accommodation of the fishermen; and, at length, a school-house was built and opened for the instruction of their children. In these undertakings kind and liberal help was obtained from Newcastle and Shields, but the originators were George Richardson and his friends.

At one of the Annual Meetings of the School, speaking to the fisher-people of the benefit it would confer on their children, he said, "The only education I ever had in my youth was from a man whose sole qualification for keeping a school was that he was *lame*, and therefore disabled for making a livelihood in any other way." But although George Richardson owed little to school instruction, and his reading in early life had been chiefly in the Bible and the writings of the early Friends, in his later life his reading was as wide as his sympathies. Seated by him one day at a dinner-table, the writer was (foolishly enough) surprised to find that he was reading a book edited by Bishop Wilberforce,—Evelyn's 'Life of Mrs. Godolphin,'—and taking pleasure in the thought that so pure and even saintly a character could exist in the corrupt court of Charles the Second. A very staunch Friend, his mind was stored with the writings and sayings of good people of·all creeds and countries. A Newcastle youth was going to reside in Ayrshire, and called to say "Farewell" to George Richardson. In parting, the old man said, "Robert, thou wilt be far from any Friends, but I hope thou wilt go to a place of worship; there have been many good divines in Scotland."

The poets, too, had their place in his affections. Addison's hymns were as much loved by him as by his cousin Isabel Casson; Milton's sonnet on his blindness was an especial favourite, and one verse of Pope's 'Universal Prayer' was often on his lips :—

"This day be bread and peace my lot,
All else beneath the sun
Thou know'st if best bestowed or not,
And let Thy will be done."

It is not, as a rule, to the aged members of a sect, or of a party, that our eyes are turned when great changes seem to be required. To this rule, however, there are remarkable exceptions, and George Richardson was one of them. In his old age, he became convinced that the Society of Friends had not taken its due part in missions to the heathen, and one of the last acts of his life was to write letters to influential Friends in different parts of England to urge this view upon them. No doubt the time was ripe for the change, yet the fact may be noted that the "Friends' Foreign Missions" to Madagascar and other countries, have all arisen since the writing of those letters.

When his cousins came to live in Newcastle, George Richardson was a man in middle life. It has been said that they came to that town while all England was debating, as it debated during 1887, how best to celebrate the conclusion of the fifty years' reign of its sovereign. The long-headed, sensible Northumbrians, instead of illuminating their towns, decided to build schools for the children of their poor. In the Royal Jubilee Schools of Newcastle, of which the first stone was laid on the 4th of June, 1810,

George Richardson took the warmest interest. He was long a worker on the Committee of the Schools, and they have not been neglected by his family.

Of George Richardson's fifty years' work for the Newcastle Bible Society, and of the 250,000 Bibles that passed through his hands during those years, the reports in our Appendix must speak. In this work he was succeeded by his son Henry Richardson, who has only recently gone from amongst us. He was a man of peculiarly gentle and retiring disposition, but his name, in conjunction with that of his wife, is known in many fields of labour, more especially in the cause of Peace. " Spend thy life actively and usefully, and much of thy time will pass pleasantly," George Richardson once wrote to one of his daughters; and " No life can be pleasing to God which is not useful to man," was a saying which he adopted. His children followed his precepts and his example.

In the midst of his busy life, he sometimes found time to call upon his cousins. On one occasion he found them in some perplexity. The street in which they lived had little traffic passing through it, and was therefore resorted to by children for their games. Persons who have lived in such streets can sympathise with our heroines. Provoked by the uproar, their servant one day rushed out and emptied a water-jug over the delinquents. Driven off for a moment, they returned in seven-fold strength, and with redoubled clamour. The tale was told to " Cousin George" on his visit. He considered the matter, and mildly suggested, " Suppose you had given them some raisins and asked them kindly to go away, might that have been a better plan ?" The spirit, if not the letter, of the advice was acted upon, and comparative peace reigned in Pandon Street.

Even our heroines Elizabeth and Hannah, who had been repelled by the narrow-mindedness of some Friends, were won to love the humble simplicity of their cousin's character, and to reverence his goodness. With his unselfish and unworldly spirit, which coveted no riches either for himself or his family, they could well sympathise. His simple, frugal habits were formed from no motive of asceticism, but simply that he might have more to give to those in need. His cousins told, as others have done, of the door of his office being besieged by the poor of Newcastle, and of his being found there distributing clothing alike to men and to women. One of their stories had a touch of pathos. His good wife, on returning from a walk with her little children, was once greeted by him with the remark, "My dear, I knew that thou hadst two cloaks, and I felt sure thou wouldst spare one of them to a poor woman who had none, so I took it from the closet where it hung, and gave it to her." Alas! the self-denying wife and mother had gone out in her oldest cloak, so her best one was given away to the poor woman.

The sisters of our narrative appear to have only resided for two years in Newcastle. They always referred to that time with interest and pleasure. Few natives of the town could have known more intimately than they its nooks and corners, its "banks" and "chares," its historic houses and its ancient "Gates," amongst which the writer was often taken when so young as to be more awed by such portentously black and gloomy buildings than interested by their antiquity.

The sisters long regretted the Newcastle "Literary and Philosophical Society," with its Lectures and its Library—even in that day a fine collection of books. But North Shields, although in such advantages far inferior to Newcastle, had attractions. Their sister Mary, having drawn them into the same county as herself, now longed to have them in the same town; and their youngest brother was a sailor, and had a ship of his own, which he sailed in and out of the harbour of Shields.

Their house in the long-vanished Pandon Street must have been near to the river Tyne; their new house in Shields stood upon its bank, and thus their furniture was easily removed by boat. Henceforward North Shields was the home of the sisters.

CHAPTER XII.

Letters.

1811—1818.

"Oh, dream of joy! is this indeed
The lighthouse top I see?
Is this the hill? is this the kirk?
Is this my own countree?"

COLERIDGE.

VISITORS to North Shields who find their way to the Fish Quay may observe, standing upon the high bank above it, a row of dark stone houses facing the south. Pleasant people lived happily in those houses fifty years ago; and in earlier and comparatively smokeless days, before the introduction of steamboats upon the Tyne, they must have been bright, cheerful abodes indeed. The row was built and owned by a Mr. Hutchinson, whose daughter resided in one of the houses to the close of her vigorous life of nearly a hundred years. In the days of its prosperity, the row bore the simple name of Hutchinson's Buildings. Now, in the time of its somewhat fallen fortunes, it has received the appellation of Tyne Terrace! The houses have long, narrow gardens in front of them, which are mostly laid out in what were called grass plats. Lawn was a word rarely used in the North of England until the introduction of the game of croquet. Only the road separates the gardens from the edge of the river-bank; and at right angles with them, facing the east, eighty stone steps lead to the road and shore below. These "long stairs" are divided into short flights by broad landings; and it is said that a couple of runaway horses, with a postchaise behind them, once galloped down them, taking each flight at a bound. An old man, perched upon a ladder mending the roof of one of the little houses, whose doors open upon the landings, was in imminent peril; but no life, human or equine, was sacrificed. The horses were found, trembling but unhurt, at the bottom of the steps. Of the fate of the empty chaise, history is silent.

At the top of the long stairs stands the "Look-out" House for the pilots; at their foot (across a road and on a little promontory) was the Sand End, where maidens were wont to stand to wave adieux to departing sailors as the ships passed down "the Narrows." On the one side of the Sand End stands the Low Lighthouse, and close by it, the Watch-house, a low building, whence a stentorian voice hails ships through a speaking-trumpet as they enter the harbour, and demands the name of the master, the port from whence his ship comes, and the cargo which she carries. Close by, too, is Clifford's Fort, then mounted with cannon, but now converted into a torpedo-station. Further along the shore, tents were pitched for bathing, and much resorted to in those early days; but now the Fish Quay with its stirring traffic, which has nearly swallowed up the Sand End, drives the bathers to Tynemouth.

Between the shore and the bank stretches that tract of level ground upon which, even in 1811, the manufactories which now cover it were beginning to arise, and which, in the commercial world, bears the name of the Low Lights; whilst beyond, nestled in its dene, lay that green spot which bears that name in this history. Whether by the shore, or by the path through the fields, Mary Richardson was within ten minutes' walk of her sister's new home.

Except in its earlier chapters, this narrative has had little help from written documents; but a small bundle of letters written by Elizabeth and Hannah Richardson during their first days in Shields to their cousin Jonathan Priestman in Newcastle, were carefully preserved by him, and have been, by the kindness of his family, placed at the disposal of the writer. The correspondence is at first very frequent. The cousins had been accustomed to meet every evening and to discuss the books they read, and other subjects of interest, and the correspondence is an attempt to make up for the loss of this daily intercourse. In reading the characteristic letters of Elizabeth, we must remember that she was now more than thirty years of age, and that her cousin and correspondent was ten years her junior. Hannah's unstudied effusions, like her letters in later life, overflow with adjectives and affection, and are somewhat diffuse

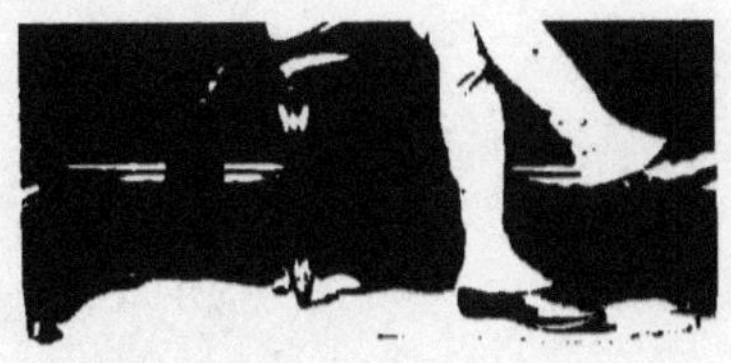

JONATHAN PRIESTMAN,

in style. But if her letters have no value as compositions, they have (unlike Elizabeth's) the great merit of being dated. By the first of the series we find that November 10th, 1811, was the first Sunday spent by the sisters in their new house at Shields. It was marked by weather not entirely unknown in that locality. After regretting the non-arrival of her sailor brother and his ship, Hannah writes:—"What a howling blast here is, and oh, how it blew in the night! I wished myself far out of the reach of the sound of the roaring of the ocean." Speaking of their first arrival at their new home, she says :—

"I found Mary very busy. The boat had just unloaded, and every-thing was safe. Nothing was broken except the pendulum of the clock. Surely nothing of the kind was ever conducted with less trouble, thanks to the kindness of our friends. Mary, with her usual right hearty good will to help us, had got all made so very comfortable, there was little left for us to do, so we all went to dine at the Low Lights the next day on roast pig! We think Ann better since she came; she complains of the cold, although until to-day we have had the weather very fine, and this is really a pleasant house when the wind is not from the east. To-day we are to have our house-warming, but with none but relations, mind; indeed they will fill our small room. I do believe we are going to be good neighbours with Cousin William, for he seems equally disposed for it with ourselves. And now I have only to add that I hope thou wilt often give us the opportunity of tasting the enjoyment which those cozy, social, long-to-be-remembered evenings which we have spent together afforded. Farewell.—H. RICHARDSON."

Let no one be surprised that anything called a house-warming should be held in a circle of Friends on Sunday. The entertainment would be simply five o'clock tea. The little party, on their return from the afternoon meeting, would gather round the table; the cakes might be varied in kind and abundant in quantity, but the guests would disperse by eight o'clock. If a similar company met on a week-day evening, the time might be somewhat lengthened, and fruit or cakes might be handed between eight and nine o'clock. The mention of "our small room" may surprise those who remember the delightful three-windowed drawing-rooms of Hutchinson's Buildings, with their magnificent sea-view. But these were on the second floor, and it is probable that the sisters, being four in number, and having many visitors, used all their upper rooms as bedrooms. The following letter from Elizabeth is evidently written later on the same day as Hannah's. It is given almost in full.

Elizabeth Richardson to J. Priestman.

"I would fain write to thee cheerily, my dear cousin, and tell thee, as I might truly do, that we seem all taking root in this new soil, but this stormy day chills all my gaiety. We got thy parcel yesterday, and thank thee for the book. Thy letter had too much of the spirit of genuine kindness to be less than welcome; but still it disappointed us, for it told us that we should not see thee to-day.

"What novices we are in the art of living happily! If thou wert sitting on thy old sofa seat, I would give thee twenty instances, all new importations from the field of observation, of people wilfully, or indolently, suffering mental pain when they might enjoy comparative pleasure; but writing is a tedious process, so I will only notice one—the case our own. Thou and we have some associations which wisdom tells us should not be broken. We have spent a part of our time in company and conversation which stimulated our mental faculties very agreeably. The opportunity for doing this daily is gone by, and at the customary hour we feel with pain that it *is* gone by. What would be so likely to banish these feelings of loneliness, perhaps of desertedness on thy part, and this want of a lost pleasure on ours, as substituting images of a different aspect? When thou hast paid us a few visits in our new home, and seen us enjoy ourselves in it, thou wilt then, I trust, have recollections of pleasant interviews at short intervals, and the consciousness would predominate that thou hast friends within an hour's ride to whom thy welfare and happiness are of importance. By dwelling on the past, rather than substituting new views of things, thou art now acting like one of these 'novices,' as I hoped to be able to prove by a plain statement when I began this; — but stop, I have not time; they will be coming in from meeting, so I will leave thee to find out all that remains unsaid, or is said obscurely. * * * *

"After all my haste, they came in from meeting before I arrived at my conclusion—William, Henry and Mary with Hannah. Our company has now gone, and now I can tell thee this house-warming is quietly, yet languidly, over. Cousin William can and will talk when set going: so can I, but having no leader to tell us what tune to play, our fiddles laid by idle, while we played on the strings with our fingers, A, B, C, &c. Hannah says, 'We shall do better when we gain some local interests; we shall then have subjects in common.' But, alas! what are 'common' subjects? Do they deserve the name of conversation?

"Thanks to our kind friends, this removing has been easily and agreeably managed. Ann's repinings become fainter daily. We have been very kindly welcomed by all our relations; much notice from the other Friends we neither expect nor covet. I wish thou couldst see how pleasantly we have spent some mornings since we got settled. Mary has come up with her work after breakfast to talk with Hannah and me, as we sat by the parlour-window enjoying the sunshine and the prospect. * * * * I am, affectionately, E. RICHARDSON."

The next letters are on literary matters. Their cousin was a subscriber to Coleridge's periodical called the 'Friend,' and sent them some of the numbers to read. He had also copied for them extracts from an article in the 'Eclectic Review' on Miss Seward's 'Letters,'* which interest both his correspondents in the highest degree. They seem, as women, to have taken an especial pleasure and pride in Miss Seward's accomplishments; and she was, no doubt, known to some of their friends at Derby. We may wonder at their admiration for letters of which the elaborately artificial style strikes us now so painfully; but we must remember their taste was formed on eighteenth century models, and that simplicity of diction is a modern invention. Miss Seward belongs to a past age, and is well nigh forgotten, whereas the name of Coleridge meets us on every hand in the literature of our own day.

Both letters being on the same subjects, Elizabeth's is given here in full:—

Elizabeth Richardson to J. Priestman.

"It was past ten o'clock when thy parcel arrived, my dear cousin. Thank thee twice over for thy quotations from the 'Review.' We will wait very patiently for the remainder until thou canst read it to us. I am very glad they are justifying themselves by giving an able critique on these letters. Probably the author's contempt for reviews and

* 'Eclectic Review,' vol. xiv., article "Anna Seward's Letters."

reviewers has proved a salutary stimulus while they affect to laugh at it. The 'masculine strength and capacity of mind' made us smile, as such expressions generally do, because they are generally very ridiculous. In this case they seem to be inappropriate. There were not any masculine qualities predominant in Anna Seward, unless we allow accurate and vigorous thought to be such, and perhaps we must, as that proceeds from judgment; but judgment in her was less conspicuous than strong imagination and highly-cultivated poetic taste. But we can talk of these things.

"None of the books we sent for were in, I suppose, as Marshall sent us Gilpin's 'Lives of the Reformers,' a very interesting work if we had been in such a course of reading at this time. I have read nothing in it but a little of the account of the eloquent and witty Hugh Latimer, who has long been a favourite with me. I often think that by running quickly from one subject to another we produce mental confusion; for this reason these books go back to-morrow, so that we may obtain something more congenial. I have looked into a few numbers of the 'Friend,' and every time I have done so, I have felt surprised that thou wast not in the practice of bringing them to us as thou received them, so that we could have discussed them together. How did this happen? How very obscure Coleridge's style is! When I read his writings I often think of a superior mind in chaotic confusion, or of a rich spring emptying itself into a disorderly reservoir, to adopt that very just thought of Anna Seward's. There is much of original thought in Coleridge, but he does not reflect sufficiently on the best manner of embodying his ideas. In minds like his we often see, when the first flow is gone by, there is a something so just, so fit, and so applicable to the subject arises, that we exclaim, 'Oh, how excellent!' Not so in some of these papers—we catch a glimpse of truths, but they are involved in lumber. But of these things, too, I would rather talk than write.

"Never more make apologies for thy letters to us—they cannot be necessary. If we do not appreciate them more by the spirit in which they are written than by the words or the manner, we do not deserve to have them. We were very well on the day thou left us, not any worse for stealing an hour or two from sleep in the morning. Hannah has been spending the morning with J. Sanders; I hope she may have time to write to thee, but the clothes have come in and we must be ironing them.— Affectionately thine,   E. RICHARDSON."

Good housewives—should any such condescend to read this record of old manners and customs—may be interested to know that at North Shields washing was paid for, not by the piece, or by the dozen, but by the stone! The bundles of clothes were weighed before they were taken away to the country to be washed. The clothes were brought home clean and dry (if the weather was favourable), but the folding, mangling, and ironing remained to be gone through. The large kitchens of old-fashioned houses afforded ample room for these processes, and the ladies of the family often assisted in the ironing. The white shawls worn by Friends, whether of spun-silk or of China crape, needed especial attention. Muslin caps and handkerchiefs, as has been said before, were rarely touched by any hands but those of their wearers.

December brought troubles to our heroines, which were communicated to their cousin in letters, supposed to be calculated to give him the "meagrims," and which need not be reproduced. Colds had been caught by running to the end of the grass-plat without bonnets, hoping to see the brother's ship come in, and meeting only disappointment. News had arrived of the illness of the youngest sister, who had been paying visits in Yorkshire, and had not yet seen the new home. These troubles soon passed, however, and better news is communicated by Elizabeth in a letter dated "Sunday evening, nine o'clock." After giving news of the invalid, she goes on to say :—

"We have visited cousin William to-day, and he was very agreeably talkative. I got some historical knowledge from him of things passing five hundred years ago. After tea, Joseph Procter came in. I asked him to send us a new poem which is published by an anonymous author of this town. This brought us some poetic criticism, and a debate between William and Joseph Procter. All this was very pleasant, and vastly more edifying than ' fat pigs and potatoes.'

"Marshall is a very careless librarian. He sent us a number of ' Nicholson's Journal,' which we had about a week since. I enclose it with this, and shall be obliged by thy procuring us a review or a magazine when there is one worth reading. If thou looks into this one, the paper on the transmission of sound through tubes is the best worth notice. I have no news for thee. This is a very still place, except as to ships, which continue to arrive in fleets, but none of them for us. Most of last week was very 'dowly' to us, but in casting up the sum total of pain and pleasure last evening, I found them more equal than I expected. This letter of Sarah's indeed brightened the close. Then I found I had to note down a new pleasure acquired, a new talent discovered, and a new book read. Little Joseph Procter came in yesterday afternoon, seemingly wishing to stay with us. I happened to be drawing, and, by way of employing him, proposed his drawing me a horse. He said, 'No, I had rather sit and look at thee.' He did so for half-an-hour, and then I proposed his trying a building, and offered him a copy. At last I overcame his reluctance, and putting him into a good method, and standing over him to watch him, in a few hours he produced a very pretty pencil-drawing, to his great delight, and my satisfaction. By this small circumstance I have discovered that it is really a very pleasant thing to instruct docile children, and moreover, that teaching is one of my talents. The new book read is Mrs. Elizabeth Montagu's 'Letters,' lively, witty, satirical, and amusing, but far, very far, behind Anna Seward's. Mary has got the 'Monthly Magazine' for October; we will keep it until thou comes; but now I think of it, we will not do so, because as Sarah will be coming in a few days, there will be no room for books in thy next visit. If we should have Isaac too, our circle would be complete; but I am sick with disappointed hope.

"I have got a letter from Hull to-night; my scientific friend was to have begun a course of lectures there on Friday last, but was disappointed by the non-arrival of his apparatus from Doncaster, so he had to stand at the door and apologise! He says, 'It is the first time I have disappointed an audience: I have been much mortified.' He wrote to me still smarting under the annoyance. It makes one smile to see a philosopher disconcerted.

"This gossiping letter will convince thee that it is well for thee that thou and I were not acquainted in my letter-writing days. At that time I rarely sent anyone less than a folio, and it is not unlikely that, in great kindness, I might have favoured thee with two! If thy business journey should be this week, contrive to stay with us over First-day; then we shall have time for details of Sarah's journey and Isaac's voyage, and the Magazine as well. It is past ten o'clock, and I have a metaphysical letter to write.—Accept my love. Affectionately, E. RICHARDSON."

The following letter from Hannah begins by giving news of the invalid, and goes on to inform her cousin that they are returning the hospitality extended to them by the Friends of Shields, with whom, in spite of the independent expressions of Elizabeth's first letter, they are evidently on pleasant terms. Well-known names occur in the letter :—

Hannah Richardson to J. Priestman.

"North Shields, December 12th, 1811.

" * * * * Yesterday we had R. and M. Spence, and M. and A. Foster, and had a pleasant, lively evening; the conversation was miscellaneous, and in part literary. This evening we have been more scientific. We had the Taylors and J. Sanders, and, just before tea, Michael Watson brought in an officer, Captain Brown (who executed the drawings for the ' Pleasures of Hope"), to see Bessy's shells, almost all of which he appeared to have some knowledge of, and he has offered to come again and name them. They brought a very beautiful and ably finished set of drawings of foreign shells of his doing, which he had made a present of to Michael; the sight of them was quite a treat. I wish thou hadst been present, and that thou couldst accompany us to-morrow, when we have agreed to go to Tynemouth to see the Captain's collection.* (Take notice, mind, that he is married.) And now be sure to remember that First-day is thy time for visiting us, the fortnight is up then, though thou hast had a business journey between. Thy presence really does us all good, and on Bessy it has a most salutary effect, and that is, surely, a sufficient inducement to one disposed to do all the good he can.—Thy affectionate cousin, H. RICHARDSON."

The next letters, written by Hannah between the frequent visits of her cousin, have little interest. One of the series is from the pen of the youngest sister. It is a letter of lively chit-chat, such as a girl would naturally write to a cousin of her own age :—

" If our writing to thee gives thee as much pleasure as thy letters give to us, we need not wait until we think we have anything interesting to tell thee. * * * * The Walkers told Sarah Spence that she would get to Paradise when she came to Shields ! She thought of their words when she

* A scientific friend informs me that Captain Brown was a well-known conchologist.

was in the Low Street, which is more likely to resemble the lower regions, I should think. * * * * It is very grievous that we cannot attend William Turner's lectures, but I hope thou wilt take notes, and treasure up all that is new, and often come down to see us, if thou should attend them."

The Rev. William Turner was the Lecturer to the Literary and Philosophical Society, of Newcastle; he was a Unitarian Minister, and highly respected in the town. By this allusion to the lecture season we may conjecture that this unfortunately dateless letter was written in the autumn of 1812, and it is evident that, although the advantages of Newcastle were still regretted, the sisters had taken root in the town of Shields. They had found out poor people to visit, and a social meeting of lady Friends for reading and needlework had been held at their house.

"Cousin William came last 5th-day, when we had the last meeting here; on seeing us all sitting round the table, he started back, saying, 'the sewing club!' However, he ventured in and stayed for an hour. He would give us something of his own (composition), if any other man would."

The "sewing" was to be enlivened by the reading aloud of original papers, and another gentleman, besides Cousin William, is mentioned as wishing to be a member.

The correspondence throws no light upon the after history of this little society. As a sewing club, its life was short; but as a clothing society, it exists at the present day. The Friends of Shields still meet in the month of November to provide warm garments for the poor, but the materials are given unmade to the recipients. As an encouragement to literary composition, it has not been the last effort of the kind in North Shields. "Essay Meetings" were held by the Friends of that town about the year 1830, and a more recent "Essay Society," which lasted from 1853 to 1865, is still fresh in the memory of its now widely-scattered members.

Whoever has been kind enough to read the foregoing letters may have observed that the name of "Cousin William" often occurs in them. In the first of the series, Hannah remarks, " I really believe we are going to be good neighbours with Cousin William, for he seems equally disposed for it with ourselves." To understand this tone of surprise, we must remember that Elizabeth and Hannah did not go to Shields as Friends; and that William Richardson was one of the most strenuous upholders of the strictest form of Quakerism in England. He was the third son of John Richardson, of the Low Lights; and his first wife was Sarah Priestman, of Marygate, York; so that he was doubly connected with our heroines. Although not a Minister in the Society of Friends, he was decidedly the leading member of that community in North Shields, and in the streets of that town, fifty years ago, he was a most striking figure. His tall, stalwart form, and strong, square, uncompromising face, were crowned by his "stayed" hat, resembling that worn by a bishop; his sturdy lower limbs were encased in knee-breeches, grey worsted stockings, and shoes with large silver buckles. A man of decided ability, he was, as has been said, of an argumentative turn of mind, and a past master in the nice distinctions of controversial theology. A great student of ecclesiastical history, it delighted him to trace in thinkers of old times, the Pelagians and Semi-Pelagians of the past, the same heretical and "unsound" doctrines which he warred against in teachers of his own day, and even in his own Society. He was a firm upholder of primitive Quakerism, believing that its founders were guided by a Wisdom which was above their own. Many who might share in this belief would yet think he carried it far. When, during a Yearly Meeting of the Society, a sentence was inserted in the "Epistle" to its members, which spoke of the Bible as "the only divinely authorised record of God's will to man," William Richardson was said to have put in a caveat at the word "only." He found no seconder, and the sentence stood.

Of the discipline of the Society, he was a very staunch defender, rarely leaning to the side of mercy. This was shown when a somewhat faulty member of the Society had married a person whose only fault seems to have been that she was not one of its members. "It is the most sensible thing he ever did in his life, but he must be disowned for doing it," said William Richardson. "We must not break our rules." These "rules" of the Society forbidding marriages with non-members might afford material for a writer of romance who wished to depict the crossing of young affections. Those which forbade the marriage with first cousins certainly influenced the lives of more than one of the daughters of the family of which I now write. But, even under "the Quaker rule," now and again, true love would have its way. A young Friend, who, in spite of much opposition, was about to marry his first cousin, came to break the terrible news to William Richardson, and listened for some time in silence while the heinous nature of the crime he was about to commit was expounded to

P

him. At length the offender said, "Well, I cannot see the matter in that light." "That is because thy heart is hardened," said William Richardson, adding the text, "Whom He will He hardeneth." This stern reproof did not, of course, convince the young man of error; and his marriage proved an important event in the history of the Society of Friends. Until it took place, in 1841, all marriages of first cousins had been followed by the penalty of disownment; and many valuable members had been, thereby, lost to the Society. But in 1841, a more liberal spirit prevailed. There were Friends who objected to visit with exclusion from religious fellowship an offence which contravened no Divine law. In the Monthly Meeting of Newcastle, of which the young man was a member, the matter was warmly debated. William Richardson and the strict disciplinarians were defeated, and the bridegroom retained his membership. The bride, however, was a member of a meeting in the County of Middlesex, and change "comes slowly up this way." Neither the decision of the Northern Monthly Meeting to retain her husband in membership, nor her own sweet qualities, saved the young wife from disownment. She was, however, warmly welcomed to her new home in the North of England. There the striking anomaly of a young creature, who in mind and person exemplified all that was lovely in Quakerism, being excluded from the privileges in which her husband shared, was not long suffered to continue. As soon as formalities would admit, she was reinstated in membership. North-country Friends travelling in the neighbourhood of London found themselves looked upon by their co-religionists in the light of daring and dangerous innovators; but their example had its influence, and the rule of the Society was altered in due time.

It will be seen from these instances that the laws of Quakerism were as sacred to William Richardson as those of Rome could be to her staunchest votary. George Richardson of Newcastle, in whose mind the "love of law" was less powerful than the "law of love," sometimes fell under the censure of his more rigid brother. Holding Bible meetings amongst the villages of the colliery districts, where Methodism is a great power amongst the people, George Richardson accepted the help of a Wesleyan minister. The next Monthly Meeting of Friends happened to be held at North Shields, and a large company assembled afterwards at William Richardson's house in Dockwray Square. At the dinner-table, the conversation turned upon the recent proceedings of George Richardson, and he was sharply taken to task by his elder brother and a Friend of Sunderland. They were very formidable antagonists, and George Richardson's young daughter, sitting by, pitied her father. He submitted to be rebuked in silence, and then quietly said words to this effect: — "If it be indeed true that Friends cannot join with others without compromising their own principles, then I have been wrong; but if, as I fully believe, Friends can unite with other Christians in forwarding objects which all agree to be good, then surely that is the better way."

The minds of the two brothers were singularly different in their power of receiving new ideas. It has been recorded in the last chapter how George Richardson, in his old age, took the initiative in advising Friends to enter upon the field of Foreign Missions. William Richardson was by no means old when the young Friends of North Shields, like those in other towns, began a Sunday School for poor children, yet he viewed the step with considerable alarm and suspicion. To say that he actively opposed it might be going too far, but it was but a grudging sanction that he gave. "Put it down as a donation," his sweet young daughter was always instructed to say when she brought the sum her father had consented to give in aid of the undertaking. He feared to be bound to support, even for a year, something which might bring in its train perilous innovation.

That the political opinions of William Richardson should lean to Conservatism seems only in the fitness of things; yet, although his life extended far into the Reform era, when his native town became a Parliamentary borough, and the removal of religious disabilities brought Friends into active political life, he never even voted at an election, holding that act to be inconsistent with the idea of being separate from the world. But if William Richardson did not wholly escape from that narrowness of view which is the besetting danger of the controversial theologian, he showed a wise liberality when he so kindly welcomed to North Shields his young cousins who had strayed from the fold of Quakerism. The event fully justified his wisdom. He and his cousin Elizabeth must have differed upon many points of doctrine and of practice, but they mutually respected each other's force of character, and continued to be " good neighbours" to each other for nearly thirty years,

In a letter written by David Priestman of Malton to his son in Newcastle, the writer speaks of our heroines as " the children of my very dear sister," and expresses his deep solicitude for their spiritual welfare. In 1812, they had the great pleasure of welcoming this dear uncle to their new home in Shields. He was accompanied by his youngest son Isaac, of whom Elizabeth, from the height of her thirty years, speaks as " a fine lad "; and rejoices that he had had the pleasure of a journey in the north, because " young things like him enjoy seeing new places so much." This passage occurs in a letter written by Elizabeth from Leeds, where she seems to have gone for medical advice for her knee. It begins with an allusion to her plans for the future.

"Thank thee for thy good wishes. I do not expect to enter upon a bed of roses, but I believe I shall increase my enjoyments. Occupation is as necessary for my mind's health as food for the body ; so much so that I am always the best in health and spirits when I have not a minute of spare time, always doing or thinking of something. Then this drawing school is only the foundation of my plan, my main project is to have it in my power to educate two children entirely, as I recollect I have before told thee I wished to do. But we can talk of this ; when I have opportunity I will tell thee all I have thought on this subject.

"My knee is much better since I came here ; I walk a mile, or two or three without inconvenience, and I am quite well and enjoying myself very much. I am frequently amused by the people I associate with, though not much interested by any. I am so in the spirit of drawing that I sit to it early and late, and sometimes, indeed, when I am weary enough, lest I should feel myself lonely without work or company. Of course I have plenty of time to read a letter, and leisure enough to feel the value of a friend's kindness ; so, if thou approves of my prompt reply, let me hear from thee again before I leave, which will not be this week, or next I think."

Speaking of associates Elizabeth makes the characteristic remark :—
"Didst thou ever feel with those milk-and-water worthies that thou esteemed them more highly in their absence than in their presence ? I could name half-a-score of whom I think so favourably that I always meet them with pleasure, yet I get so tired of their company that I part from them without wishing the time lengthened by a second."

We can scarcely wonder that Elizabeth fears this letter "breathes somewhat of my old and sinful nature."

The next (also from Leeds) is chiefly devoted to the expression of her views upon different types of character, and is evidently called forth by some remark made by her correspondent.

"It is tolerably easy to arrange those whom we are acquainted with into classes, but to fix them in their proper genera and species requires a knowledge of minute traits which can rarely be obtained—by me at least. To the two or three general observations which I have made on different classes thou art very welcome.

"There is one class of beings in the world who are distinguished by their susceptibility in receiving impressions from the influence of other minds ; and also, by their habit of yielding more to the impulse of feeling than to the dictates of judgment. The advantages these persons possess over others are in the facility with which they imbibe knowledge, in their exemption from selfishness, and in the interest which they excite. They excite more interest than confidence, for we do not rely upon the stability of things whose nature it is to change, and these persons must vary in the lighter qualities of their minds by the different influences they yield to, even though the more important ones are fixed by conviction and sound principle. Their chief defect lies in a want of the habits of observation and of reflection ; from these we gain judgment which always produces firmness of character in proportion to its extent.

"There is another class of persons whose actions appear to proceed from thought, not from impulse of feeling. They mark the tendency of things, and they use with caution those means which are most likely to effect their purpose, and they perceive where these means are weak, and where they are strong : against the weak part they form a guard, or, if that cannot be done, they provide the best remedy which the case allows. These persons inspire us with confidence, but (unless they are our near connections and in habits of kindness) not with interest, or with lively regard.

"I have sometimes thought the best line for each of these classes to pursue is to strive to become like the opposite one. By this means each may gain a little of what they are most deficient in without becoming artificial characters ; provided always it is real amendment, not a change in appearance only, which they wish to effect. To know ourselves and justly to appreciate our qualities is, (as we have often observed), a most desirable attainment ; it is what we may strive for through life without gaining ; but ' every little helps,' and thoughts suggested by others which lead us to make observations for ourselves are useful. Accurate observation is the first step in this science ; if thou wilt favour me with some of the results of thine, I shall be encouraged to give thee more of mine at some suitable opportunity."

Jonathan Priestman highly valued all his cousins' letters, but it may be that the one which concludes the series was the most treasured of them all. He had written to inform his correspondents, under the strictest seal of secresy, of his engagement to be married. The letter he received in return is on a sheet of folio paper, upon which the three sisters wrote in turn. Elizabeth's opening sentence, "Half-an-hour ago we received thy letter, need I say that its contents gave us the most lively pleasure ?—I might call it joy," gives the key-note to all the letters, but Hannah's delight at the news, and her ardent hopes and wishes for the happiness of the cousin whom she seems to have loved as closely as a brother, are expressed in no such measured language ; while the simple sentences of the youngest sister breathe the same spirit. All the sisters express the warmest approval of their cousin's choice of a wife. " There is no one to compare with her ; " " There is no one I have so coveted for thee " are the expressions they use. Nor is there the slightest trace in the letter of a thought which must have been present to the minds of all the writers, that, although the bond of friendship between them and their cousin was only to be broken with their lives, the time was over when he would turn first to them for sympathy in his joys and sorrows. Speaking near the close of his life, and when left the sole survivor of the group of friends, Jonathan Priestman told the present writer of his having received this letter, and how he saw in it a proof of the " noble unselfishness " of character which, in his opinion, marked the three sisters.

The letter bears the Newcastle post-mark of April 15th, 1813. Jonathan Priestman was married to Rachel Bragg in the following year. Change had come also to his cousins. Their eldest brother was left a widower with four little children, and Ann, the eldest sister, who had never been reconciled to the cold of the north-east coast, went to reside with him at Stockton. She never returned to Shields, and died at Durham in 1834. Her beautiful handwriting, acquired at York School, is in a book in the writer's possession, ' The Horkey,' by Thomas Bloomfield, a poem which has been republished in our own own day with fresh illustrations.

It was probably in 1813 that Elizabeth carried out part of her plan, and opened a drawing school at their house in Hutchinson's Buildings. The undertaking met with a favourable reception, and married ladies as well as young girls became her pupils. This brought her in contact with the general society of North Shields, outside the pale of Quakerism, and a glance at that society in former days may be permitted.

CHAPTER XIII.

North Shields and Sunderland in former days.

"Yon shrouded figure, as I guess,
  By her proud mien, and flowing dress,
  Is Tynemouth's haughty Prioress,
    And she with awe looks pale."
Sir W. Scott.

"And now the vessel skirts the strand
  Of mountainous Northumberland.
    *   *   *   *   *
Monk Wearmouth soon behind them lay,
And Tynemouth's Priory and bay:
They marked, amid her trees, the hall
Of lofty Seaton Delaval:
They saw the Blythe and Wansbeck floods
Rush to the sea through sounding woods;
They passed the tower of Widdrington,
Mother of many a valiant son;
At Coquet-Isle their beads they toll
To the good Saint who owned the cell;
Then did the Alne attention claim,
And Warkworth, proud of Percy's name;
And next, they crossed themselves to hear
The whitening billows sound so near,
Where, boiling through the rocks, they roar
On Dunstanborough's caverned shore,
Thy tower, proud Bamborough, marked they there,
King Ida's castle, huge and square,
From its tall rock look grimly down,
And on the swelling ocean frown."
Sir W. Scott.

In the year 1280 the Burgesses of Newcastle obtained a precept from the Sheriff of Northumberland to summon the Prior of Tynemouth before King Edward the First in Parliament. The offence of the Prior was that he had tried to raise into a little town the few "shiels," or fishermen's huts, which had clustered for shelter under the high bank of the river

Tyne. The Prior had encouraged trades to be carried on, and a market to be held on Sundays; and had built a wharf where ships could load and unload; "making a port where there was no port before, and thus injuring the King and the Burgesses of Newcastle." The case was tried in the King's Bench in 1292. The Prior defended himself ably, but the judgment of the court was given against him, and the buildings and wharf were ordered to be removed. For centuries the poor little town was kept down by the heavy hand of its powerful neighbour, and was not allowed to bake its own bread, or to brew its own beer. Not until the nineteenth century did it obtain the right to hold a market and fairs of its own.

Much might be written of the early history of Tynemouth Priory, which stretches back to the first days of English Christianity, when log rafts* were floated down the Tyne for the Chapel which King Edwin was building upon the cliff at its mouth. It is said that Edwin's daughter Rosella (a name commemorated in North Shields) entered the religious life at Tynemouth; it is certain that there were nuns there in the eleventh century, and an Abbess, Virca, who presented Saint Cuthbert (yet alive) with a rare winding sheet, in emulation of a holy lady called Tuda, who had sent him a coffin ! †

Edwin's wooden chapel was rebuilt in stone by his successor, Saint Oswald, and there it is said that the sainted king's mutilated remains were brought for burial after his defeat in 642 by the old heathen King Penda of Mercia, who plays so terrible a part in the early history of Northumbria. Oswi, Penda's conqueror, was the Patron Saint of Tynemouth Priory. It had a little oratory to the Virgin, and in after years we are told the seal of the monastery bore a representation of Christ, the Virgin, and King Oswi, and an inscription which is thus given in an old history : " Sigile, commune prioratus Sancte Marie and beati Oswini de Tinmutha." So great was the reputation of the Priory for sanctity, that even the marauding King, Malcolm of Scotland, spared it in his ravages; and he and his son are buried within its walls in company with more saintly personages,— Oswi, King Edred, and Henry, the holy hermit of Coquet Isle.

In the middle ages, the Priors of Tynemouth (although not allowed to establish markets near to the Tyne) were persons of great importance,

---

* Green's ' Short History of the English People,' p. 25.
† Sir Walter Scott's Notes to ' Marmion.'

and the King's Justices did not enter their "liberties." The old story of the Monk's Stone is probably true in its leading features, and it throws a light on the rough life of those days. A monk of Tynemouth catering for the Prior's table, or actuated by more personal longings, had wandered some miles north of the monastery, and attracted by savoury odours, entered the kitchen at Seaton Delaval while the dinner was cooking. Amongst other viands, a whole hog was being roasted. The monk placed his affections upon the head, and regardless of the anger of the servants, cut it off, put it in his wallet, and carried it away in triumph. The enraged servants durst not by force resist the holy man, but when the young and fiery Lord of Delaval returned with his friends from hunting, and found that what he considered the best part of his dinner was gone, he speedily remounted his horse and rode towards Tynemouth. He overtook the monk about two miles from the monastery, and so soundly beat him with his hunting gad, that he crawled home to his cell to die.

The contention was sharp between the temporal and spiritual lords, and in those days the boldest spirits had to bend before the power of the Church. Young Delaval paid with his lands for his outburst of temper, and it is said that the Manor of Elsig near Newcastle, afterwards a summer residence for the Priors of Tynemouth, was part of the forfeit he paid. The high, slender stone, still standing in a garden near Monk Seaton, was said to have been erected to mark the spot where Delaval overtook the monk. Others believe it to have been the shaft of an ancient cross, or boundary mark, which was made use of for the rude carvings of men and animals made to commemorate the event; and for the legend familiar to Northumbrian children fifty years ago :—

> "O horridde deede,
> To kill a maune for a pigge's heede."

After the dissolution of the Monasteries, Tynemouth Priory continued to be the Parish Church of the district until the time of the civil wars. During that troubled period, the strength of the fortifications around the cliffs of Tynemouth made its Castle a place of military importance, but rendered the venerable Priory, within the same enclosure, little suited for a place of worship. It is strange to think of the inhabitants of Shields resorting to it for that purpose during the intervals of sieges and conflicts. Readers of Carlyle's 'Cromwell' may remember that within the walls of Tynemouth

Castle the stormy career of Colonel John Lilburn came to its tragic close; and that the whole garrison, which had revolted with him from the Parliament to the King, was put to the sword. It need not surprise us that in 1657 it was decided to build a new Church in a more peaceful locality, a mile distant from Tynemouth and its Castle, and in a central position for the townships of North Shields, Preston and Chirton. This edifice was originally of brick, but was afterwards rebuilt with stone. It was consecrated by Bishop Cosens in 1668, and is still the Parish Church of North Shields.

Before this time, the Society of Friends had established itself in the district. It had two burial grounds, one near to the fishing village of Cullercoats; another to the west of the town of Shields, beyond the Bull Ring. To one of these graveyards, the corpse of a Friend, George Linton, was being taken for interment, followed by his family, when the procession was stopped, and, in the words of the Register of the Meeting, "the body by the fury of the tymes, was, by relations and soldiers, carried away from Friends, and lieth buried in the down end of Tynemouth Kirk, the month and day not certain, but it was thought the eleventh of twelfth month, 1668." We may feel thankful when religious fanaticism confines its acts of violence to the dead; and doubtless the "relations and soldiers" thought they were doing good service to the departed George Linton when they secured for him burial in a place once held so sacred as Tynemouth Priory.

About the time of the accession of George the Third, North Shields was described as "a poor, miserable place." It then possessed only two tiled houses, and the town consisted entirely of the narrow street along the margin of the Tyne. But the advantages of the position at the mouth of so fine a river were becoming recognised, and the movement northwards of so many Whitby shipowners, chronicled in a former chapter, added to the population of the place where so many of them settled.

In 1763 the building of Dockwray Square was begun. This was a great event in the history of North Shields, being the commencement of the high town. A number of persons agreed upon a site, and the plan of a square was drawn. Each intending resident then bought a piece of the ground, and built upon it his own house, or two houses, of whatever size and height seemed best to him. The result was a square with one side open to the river, and the three remaining sides consisting of houses of irregular height and structure, but considered to be very "elegant" in those early days. For some time they were the only houses upon the bank, but by degrees streets and shops began to arise, and other groups of dwelling-houses. We have seen in a former chapter the origin of Northumberland Square; and Walker Place was built upon the land of another native of Whitby, whose coming to North Shields, and whose possession of property in the place have been already mentioned.

Pleasant traditions of social life in North Shields during the later decades of the eighteenth century have drifted down to our times. Cheerful little supper parties were given amongst neighbours during the long winter evenings, and more formal and stately groups gathered around dinner tables at the then fashionable hour of three o'clock. That much good cheer prevailed, and that much care was devoted to its preparation, is evident from the numerous recipes which have been preserved. Neighbours seem to have handed them to each other as valuable possessions, and although the ink with which they are written may be faded, and the paper yellow with age, yet the clear handwriting of that day causes them still to be legible, so that it would be possible to prepare a calf's head, or to compound a "cure for the Rheumatism," from these recipes, sent "with Mrs. M.'s compliments," a hundred years ago.

In this society, as has been said, the family in the Pew Dene had no part. They preferred their own secluded life, but with Friends who lived " on the bank " (as the new town of Shields was called) it was otherwise, and they mixed freely in the social life of their neighbours. One of these Friends was a great lover of books, and a fair classical scholar. By his neighbours he was considered to be a poet, and fifty years ago old ladies were fond of repeating his rhymes to the too heedless ears of his descendants. Some of his verses appeared in the 'Gentleman's Diary' and the 'Ladies' Diary,' publications which appeared at Christmas, and afforded to amateur authors the same facilities for publishing their effusions in prose or in poetry which the 'Annuals' of a later day offered on a far more brilliant scale. But the verses of their old neighbour which the ladies loved to repeat were on little occurrences in their own circle—a birth at one house, a marriage at another, a punning rhyme or a riddle. He had no daughter, but many sons. At that time the chief school in Shields for the education of young children was kept by a Miss Weir. She lived at the back of Dockwray Square, and her school was attended by the children of its inhabitants. She had about thirty scholars, of whom about two-thirds were generally girls, and the remaining third little boys. A woman of spirit, and of great force of character, she ruled her boys and girls with energy, and on the whole with justice. There was no disorder in her school. In her boys she took an especial interest. One morning, a good tempered little fellow, a son of the poet, was going to school as usual, when he passed two boys of the rougher class. One of these said to the other, " Now you dare not go and give young B. a thump on the head ? " " I dare! " said the boy thus challenged, and he instantly darted forward and gave the blow. The young Friend, stung by the sudden assault, turned upon his assailant, overcame him, and soundly thrashed him, the originator of the quarrel standing by to see fair play. Having removed all trace of the conflict, the victor walked quietly into school, when to his amazement the schoolmistress addressed him by name : " Ah, you did not think I was watching you," she said, " but I was so glad to see you beat that big fellow; I did not think you had so much spirit in you ! "

In Dockwray Square resided a lady of strong will and determination of character, who has left some descendants of remarkable ability. She once paid a visit to Miss Weir, to remonstrate with her upon having so many boys in her school, and to make some complaint against them, from which the sons of her neighbour were not excepted. There was something in this speech, or the manner of it, which aroused the ire of the old school-mistress, and she rose up to her full height and thus addressed her visitor before all the listening pupils :—" Take away your daughters as soon as you please, Mrs. H. ; I will part with all my girls sooner than with one of my boys ! " It is probable that the imperious lady did not " take away " her daughters, for one of them, a dear little girl of five years old, was wont to sit on a form between two of the boys complained of, who took care of her and helped her with her sums when they were too difficult for her tender years. Some of these boys went afterwards to a school in the town kept by a Unitarian Minister, but he never took the place occupied in their respect and loyalty by Miss Weir. They often said that (except for his Greek and Latin) their new master was far inferior to their old school-mistress, who could have given him many a lesson in his calling.

Some writers of our time look back to the days of the French War as to a glorious epoch, when this little island stood against a world in arms, and when the news of great naval victories came to our shores in constant succession. This was certainly the view held by the majority of the shipowners of North Shields while the struggle was going on, and it is not the work of the present writer to contravene it; but it may be well to remember that there was another side to the brilliant picture. The old town of Shields saw many a desperate conflict between the inhabitants and the press-gang; and informers were often very roughly treated, especially by the sailors' wives. Finer arches than any which now remain of Tynemouth Priory were destroyed by the rulers of the day to make room for their hideous barracks, and the little Chapel at the east end, which was then in fair preservation, had its windows walled up that gun-powder might be stored therein. Wheat, which was only three shillings a bushel when John Richardson had his Seghill Farm, rose to a guinea during the war, and the suffering of the poor was terrible. In the town of Shields, the tide of political feeling ran high, and the kindly intercourse between neighbours was for a time interrupted. Few, indeed, were the opponents of the policy of Mr. Pitt, and they needed to have all the courage of their opinions. Only five persons (one of whom was our friend the poet) accompanied Mr. Charles Grey when, during a contest for South Northumberland, he canvassed for votes in Dockwray Square. Scant courtesy did the group receive, and one shipowner closed his door roughly in their faces. In a small house in a corner of this Square there lived a man whose habits of life were retired, and whose means of livelihood were not evident to his neighbours. He was, therefore, conjectured to be a spy sent down by Mr. Pitt to look after the proceedings of this very small group of Whigs.

Even amongst the Society of Friends opinions were divided. The builder of the great mansion, then in the height of his prosperity, said in the heat of argument with his Whig neighbour, " Why, I would go myself to fight the French, if it were not for my peace principles! " It was a troubled time for the Society in the North of England. Many of its members at Whitby and at North Shields were shipowners, and they were placed in a very difficult position, and the rules of the Society were rigidly enforced against them. When in later years the question was asked why

some well-known families were no longer Friends, the answer was always,
" Their father was disowned for carrying guns on board his ships."   In
many instances this severity seems to have involved a loss to the Society.
The difficult position of shipowning and sea-going Friends was so notorious
that it gave rise to many curious stories. The Friend who cut off the hand
of the first man who attempted to board his ship, with the remark, " Friend,
thou hast no business here ! " belongs evidently to the realm of pure fable.
A better invented, if not a truer story, is that of another Friend, also on
shipboard, who, seeing a conflict to be inevitable, retired to the cabin
disclaiming all complicity in the matter. Watching from the cabin window,
he saw an error about to be committed ; seamanship prevailed over
Quakerism, and he called to the man at the helm, " I have nothing to do
with it, but if thou *dost* mean to hit her, then starboard, John ! "

As time went on, and its wealth increased, North Shields gradually
became a less miserable place ; but its progress was delayed, not only by
the jealousy of the Newcastle Corporation, but by the inertness of its
own inhabitants.   For every step in improvement, a hard battle had to be
fought.   It was a great shock to all preconceived opinions when some
daring innovators proposed to dispel a little of the darkness of the streets
during the long winter evenings by a few oil lamps.   The project was
thought most revolutionary, and a crowded meeting was held to oppose it.
Eloquence might be lacking amongst the opponents of change, but strength
of lungs was present in full force, and the strugglers for light were howled
down.   One worthy stood upon a form, waving his arm and shouting " Nee
leets ! Nee leets ! "   This man was thought to be so brave a champion of
the good old cause of darkness, that some say a testimonial was given to
him for his exertions, but upon this point history does not speak with
a certain sound.   The victory won at the meeting was not a lasting
one.   The oil lamps were soon hung in the street, and gas lights followed
in their turn.

Early in this century a company of about a hundred and thirty persons
founded the Subscription Library in Howard Street.   The building which
contained it, and which is distinguished by the Town Clock, was erected in
1807.   The collection of books, if far inferior to that of Newcastle, was a
very good one, in which persons of varied taste might each find congenial
mental food.   While the founders were arranging their first books, one of

the Philistine party entered the room, and scowling at the group said,
" Men of Shields, what business have you with any books but your ledgers ? "

In those early years of the century there was much intercourse, social
and commercial, between the towns of North and South Shields, but the
only means of crossing the Tyne was by rowing boats. This, when the
river was crowded with shipping, must have been a trying ordeal for timid
persons. The Friends of Sunderland, travelling in large numbers and in
all weathers to attend their Monthly Meetings at North Shields, found the
crossing of what they spoke of as " the great gulf " a most formidable part
of their journey. There were stories of people who, wishing to reach North
Shields from the opposite shore, drove round by Newcastle Bridge. A tunnel
under the river Tyne or a suspension bridge across it were suggested.
The execution of these projects, however, remains unattempted even at the
present day. About the year 1830, a few inhabitants of the two towns
joined together to endeavour to surmount the difficulty in a more practical,
if in a humbler fashion. This was by a Steam Ferry Company, the ferries
being large flat boats, capable of accommodating four carts or carriages at
once, and conveying passengers for a penny each. The undertaking had, of
course, its enemies, and the loss of employment to the poor old watermen
was put prominently forward by the opponents of all change. It was a
proud day for the directors when their first boat load of passengers and
carriages steamed away from the landing place at North Shields. As they
watched its progress, an opponent thus addressed one of them :—" This
is begun in folly and ignorance, and it will end in disappointment and loss."
The prophecy was not a true one, for the Steam Ferry proved a benefit to
all parties concerned in it, especially to the public; but the directors in
their turn lived to find themselves behind the times. Twenty years had not
elapsed when a new company was started to run a smaller boat directly
across the Tyne for the charge of a halfpenny. The old company went to
Parliament for powers to stop the opposition, but the day of monopolies was
over. Amalgamation was advised and agreed to, and both the ferries ply
to this day.

In the year of King George's Jubilee, North Shields, like its neighbour
Newcastle, founded its Jubilee Schools, and some years afterwards Thomas
Kettlewell founded his Charity School for boys.

In 1820 an angry mob swept through Dockwray Square, its leader carrying a green bag stuffed with straw. This was taken to a waste place and burned with every mark of execration. It represented the green bag in which the evidence against Queen Caroline was brought into the House of Lords; and in that way the rough, yet generous, English populace gave vent to its feelings of sympathy for one whom they only knew as an ill-used woman.

In 1832, the Reform Bill of Earl Grey raised the town where he had had such warm adherents and such bitter opponents, into the Parliamentary Borough of Tynemouth. In 1849 it became a Corporate Town, and in 1850 a Port with a Custom House. But with all these changes, North Shields was still an old fashioned place in the middle of this century. A George Eliot, had such a person lived in Northumberland, might have found figures for her portrait gallery among the old shipowners who walked upon the Library flags, or who leaned over the railings by Dockwray Square watching the coming in of their ships. There was the typical old Tory, who thought his fellow-townsmen as unfit to exercise the municipal franchise in 1850, as he had thought his fellow-countrymen were for the parliamentary franchise twenty years before; who, rarely seen inside a church, yet upheld the Establishment as an Engine of State, and thought Dissenters should be compelled to attend its services " at the point of the bayonet." To him Sir Robert Peel was a traitor, the old Austrian Despotism a paternal Government, and the Emperor Nicholas of Russia the "last gentleman left in Europe." Then there was the other hale old shipowner, who, at four score, disdained to defend himself from an October gale because " he never *had* put on his great coat until November, and he never would." Then there were the dear old ladies with their handsome dresses and well-appointed houses, their active habits and early hours, their shrewd sense, and sharp tongues. True, their range of knowledge was limited, and to take the workhouse children for a picnic was " demoralising," for in *their* youth did *they* ever have any change ? Foreign countries were of course better known to them by report than to people in inland towns, but their patriotism was local and insular. It was a true son of North Shields, who, after a sojourn in some beautiful Continental city, said, " Oh yes, it is really a very nice place—for an outlandish place, you know."

But if the elder ladies of North Shields forty years ago stood firmly upon the old ways, they were very faithful to their old houses, their old servants, and their old friends. " The old set," on their lips, meant the families whose friendship dated from the days of their fathers and grandfathers in the last century; and any scion of such families, even in poverty or misfortune, was more sure of a welcome from them than a more recent and richer acquaintance. Commercial misfortune through the successive failures of large Joint Stock Banks fell heavily upon the North of England in the Forties and the Fifties of this century, and the old families of North Shields were especial sufferers. During that period poverty became almost a mark of distinction, and moneyed people made little or no parade of their wealth. Few, indeed, were the private carriages in North Shields; and when some new comers to the town introduced champagne at an evening party, heads were gravely shaken. " No good would come of it. The old set had never had champagne at *their* parties."

The Crimean War, and still more the years from 1868 to 1874, when English prosperity advanced by leaps and bounds, wrought a great change in North Shields. Old inhabitants who returned to visit it hardly knew the place or the people. Carriages rolled about the streets, late dinners had come into fashion, and many families had left their ancient abodes in Dockwray Square for the crescents and terraces which had arisen on the cliffs of Tynemouth where primroses used to grow.

The recent period of adversity has not spared North Shields. It is sad to think of privation amongst its industrious working population, sad too to see the cliffs of Tynemouth disfigured by aquariums and skating-rinks, and the venerable Priory, now as formerly, suffering from "the attacks of time, and of military barbarity." But the greatest lover of the old times cannot be blind to the manifest improvements in North Shields. Duke Algernon of Northumberland built for it new churches, and chose for them active and enlightened clergymen. The town is well and efficiently schooled. The streets are intersected by wide thoroughfares, are well kept, and are purified by sea water. Even the old town, no longer comparable to the lower regions, is thought by strangers to be quaint and picturesque. In promoting these improvements, members of the Society of Friends have not been idle; and when the list of workers for the good of the town of Shields, and for the improvement of its magnificent river comes to be made up, the name of a descendant of John Richardson of the Low Lights will not be forgotten.*

* Written before the death of John Richardson Procter.

To parody a sentence used of far greater towns across the Atlantic, "Newcastle speaks one language, North Shields another, and Sunderland a third, and though the several dialects have only slight differences of inflection, their moral accents render each a little difficult for the others." The "moral accent" of Sunderland was decidedly different from that of North Shields half a century ago. The people of Sunderland were remarkable for their progressive and enterprising spirit, their houses were built with some attention to external adornment, their streets were handsome, their smaller river and harbour were made the very best use of by the formation of docks and piers before any steps were taken to improve the Tyne. The ladies of Sunderland were dressed, if not more handsomely, yet with more style, and walked with more dignity than those of North Shields, carriages were numerous, hours were later, and society altogether more fashionable on the banks of the Wear than on those of the Tyne.

Those who had family ties to Sunderland held the place in warm affection, and treasured the old tales of the town and of its neighbourhood. That of the country woman who, when nearly a hundred years old, was wont to say, "I think God Almighty has forgotten me"; and of the clever man who, feeling his memory fail, said to a younger and feebler person, "I have forgotten more than thoo wilt ever learn," have been preserved in Sir Henry Taylor's Autobiography. A Sunderland working-man had with praiseworthy industry learned to read in mature life. A lady visitor congratulated the workman's wife upon her husband's new acquirement, saying, "How nice it will be for him to be able to read his Bible." The poor woman's answer sometimes recurs to me when I meet very "advanced" and "enlightened" people :—"Oh, the Bible, ma'am! He has got *far* past the Bible! He reads the papers!"

It was in the shop of a Sunderland draper that the pitman's wife was shown stuffs of divers pretty shades—blues, greys, and greens. Nothing attracted her fancy until a material appeared in which the primary colours predominated. Then she pushed away the delicately tinted fabrics with the exclamation, "Take away all your gaudy colours, plain reed and yaller for me!"

The pitman, who, when asked if he would swear to some fact, answered "Sweer! why I'll sweer *oot* for oor Maister Pemberton, I'se like;" is a person of an utterly past time. And in these days of secret voting, it is curious to remember how, at a county election, the voters from the Colliery districts when asked "Whom do you poll for?" would say "Who for? Why for Maister Lambton, to be shower!" in tones that could be heard far and wide. The pit district in its tales, its dialect, and its customs, had a distinct character of its own. This has sometimes been misunderstood by strangers; but in our day, the highly cultivated men who, in connection with the scheme of University Extension, visit so many parts of England, have found nowhere so warm a welcome, such appreciative audiences, or such marked success as amongst the miners of Northumberland and Durham.

A Sunderland man who had been the architect of his own fortunes, while waiting in the London office of Mr. Lindsay, the great shipowner, was attracted by the appearance of a gentleman who was absorbed in copying figures from the records of shipping. At length the successful Northerner, laying his strong hand upon the shoulder of the man whose intense industry had impressed him, said, "Thoo writes an uncommon nice hand, ma frind, and thoo maks good, clear figures, and thoo has a sensible-like face. I do not know what they give thee here; but just say what thoo'll tak to come into ma office in Sunderland, and thoo shall have it!" "We must ask Mr. Lindsay about that," smilingly answered the supposed clerk, and the shipowner appearing upon the scene, introduced the parties. The handsome offer of the clerkship had been made to the Right Hon. W. E. Gladstone, then (about thirty years ago) Chancellor of the Exchequer.

Earlier in the present century, an inhabitant of Sunderland had devoted much of his time, his energy, and his money to the service of one Dissenting Sect. In his old age, he differed from his fellow-members upon some point long forgotten; the whole congregation turned against him, and he was left alone. The general public knowing nothing of the matter in dispute, saw only the gross ingratitude shown by the congregation to its benefactor; and a Churchman meeting his Dissenting neighbour in the street, gave utterance to the general feeling of sympathy. "Indeed," replied the old man, "it is very hard to bear, and it grieves me so much that I sometimes think I will just give up religion altogether and go to Church!"

Going somewhat further back in the history of Sunderland, we find one of its inhabitants whom Mr. Ruskin might think worthy of remembrance for his good and lasting workmanship. Some years ago it was the fate of the writer of this book to be present at a sale of household furniture in the village of Ayton, so often referred to in the earlier chapters. The furniture was old, and had formerly belonged to a member of the Richardson family. He had bequeathed it to its last possessor, and the sale was held in a field near to the cottage where she had lived. One of the articles offered for sale was a clock ; it bore the name of the maker, John Ogden, Sunderland, and the date of 1640. It sold for several pounds, and an attempt afterwards made to buy it failed. The purchaser of the clock at the sale had taken it to his home in the south of England, had found it keep excellent time, and refused to part with it. The clever artificer who had made the clock two hundred years before, joined the Society of Friends in its earliest days, and his Quakerism was as thorough-going as his workmanship. After the Restoration, Holy Days were observed with especial care, and oral tradition relates that on such days as Christmas Day and Good Friday, John Ogden would open wide his door, and show himself busily engaged with his clock-making in evidence that he, at least, was keeping no Holy Day. We may think his zeal excessive, and perhaps out of taste. What on the other hand would he think of our workmanship ? Will our clocks keep good time for two hundred years ?

The art of the " horologer," to use the old fashioned word, seems to have been hereditary in the Ogden family. Some of the name carried on that business in Wensleydale, where their memory still lingers, but our business is with the immediate descendant of our former friend, John Ogden, who lived in Sunderland during the eighteenth century, and pursued the same craft as his grandfather. He died in middle life, leaving a numerous family. His widow was a clever and energetic woman, and she used every exertion to support her family in comfort. Amongst all the new employments for women, we have not yet heard of a lady horologer, but I am told that the name of Jane Ogden was well known upon clocks, for she continued her husband's business. She was able to bequeath money to each of her children, and was wont to say that " it ought to do them good service, for it had been very honestly come by." She had one son and several daughters, whose descendants are scattered about the world in many walks of life, more of them being clergymen and clergymen's wives than members of the Society of Friends.

Her daughter Jane was long remembered in Sunderland, in which town she resided during her long life of ninety years. A woman of great spirit and vivacity, with striking features, fair complexion, and reddish-yellow hair, she was probably good-looking in her youth, and certainly attractive. "Charming Jennie Ogden" was scratched upon the window-pane of an inn in the county of Durham, and found there many years after by a company of grave Friends (one of whom was her husband) as they waited for fresh horses in the old posting days. She married Solomon Chapman, one of the family so well known in Whitby for four hundred years, and mentioned in a former chapter of this book as having intermarried with the Richardsons. He became a minister in the Society of Friends, and was somewhat formal and sententious in speech.* This formality often contrasted oddly with his wife's energy and quickness. It is told that she once came late into a Quarterly Meeting at Darlington, and looked for a seat about half-way up the meeting-house. A Friend at the top of the meeting called to her "Come forward!" and her husband, rising from his seat in the minister's gallery, unadvisedly added, "Jane Chapman, come forward!" The high-spirited woman, indignant at being thus publicly named, turned sharply round, went to the bottom of the meeting, and took her seat upon the very lowest form! The muscles of the gravest Friends were severely tried, and when Solomon Chapman met his wife at dinner at a Friend's house later in the day, he thus addressed her:—"Thou showedst in the face of the whole Quarterly Meeting thy disloyalty and disobedience to thy husband!" He was both fond and proud of her, but her impulsive ways must have been a sore trial to him. When she was more than usually defiant of his authority, he would say, shaking his head at her with mock gravity, "Ah, thou wert always a rebellious subject, even from thy very birth!" From this it was conjectured that she was born about the year 1745. As a rule, she and her husband were reticent on the subject of their age. Solomon Chapman suffered as much from his Old Testament name as did a late brilliant politician and literary man, and veiled it as carefully under its initial,

---

* His directions to a servant in a house where he visited are still remembered:—"Bring me two jugs of water in the morning,—one, not warm, but hot; another, not hot, but warm. Knock at the door, then open it, and proclaim the hour in an audible voice!"

S. Chapman being the only name he could ever be induced to give. Fortunately for him, he and his wife were known to a very large circle as "Uncle and Aunt Chapman."

A nephew who came to Sunderland once a week on business was accustomed to dine at their house. On his marriage he (naturally) arranged to go home to dine with his wife. "Uncle Chapman," meeting him in the street, said to him, "William, it is said that a man shall leave his father and mother, and cleave to his wife; but it is nowhere said that he shall leave his uncles and aunts!" He would sometimes administer little reproofs, in his formal way, to what appeared to him undue levity, or conformity to the world's fashions. His wife, on the contrary, exercised a most generous tolerance, even for the more serious failings of frail humanity. "Really, Aunt, how canst thou defend such persons?" was said to her with respect to some noted offenders. "There are plenty of people to speak against them without my help," she would reply. This tolerance was carried far, when she refused to discard her old family doctor, whose habits of intemperance had become notorious. "How canst thou admit such a drunken man into thy house?" enquired her horrified friends. "He is far cleverer when he is drunk than other folks are when they are sober," was "Aunt Chapman's" (most reprehensible) reply. Like everyone else, she bought her fish of the women who brought it to the door in their creels, and drove a bargain with them. On one occasion, the fishwoman, after abating a little of her demand, said, "Eh, Mrs. Chapman, hinnie, but we're badly off just noo; the bairns have been poorly, and the fish has been scarce." Back into her dining-room stepped the impulsive woman, who had been haggling over a few pence, and taking a scarcely-touched fillet of veal off the table, packed it up to be taken home in the fisher-woman's empty creel. Her husband's hot-house grapes (rare luxuries early in this century) were always at the service of the sick.

Of a light, spare figure, and very quick in her movements, "Aunt Chapman" was, like many ladies of that day, of very independent habits. When ninety years old, she had to accept a little aid from a servant. As she laid her hand upon "Betty's" arm, she turned and said to a bystander, as if apologising for such weakness, "At stern necessity's supreme command!"

From their age, their childless position, and their great hospitality,

"Uncle and Aunt Chapman" were the centre of a very large circle of relatives and friends, by whom their house in Sunnyside, with its double flight of steps to the front door, its old servants, its pet dog, and its parrot were long remembered. The dog, it was said, preferred visitors who wore the Quaker garb, but the spirit of the master, and still more that of the mistress of the house, was truly catholic. Poor and lonely relatives from quiet old Whitby met the dwellers in the busy towns of Durham and Northumberland, and clergymen of the Church of England mingled freely with members of the Society of Friends. When the aged couple died, the wife in 1834, the husband in 1838, the place they had occupied in society was left vacant. No other persons could unite the differing elements which had composed their circle, and friends and relatives drifted apart.

Most of those who met at the house in Sunnyside, upon whose recollection this sketch is based, and for whose dear sakes it is written, have long passed away. Among the loved and honoured descendants of the Ogden family still remembered, Dr. Joseph Brown, the skilful physician, and cultured and kindly man, may here be mentioned.* When only six years of age, being on a visit at Sunnyside, he saw from the window a gentleman run up the steps, shouting in the wildest excitement, "The King of France is taken!" News of the capture of Louis XVI. at Varennes had reached the town, already agitated by the tidings of his flight from Paris. Twenty years after, Dr. Brown, then Surgeon on the Duke of Wellington's staff, witnessed the return to Paris of the unfortunate King's brother, Louis XVIII. Sunderland has had many other worthies. Clarkson Stanfield was born there, and took his first sea-sketches from its pier. Dixon, the cork-cutter, Ruskin's friend, is worthy of mention. It was the birth-place and youthful home of the gifted dramatist and genial Editor of 'Punch,' Tom Taylor; and the residence throughout life of that Christian gentleman and large-minded philanthropist, Edward Backhouse, who died in 1879, and to whose wise liberality the pleasant and prosperous Sunderland of our day owes a debt of gratitude.

This history must now return to its legitimate objects.

* See Appendix.

CHAPTER XIV.

Changes.

1818—1889.

"The burden and heat of the day."

An attempt was made in the last chapter to recall some traditions of society in North Shields in former days. That society, less addicted than some circles of more pretension to the worship of wealth, always gave due honour to intellect. Elizabeth Richardson's taste in drawing and painting was at once recognised by the ladies who attended her drawing school; and her spirit and vivacity rendered her a pleasant addition to the social circles into which she was welcomed. She had never dressed fashionably, and now appears to have resumed the Quaker garb; no doubt to mark her preference for the religious body whose worship she attended; and also, it may be, because she was thereby exonerated from following the changes of fashion. But (except in her own family circle), she never resumed the peculiar Quaker phraseology, and would say with characteristic directness that there was no more harm in saying "Mrs." or "Miss" than in saying "table" or "chair." Her speech was always more forcible in expression than was usual with those accustomed to the guarded language of Quaker homes. Not being a member of the Society she was liable to no reproofs, not even to one so gentle as was given to a young Friend who allowed the word "horrid" to escape from her lips. "My dear Cousin, would not some mitigation of thy language be desirable?"

When, in 1817, Elizabeth took a house in Dockwray Square, and there opened a school for the general education of girls, it was largely attended by the daughters of the principal inhabitants of North Shields. She conducted this school for twenty-two years, and it is believed to have powerfully influenced the minds of many who passed through its course.

This was especially the case with those girls who knew that in their homes the character of their instructress was respected and admired, and that her authority would invariably be upheld.

Dr. Arnold was once touched by the appeal of a boy of slow capacity, who looked up into his face and said, "Why do you speak so angrily, Sir? Indeed, I am doing the best I can." One could wish that some girl had had the courage to make such an appeal to Elizabeth Richardson, for it cannot be denied that she was impatient with the dull, and did not make sufficient allowance for the timid. She had a few boys in her school, who held a very different position in it from that occupied by their fathers in the school of Miss Weir, as described in the last chapter. A strenuous upholder of the rights of her own sex, it is doubtful if Elizabeth Richardson held the balance quite evenly. Far from showing any favour to her boys, the personal recollections of the writer, and the early traditions of the school, leave an impression that exceptionally hard measure was dealt out to them. Indeed, it must be conceded that in her younger pupils the strongest feeling she inspired was that of awe. It was in those who remained long under her care (many having no further instruction,) that she inspired regard and affection. Some of these ladies looked back to the time which they passed under her tuition with pleasure and pride ; and so highly did they esteem her character and usefulness, that when they in their turn had become mothers of families, they wished for a similar instructress for their daughters. Many years afterwards two sisters opened a school in Shields. They were strangers in the town, but their school had for a time a marked success, simply because they were members of the Society of Friends, and it was therefore supposed they would be "like Miss Richardson."

Yet the education given by this long-remembered schoolmistress was a very plain one. The hours were from nine to twelve, and from two to five o'clock. Order and punctuality were rigidly enforced. The lessons appointed the day before had to be repeated without an error. They were in spelling, "Tables," Geography, and Lindley Murray's English Grammar. A master came for an hour to superintend the writing and "ciphering" of the elder girls. The rest of the morning was devoted to parsing, and to working problems on the globes. In the afternoon, the boys sat at their desks at arithmetic, the girls on forms at needlework. A young teacher gave any instruction needed in that art, and taught spelling, Tables and verbs to the little ones in classes. The elder girls read aloud in turn, and it was the earnest endeavour of their instructress to impart some intelligent interest to their readings in prose, and to infuse some spirit and enthusiasm into their reading of poetry. Now and then an extract from Byron or Scott brightened the long hours ; but how welcome were the short winter days of Northumberland when darkness closed in at four o'clock, and long before that hour murmurs of "Please ma'am I can't see" were heard from different parts of the room, in the rising inflection of the Border County.

Once a week there was a lesson in Scripture, and when wished, the Church Catechism was taught. Elizabeth held her drawing-class on Saturday afternoons. French and music were taught by masters, and there was a piano in the dining room, an object of great interest to little Friends, who would sometimes, by softly touching it, " snatch a fearful joy."

It is clear that this school was only raised above the level of others of its day by the energy of its mistress, and by her intense interest in the progress of every individual pupil. This personal interest was one cause of the high estimation in which Elizabeth Richardson was held, and it is probable that the entire absence of self-seeking in her character was appreciated both by her pupils and their parents.

Her holidays were complained of, not for their length, but for their brevity. A week or ten days at Christmas, three days at Easter, and a month at Midsummer was the moderate allowance. The prizes given in the school were out of all proportion to the fees charged. During the Thirties, the 'Annuals' were in the height of their glory, and the best of them (including Lady Blessington's 'Book of Beauty') were sent down by a Newcastle bookseller to Elizabeth, that she might select from them the prizes for her elder girls. Some of her young relatives were allowed to see these books which, with their exquisite engravings, their verse, and their prose fiction, opened a new world of delight to Friends' children. To them the coming of the 'Annuals' was the chief joy of Christmas.

In the year 1838, one of the last years of the school, the daring proposal was made by a pupil, "to present Miss Richardson with a piece of plate." The idea was warmly taken up, and the money was soon raised. A plain, handsome silver sugar basin was purchased, and a suitable inscription was engraved upon it. The secret was well kept, for even the youngest pupils understood the character of their schoolmistress well enough to know that, had any hint of the project reached her ears, a speedy stop would have been put to their proceedings. Indeed, there was some fear that the sugar basin might be flung at the person presenting it; and there was no desire to fill that prominent position. It was undertaken by a tall, quiet girl, who, on "breaking up" day, went forward with the simple words, "If you please, Miss Richardson, the scholars give you this," holding out the sugar basin. The answer came in accents of dismay, "The scholars, my dear ! I never was so much shocked in my life !" The surprise and annoyance were unmistakeable, nor can any after expression of thanks or of gratitude be remembered. The donors may have derived some pleasure from their gift, but the recipient experienced none. It grieved her unspeakably to think of money being collected on her account, and persons asked to give who could ill afford it, and who yet could not refuse to contribute to a present for one whom they regarded as a friend. The sugar basin was never exhibited by the person to whom it was presented, nor was it ever seen upon her tea table; but she, of course, preserved it, and it is now in the possession of the writer of this book.

Elizabeth made no fortune by her school. When she relinquished it at the Christmas of 1839, she did not sell it, but gave it away to a young person who had been employed by her as a teacher. At different times while she had this school, Elizabeth Richardson had a pupil as boarder. One, who, from her sweetness of disposition was an especial favourite with all, became in after years the wife of the Hon. and Rev. R. Eden, Rector of Bishop Wearmouth. Another sprightly, affectionate girl had a chequered career, and also married into a titled family. At one time Elizabeth had an orphan niece to live with her; a very pretty girl, beyond the age of pupilage. She was long remembered in the social circles of North Shields.

While Elizabeth Richardson was engaged in teaching her school, and mingling in the general society of the town, her sister Mary was living an equally active and useful life in a more secluded circle. All the descendants of John Richardson, the families of his sons Isaac and George in Newcastle, of his son John in Sunderland, and of his daughters, Margaret Unthank and Elizabeth Procter looked to the house at the Low Lights as their home. Mary Richardson fully realised that presiding over the household of the youngest son, who lived at the old place, she was bound to make all welcome.   Not only was this her duty, but it became her pleasure ; and it is somewhat remarkable that with every member of that large circle, she maintained relations of affection and of kindness to the end of her life. A young Friend of the South of England, who married into the family, was heard to say, " I shall never like Cousin Mary, she is so blunt in her manner."   Yet this lady became one of " Cousin Mary's " greatest friends.

From those early days when, little more than a child herself, Mary cared for her young motherless sisters and brother, her devotion to children was remarkable.   Although in her household the worship of cleanliness and order was carried to a great pitch, and her dearest friends feared to call on " washing days " or when their boots were exceptionally dirty, her tolerance of disarrangement and disorder, if it was caused by children was a well-known fact.   They always were fond of her.   When fever broke out in any of the families, it was usual to send the rest of the children to the Low Lights, where it was known they would be happy and well cared for. One little girl was sent from Newcastle on a visit to that hospitable house that she might have the benefit of sea bathing.   For this purpose she was taken by her " Cousin Mary " to one of the tents on the beach and undressed ; but when the child saw the expanse of water into which she was to be plunged, she shrieked with terror.   Her indulgent cousin, instead of forcing her into the waves as some sterner persons would have done, soothed her childish distress, dressed her again, and took her home without even a scolding.   Whether " Cousin Mary " was right or wrong in this matter need not be here decided ; the little child of that day, now in her age, only remembers gratefully her cousin's kindness.

In those families the tradition of affection and respect for " Cousin Mary " seemed to be handed on from one generation to another, just as the toys in a certain cupboard in her bookcase pleased the boys and girls of those who had played with them in their own childhood.

How warmly Mary welcomed her sisters to Shields has been seen by their letters.   Her home had many attractions for them, and one undoubtedly was that flowers grew in her sheltered garden, which they tried in vain to raise in the wind-swept enclosures of Hutchinson's Buildings or in the tiny front gardens of Dockwray Square.   The woods and wild flowers of Yorkshire and Durham were missed by the sisters when they settled on the bleak coast of Northumberland. But in the spring, primroses grew abundantly on the sea banks between Tynemouth and Cullercoats : and in June, the small Burnet rose covered with its delicate pink or white petals, the grassy sandhills on the south side of the river Tyne. Further on the Durham Coast, Marsden Rock, standing out in the sea, with its base hollowed into arched caverns by the constant fretting of the waves, was a favourite excursion. Of one walk to that place a tale is told. The sisters and some friends crossed the Tyne in a rowing boat, (it was before the days of the Steam Ferry,) and landed upon the hard sand near the mouth of the river on the Durham side, from whence the walk to Marsden is about three miles. Mary's active hands had packed a basket with good things of her own making, including (in those pre-Teetotal days) one or two bottles of her excellent currant wine. On reaching Marsden, this basket was deposited in a cleft of the rocks, and the group pursued its way, exploring the little bays and coves with which the coast is indented, and (if Elizabeth was of the party) probably cutting some of the flexible lime-stone. Their ramble proved longer than they intended, and the afternoon was far advanced when they returned, hungry and tired, to the place where they intended to dine, probably the "velvet beds." An active youth, afterwards known as "John Richardson of Langbarugh," climbed up the rocks to the place where the basket containing the dinner had been hidden. The basket, indeed, he found, and waved it (empty) above his head, exclaiming "all gone!" The famishing party were incredulous, but it was too true. It was remembered that some men with guns had been seen. Doubtless they had enjoyed the luncheon and the currant wine. Peter Allan had not then excavated his dwelling in the rock where tea can now be procured, and the party had to return hungry to North Shields.

A more serious misadventure befel Mary and Hannah, and a young Friend from the south of England. This lady was unfamiliar with the rough coast of Northumberland, and unused to climbing over its rugged rocks. Her satin shoes and silk stockings were ill-fitted for rough walking, and the three friends rested in one of the little bays north of Tynemouth. The London lady, if a poor pedestrian, was a charming companion, and in her society Mary and Hannah forgot that the tide was rising. Suddenly they awoke to the fact that the waves were dashing over the rocks by which they had come. The bay in which they sat they knew would be covered by the sea at high water. The banks so populous now, were lonely then, and they called for help in vain. To ascend the cliff seemed impossible, but Hannah resolved to attempt it. The thought of this terrified Mary more than the rising tide; and she knelt on the shore at her sister's feet, entreating her to remain and let them all drown together, rather than run the risk of being dashed to pieces by falling from the cliff. Hannah, however, was unshaken in her resolution, and her habits of climbing in her childhood stood her in good stead that day. She reached the bank in safety, went to the Castle, and came back accompanied by two soldiers. Mary and her companion (in her satin shoes) were drawn up the cliff by ropes.

In a former chapter it has been stated that in 1820, three of the orphan children of Joseph and Elizabeth Procter were received into the home at the Low Lights by their "Uncle Henry" and their "Cousin Mary." These were Mary's children by adoption and affection, and well in after years did they repay her love and care. Another group of children in North Shields were very dear to her. Descendants by their mother of the Cleveland Richardsons, they have their place in this history. About the time Mary came to reside at the Low Lights, her cousin Mary, eldest of the Langbarugh girls, was married to Joshua Wilson of Sunderland. He died early in life, and Mary Wilson was left a young childless widow in a large house in Bishop Wearmouth Walk. It is said that she, one day, asked who the handsome young man was who rode past her house every Wednesday? She was told that this young man was William Brown, a partner in Willington Mill, who came to Sunderland every Wednesday on business, and always dined at the house of his " Uncle and Aunt Chapman " in Sunnyside. Not long after this Mary Wilson went to stay awhile with her cousin at the Low Lights. The two Maries, no doubt, visited many places of note near Shields, but they paid one visit to a place then quite unknown to psychic fame, Willington Mill, where the youngest partner resided. Here it was that he was first introduced to Mary Wilson, and the acquaintance thus formed resulted in a marriage in the year 1807. Mary Wilson was a few years her husband's senior, but the marriage was one of the greatest affection. They settled in a house in Dockwray Square, where eight children were born to them, of whom three died in early life. Mary Brown was on terms of pleasant intimacy with her neighbours in North Shields; but her cousin Mary was her closest friend, and her children were always welcome visitors at the Low Lights.

A warm-hearted, impulsive woman, Mary Brown was deeply mourned when she died in 1817, leaving five very young children. Four years afterwards, her husband married Sarah, the youngest daughter of Henry Richardson of Stockton. Those who knew the heroines of this book in their home at Newcastle and at Shields, were wont to say that the gentle nature of the younger sister gave the touch of repose needed to complete the picture of a happy household. With the elder sisters, a visitor might feel that he was interrupting some current of thought or of action, but from the youngest he was sure of a pleasant smile of welcome. Of a loving and unselfish disposition, she was peculiarly fitted for a stepmother. She had her joys and sorrows in the old house in Dockwray Square. Like her mother at Whitby, so many years before, she lost her first children (three boys) in early life, and was left childless. Lonely she was not left, for her husband's children, to whom she was a most affectionate mother, warmly returned her love. She had afterwards a daughter, who has survived to gather these old memories. It was Sarah Richardson's lot in life to make one home happy; this Biography is concerned with the varied lives and widely differing experiences of her energetic elder sisters,

Of Hannah little has been said in recent chapters. It is not to Biographies of Friends who were born in the last century that we look for sensational religion; and the word conversion was rarely upon their lips. But by whatever name we may call it, there can be no doubt that between the years 1808 and 1813, a change took place in the character of Hannah Richardson which materially affected her views of life and of duty. At the time of her father's death, she was a gay, fashionable young lady. We are left entirely to conjecture in the matter, but that leads to the belief that during the two years the sisters spent in Newcastle, any adverse feeling towards Friends passed away from the minds of Elizabeth and Hannah. When they went to live in North Shields it is clear that they all attended the Friends' meeting, but Hannah's letters are still dated " November " and " December " instead of " 11th month " and " 12th month." During the following years she appears to have become more and more attached to Friends, adopting even the minor peculiarities; and in 1814 she applied to be " reinstated in membership." If, as is supposed, she had entertained what would now be called " advanced " opinions, she must have satisfied the Friends who " visited " her that she was convinced of the truth of

Christianity, and sympathized with that simple form of it professed by the Society. It was not by words, however, but by her whole after life that the change was shown. It was about this time that Elizabeth was establishing her drawing school, and entering into the general society of North Shields. Hannah seems to have felt that this course was not the one for her, and the sisters, so long united, took separate paths in life, although the tie of affection between them always seemed to be especially close.

In the same spirit in which a Roman Catholic lady might have taken the veil, or an Anglican might have entered a sisterhood, Hannah seems to have chosen a course in life very different to that which she had before pursued. An expression dropped in one of her letters,—a wish for humility,— gives some clue to the workings of her mind. It may be that she felt she had erred through pride and self-will ; and it is certain that she deliberately placed herself in a position in which her will would be subjected to that of others.

An aged, childless couple in the neighbourhood of York wished for a young Friend to read to them, to write for them, to superintend their household affairs, and to act to them the part of a daughter. Hannah offered herself for this post.

CHAPTER XV.

Lindley Murray.

1745—1834.

> " Great gains are mine, for thus I live remote
> From evil speaking : rancour, never sought,
> Comes to me not ; malignant truth or lie.
> Hence have I genial seasons, hence have I
> Smooth passions, smooth discourse and joyous thought :
> And thus from day to day my little boat
> Rocks in its harbour, lodging peaceably.
> Blessings be with them, and eternal praise,
> Who gave us nobler loves and nobler cares,—
> The poets,—who on earth have made us heirs
> Of truth and pure delight by heavenly lays ! "
>
> WORDSWORTH.

LINDLEY MURRAY, the well-known grammarian, was born in 1745, at Swetara in Pennsylvania, at which place his father had a flour mill. In a memoir of his life upon which this sketch is based, Lindley Murray speaks of his mother as "remarkable for mildness, humanity, and liberality of sentiment." When five or six years old, he remembers " being some time at the Academy of Philadelphia, the English department of which was then conducted by the truly respectable Ebenezer Kinnersley." Lindley Murray regrets that his "continuance in that seminary was of short duration," and remembers " to have read there with pleasure some passages in the ' Travels of Cyrus,' and to have been agreeably exercised in the business of parsing sentences." But in the same Johnsonian language he records of himself that he was a " mischievous child " and a " heedless boy."

His father became a merchant, and in 1753 settled with his family in New York. The memoir says, " In this city I was placed at a good school, and made the usual progress of young learners. Being extremely fond of play, I believe I neglected no opportunity of indulging this propensity." He believes that he "never failed to perform his tasks," but makes the confession, " sometimes I absented myself from school to enjoy a greater degree of play and amusement."

At the early age usual at that day, young Murray (who was the eldest of twelve children) was taken from school, and placed in the counting-house of the firm of which his father was the leading member—Murray, Sansom and Co., of London and New York. Like many another boy, when school days were over he longed for more time for study, and with the " otherwise mindedness " of youth, " wished to be anything rather than a merchant." His father, however, thought this the best career for him, and kept him very strictly to business. He was a very lively boy, and the restraint placed upon his natural disposition, both in and out of office hours, seems to have been very irksome to him. When he was fourteen years old, a circumstance occurred which is not without instruction for parents as well as for children. It shall be told in his own words :—

" Though my father, as the events already mentioned demonstrate, had an earnest desire to promote my interest and happiness, yet he appeared to me in some respects, and on some occasions, rather too rigorous. Among other regulations, he had, with true parental prudence, given me general directions not to leave the house, in an evening, without previously obtaining his approbation. I believe that his permission was generally and readily procured. But a particular instance occurred, in which, on account of his absence, I could not apply to him. I was invited by an uncle to spend the evening with him; and trusting to this circumstance and to the respectability of my company, I ventured to break the letter, though I thought not the spirit, of the injunction which had been laid upon me. The next morning I was taken by my father into a private apartment, and remonstrated with for my disobedience. In vain were my apologies. Nothing that I could offer was considered as an extenuation of my having broken a plain and positive command. In short, I received a very severe chastisement, and was threatened with a repetition of it for every similar offence. Being a lad of some spirit, I felt very indignant at such treatment under circumstances which, as I conceived, admitted of so much alleviation. I could not bear it ; and I resolved to leave my father's house, and seek in a distant country what I conceived to be an asylum, or a better fortune. Young and ardent, I did not want confidence in my own powers ; and I presumed that with health and strength, which I possessed in a superior degree, I could support myself, and make my way happily through life. I meditated on my plan; and came to the resolution of taking my books and all my property with me to a town in the interior of the country, where I had understood there was an excellent seminary, kept by a man of distinguished talents and learning. Here I purposed to remain till I had learned the French language, which I thought would be of great use to me, and till I had acquired as much other improvement as my funds would admit. With this stock of knowledge, I presumed that I should set out in life under much greater advantages, than I should possess by entering immediately into business, with my small portion of property and great inexperience. I was then about fourteen years of age. My views being thus arranged, I procured a new suit of clothes, entirely different from those which I had been accustomed to wear, packed up my little all, and left the city, without exciting any suspicion of my design, till it was too late to prevent its accomplishment.

"In a short time I arrived at the place of destination. I settled myself immediately as a boarder in the seminary, and commenced my studies The prospect which I entertained was so luminous and cheering, that, on the whole, I did not regret the part I had acted. Past recollections and future hopes combined to animate me. The chief uneasiness which I felt in my present situation must have arisen from the reflection of having lost the society and attentions of a most affectionate mother, and of having occasioned sorrow to her feeling mind. But as I had passed the Rubicon, and believed I could not be comfortable at home, I contented myself with the thought that the pursuit of the objects before me was better calculated than any other to produce my happiness. In this quiet retreat, I had as much enjoyment as my circumstances were adapted to convey. The pleasure of study, and the glow of a fond imagination, brightened the scenes around me. And the consciousness of a state of freedom and independence, undoubtedly contributed to augment my gratifications, and to animate my youthful heart. But my continuance in this delightful situation was not of long duration. Circumstances of an apparently trivial nature concurred to overturn the visionary fabric I had formed, and to bring me again to the paternal roof.

"I had a particular friend, a youth about my own age, who resided at Philadelphia. I wished to pay him a short visit, and then resume my studies. We met according to appointment, at an inn on the road. I enjoyed his society, and communicated to him my situation and views. But before I returned to my retreat, an occurrence took place which occasioned me to go to Philadelphia. When I was about to leave that city, as I passed through one of the streets, I met a gentleman who had some time before dined at my father's house. He expressed great pleasure on seeing me, and inquired when I expected to leave the city. I told him I was then on the point of setting off. He thought the occasion very fortunate for him. He had just been with a letter to the post-office, but found that he was too late. The letter, he said, was of importance; and he begged that I would deliver it with my own hand, and as soon as I arrived at New York, to the person for whom it was directed. Surprised by the request, and unwilling to state to him my situation, I engaged to take good care of the letter.

"My new residence was at Burlington, about twenty miles from Philadelphia. I travelled towards it rather pensive, and uncertain what plan to adopt respecting the letter. I believe that I sometimes thought of putting it into the post-office; sometimes of hiring a person to deliver it. But the confidence which had been reposed in me, the importance of the trust, and my tacit engagement to deliver it personally, operated so powerfully on my mind, that after I had rode a few miles, I determined, whatever risk and expense I might incur, to hire a carriage for the purpose, to go to New York as speedily as possible, deliver the letter, and return immediately. My design, so far as it respected the charge of the letter, was completely accomplished. I delivered it, according to the direction, and my own engagement. I was, however, obliged to remain in New York that night, as the packet boat, in which I had crossed the bay, could not sail till the next morning. This was a mortifying circumstance, as I wished to return very expeditiously. The delay was, however, unavoidable. I put up at an inn near the wharf from which the packet was to sail in the morning, and waited for that period with some anxiety.

"I thought I had conducted my business with so much caution, that no one acquainted with me, had known of my being in the city. I had, however, been noticed by some person who knew me; and, in the evening, to my great surprise, my uncle, whom I have mentioned before, paid me a visit. He treated me affectionately, and with much prudent attention; and, after some time, strenuously urged me to go with him to my father's house, but I firmly refused to comply with his request. At length he told me, that my mother was greatly distressed on account of my absence ; and that I should be unkind and undutiful if I did not see her. This made a strong impression upon me. I resolved, therefore, to spend a short time with her, and then return to my lodgings. The meeting which I had with my dear and tender parent was truly affecting to me. Everything that passed evinced the great affection she had for me, and the sorrow into which my departure from home had plunged her. After I had been some time in the house, my father unexpectedly came in : and my embarrassment, under these circumstances may easily be conceived. It was, however, instantly removed by his approaching me in the most affectionate manner. He saluted me very tenderly ; and expressed great satisfaction on seeing me again. Every degree of resentment was immediately dissipated. I felt myself happy in perceiving the pleasure which my society could afford to persons so intimately connected with me, and to whom I was so much indebted. We spent the evening together in love and harmony : and I abandoned entirely, without a moment's hesitation, the idea of leaving a house and family, which were now dearer to me than ever.

"The next day a person was sent to the place of my retreat, to settle all accounts, and to bring back my property. I was taken into still greater favour than formerly ; and was never reproached by my parents, for the trouble and anxiety which I had brought upon them. My father probably perceived that I felt sufficiently on the occasion ; and he was, perhaps, conscious that the discipline he had exerted, was not altogether justifiable. When I reflect on this rash and imprudent adventure ; on the miseries in which it might have involved me ; and on the singular manner in which I was restored to the bosom of my family ; I cannot avoid seeing the hand of Divine Providence in my preservation ; and feeling that I ought to be humbly and deeply thankful for the gracious interposition.

"Before I quit this subject, I must observe, that soon after I had left home, inquiries were made to discover the place to which I had retreated. I knew that this was the case : but I had made up my mind not to return, and subject myself again to a treatment which I had felt to be improper and unmerited. I therefore declined all the proposals and entreaties of individuals who were friends to the family, and who endeavoured to shake the resolutions I had formed. And I am persuaded that, at this period, nothing would have induced me to relinquish them, but a security against the repetition of the harsh discipline which I had experienced. I rejoice, however, that a train of events so unexpected, and so contrary to my fixed purposes, happily brought me again to the paternal mansion, and settled me safely under its protection.

"A short time after I had returned to my father's family, I solicited the privilege of having a private tutor, to instruct me in classical knowledge and liberal studies. With this request, my father very generously complied. A tutor of talents and learning was procured for me : and I pursued this new career with great alacrity of mind. I sat up late and rose early, in the prosecution of my studies."

Lindley Murray speaks with great modesty of his attainments under this tutor, but the course of study certainly contributed to the happiness of his after life. He joined a debating society, and, when about seventeen years old, wished to study for the law. His father, whose heart was still set upon his being a merchant, was slow to give way upon this point, until at length the youth stated his case in writing with such cogent arguments, that, on the paper being shown to an eminent counsel, he not only pleaded the boy's cause, but asked to have him as a pupil. To this gentleman, Benjamin Kissam of New York, Lindley Murray was articled, and he had for his fellow pupil John Jay, afterwards Governor of the·State. Of the "integrity and eminence" of his "truly respectable" instructor, and of the talents and virtues of the "meritorious person" who was his companion, Lindley Murray speaks in the highest terms. He allows that even the study of the law "contains many barren and uninviting tracts," but it was the profession of his choice. In the year 1766, when he was twenty-one, Lindley Murray was called to the American bar, and about the same time he was married to a good and amiable woman. Happy in his home and rising in his profession, his prospects were bright. But this brightness was soon overcast. The war with England put a stop to business in American courts of law, and in 1776 the British troops took possession of New York. About this time Lindley Murray had a severe fit of illness, which left a weakness in the muscles of the limbs. During the war, he and his wife resided for some years at Islip on Long Island, and, after the success of the American arms, at a place called Bellevue, three miles from New York, on the beautiful banks of the river Hudson. This home Lindley Murray speaks of as a "paradisaical spot." But it did not restore his health. Visits to the mineral springs of New Jersey, to those of Bristol in Pennsylvania, and to the Moravian settlement at Bethlehem were paid, but in vain. At length a physician proposed a residence of two or three years in England, so as to escape the hot, exhausting summers of America; the climate of Yorkshire being especially recommended. This advice was at once acted upon. Lindley Murray says, " Dear as were our relatives and friends, and our native land, we resolved to forego the enjoyment of them. But hope cheered us with the prospect that the separation would not be long; and that we should return to them, with renewed health and spirits, and capacities of greater happiness in their society. My dear wife did not hesitate a moment, in resolving to accompany me to a distant country; and to render me every aid, which her affection, and solicitude for my happiness, could suggest.

"Soon after our determination was made, we prepared for the voyage. The trying scene now commenced of taking leave of our relations and friends. Many of them accompanied us to the ship, in the cabin of which we had a most solemn parting. An eminent minister was present at this time, for whom we had a particular esteem and regard, and who prayed fervently on the occasion." This parting proved to be for life.

It was in 1784, the year in which peace was signed between England and America, that Lindley Murray and his wife left their native land, and after a voyage of five weeks landed at Lymington, in Hampshire. They were not strangers in England. The memoir says, " In a few days after our landing we reached London. Here we were cheered with the society of a number of our friends whom we had known in a visit we paid to this country in 1771. We continued in and near London for about six weeks, and then proceeded for Yorkshire." After visiting many places in that county, Lindley Murray bought a house and garden in the village of Holdgate, near York. Here he settled in 1785, and at first so improved in health, that he looked forward to returning in a few years to America a vigorous man. This hope, however, was never realised. The improvement from change of climate was but temporary; it was found that exercise caused suffering, and weakened rather than strengthened the limbs, and his infirmities gradually increased upon him until he could only walk from his house to his carriage. Hope of returning to America, never formally relinquished, became fainter as time went on. Lindley Murray writes in 1806, " Two and twenty years have passed away since we left our native land, and little hope remains of our ever being able to visit it again. But resignation is our duty. And this should be the more cheerful, as we have been so long preserved together by Divine Providence, in this happy country ; where we have been abundantly blessed, and for which we can never be sufficiently grateful.

"Our attachment to England was founded on many pleasing associations. In particular, I had strong prepossessions in favour of a residence in this country ; because I was ever partial to its political constitution, and the mildness and wisdom of its general system of laws. I knew that under this excellent government, life, property, reputation, civil and religious liberty, are happily protected ; and that the general character and virtue of its inhabitants, take their complexion from the nature of their constitution and laws. On leaving my native country, there was not, therefore, any land on which I could cast my eyes with so much pleasure ; nor is there any which could have afforded me so much real satisfaction, as I have found in Great Britain. May its political fabric, which has stood the test of ages, and long attracted the admiration of the world, be supported and perpetuated by Divine Providence ! And may the hearts of Britons be grateful for this blessing, and for many others by which they are eminently distinguished !"

When it became evident to Lindley Murray that his life would be that of an invalid, he seems to have been anxious to avoid becoming too much engrossed by his own condition. His daily drive was continued for years, so that he might see " the busy or the cheerful faces of his fellow-men." It was not long before he began to occupy himself with writing, and his first work was called 'The Power of Religion upon the Mind.' It is, to use his own words, "a collection of the testimonies of great and good persons in favour of piety and virtue," and of their "sentiments on the subject of religion and futurity as they approached the close of life." He says, "As I wished to form it upon liberal principles, and render it acceptable to readers in general, I was careful to introduce characters of various religious professions, and of different ages and countries." This book was printed at York in the year 1787. The first edition of five hundred copies, neatly bound in leather, was distributed at the author's

L

own expense. He says, " I sent them to the principal inhabitants of York and its vicinity; and accompanied each book with an anonymous note requesting a favourable acceptance of it, and apologizing for the liberty I had taken." The publication was well received, and several editions were printed in London. When a sixth edition was called for, Lindley Murray enlarged and improved the book, and placed his name on the title page, and then gave away the copyright to a London publisher, hoping in this way to attain the end he had in view of making the work useful.

Amongst " the enjoyments and advantages yet left " to him in his invalid state, Lindley Murray counts " the society of worthy and intelligent friends." He was a man of very liberal views, and had friends and relatives in America who belonged to different religious communities, but this remark probably applies chiefly to the members of his own Society.

The Friends of York have been for more than a century a very appreciable element in the population of that city. " Ah ! Quakers are very good subjects; I wish I had more of them in my kingdom," was the exclamation of the King of Prussia when he distinguished persons in a quaint garb amongst the crowds who welcomed the Allied Sovereigns to London in 1814. And not only are Quakers good subjects, but they are generally good citizens; and the Friends of York felt that they were " citizens of no mean city." It was in no bounded or backward spirit that they interpreted the duties which devolved upon the dwellers in the old Roman Capital in the days of its humbler fortunes. Not only were they prominent in promoting the welfare of its living inhabitants, but in caring for the memorials of its past. They were earnest and energetic members of the York Philosophical Society, which rescued St. Mary's Abbey from the hands of the spoiler, and enclosed it and the Multangular Tower in a fair garden, and gathered into its Museum the coins and the weapons of the masters of the world, and even the very mirrors and tresses of the long-forgotten Roman ladies. A certain largeness of view always seemed to characterise the Friends of York amidst their strict conformity to the customs of their sect. They were proud of their magnificent Minster, although they knew it but from the outside. Few of them would compromise their testimony that reverence was due to the Almighty alone, by doffing the hat beneath any portal raised by human hands.

The interests of York have always been very varied. " I am afraid

that York to me means simply Mr. Backhouse's Nursery Grounds," said an
enthusiastic flower grower of our own day, when he was told of the ancient
churches of the city. And in the early days of Lindley Murray's life at
Holdgate, York, to many a lover of humanity all over the world, meant the
place where William Tuke was endeavouring to prove, by practical experiment, that some forms of mental disease might be cured by judicious
kindness, and that some brightness might be shed even over the darkened
lives of the hopelessly insane. Another undertaking of the Tuke family
was a source of interest and pleasure to Lindley Murray. This was the
School for girls mentioned in an earlier chapter of this book. The historian
of the school says, (speaking of Holdgate) " In this pleasant home Lindley
Murray was compelled to lead a quiet sedentary life, so he devoted his time
chiefly to reading and writing. He took a great interest in the school, and
was often consulted as a literary oracle by his friends there. The teachers,
Ann and Mabel Tuke, and Jane Taylor, who were intimate friends as well
as colleagues, feeling their inability to teach grammar, applied to him for
aid; and during a succession of winter evenings he gave them regular
lessons, much to their own enjoyment and the benefit of their pupils.
The walks to Holdgate, as well as the lessons, were noteworthy, for the
road was dark and rough; but the young pedestrians, shod in pattens, and
escorted by a man carrying a lantern, bravely and cheerily wended their
way to their preceptor's home, where their presence was both welcome
and enlivening."

Although a hundred years have passed since then, we can picture the
scene, and almost seem to hear the voices of those lively girls as, casting
aside cloaks and pattens, they passed from the darkness of the steep
Holdgate Lane into the cheerful parlour, where they brought the freshness
of youth and health, and of active work into the quiet lives of their genial
instructor and of his kind, hospitable wife. "A little later," says the
historian, " we find three of the teachers uniting in a 'humble petition to
the Right Hon. Lindley Murray, teacher of the English language, &c., &c.'
After stating the inconvenience they have experienced ' from the want of a
complete English Grammar, with examples and rules annexed,' and
expressing their faith in ' the incomparable abilities of their able preceptor,'
they humbly solicit the preparation ' of his materials for a work so
important; and in the execution of which they will gladly afford him their

feeble assistance. And his petitioners will, as in duty bound, desire (also pray) that his labours may be amply rewarded by the manifest fruits of its utility to the present and succeeding generations.'" Lindley Murray's reply to this petition is a doubtful one, but it contains the sentence that he "entertains such a respect and affection for his dear friends, Ann Tuke, Mabel Tuke, and Martha Fletcher, that it would be no easy matter for him to refuse any request that they might think proper to make." So in the words of the Historical Sketch, "It was to this playful yet earnest appeal from the teachers, seconded and strengthened by the representatives of other schools, that we owe the Grammar, which for half a century was decidedly the most useful and popular class-book in England; we think deservedly so when compared with its contemporaries, and judged by the standard that prevailed at the time. It was published in 1795, and the profits of the first edition were devoted to the benefit of the school.'"*

When Lindley Murray published his Grammar, he had no expectation of its being used except at the York Girls' School and at a similar establishment at Clonmel. Its general acceptance was a source of both pleasure and surprise to him, and to correct its many editions for the press gave him interesting employment. He had many attacks of severe illness, during which his life was despaired of, but when these passed away, he again resumed his pen. A list of his many publications will be found in the Appendix to this book. The children who, fifty years ago, toiled over the large and small print of his octavo Grammar, found it a somewhat weary pilgrimage through which the examples in Prosody loomed like the Delectable Mountains at the end of the journey. The Exercises upon the same volume caused many a sigh. But the 'English Reader' revives more cheerful memories. A less amusing and varied collection than 'Enfield's Speaker,' it was yet read for pleasure by some children at that remote period.

The great sale of Lindley Murray's works brought large profits to his publishers and to himself. His relations with these gentlemen were very agreeable, and they wished to have his portrait painted at their expense. This proposal, in accordance with the views of most Friends of that day, he declined. He was not a rich man in the modern acceptation of the word,

* 'Historical Sketch of York School,' by L. Rous.

the income from his property in America rarely exceeding £600 a year.
This sum he considered to be more than sufficient for the modest comfort in
which he lived at Holdgate, and the money which the Messrs. Longman
paid him for his copyrights all went to increase his charities.   These were
varied and judicious, including the payment of school fees for many poor
children, and the quiet giving of help to persons in straitened circumstances.
One trifling act of kindness is still remembered in York.   Within sight of
his house, a footpath ran over some fields to the city. Lindley Murray kept
this path in repair at his own expense, and placed seats upon it ; and it gave
him pleasure when, by the aid of a glass, he could see that these seats
afforded rest to some tired wayfarer.   As to charities of wider scope, many
a visit was paid to Holdgate by the Friends of York, who, coming out of
their busy lives into the hush of the invalid's room, with their minds full of
benevolent projects, never failed to find there sympathetic interest, wise
counsel, and generous aid.

His writings brought him reputation as well as money.   In his native
city of New York he was elected an honorary member of the Historical
Society, and of the Literary and Philosophical Society.   An impression
prevailed that he was a schoolmaster, and distinguished foreigners wished
to place boys under his care, whilst English noblemen wrote for his advice
with respect to their sons.   Many visitors sought the secluded village of
Holdgate to seek an introduction to him, one name mentioned being that
of the Earl of Buchan, whose appearance in odd boots at an Edinburgh
breakfast table is recorded in an earlier chapter.   A letter from the famous
Dr. Hugh Blair of Edinburgh addressed to Lindley Murray, and expressing
in words of stately eulogy, the admiration felt by the great Edinburgh
Divine for the writings of the Quaker recluse, is printed at the end of his
Biography.   Of these honours we now read with calmness, but the record
of one visit shall "brighten this poor page."   In the year 1803, the
versatile, much married, truly patriotic Irishman, Richard Lovell Edgeworth, and his daughter Maria, of happy memory, on their return from
Paris, passed through the city of York. During the evening they appeared
quite unexpectedly at Holdgate, and have recorded the impression made
upon them by the fine personal appearance, the unassuming manner, and
pleasant conversation of Lindley Murray, in whom they probably expected
to find the stiffness and formality of the pedagogue.   They remarked on the

" benevolent looks of Mrs. Murray as she offered us cake and wine ; " and considered the inmates of Holdgate " the most striking example of domestic happiness, and of religion without ostentation or the spirit of dogmatising which we had ever beheld."

Amongst the visitors who sought Lindley Murray, those who came from his own country were naturally especially welcome. Professor Silliman of Yale College, who travelled in England in 1805, recorded, in the volume he published, a visit to Holdgate. He says, " I was fortunate in finding Mr. Murray able to converse with freedom, for, at times, he is unable to utter even a whisper, and is compelled to decline seeing his friends . . . . One would suppose that a situation so peculiar would naturally induce a degree of impatience of temper, or at least of depression of spirits ; but I know not that I have ever seen more equanimity, and sweetness of deportment, joined with a more serene and happy cheerfulness, than in this instance. When the painful circumstances of his situation were alluded to, he expressed his gratitude to Heaven for the many comforts and alleviations which, he said, he enjoyed under his confinement. You would not judge from his appearance that he is an infirm man, for his countenance is rather ruddy, and it is animated with a strong expression of benevolence. His person is tall, and well formed ; and his manner of conversing is modest, gentle, easy, and persuasive . . . . . Mr. Murray belongs to the Society of Friends, but both he and Mrs. Murray have so tempered the strictness of the manners peculiar to their Society, that they are polished people, with the advantage of the utmost simplicity of deportment."

Fourteen years later, another American traveller, John Griscom, Professor of Chemistry in the New York Institution, chronicles in his ' Year in Europe ' a call at Holdgate. This visitor, coming from the same town as Lindley Murray, and being acquainted with his relations there, the conversation was full of interest to both interlocutors. Professor Griscom says, " It is thirty-four years since this worthy pair left their native shores, but their feelings are still American, and to listen to a particular relation of the enlargement of our cities, and the progress of the country, afforded them evidently the most lively satisfaction." Commenting with surprise, like other visitors, upon the cheerfulness of Lindley Murray, the New York professor says, " I have been informed by persons who were his youthful contemporaries, that he was possessed by nature of great vivacity

of feeling, and passions not less difficult to control than those which fall to
the ordinary lot of humanity."   After speaking of the way in which this
" waywardness of nature " was overcome, and of the sweet expression upon
Lindley Murray's countenance, the visitor continues, " He has been blessed
with a most amiable and intelligent wife, the companion of his early years,
and the faithful and sympathising partner in all that concerns him.   A
young woman who serves them as housekeeper, appears also well qualified,
by the respectability of her character and attainments, to perform the duties
of an almost filial trust."

In this young woman of "respectable character and attainments," it is,
for a moment, a surprise to recognise our lively heroine, Hannah.   Somewhat changed from the stylish girl in the gypsy hat and feathers, we now
behold her in the neat close cap of Quakerism, writing from Lindley
Murray's dictation, reading aloud to him slowly and distinctly, and
presiding over his household.   When she became a resident at Holdgate,
Lindley Murray was entirely confined to the house, his strength being no
longer equal even to his daily drive.   "His gentle wife," writes a correspondent, "was so entirely devoted to his companionship that she rarely
left the house, and their sprightly and energetic young friend (Hannah)
formed a needed link between them and the outer world."   Every morning
her tall, lissom figure was seen on the road between Holdgate and York,
her feet shod with pattens if the weather was wet, her hand carrying a
basket, her walk full of energy and directness of purpose.   Her lightness
of heart did not depart with her feathers; nor did her quiet dress dull her
spirits.   Not only in the seclusion of Holdgate, but in many a home in
York, her cheerful presence was welcome.   It is still remembered how her
coming was watched for in houses which she passed in her daily walk; and
how her friends would rush to door or window to beg for a few minutes of
her company; but, beyond the time required for loving greetings and
enquiries, she might not prolong her stay.   The invalid almost counted the
minutes until her return with his letters, his daily paper, his ' Newcastle
Chronicle ' once a week, and the news of his friends.   Some marvelled at
the way in which his messenger curbed her natural inclinations and
strongly social instincts, and bent her will to that of another.   But if
this caused her a struggle, it was known to herself alone.   In the eyes of
children, to whom Holdgate seemed almost a sacred and inviolate spot, she

seemed the bright intermediary who admitted them within its precincts. The same correspondent writes, " We oftener enjoyed this privilege from dear cousin Hannah being as the daughter of the house, and always giving us a welcome, and knowing how to give pleasure to the young without inconveniencing the venerable pair around whom there seemed to be a halo of repose as they sat side by side in the cheerful drawing room through which perpetual sunshine seemed to stream ; for the window at one end looked over the road to the meadows on the banks of the Ouse, and that at the other end over the beautiful garden with its broad gravel walk leading up to the summer house of somewhat classical construction, with glass walls lightly supported by wooden pilasters ; the roof, elegant in form, was surmounted by a vane. Fine cherry trees stood on the lawn around it, the fruit of which seemed delicious, and as the westering sun gleamed through their branches and rested on the luxuriant growths of fragrant flowers, the whole seemed like enchanted ground to the young imagination."

Holdgate was the home of Hannah Richardson for twenty years. During most of this time, there was only one female servant, a Friend called Mary Hollingsworth, whose beautiful complexion, happy countenance, and spotless Quaker dress, added to the charm of the household. One of Mary's duties was to bake with the household bread, large soft biscuits, so that beggars who came to Holdgate, if not relieved by money, might never be sent away hungry. So closely in readiness did Mary keep these biscuits, that it is said she slipped one into the hand of the genial minister, James Backhouse, when he came to call upon her master !

During the last twelve years of Lindley Murray's life, from 1814 to 1826, he became increasingly dependent upon Hannah Richardson as his reader and secretary. His literary labours were then nearly over, only two small books being published during that period, one on the ' Duty and Benefit of a Daily Perusal of the Holy Scriptures,' the other being ' Selections from Bishop Horne's Commentary on the Psalms ; ' but he still delighted to listen to the poetry or the prose of his favourite authors. His correspondence with his family in America came, in the end, to be conducted entirely by Hannah, and formed an important part of her duties. Lindley Murray, the eldest of his father's family, and a confirmed invalid, survived in his quiet Yorkshire home the brother and many sisters whom he left in America in the full enjoyment of vigorous life. At first, his father was his chief correspondent, but after his death in 1786, this post was taken by his brother, John Murray. For more than thirty years, Lindley Murray was indebted to this brother for the entire management of his property in America from which his income was derived, and for constant intelligence of his family. John Murray seems to have resembled his eldest brother Lindley in his lively disposition, in his mental activity, and in his desire to benefit his fellow-men. Engaged like his father in mercantile pursuits, he early gained a competency and then retired from business; devoting the remainder of his life to benevolent objects, such as hospital management, free schools, prison reform, the prevention of pauperism, and the abolition of slavery. His energies had abundant scope in the growing city of New York; and his death in 1819 was mourned as a heavy loss by his fellow-citizens as well as by the brother in a far distant land who owed so much to his kindness. John Murray left two sons, with one of whom, Robert Murray, as well as other members of the family, Hannah Richardson corresponded for many years. Long after the venerable pair at Holdgate were gathered to their rest, Hannah continued to receive tokens of esteem from the unknown friends who loved her for their sake. Albums full of extracts from the then little-known Poets of America, drawings of its then unfamiliar scenes, and other presents from that far country were ever and anon sent to her. In 1846 Robert Murray visited her at the Low Lights where she was staying with her sister Mary. The meeting of two persons who had so long corresponded with each other was full of interest. Robert Lindley Murray (whose name especially recommended him to Hannah and her sisters) accompanied his father. The visits of cultured American gentlemen were then rare events in the North of England, and this visit was long remembered.

Lindley Murray died in 1826, at the age of eighty-one, having lived forty-one years at Holdgate. He was a man who attracted the love and reverence of those around him in no common degree, and his loss was mourned by Hannah Richardson as that of a father. For eight years she continued to live at Holdgate, and to be the loving friend and companion of his widow. Hannah Murray must have been a remarkably sweet and unselfish woman. When she accompanied her husband to England, she left a father and other dear relatives in America, and for many years spoke of that country as her home; but she never asked to return or murmured at her exile. For years she hardly quitted the two rooms by which her husband's life was bounded, but on his death she resumed the ordinary habits of life, so far as that was possible at seventy-eight, even walking from Holdgate to attend the Friends' meeting at York. She lived until 1834, and then Hannah Richardson's long sojourn at Holdgate was ended. She would probably have said that those twenty years were the happiest time of her life, and every thing and person connected with that time seemed to have a charm for her. If anything could have reconciled her to the idea that she would ever be made the subject of a biography, it would be the knowledge that one chapter in the book would be devoted to the memory of Lindley Murray, and another to the history of an Institution to the welfare of which we shall now find her devoting herself.

For some time after the home at Holdgate was broken up, Hannah resided in York, but although her youth was past, she was still a vigorous woman, and full of energy and the desire to work for others. The large Friends' School at Ackworth was passing through a period of difficulty. A Principal who bore the title of "Governess" was needed for the girls' side of the school. Hannah Richardson offered "her poor services" until a fitter person could be found to fill the place.

CHAPTER XVI.

Ackworth School.

1778—1846.

" Not vainly the gift of its founder was made,
  Not prayerless the stones of its corner were laid,
  The blessing of Him who in secret they sought,
  Has owned the good work which the fathers have wrought ! "

J. G. WHITTIER.

" The great business of man as a member of society is to be as useful to it as possible, in whatsoever department he may be stationed."

JOHN FOTHERGILL, M.D.

THE name of the Foundling Hospital is very familiar to all who live in the valley of the Thames. "This is a foundling, ma'am," is often said to a visitor by a mother of many little ones, and the child thus indicated is frequently the best dressed and the healthiest looking of the group. Very tearful are the partings when the little charges are delivered up to the Hospital Authorities at the age of five, and long do the children remember the country cottages where they firmly believe they were born. And even when old enough to know that no tie of kinship exists between them and the inmates of the old home, the tie of affection draws them back to it. A good woman, the mother of twelve children, once had room for a foundling, and it is still a festive day in her household when the boy returns in his stalwart manhood to visit the only mother he ever knew. To see the children at the Hospital, seated at their long table, eating their Sunday dinner, is one of the pleasant sights of London; to attend service in their Chapel, where their well-trained voices are supported by their magnificent organ, is a treat to all lovers of music. (Query, how did the genial and gifted organist derive his musical talent through the long lines of his good Quaker ancestry ?)

The early history of the Foundling Hospital is connected with another art than music. When Hogarth painted the honest, open face of its founder, Captain Thomas Coram, the great artist said he had never painted a portrait with so much pleasure. Other artists gave their works to adorn the building, and were elected Governors of the Hospital. An Exhibition of paintings held within its walls from time to time was a fashionable resort in the days of King George the Second, and carriages then waited in Lamb's Conduit Fields as they now wait in the court yard of Burlington House. And as the Exhibition of the Royal Academy had its precursor at the Foundling Hospital, so had the famous Academy Banquet. Artists and patrons of art dined together annually at the Hospital, and the entertainment was called the " Artists' feast."

The year 1757 seems to have been a very prosperous one at the Foundling Hospital. In that year one hundred and fifty-two persons celebrated its " Artists' feast," and at the same date, the Governors of the Hospital purchased a large estate at Ackworth in Yorkshire. The institution was then rich in subscriptions, and aided by a grant from Parliament, and the Governors desired to found branch establishments, so that the children might be distributed over the country. Such branches had already been opened at Westerham, Chester, and Shrewsbury, but the one at Ackworth was to be on a larger scale. An estate of eighty-four acres was purchased from Sir John Ramsden ; and a number of children were sent down at once to a house on the property called Seaton's Farm. This house was soon found to be too small, and the Governors commenced to erect the large stone building afterwards to be known as Ackworth School. The east wing was first built, and the gilded lamb which surmounts the vane on its summit still testifies to the benevolent purpose of its founders. The architect was a Mr. Watson, but Dr. Timothy Lee, the Rector of Ackworth, a firm friend of the Foundlings, designed the centre. The west wing was then built, and the colonnades which connect the different parts of the building. The estate was increased by purchase and exchange, until in 1760 it amounted to a hundred and four acres. The water supply was planned and worked out by the great engineer Smeaton, builder of the Eddystone Lighthouse. The clock was a very fine one, striking the hours on a bell which was heard all over the parish. The building was supposed to accommodate five hundred children. These were brought down in detachments of about fourteen by two or three nurses in a large caravan, which cost forty-two pounds, and performed the journey in seven days. The ingenious and kindly Dr. Lee contrived a hammock for it. The historian of Ackworth School, writing of this early time says :—

" On the arrival of the caravan at Ackworth, the country nurses of the district around trooped up to receive such of the infants and young children as should be apportioned to them. Great care was urged by the London Governors in the selection of these women. They were to be ' careful and tender.' No instance is on record of their being unkind, negligent, or cruel. Yet the number employed was very large. At one time (1776) there were thus placed out 233 of the sickliest children, namely, at Ackworth 64, at Badsworth 43, at Hemsworth 99, at Wragby 23, and at Pontefract 4. About this time there were from seven to eight hundred children at Ackworth. The price paid to these nurses was one shilling and ninepence a week. No nurse was permitted to have more than one unweaned child, nor more than one who could not walk. This created a considerable industry in the surrounding villages, and the amount of money earned by the villagers during one quarter of 1766 was £324 5s. 0d."* It would appear that this experiment of boarding out the little foundlings in the homes of cottagers was a successful one.

In Ackworth Hospital itself, a woollen manufactory was established in 1759, and so quickly did the children learn to spin and to weave, that their blankets and clothes were in great request. In 1762 the profits of their labour were entered upon the balance sheet at £500, which seems as incredible to us as it did to some members of the London Board. Dr. Taylor White wrote for particulars " for the conviction of the hereticks."†

But the great object which the Governors had in view in their Ackworth establishment, was to apprentice the children to the farmers and manufacturers of the Northern Counties. The local Committee, a numerous body, containing many persons of high rank, advertised their apprentice system in the newspapers, adding the clause, "Masters must be of the Protestant religion." A member of the Society of Friends residing at Richmond, applying for an apprentice, the matter was referred to the London Governors, who replied, " We have no sort of objection to a boy's

* ' History of Ackworth School,' page 7.
† Ibid. page 8.

being bound apprentice to a Quaker." The same body, however, hearing that the Ackworth Committee proposed to apprentice a boy to a chimney sweep, at once forbade it, adding, "This Committee has never placed a boy with one of that profession, and does not think it for the credit of the charity so to do."* Apprenticeship was a serious matter to those little ones. The poet sings of "My seven long years," but the indentures are preserved at Ackworth of a foundling who was apprenticed to a pavior of Pontefract from the age of six to that of twenty-four!† The hospital authorities always inserted a clause binding the master to give wages of £5 a year to his apprentice after he attained the age of twenty-one, and in 1768 Parliament passed an act which terminated apprenticeship at that age. The children were sent forth in their garments of strong cloth and leather, each with a Bible and prayer-book, and the masters were expected to give them some education. Little of this, it is to be feared, fell to their share. Every effort was used by the London Committee to obtain good masters; certificates of character were required from responsible persons, and the steward was advised to inform himself as to "what care the applicants had taken of their own children." But when the demand for apprentices became so great that there was an instance of a hundred and sixty-six leaving Ackworth Hospital in a single day, such careful investigation of each case became impossible, and it is probable many children found unkind, and even cruel, masters. This danger was increased by the action of the Government, which proposed to the Governors to give a fee with their apprentices, and gave an additional grant of money for the purpose. The historian of Ackworth School says:—

"At the instigation of the Government of the day, the Committee, in 1765, introduced the practice of giving fees with their apprentices—the object being partly to enable the hospitals to place out their more unsound children, and partly to get all out of hand at a cheaper rate by getting them off earlier. In addition to its grant of £28,000 for the general purposes of the London hospital, Parliament that year granted £1500 for fees of this kind, and the following year increased the amount to £2000. Perhaps no more attractive plan could have been devised for bringing in unsuitable applicants for apprentices. Indifferent characters, living from hand to

---

* 'History of Ackworth School,' page 10.
† Ibid. page 10.

mouth, saw in it a temporary lull from their troubles, and too frequently extorted, from easy vicars and municipal officers, certificates of conduct, and carried away apprentices and apprentice fees. The latter they soon drank or squandered, the former they too often cudgelled and starved. One instance occurs in which a successful scoundrel received three or four children at once, with the appropriate douceur. On the strength of the latter, he abandoned his home for ever, leaving the children for his poor wife to keep." *

In 1765, seventy-four little girls, about seven years old, were articled to a Leeds manufacturer, who proposed to employ them in carding and spinning some peculiar kind of wool. He built a large room for them, called the "Industrial Foundlings' Hall." His business proved unremunerative, and it was a time of dear bread. In 1768 he wrote to the Ackworth Committee, telling them he was losing £3 a week by the children, that twenty-two out of the seventy-four had died, and begging that some might be taken back. The Ackworth Committee communicated with the London Governors, who ordered that some one should go at once to Leeds " to preserve the children, who seemed in a perilous condition."† They were brought back to Ackworth in sad plight. This was from pure misfortune. The action of the Governors was equally prompt if cases of cruelty were brought to their notice. In these cases the perpetrators were prosecuted, and punished so far as lay in the power of the Governors. There were bad boys as well as bad masters. A letter describing one is given here. Vigorous English seems to have been written in Cleveland in the eighteenth century.

" Sir,—I received your letter yesterday, and in answer to it am sorry to tell you Thomas Revel, apprenticed to David Lincoln, of this place, does no credit to the Foundling Hospital. He is one of the most Subtile, Lying, Mischievous, Thievish, incorrigible Rasscals, perhaps, in the whole Kingdom. The only reason I know of for his going to Sea was because he was no longer fit to live upon land. He is addicted, I am afraid, to every vice a Boy of his Age can be capable of. After frequent complaints had been made of him, to no good purpose, it was thought proper by Mr. Turner and Mr. Dundas to make a Trial of him at Sea. Accordingly, Mr. Dundas (with the Boy's own consent) had him put on board one of Sir Lauce.

* ' History of Ackworth School,' page 15.
† Ibid. page 11.

Dundas's Allum Ships, from which I find he has deserted, and found the way to his old nurse. What sort of a Nurse she has been, or how long she nursed him, I don't know, but if he had been nursed for two Seven Years in Bridwell you could hardly have supposed him a more compleat young Villain. It would be impertinent in me to advise how to dispose of him, but I cannot help saying, I hope we shall never see him at Guisborough again.

"If the Governors should think fit to remit him to his former Master (who, by the way, I believe, was a very good one), he will be obliged to make use of such means as the Law directs to be freed from him, as he is a dangerous Person to have in his Family. And if he should be received again into the Hospital, he will be a means of corrupting the whole Society. He says, it seems, that he likes Land better than Water, but he will stay long upon no Ground, I promise you. I daresay he has taken leave of his Nurse Steere before this time, at least for a while. If he is manageable at all, I should suppose it must be on board one of his Majesty's Ships of War. The boy I took from your Hospital is a very fine one. I beg my compliments to Dr. Lee, and am Sir, Your most obedient Servant, W. L. Williamson. (Guisborough, March 10, 1771)." *

This boy must have been like the foundling introduced to us by Mr. Walter Besant, a "Rogue in Grane."† But there were many of a different stamp. "In 1772 Sir James Lowther, who had had many children from Ackworth—taking boys for banksmen and overseers at his collieries, and for sailors and farm labourers, and the girls for servants and operatives in the carpet factory he had established near his own estate in Westmoreland—being present at the London Board, spoke in terms of such praise of the Ackworth children, that Sir Charles Whitworth wrote to Dr. Lee, of Ackworth, saying, 'Sir James paid great compliment to your hospital . . . . in the goodness of the children, and the cleanly and orderly manner they were educated.'" ‡

We may hope that of the two thousand three hundred children apprenticed from Ackworth, the greater number found their fitting places amongst the hardy and industrious population of the Northern Counties.

---

* 'History of Ackworth School,' page 16.

† 'All Sorts and Conditions of Men,' by Walter Besant.

‡ 'History of Ackworth School,' page 15.

This was the intention of the London Governors, and grievous was their disappointment when they had to close the branch for want of funds. In 1759, a warning came from the Government that the Parliamentary grant of £30,000 a year would soon be withdrawn. Arrangements were made at once to close the branches at Westerham, at Chester, and at Shrewsbury, and to transfer their children to Ackworth. The latter institution was thus filled by the residuum of all the houses, the sickly and deformed children whom no one would take as apprentices. If only for these, it was earnestly desired to retain the Hospital at Ackworth, where milk was threepence a gallon, and coal one-seventh of the price it was sold for in London. Every effort was made to raise the poor little waifs into a state of health to fit them for country employment. Detachments of them were sent to Ilkley for change of air and to drink the water. In 1773, the Government grant being withdrawn, and subscriptions having so far diminished that every consideration had to give way to the necessity of supporting the Parent Institution in efficiency, the children were reluctantly taken away from Ackworth. The most sickly were left until the close; then, in July, the last group of these poor, forlorn wrecks of humanity were carried away to London; and the towns on the great North road knew the little foundlings and their caravan no more.

Now arose the question, "What is to be done with the property?" The London Governors thought the estate would sell better if the building was pulled down, but to this proposal the country Committee would not listen for a moment. The Rector of Ackworth would not hear of the destruction of "a structure so noble, so strong, and so well constructed, that it might be converted into a palace for a nabob or a barrack for a regiment." Part of the land was disposed of, and the fine clock was bought by the Marquis of Rockingham for £50. The building stood empty for five years, and foxes reared their cubs in its empty corridors.

In 1777, Dr. Fothergill, a London physician, visiting his native county of Yorkshire, saw the plan of Ackworth Hospital, and heard that it was to be sold far below its value. A benevolent bachelor and highly cultured man, he was anxious to promote education amongst the Society of Friends, of which he was a member, and he at once saw the opportunity of securing such admirable premises. The place which had cost the Foundling Hospital £17,000 was to be sold for £7000; and £6800 had already been offered for it. No time was to be lost, and Dr. Fothergill and some other Friends came forward to advance the money and secure the purchase before the sanction of the Yearly Meeting of the Society could be obtained.   The contract between the Hospital Authorities and Dr. Fothergill was signed in the autumn of 1777.   Thus the fine pile of buildings raised in the flush of hope by one group of philanthropists, and by them abandoned in disappointment, fell into the hands of another group, who began within its walls an Institution which has flourished for a hundred years.   But those who succeeded were not more noble, self-denying and devoted than those who failed.   In these days, when philanthropy is in fashion, the name of Sir Charles Whitworth should be held in honour, although his ways may differ from our ways.   He thus writes to Dr. Lee:—

"Lady Whitworth, as well as myself, attend the Breakfasts every morning at half after seven and hear their public Prayers, and are frequently present both at the dinners at twelve, and their suppers at six, after the latter of which they rehearse their Evening Prayers.   I likewise hear the Catechism three or four times a week, all which attendants are amusements, and I flatter myself of Utility, as well as keeping the Children in Order and Decorum."*

Other devoted workers were Dr. Taylor White, before mentioned, and Mr. Collingwood, the Secretary of the London Hospital, whose name sounds pleasantly in Northumbrian ears.   John Hargraves, the steward of the Ackworth Hospital, was said to have performed his duties with "great tenderness and humanity."   He died before the branch was closed.   We would fain know whether the active and philanthropic Rector ever visited the building after children of a sturdier growth had replaced his poor little protegées; but it is on record that Sir Rowland Winn, of Nostel Priory, happening to go when the little Friends were at their dinner, said, with tears in his kind eyes, "Why could we not have had *our* children as healthy and as happy as these?"

In this record of North Country people, room may well be found for some account of the distinguished Yorkshireman, John Fothergill, the honoured Founder of Ackworth School.   His family had been long settled in Yorkshire.   When, in 1068, the Conqueror took the city of York, his general in the field bore the name of Fothergill.   This Norman Knight, like so many of

* Drake's 'Eborecum' as quoted by J. H. Tuke in his 'Sketch of the Life of Dr. Fothergill.'

William's followers, married an Englishwoman, a certain "faire Isabel Poulton," or Boulton, who brought her lord the manors of "Sedber and Garsdale."

In the part of Yorkshire which those names indicate, the wild and beautiful valleys which run between that county and Westmoreland, there lived for hundreds of years families of the name of Fothergill, who, although doubtless descended from the Norman warrior and his English heiress, were peaceful folk, quite unknown to fame until the preaching of George Fox stirred the stillness of their valleys, and brought their names into the records of Quaker history.

Dr. Fothergill was born at Carr End, the house upon his father's small estate on the banks of Semmer Water in Wensleydale, in 1712. His father, John Fothergill, and his brother Samuel, were devoted ministers of the Society of Friends. Dr. Fothergill was not a preacher, but his whole life was a sermon upon a saying of his own which stands at the head of this chapter: "The great business of man as a member of society, is to be as useful to it as possible, in whatsoever department he may be stationed." In his early life, Dr. Fothergill lived much with his mother's family, the Houghs of Cheshire, people of larger means and more knowledge of the world than the simple dalesman, his father, whose anxiety was so great for the spiritual welfare of his children, that he had no thoughts to bestow upon their temporal advancement. The boy went to a day school at Frodsham, and then from the age of twelve to that of sixteen to the Grammar School of Sedbergh, little more than ten miles from his father's house. To this school, established in 1528 by Dr. Lupton, Provost of Eton, there is no doubt young Fothergill owed much. At sixteen he was apprenticed to Benjamin Bartlett, an apothecary of Bradford, who, being a minister in the Society of Friends, had travelled with young Fothergill's father. The boy was fortunate in his master; Bartlett seems to have been a man of refined manners and liberal sentiments, and his house was an excellent school for learning the art of surgery and acquiring a knowledge of medicines. This good man saw that in his old friend's son he had a pupil of great promise, and generously liberated him before his articles had expired, so that he might go earlier to Edinburgh. There he was under Drs. Munro, Alston and Rutherford, all pupils of Boerhaave of Leyden. Young Fothergill's energy and application attracted the notice of these Professors.   He had no higher ambition than to be a country doctor, but by Dr. Munro's advice he changed his plans, and after taking his degree of M.D. at Edinburgh, he came to London and entered as a pupil at St. Thomas' Hospital in 1736.   After travelling in Holland and Germany, he settled in White Hart Court, Gracechurch Street, as a physician.   For some time his work was chiefly amongst the poor, but in 1748 a circumstance occurred which brought him before the public.   A malignant form of sore throat prevailed throughout Europe, and it became an epidemic amongst all classes in London.   Many persons of rank died of the disease, and the alarm created was very great.   Dr. Fothergill appears to have had the courage to introduce new methods of treatment, consisting largely of antiseptics.   The fame of the cures he effected brought him a large and lucrative practice, and his Treatise on "Putrid Sore Throat attended by Ulcers" still further established his reputation. The son of the poor Yorkshire dalesman now found himself in the first rank of London physicians.   The following letter is to his brother in Wensleydale, written in the beginning of this time of prosperity, when he was forty-one years old :—

"London, 12, 1, 1753.

"Dear Brother,—. . . . . . My time is much less my own than ever, and if I live must still be less so for a season.   My business is not the most gainful.   Many, very many, I attend as a duty, which costs me labour and some thought, yet all my business is not of this kind.   I have a greater income than ever I expected, but my expenses are likewise large, and as it is but very lately that I was fairly upon a level, so it will be long, if I live, ere I get so much as to maintain me with less labour.   I generally go out at nine, and am traversing the streets till two or past.   I then come home to dinner, and, if not called out before, I begin again about four, and have something to do till between seven and eight, now and then till nine. It would perhaps surprise thee to hear that the last year afforded me not less than £1800, and that I spent not much less than £1000, yet this is not far from the truth.

"I imagine that my business is greatly magnified; but so intimate a friend, so near a relation, ought to be better informed.

"When I consider my beginning, progress, and present condition, a youth, a stranger, with little money, without friends, being utterly unknown in the place, and that from thence in the space of about seventeen years, two of which were wholly spent in improvement here, I should be favoured so far, it raises many a serious and sometimes grateful consideration and acknowledgement to a Power whose great name I am not worthy to mention.

"Thy son I hope will be taken suitable care of at Coz Gilbert Thompson's. The expense I shall cheerfully defray. As to Jane, I shall do my part, and do it with pleasure, in order to convince thee of the unfeigned affection I bear thee as my brother and my father's son. Thy kind presents at length came safe and were acceptable . . . . Farewell, and be assured that I am thy affectionate brother, J. FOTHERGILL. Pray remember me to the worthy Justice (Metcalf)." *

The following words embody the views with which he began his practice in London :—

"My only wish was to do what little might fall to my share as well as possible, and to banish all thoughts of practising Physic as a money-getting trade, with the same solicitude as I would the suggestions of vice and intemperance." The way in which Dr. Fothergill acted up to this high ideal during his long career, made him the object of much love and reverence. With great delicacy he would refuse fees, sometimes from persons whom others thought well able to afford to pay them, and especially from the clergy of all denominations. There were instances in which he not only refused to accept money, but gave handsome sums to persons whom he found overwhelmed by misfortune and sickness. One of these gifts amounted to £1000.† The physician, who, when attending in poverty those whom he had known in affluence, gently pressed a cheque along with his prescription into the hand of the patient, must have been, indeed, a welcome visitor, and such is said to have been the not infrequent habit of Dr. Fothergill. The money he disdained to amass for himself made many persons happy. In his loving letters to his brothers, it is remarked how constantly the phrase occurs, "I will cheerfully defray all expenses," whether it be for planting trees around the old home in Wensleydale; keeping up the day school near to it; apprenticing a nephew to his own profession, or giving a marriage portion to a niece.

To sea-faring men he was wont to say, "I prefer plants to money,

* 'Sketch of the Life of Dr. Fothergill,' by J. H. Tuke, page 60.
† Ibid. page 50.

bring me plants!"   A collector of objects in many sciences, he is especially honoured by botanists. He wished to introduce into England and her colonies plants useful for medicine or commerce, and for this purpose he brought a house and grounds at Upton, near Stratford in Essex, afterwards the hospitable abode of the great banker, Samuel Gurney, and now a "People's Park."

Dr. Fothergill's garden was thus described by a contemporary :—

"On the banks of a winding canal rare and exotic shrubs flourished. In the midst of winter, evergreens were clothed in full verdure, without exposure to the open air ; a glass door from the house gave entrance to a suite of hot green-houses nearly 260 feet in extent, containing upwards of 3400 species of exotics, whose foliage was a perpetual verdure, and in the open ground in summer, nearly 3000 distinct species of plants and shrubs vied with the natives of Asia and Africa.

"That science might not suffer a loss when a plant he had cultivated should die, he liberally paid the best artists to draw the new ones as they came to perfection ; and so numerous were they, that he found it needful to employ three or four artists in order to keep pace with their increase. His garden was known all over Europe. Foreigners of all ranks asked permission to see it." *

We are told that he employed fifteen gardeners at Upton, and established a correspondence with every part of the globe, and offered premiums to captains of ships for medicinal plants, notably the " Winter's Bark " and the Cinchona. At Upton were seen the Kalmias, Rhododendrons, and other American plants now so well known. But Dr. Fothergill had little leisure to enjoy the place. Although Upton, in his day, had " a forest on one side of it," it was too near London for him to have much quiet in his home there. It was often dark when he arrived, and he visited his beloved plants by the light of a lantern.

Before this time of Dr. Fothergill's life he had given up all idea of marriage, and about 1750 he sent for his sister Ann to live with him. The change from Wensleydale to the home of a London physician must have been great indeed. It is thus described in a letter :—

"I have my health at present just as well as before I came here, being

<hr>

* J. H. Tuke's 'Sketch of the Life of Dr. Fothergill', page 65.

under the care of a kind, affectionate brother and physician, who often orders some little thing or other to recruit my constitution, and endeavours to inspire (me) with cheerfulness and ease." She goes on to describe the life in her new house :—

"A new scene of life it is to me, where a multitude of occurrences attend to engage, divert, or amaze. Singular I am, and so I hope to continue, in my dress; the antic folly I observe does not incite me to imitate. Brother's extensive acquaintance and esteem exposes me at present to a pretty deal of company . . . . He has employ for every hour of his time, and is anxiously careful to execute his business well, that so much intense study and fatigue keeps him very thin, and he is generous beyond a wish. I came here in great fear. I find I am very deficient ; but brother is not for dismissing me."*

Far from wishing to dismiss this good sister, Dr. Fothergill writes in 1755 :—" Sister Ann is still poorly, but I hope she will soon be restored to her usual, if not better, health, and be long my sister, my companion, my friend, and my example."† The biographer says :—" Then we find pleasant intercourse constantly kept up between the family at Carr End and White Hart Court. Sister Ann sends clothes for the family, and they in return send Yorkshire hams, hung beef, oatmeal, which they cannot obtain in London, and which she says, 'make an agreeable part of many a regaile. I borrowed a bake stone, scarce expecting to see such a thing in town, and made some oate bread, which several thought a choice regaile, and of which, luckily, the Doctor is very fond, and which often makes up the greatest part of his supper.' " ‡

One wonders what was thought of " Sister Ann " by some of her brother's visitors. Had she much of the Wensleydale speech ? and was her dress singular beyond that of the London Friends ? Within doors, she would certainly wear the white muslin cap and kerchief ; the short sleeves and mittens, and the apron, sometimes of white muslin, sometimes, oddly enough, of green silk or camlet, which formed part of the dress of that day. Her out-door costume would not include the close silk bonnet familiar to us all. The head gear of plain Friends then was a beaver hat with large brims, said to be very becoming to some faces. Amongst the last to wear

---

* ' Sketch of the Life of Dr. Fothergill,' by J. H. Tuke, page 58.
† Ibid. page 56.　　　　　‡ Ibid. page 59.

these hats were two well-known ministers, Deborah Darby and Susanna Horne. It was one of these ladies who, in an interview with Elizabeth Gurney (afterwards Mrs. Fry), told the lively and gaily dressed girl that a useful life lay before her. "Thou wilt be eyes to the blind, feet to the lame," were the words used.

If we are left to conjecture as to the appearance of Ann Fothergill, a minute description has been preserved of that of her brother in his later years. It was written by a great-nephew :—

"Dr. Fothergill was pious, generous, and benevolent, rather above the middle height ; very delicate and slender, of a sanguine temperament ; his forehead finely proportioned ; his eyes light-coloured, brilliant, acute, and deeply penetrating ; his nose rather aquiline ; his mouth betokened delicacy of feeling, his whole countenance expressed liability to irritation, great sensibility, clear understanding, and exalted virtue.

" He usually wore a large low three-cornered hat, a white medical wig, with rows of small curls descending one under another from near the crown to his shoulders ; a coat, waistcoat, and breeches of nearly white superfine cloth ; the coat without any collar, large cuffs, and two of the buttons buttoned over his breast ; the waistcoat with long flaps ; the ends of his cravat were buttoned within his waistcoat ; the stockings he wore were silk, and the colour of his clothes ; his buckles were small.

" His coach was dark green, with wheels of the same colour ; the horses were tall black ones, with very short dock'd tails after the old manner. His coachman was exceedingly lusty : he weighed at least sixteen stone ; his livery was a plain cocked hat, a white wig, a light drab coat with a velvet collar the same colour, and bright haycock buttons. My great-uncle left him £50 per annum. Dr. Fothergill had a little stiffness in his address ; when he walked along the streets he leaned forward a good deal." *

The big coachman, the green coach, and the black horses made many journeys to the North of England. In 1763, the Doctor and his sister paid a visit to Scarborough, and proposed visiting their old home, driving by way of Thirsk. The brother is asked to meet them at that place, and they hope to reach Askrigg or Bainbridge in a day and a half. "We fancy we can get to Bainbridge in our carriage, and leave it there, or at Askrigg, with our horses and servants ; only the saddle horse to carry me, and thou

* 'Sketch of the Life of Dr. Fothergill,' page 101.

must get one, either double or single, to carry sister * * * * Give thyself
no uneasiness about our entertainment. Nothing will come amiss to us
but thy family's too great concern for our accommodation. Remember we
have lived there, and yet can do so with great content if you will permit it."*

Those who know Wensleydale will sympathise with the wish of the
biographer. "We should like to have seen the calvacade, as leaving the
admiring awe-struck crowd of villagers at Bainbridge, it wound up the hilly,
rocky road to Carr End. The great London Doctor, with cocked hat and
big wig, in light drab suit and drab silk stockings, sitting upright on his
horse, with sister Ann in light drab bonnet, and habiliments of the plainest
sort on a pillion, escorted by brother Alexander, let us hope in Dalesman's
costume."†

In 1767, Dr. Fothergill removed from White Hart Court to Harpur
Street, so new a street that the house was still unfinished. He wrote of
this change :—"We find a great difference between Harpur Street and the
City; we have almost an hour more daylight. I keep at home to see
patients only on Third and Fifth day afternoons, by which means I have
Second, Fourth and Sixth day afternoons more at liberty, and I hope
gradually to lessen both my business and all my incumbrances."‡ He now
proceeded to let his house at Upton, retaining his interest in the garden.
Desiring a quiet place more remote from London, he took Lea Court, in
Cheshire, and retired there every autumn to entertain his intimate friends,
and make up the arrears of his scientific correspondence. This extended
all over the world, but his interests were not confined to science.

Dr. Fothergill was said to be "truly a public character." Associated
with John Howard in his work, and with the members of his own Society in
caring for the French prisoners in England, so numerous during the Seven
Years' War; appointed by Government to enquire into the mortality among
Spanish prisoners at Winchester; he yet found time to advocate cheap
public baths for Londoners, cheap fish and potatoes for the poor, and to
write more than a hundred letters to the papers on the state of the London
streets. He was the first to write a monthly account of the weather in
London, and contributed it to the 'Gentleman's Magazine.'

A man of warm feelings, he took a keen interest in national affairs.

---

* 'Sketch of the Life of Dr. Fothergill,' page 72.
† Ibid. page 72.   ‡ Ibid. page 72.

This was by some persons considered a fault in him, but we shall hardly agree with those critics. Probably few persons now remember that even in the present century it was usual to speak of the French as " our natural enemies." " Man," wrote Dr. Fothergill, " can never be the natural foe of man. Habit has rendered the language of ' natural enemy ' familiar to national prejudice as regards France, yet even France might be united to us by interest and friendship were we to encourage mutual intercourse in trade, instead of interdicting it by severest restraints. * * * * Whilst she takes of our woollens, our hardware, or other heavy articles, we might receive in exchange her wines, and other articles which the gaiety of the people, or the constitution of the soil, seem better adapted to produce."*

But if it seemed in the eyes of wise men a folly for English people to fight with their nearest neighbours, what must it have seemed when they fought with their nearest relatives ? When we read of the old days in the " Province " of Virginia, we feel that the Fairfaxes, the Washingtons, and the Carys, were simply English country gentlemen, to whose wives and daughters the English fashions were sent half yearly, who drove in English carriages, whose servants wore English liveries, the soil of whose fertile lands was turned by English tools, and whose churches were built with English bricks. And between Friends who lived on either side of the Atlantic, the intercourse was constant and the tie unbroken. Dr. Fothergill's father and brother both visited America many times, and the Doctor's house in London was always open to American ministers who came to preach to their brethren in England. Invalids, attracted by his fame, crossed the Atlantic to obtain his advice, and his many correspondents did not confine themselves to noting the growth of plants, but kept him alive to the state of public feeling in the Provinces. He was warmly attached to his American co-religionists, whom he had assisted with their schools in the growing cities of New York and Philadelphia, and their troubles touched him nearly. At the time of the imposition of the Stamp Act, he published a pamphlet of thirty pages entitled ' Considerations relative to the North American Colonies.' In this admirable work occurs this passage :— " Colonies sprung from Britain will bear much, but it is to be remembered

* ' Sketch of the Life of Dr. Fothergill,' by J. H. Tuke, page 62.

that they are the sons of freedom ; and what they have been early taught to look upon as virtue in their ancestors, will not soon be forgotten by themselves; nay, they will the sooner be apt to vindicate their wrongs."[*]

When the struggle became imminent, and Benjamin Franklin came to England to attempt to avert it, he and Dr. Fothergill became intimately acquainted. One evening in October 1774, after an unusually fatiguing day amongst his patients, Dr. Fothergill sat up all night drawing up a paper as a basis of agreement with the Colonies. A messenger was sent in the early morning, from his house in Harpur Street, to that of his friend David Barclay, in Red Lion Square, asking that they should "see each other before nine o'clock." The paper is said to have been "honourable alike to Dr. Fothergill's clear understanding and judgment, and the impartiality with which he viewed the points in dispute." It was, in its main points, accepted by Franklin, and Lord Clarendon laid it before the Government. That the effort was fruitless we know too well, but it is good to remember the protests made both against the beginning and the continuance of the conflict. A general assembly of Electors of Yorkshire was held at York in December, 1779. Dr. Fothergill wrote a letter to his friend the Rev. Henry Zouch, Vicar of Sandal, evidently to be read at the meeting ; the letter denounced in no measured terms the evils which the war was causing, and urged Yorkshiremen, in the name of "the honour of our county, the good of the country in general," to "pray that peace be restored between us and America."

So enlightened a man as Dr. Fothergill, naturally desired to promote education amongst his co-religionists as well as amongst others, and in England as well as in America. From the earliest days of the Society, George Fox had an earnest care for the instruction of the young. Himself unlearned, he had many University men amongst his converts, and this class provided him with efficient schoolmasters, who trained others to fill their places, so that the tradition of culture never died out amongst Friends, although for nearly two hundred years their conscientious scruples excluded them from the Universities. There were towns where Friends were so numerous that they supported day schools of their own, and we hear of many boarding schools in different parts of England during the eighteenth century, but there were large classes who were out of the reach of those

---

[*] 'Sketch of the Life of Dr. Fothergill,' by J. H. Tuke, page 79.

advantages. Between the years 1700 and 1740, London Yearly Meeting addressed the Society no less than twenty-seven times on the duty of providing for the education of the children of its poorer members, or as the Friends put it with their gentle courtesy, of " those not in affluent circumstances." Yet little seems to have been done until 1777, when the prompt action of Dr. Fothergill in securing the vacant premises of Ackworth Hospital provided space for a large boarding school for the class indicated.

The Yearly Meeting of 1778 ratified Dr. Fothergill's contract with the Hospital Authorities, and the purchase money of £7000 was soon raised. Of that, and of the annual subscriptions, London and Middlesex Quarterly Meeting bore by far the largest share. Ackworth School, like Ackworth Hospital, was to be managed by a London Committee and a country Committee, each consisting of twenty-eight members. This dual government lasted until 1869. The building required some alteration to make it fit for a school : part of the east wing was converted into a meeting house, and the whole edifice was repaired and put into working order. While this was being done, a Friend named Robert Arthington offered to reside upon the premises to superintend the work, and his offer was " kindly accepted " by the Committee. When in a year and a half the building was ready for occupation, and the Committee were busily engaging " cooks at £7 per annum, chambermaids at £5, and housemaids at £4," an " expert shoemaker," a tailor, a mantua-maker, a farmer, a master and a mistress, they were slow to fill up the office of Principal of the Institution, hoping, in the words of the History, that " some well qualified Friend of leisure and experience might feel himself drawn to offer his services as Treasurer, live in the school, and exercise the happy control over the household which they, at that time, appear to have thought they could scarcely expect from a salaried officer."*

The Committee were not disappointed in their hope, for Ann Fothergill, writing to her niece Sarah, the wife of Dr. Hird of Leeds, says :—

" 1779, Tenth Month, 28th . . . . . My brother has prevailed on Nancy (Hill) to go to Ackworth to teach the girls there, at least for the present, and likewise prevailed with her father to accompany her thither, and stay a few weeks himself to superintend and assist in establishing good

* ' History of Ackworth School,' page 36.

order in the beginning.   They set off last evening in the coach with five or
six girls under their care, so that if it suits thee to go to Ackworth next
Second day, if they get safe down thou would receive late intelligence of us,
and it would be satisfactory to them to see a cordial face they know."[*]

Ann Hill (the "Nancy" of this letter) became a permanent mistress
at Ackworth, and the "few weeks" of her father's proposed stay were
lengthened into ten years.   He and his wife are said to have been
"eminently amiable, genial, and earnest people," and under their benign
influence the school opened brightly.   There were few scholars from the
North of England.   The first came from Poole in Dorsetshire, and others
soon followed from Cornwall, Wales, and even from Scotland.   Hundreds
of Friends' families were then engaged in farming, and scattered in remote
places in rural England, and to them the school was a great boon.   Some
thought the fees too high.   One of the Lothersdale Friends wrote that it
was "a contradiction in terms to say the school was for the children of
Friends not in affluence, and then to charge eight guineas."   Some of the
Committee held the same opinion, and wished the terms could be reduced
to four guineas; in the meantime it was agreed to help in the travelling
expenses, by the offer of twopence a mile for every mile exceeding fifty.
This was a wise and a kind provision, and during the first year £180 was
dispensed for travelling expenses, the children coming from distances of
which a hundred and twenty miles formed the average.

Many Friends recorded their pleasure in the opening promise of Ackworth School.   Here it may suffice to give part of a letter on the subject
from Dr. Fothergill to the celebrated chemist, Dr. Priestley, whose name
is still remembered not only for his scientific discoveries, but also for his
sufferings at the hands of the Birmingham mob, who burned his house,
his library, and his scientific apparatus, because he was a Unitarian.

Dr. Fothergill to Dr. Priestley.

"Near Middlewich, Cheshire, 24th of Eighth Month, 1780 I
called at Ackworth on my way hither, and find we have made a pretty
prosperous beginning.   Above eighty girls and a hundred and fifty boys
are got together in less than ten months' time.   The head of the house is
made for it, and teachers we are making as fast as we can.   The children

* 'Life of Dr. Fothergill,' by J. H. Tuke, page 93.

are already moulded into excellent order, clean and attentive. The beginning is prosperous, the event must be left."

"It is my fervent wish that all the professors of Christianity may be more anxious to live Christian lives, than either in advancing the consequence of a sect, or reflecting on our fellow-servants and our brethren, the sons of the same Father. To establish young minds in Truth, and erase the prejudices that may have been sown, is a great object with me . . . . . Reading, writing, and arithmetic for the boys, and for the girls the addition of necessary female employments, are there taken care of. To give them an early inclination of acting uprightly, doing to all as they would desire others to do to them, even in the most trivial concerns of life, is a matter I very much wish to have *kneaded* into all their instruction. If they can act so as to avoid the reproaches of their own minds in the first place, and then be able to act such a part as to feel an interior approbation, they never will slide far from the paths of rectitude."*

This letter, so characteristic in its moderate and guarded language of a member of the Society of Friends, and in its tone of the liberal, truly catholic spirit which distinguished some of the highest minds of the eighteenth century, was written near the close of its writer's life. His removal from White Hart Court to Harpur Street did not diminish his work, for if it lessened the number of his city patients, it added to those from the West End who were not accustomed to delay or denial. In 1775 it is said he had sixty patients on his list, and his sister says:—"My brother is at the full stretch continually, of what his faculties of both body and mind can sustain. He drags himself about from eight in the morning to near five, which is now our hour to dine. He eats a morsel in almost impatient hurry, and is out again about six till near nine or ten; then comes home, scarce able to get upstairs, and then sits down to write until eleven or twelve." And again, she speaks of the "anxious fatigue and solicitude impressed on his countenance."†

During 1780, the last year of Dr. Fothergill's life, his sister describes their journey from Ackworth to Lea Hall :—

"17th Eighth Month, 1780 . . . . . We got well to Halifax before twelve, ordered dinner early, to go on as fast as we could. But so many

---

* 'Life of Dr. Fothergill,' by J. H. Tuke, page 96.
† Ibid. page 74.

were apprised of my brother's coming, that he had a number of apothecaries and patients presently, that put him almost out of patience, and detained us until four o'clock, though he left divers unsatisfied. Some urged his staying all night that he might see more, which was no part of his plan, and then to Littleborough that night; and to Manchester about nine next morning, where my brother was that day employed unceasingly."[*]

In October there was another visit to Ackworth, and in December his useful and busy life was ended. The quiet time he desired after his "excessive labour," and "the excessive hurry he had long lived in," never came to him, but he died "grateful to every one for what had been done for him, and desiring blessings upon us with his last intelligible voice," wrote the devoted sister. It is said that six hundred persons called or wrote to enquire after him during his illness, and his death was regarded as a national calamity. Of the many eulogiums on his character, the brief one of Franklin may be quoted here. "If we may estimate the goodness of a man by his disposition to do good, and his constant endeavours and success in doing it, I can hardly conceive that a better man than Fothergill has ever existed."[†] It is said that he never sat for his portrait, yet many exist, and one is by Hogarth. All show the same nervous, delicate, and sensitive face. We are told that "his manners were highly pleasing, and his demeanour in a sick room was singularly fitted to inspire confidence."[‡] It was said that his income from his profession was £8000 a year, and that he left £80,000. He left, in fact, little more than a fourth of that sum, and how much he gave away and remitted in fees will never be known. In these days of great sales it may be of interest to record that his library took eight days to sell by auction; that his collection of engravings of English portraits sold for £90; that his collections of shells, insects, &c., were sold to Dr. Hunter for £1500; and that the paintings on vellum of his rare plants were sold for £2300 to the Empress Catherine of Russia. Besides his donations to Ackworth, he bequeathed to it £100 a year for five years, and £50 a year "for ever."

One of the early friends and supporters of Ackworth School was William Tuke, mentioned in a former chapter as being the Founder of the

---

* 'Life of Dr. Fothergill,' by J. H. Tuke, page 95.

† Letter from Dr. Franklin in Paris, to Dr. Lettsom.

‡ Aikin's 'Biographical Dictionary,' Article Fothergill.

"Retreat" at York, and as taking, with his wife, the superintendence of the Girls' School in that city. His elder daughter Sarah has left an account of both schools. It has been said that in Sarah Tuke, "the manners of a duchess were combined with the piety of a saint!" When only sixteen years old, she was allowed to help in nursing John Woolman, who died of small-pox at Thomas Priestman's house in Marygate in 1772. The patient sufferer, dying in a strange land, said to his young nurse, "My child, thou seems very kind to me, a poor creature; the Lord will reward thee for it." Sarah Tuke's short life was one full of good works of every kind. In 1782, she was married to Robert Grubb of Clonmel, and four years later, she and her husband went to live at that place, to establish a boarding school for girls, afterwards called "Suir Island School." The letter describing Ackworth was written in 1786, just before Sarah Grubb left England. It is dated "Foston" (a name afterwards famous as that of Sydney Smith's Yorkshire vicarage), and the letter is addressed to a friend in America. It is in six sections, and is a minute description of a well-ordered school. The officials in charge of each department, of the farm, the garden, the dairy, and the washing mill "wrought by a horse," are passed in review, as well as the tailor, the mantua-maker, the shoe-maker and the baker. Within doors, under the Treasurer and his wife, were the housekeeper, the "steady matron in the station of nurse," the chambermaids and under-servants, male and female, and the two cooks who so arranged their work, that "on meeting days only one person stays at home to keep the coppers boiling." For the boys there were four or five masters, and four schools for Reading, Writing, Arithmetic, and English Grammar. There were some Apprentices, and "ten or twelve of the eldest and more solid boys" were chosen monitors. One of the duties of these monitors was, when the boys were collected in the colonnade before meals, to "survey them behind and before, taking care that their buckles are in order, their hair combed, and if any be dirty to send them to wash." The quiet meals with the solemn silence before and afterwards are described. The girls had four mistresses, who taught them "sewing, knitting, spinning flax, reading, and the English Grammar." Writing and Arithmetic were, when Sarah Grubb wrote, taught by a master, but a mistress was soon after-wards found qualified to undertake the work. The girls assisted the mantua-maker and the laundress, and in the house work. The orderly state of the girls' "lodging rooms," "scarcely an article of clothing out of its proper place," and the "healthy cheerfulness and decorum" which prevailed throughout are dwelt upon, as well as the reverent observance of "First days." On that day, the whole household met together; in the morning and afternoon in the Meeting House for Divine Worship, in the evening in the Boys' dining room for the reading of the Scriptures. The post of reader was taken in turn by a master and a boy, a mistress and a girl; and the day closed solemnly.

Sarah Grubb says, "The children's dress, if not so when they come, is modelled to a certain simplicity." "An exact uniformity in colour, &c., has not been adopted." A superintendent of later years, Thomas Pumphrey, has described the dress in these words:—

"In the early days of the school, its juvenile groups might have reminded us of the pictures of olden time, when the cocked hat, the long-tailed coat, the leather breeches, and the buckled shoe were the dress even of boys. The girls figured in white caps, the hair turned back over them, or combed straight down on the forehead, checked aprons with bibs, and white neck handkerchiefs folded neatly over their stuff gowns in front. Their walking costume was a kind of hat, the pattern of which we are unable to indicate, and a long cloth cloak, with coloured mits reaching to the elbows."*

This dress, which differed little from that of others at that time, was preserved at Ackworth until it made its little wearers peculiar. The white caps and white kerchiefs were long retained by the girls, giving to them as they drifted softly into meeting, filling form after form, the appearance of a fall of snow. Leather breeches were worn by the boys until 1820, when they were exchanged for corduroys. One leather pair was long retained for "temporary penal use," in the case of boys who inked their trousers!

The picture of Ackworth School drawn by Sarah Grubb, for her friend in America, probably represents very truly the course of the external life of the school for half a century. During that time, its prosperity had many ebbs and flows. A falling off in numbers about 1788 caused the Committee to examine into the working of each department, and one master was "tenderly acquainted" with the fact that he did not suit. John Hill was

---

* 'History of Ackworth School,' page 43.

an old man when he became the Head of the School, and towards the close of his term of office some of the boys seem to have taken advantage of the mildness of his character. Traditions of the exploits of these boys descended to later generations as from a sort of heroic age. One daring spirit, who had climbed higher than his fellows up a leaden spout in the corner of the pediment in the very centre of the main building, and thereon cut his initials, was elected King of the School. A perfectly absolute monarch, his commands were obeyed, although they involved transgressions of rules, and even attempts to escape from the school. In 1789, John Hill begged to be released from his post on account of his age and infirmities, and the Committee presented him with two hundred guineas as a testimony of their " esteem and regard." When John Hipsley, a vigorous disciplinarian, succeeded to the post left vacant by the mild old man, the Royal personage just mentioned did not escape the rod.

Far from wondering at an outbreak of lawlessness in a school of which so idyllic a portrait had been drawn two or three years before, we may rather wonder that such outbreaks were not more frequent. " Play and mischief " it has been said were almost the only outlets for boyish spirits and emulation. The number of studies was very limited. We have seen in a former chapter how few were the children's books in a Friend's family a hundred years ago, and far fewer were those which passed the censorship of the Committee appointed to draw up a list for the Ackworth children to read in class and at other times. The Committee deliberated for months, and then ordered ten copies of each of the following books :—

' John Richardson's Journal,' ' John Woolman's Journal,' ' Richard Davis's Journal,' The last edition of ' Dying Sayings,' ' William Penn's Travels through Holland and Germany,' Thomas Sweeting's ' Fighting Sailor,' ' John Roberts' Life,' Sewell's ' History of the Quakers.'

No word of disrespect shall here be written of any of these works. Did not Charles Lamb declare the last volume to be " worth all Ecclesiastical History put together " ? and did not the same beloved and genial humourist exhort his readers to " get the writings of John Woolman by heart, and love the early Quakers ? " But the narrow list makes the hearts of all book lovers ache for the poor little Ackworth children of 1783 !

In ten years' time, some additions were made to the collection. Twenty-five copies of the ' Beauties of Sturm ' still further depress our spirits ;

'Collections of Debates on the Slave Trade,' 'Reflections and Maxims,' 'Extracts and Original Anecdotes,' and 'Guthrie's Geography,' afford a little more variety, whilst 'Goldsmith's History of England,' and Dr. Aikin's 'England Delineated' must have had the fascination of romance. A brighter time came with the close of the century, and the publications of Lindley Murray. When we take up his 'Reader,' and imagine little Friends making acquaintance with 'Damon and Pythias,' with 'Cicero against Verres,' and 'Adherbal against Jugurtha,' and with the prose and poetry of Goldsmith and Addison, we need not wonder at the honour in which Lindley Murray was held both by young and old.

In 1796, it was proposed to establish a School Library, and the "Society" was appealed to for donations of books or money. The appeal was liberally responded to. The gift books had to pass through the censorship, but the nucleus was formed of a good collection of solid literature, from which poetry was not excluded. In 1826, thirteen years after, the masters, greatly daring, applied for eleven copies of 'Evenings at Home' for occasional reading in the School. The request was granted by the Committee.

The third Treasurer and Superintendent of Ackworth was Dr. Jonathan Binns, who, in 1795, gave up a large and lucrative practice in Liverpool to undertake the office to which he felt himself called. His medical skill and devotion to the children in sickness were long remembered. He compiled the famous 'Ackworth Vocabulary,' which was prized in many schools, but held almost sacred at Ackworth. It and a Bible were the only books allowed to boys who were in solitary confinement, and the 'Vocabulary' was the one volume not " of a religious tendency " allowed to be used on " First days." Dr. Binns was a very efficient Superintendent, but during his term of office and that of his predecessor there was some conflict between different authorities, and the Committee found there were drawbacks to gratuitous service, even when rendered by able and devoted men. They resolved to separate the offices of Treasurer and Superintendent, and that the latter post should be filled by a salaried officer. Dr. Binns had had a secretary, Robert Whitaker, a highly educated man, and an experienced schoolmaster, who had entered the Society of Friends " by convincement." On Dr. Binns' resignation in 1804, Robert Whitaker became the first salaried Superintendent of the school.

Both the London and the country Committee were subject to the authority of the General Meeting held every summer at Ackworth. At that of 1795, a schoolmaster from the South of England " hinted a fault " to the boys' reading. He thought the " rising cadence " was defective. The General Meeting appointed a Committee to hear the masters read. They acquitted themselves to its satisfaction, one young man throwing down his book with an indignant gesture. Soon after this, one of the mistresses was sent to York " to read before Lindley Murray, from whose judgment there was then no appeal. His report was so flattering, that he suggested it should not be shown to the subject of it, lest it should conduce to too much exaltation."*

The relation of the two Committees was not always harmonious. Once the London Committee thought the boys' clothing cost too much, and politely enquired, " Is the tailor an experienced artist ? " When, in 1786, the boys' need of a covered playground was acknowledged, the country Committee proposed a plain stone shed. The London Committee, in alarm, sent down an architect to see if a wooden erection would suffice. He reported that in Yorkshire stone was cheaper than wood. Then the London Committee, yielding gracefully, proposed that the new " shed court " should have pillars and a pediment, so as to be in keeping with the main building. Upon the whole, the London Committee leant more to the elegancies of life than did their Northern brethren.

The last recorded difference of opinion was in 1836. The country Committee proposed that " the use of beer at the children's table should be discontinued." The London Committee moved as an amendment " that the beer be made better." The Northerners won the day, and the brewhouse was converted into a water tank. But this was in modern times. We are apt to forget that Friends were not always so abstemious as they are now. Good Dr. Fothergill's order for wine to be laid down in his cellars at Lea Court was a liberal one, and the early Ackworth Committees closed their labours in an evening (incredible as it may appear to us) amidst the smoke of long clay pipes, and the aroma of hot spirits and water.

The dark days of the long French War were memorable at Ackworth. In one year of scarcity, 1795, the Superintendent's son was sent to

* J. S. Rowntree's ' Sketch of Ackworth School,' page 40.

Pontefract " to buy corn for the household at any price," and the moment
the market bell rang he placed his hand on the farmer's sack to secure it.
During those years, members of the teaching staff were at different times
drawn for the militia, and in 1814 three of the establishment were
imprisoned at one time in the Wakefield House of Correction for refusing
to serve. Through the presence on the bench of one enlightened magistrate
they escaped being thrown amongst criminals; but their privations would
be thought severe enough in the present day.

The best description of a boy's life at Ackworth during the first years
of this century is given by William Howitt in his delightful ' Boy's Country
Book.' (Why is there not a new edition of it for boys of this day ?)

The son of a man of property in a secluded part of Derbyshire, William
Howitt grew up in the freedom of open air life, amongst simple, honest
country folk, sharing with the village children in the sports and pursuits
which he so charmingly chronicles. He went first to a Dame School, and
then to one kept by a merry little man, the baker of the village. This
schoolmaster was wont to come whistling out of his hot bakehouse to hear
his pupils read; and to set them their copies in the intervals of " setting "
his bread. When young Howitt was ten years old, a certain " Cousin
John," who plays an important part in the narrative, began to look at the
boy's copy books, and enquire about his ciphering, "and always ended by very
loud and long praises of a certain great school at Ackworth in Yorkshire,
where he had been not long before to a general examination of the scholars,
and came back brimful of it. As it was a school belonging to the Society
of Friends, and one that my father and Cousin John were liberal con-
tributors to, and had been for years, he did not see why my father should
not have some benefit from it. It was for all or any in the Society; for rich
and poor—all were treated alike there; and the nonsense about rank and
money that got only too soon thrust into children's heads, never was heard
of . here. Besides that, there certainly never was such a school for laying
a sound and thorough foundation in all the branches of English education,
' and when that is done, Cousin Thomas, thou knowest,' said he, ' thou canst
top the lad up in Latin and Greek, and such like, if thou thinkest
necessary, somewhere else.' "

"The upshot of the business was, that I was duly entered on the rolls
of the school, and exactly as I was eleven years of age, Cousin John

had the unqualified satisfaction of conducting me thither."* After a tearful leave-taking of the home and its inmates, and of the kindly villagers, the travellers,—Cousin John on a tall black horse, young Howitt on his little pony,—set out on their journey from Derbyshire to Ackworth; and on the evening of their second day's ride, came in sight of the large stone building. "We went to the inn in the village for the night; and after breakfast next morning we set out to walk up to the school. As we drew near it, we overtook a poor man and his son. Cousin John asked the poor Friend whether he was taking his boy to school. He said, 'Yes,' and that they had come seventy miles to it on foot. As I have said, rich and poor alike belonging to the Society of Friends went there. If a man could not afford to send his children himself, the Society sent them for him. It had given this boy admission to the school, and his father being a very worthy honest man, though exceedingly poor, thought that if he could do nothing else to testify his gratitude, he could save the expense of his son being sent by coach, which the Society would otherwise have done. He therefore had set off with the lad on foot to walk this seventy miles. He was a very thin delicate-looking man, in clothes that had evidently seen a good deal of service; but his son was a stout hardy-looking lad of about ten years old. The poor man had very little money to take him on his journey, but he told Cousin John that he had the names of several wealthy Friends who lived on the road given him, and when he came to any of their houses he had only to mention the names of the Friends that had told him of them, and he was sure of a hospitable welcome to bed and board. So he told Cousin John he and the lad had jogged on together, and had arrived in little more than two days. 'And were you not very tired?' asked Cousin John. 'Why, rather,' answered the poor man; 'my son Joseph complained a good deal yesterday' . . . . . . Here we were arrived at the gates of the school. The poor man turned into the Superintendent's office, and Cousin John went to enquire for the farmer with whom he was acquainted. Before, however, that I proceed with my own narrative, I must add that we saw the poor man going away again, and Cousin John said with great surprise, 'What, are you leaving your son already?' 'Yes,' said the poor man; 'I am wanted at home; I am losing time, and it

* 'The Boy's Country Book,' page 239.

signifies nothing staying. I have turned the lad up amongst his school-fellows, and he looked rather scared, to be sure, but he'll soon get over that.' So wiping a tear away with the back of his hand, that he would not have to be seen, he bid us good bye, and turned away.

"'There you see, Will, what little ceremony a poor man is obliged to make. I know that poor fellow's heart aches to leave his child in this sudden way; but, as he says, it does not signify, go he must. And for my part, I am truly thankful that a poor man has such a place as this to send his son to. I hope, Will, you will take a bit of notice of this lad sometimes,'

"I soon afterwards found that the lad did not need much notice; for he was a bold, hardy-spirited lad, that could take care of himself; and there was no distinction between rich and poor within the bounds of that school.'"*

The poor man's son was in his right place, for it was for him and his fellows that the school was founded. The good education given attracted others, as we see in the case before us, and the mingling of classes was good for all. William Howitt continues his story :—

"Here then I was about to take my place in this great school; and though my introduction to it was very different to that of this poor lad, I was, like him, a little scared. The vast building, which to my eyes, accustomed to the simple houses of villages, seemed a palace; the huge rooms, the long passages and halls; the vast number of boys, all at active play on the green, 180 of them;—all was strange, and fell with a depressing weight on my spirit. Cousin John did everything to make it easy for me. He did not take me and turn me at once amongst the busy crowd of lads, but he went round and shewed me the whole place—the lads' gardens; the great garden of the school; the schools themselves; the dining rooms, kitchens, farmyards—everything. He introduced me to the Superintendent, the masters; nay, to the nurse and matron—to everybody that he thought might be a friend to me at one time or other; and it was not till bed-time that he took his leave. But soften the thing as he might, the change from the endearments and comforts of home was striking and cheerless enough. A vast wide house, with long stone passages; large numbers of strange boys; a severe discipline; cold hard beds at night;

* 'The Boy's Country Book,' page 246.

cold rising in the dark early mornings ; no hats allowed in the playground in winter—and the winters there were very sharp ; no approach to the fire on holy-day afternoons till after dark-hour ; and on rainy days, our play-place, an immense open shed, supported in front by Tuscan pillars, where, thrusting our hands into our bosoms, we used to huddle together by scores to keep one another warm—and happy was he that got deepest into the throng.   Could anything be more comfortless ? "*

In this list of Ackworth hardships, the Bath is not mentioned.   This Bath, a pleasure to vigorous boys, was a terror to the timid.   It was nearly a mile distant from the school, and was about twelve feet square.   It was surrounded by a wall, and fed by a cold chalybeate spring. The boys used it three mornings in the week, and the girls on the other three mornings. For the girls, a dressing room was provided, but it was not used by the boys, who laid their clothes on the ground,—dry, damp, or snowy, as it happened,—outside the wall.   For young boys roused from sleep soon after five o'clock, and just warmed by their walk, to be expected to jump into the deep red water, was a trying ordeal.   If they hesitated, they were thrown in by some of the younger masters, caught by an elder boy and helped out on the shallower side.   There were no towels, they ran about until they were dry, and then dressed, and went home to an hour's spelling before breakfast. Thus the day was begun in a manner truly Spartan, a word very much used by those who describe Ackworth in its early days.   These writers tell of the long cold corridors, the concrete floors, and stone steps, the washing in a cellar, the wooden trenchers for food, the tin cans for beer or water, the homely dinners—hot fresh meat only twice a week, "Lobscouse" on two days, and on the other days puddings, not always of a tempting character ; a plain and even a hard regimen, but not harder than that of Christ's Hospital in the school days of Coleridge and Lamb ; and we have heard that even in the present century Eton College was no luxurious abode for the sons of clergymen and gentlemen who were entered on the foundation, yet the privations endured by those young collegers did not prevent them from rising to high honours in English life.

William Howitt was no grumbler.   Having stated, once for all, the hardships of Ackworth School, he goes on to say :—

* 'The Boy's Country Book,' page 248.

"I found myself very comfortable. Amongst so many boys it was easy to find some of kindred tastes. I began to be as fond of books, and the delightful knowledge they opened up to me, as I had been of birds'-nesting, and riding on asses and horses. A little knot of us were great gardeners.

"By the good nature of some boy leaving the school, I was put into possession of one of the best gardens in that beautiful plot of gardens of which I have already spoken. Here, with the help of my young friends, I built a grand garden-house of mud, and made beautiful clatty sides (as we called them) to the garden. Here we sat, or rather lay in the walk, on summer days, and told tales of our early days, before we came here. Here, too, we read, and discussed a deal of natural and moral philosophy— for we had a good school library to go to, and had a great philosophical fit upon us. Here, too, we read and recited a vast deal of poetry, for poetry was in high estimation all through the school. We had Wiffen, the future translator of Tasso, amongst us; and I had the honour also to be considered a very promising poet of thirteen. Well, those were delightful days, helping each other with our gardens, reading, and talking of all that we read, and at other times joining in all the active sports of the school. There was a famous troop of lads to engage in any play, and I have often seen the whole number—180—making one long line at leap-frog, or busy at prison-bars, or run-across, making a clamour and a hum that was heard a mile off. That run-across was a grand play. Across the middle of the green ran a paved walk; under the windows of the boys' dining-room was another; the space between these was occupied by one half the boys at play, whose business was to seize any of the others who attempted to run across. If the runners got across to the pavement under the windows, they were safe; if they were caught and detained while the captor counted ten, they were prisoners, and were on parole under the dining-room till any other of their party running across could touch them, which gave them a right to attempt to run back again. The apprentices, that is, young men who have been scholars in the school, but were now apprenticed as teachers, joined us, especially one named Richard Boxall. Boxall was an enthusiastic reader of Homer, and had diffused this Homeric admiration amongst us all. We were Greek and Trojan mad, and of course we divided our two bands in this game into

Greeks and Trojans.   Many a good coat- and shirt-collar have I seen wrenched away at one pull in that favourite game!"*

William Howitt does not mention the skipping, which, whether with a long or a short rope, was a favourite pursuit. "Thribble skipping" arose to the dignity of a fine art, and boys who excelled in it stinted their appetites at dinner, lest their agility should be diminished. For the country-bred lad there were other pleasures:—"One of the greatest treats which we got, was to go, a party of half-a-dozen of us, occasionally to help in the farm, to make hay, or reap corn. Cousin John had contrived that I should have the benefit of this occasional treat; for he had taken me to the worthy old farmer of the establishment, Samuel Goodwin, and said, 'Friend Samuel, when you want a lad to make hay or reap corn, this is the man for you.' Good old Samuel soon tried me, and was so well pleased with my accomplishments that he had me out on all possible occasions, and anybody may judge what a treat it was to me to get out of the bounds, which were never passed except on special occasions, and to enjoy the green fields and all their favourite objects. The farm was large, for the establishment was large, having altogether not less than 350 people to support. There were twenty cows to supply milk, and everything in proportion. Sometimes we were on the hills not far from the school, and at others a mile off, at what was called the Low-farm. Here we helped to make hay, and to eat great hunches of bread and butter at lunch-time, and drink cans of beer, sitting on the green sward; and when we got a little opportunity, were very busy at the side of a clear, shallow brook that ran through the meadows, looking after fish; and in very hot weather have actually run up and down it with our shoes and stockings on, and thought it delightful. Nobody can tell how pleasant those times were, except boys like us that seldom got out of the dry play-grounds, and now could hear the hum of the boys there, and yet enjoy this silence and field liberty. These things lead me back forcibly into the past, and bring before me vividly the characters and scenes of those school-days. I think there was more singularity of personal character in the school at that time than may occur again. We had children from all parts of the United Kingdom, from Guernsey, America, and Russia. The generation of lads which preceded us had been

* 'The Boy's Country Book,' page 252.

of a bold and insubordinate cast; they seemed to us to have been 'giants
in the land,' and the traditions of their exploits were our themes of fear
and wonder. They had elected a King—it was he who had dared to climb
the highest up the leaden spout in the corner of the pediment in the very
centre of the main building, and there cut his initials. I observe they are
there to this day. Under his orders they had committed many a daring
transgression, for his sway was absolute. They had planned schemes of
escape, and put their plans into execution, but always, with one solitary
exception, were brought back again and punished, a result morally
certain, for not being allowed to possess money, nor to wear hats, their
appearance and purses were equally hostile to long flight. Many a time
has my indignation been roused by the recital of the treachery of an old
Friend, who, beholding a troop of these bare-headed, moneyless, and foot-
sore boys, passing through his town, had entrapped them by an invitation to
dinner, in their case an irresistible bait, and then sent them back. Often,
too, have I wept at the pathetic story of a poor lad, who, having reached
the house of his companion, while he sat on a fine summer day, with him
and his mother, shelling peas in the garden, was pounced upon by the
pursuer and driven back, like a stray sheep, along the hot and dusty road,
—a long and dreary way, and with a heart full of weary expectations.

"Besides these serious attempts at running away, there were certain
daring lads who enjoyed running off occasionally for a lark. Poor Wiffen,
I remember, made one of them. The party was out two nights and a day,
and could not be found, though they were never more than a mile off. It
was a great amusement to hear them tell their schemes and 'hair-
breadth 'scapes.' How they slept in a haystack round which the masters
who were in quest of them went; how they heard all their cogitations
and conjectures, and were nearly betrayed by one of the lads being taken
with a disposition to laugh; how they came one of the nights and slept
on the forms in the writing-school, through which the masters passed
without seeing them; and how they agreed to surrender on the capture
of any one lad, and were eventually seized in a turnip-field, supping on
cold turnips, and very glad to be caught."*

Like other writers, William Howitt remarks upon the "complete
isolation of the children at Ackworth. They have ample and airy play-

* 'Boy's Country Book,' p. 256.

grounds, but are as perfectly separated from the world as if they were not in it. Owen of Lanark himself could desire nothing more secluded. As no vacations are allowed, the children are often three or four years there, and during that time see nobody but members of the family, and occasional visitors."

"Yet," he goes on to say, "though the children are thrown entirely upon their own resources for amusement, these resources never fail. Besides ordinary play, and means of play, there are their gardens; and a gardener and seedsman attend in the spring for every boy to lay in his stock of seeds and plants, which are paid for by the Superintendent, their general treasurer. Then there is a flagged walk of some two or three yards wide, and reaching from the centre building to the garden, a considerable distance; a charmed promenade, marking the separation betwixt the boys' and girls' green, where the relatives of each sex may meet and walk together, and where only they can meet for conversation, being kept as completely apart in the opposite wings of the building as in two distinct establishments. It is beautiful to see brothers and sisters, and cousins (a relationship, I fancy, somewhat liberally rendered) there walking and talking, with linked arms and words that never cease.

"In winter, whenever a frost sets in, down this walk the lads pour water, and have in a short space, a most glorious slide, whereon one hundred and eighty of them, driving impetuously, soon produce a scene of animated glee. The moment snow falls, they all set about treading it down, and speedily convert it into a broad surface of ice. There, with skates made of narrow strips of wood, they skim about with extraordinary celerity; and some, forming a team of boy-horses, imitate in imagination the Grecian heroes before Troy in their rapid cars. Round the evening fires, they tell tales and repeat verses, and in bed too; and I well remember that in one room, a room of more than twenty beds, Wiffen and myself alternately officiated as tale-makers.

"What are all their within-bound enjoyments, however, to their monthly rural walks? To a stranger, nevertheless, in my time, they must have presented a most laughable spectacle on these expeditions. The bell rung, they ran to collect in the shed; they drew up in two long lines facing each other, perhaps two yards apart. Large wicker baskets were brought forth from the store-room, piled with hats of all imaginable shapes and species; for they were such as had been left by the boys from the commencement of the institution; they wear none except on these excursions—and there they were, broad-brims, narrow-brims, brown, and black, and white; pudding-crowns, square-crowns, and even sugar-loaf-crowns, such as Guy Faux himself wore. These without ceremony were popped upon the heads of boys at random; little ones were left sticking on the very summit of great round-headed lads, ready to fall off at the first move, and great ones dropping over the noses of little ones. Away they went, however, as happy and picturesque as possible. And, oh, the pleasant memories I have of these excursions! The moving along green and bowery lanes; past cottages and cottage-gardens; past groups of villagers all radiant with smiles—and well might they smile at our grotesque array; past great waters, and woods, and gentlemen's houses, to a common—such a common! It seems to me that it was boundless, and full of all sorts of pleasant and wonderful things. There, at the lifting of a hand, a shout broke out like the shout of an army; and we dispersed in every direction. There, too, when it was time to return—a time, alas! that pounced upon us sadly too soon—a handkerchief hoisted on a pole, upon some eminence, a shout raised by a little group collected with some difficulty, became the signals of retreat; and every minute the group grew and grew, and every moment the shout swelled louder and louder, and parties of 'hare and hounds' came panting up, all warmth and animation; and stragglers were seen toiling wearily from far-distant nooks, till the last, some embryo poet very likely, roused at the latest minute from some brook-side reverie, arriving, we marched homeward."*

The rulers of Ackworth School were kind and generous employers. The salaries they paid, if to us they seem small, were above the standard of the day; they gave liberal donations in years of scarcity to those masters who lived in the village; and they provided for their servants in age, whether they had worked for them with hand or with brain. Most of the officials named by William Howitt had been in the school from its commencement, twenty-five years before, and seclusion had intensified their peculiarities.

"Our masters and officers were men of a day decidedly gone by—men of old-fashioned garments, and primitive lives and eccentric habits. There

* 'Boy's Country Book,' page 261.

was William Sowerby, an old preacher—a man in a long homespun coat, buttoned to the chin, who was in no office, but delighted to be there—a man of whom Crabbe might have said,

> "And never mortal left this world of sin
> More like the being that he entered in:"

a creature as tender and innocent as a lamb, who wandered about the house and schools, from place to place; met us at coming out, dropped a word of advice to us, preached to us at meeting of 'onions and garlic in the flesh-pots of Egypt,' and worked with us in the fields. The very gardeners, Matthew Doney and Tommy Briggs, were characters. . . . . Joey Crowther, the lamplighter and prince of the washing mill, a little, broad-built man, the sound of whose wooden clogs is in my ears at this moment, was a perfect humorist."[*] Association with these original, cheerful people evidently mitigated the dulness of school routine to many boys.

When the first pupils came to Ackworth in 1779, the only master they found there was a young man called Joseph Donbavand. He had been appointed by Dr. Fothergill. When pupils increased, and masters were appointed for the different schools, Joseph Donbavand became the writing-master. He was supposed to have attained perfection in his own art, and he sent out many generations of good writers from the school. His copies, published in 1802, were the pride and glory of Ackworth, and the despair of all succeeding caligraphists. He was always called "Master Joseph," for the Friends, who disallowed empty and flattering titles, inculcated the use of any which denoted an office, as "Queen" or "Justice" in the great world, "Master" or "Mistress" in the little world of Ackworth. A tall, fine-looking man, "kind-hearted to a fault," quick to forget a quarrel, fond of a joke and of snuff, "Master Joseph" is a striking figure in all Ackworth reminiscences, but William Howitt's is the most vivid portrait.

"The masters were strongly marked characters. There was Master Joseph,—properly Joseph Donbavand, the senior writing-master,—a tall, slender man, with a long, thin countenance, and dark hair combed backwards. What scholar that ever knew him does not remember the good-natured eccentricities of his character? Who does not remember his snuff-box, opened with its three systematic raps; and the peculiar jerk

---

[*] 'Boy's Country Book,' page 257.

of his elbow when he felt himself bound to refuse some petition?   He was
a most perfect master of penmanship, and, in our opinion, not less of the
art of swimming, which he often told us he had been taught by a frog,
having one end of a string tied to its leg, and holding the other in his
mouth, and thus pursuing it and imitating its movements.   It was his
favourite humour to do a kind act with an air of severity.   'Get away
with thee,' he exclaimed with an emphatic elbow-jerk, to a very little boy
sent to him to be caned: ' *thee* be caned! why, thou art a coward—thou
art afraid to go into the bath!   Get away with thee!'

"There was Thomas Bradshaw, the senior reading-master, a little
stiff man, with a round well-fed face, and a very dry and sibilant voice.
His hat was always three-cocked, his clothes always dark brown, his
gaiters black.   We looked upon him with awe, for he had been a naval
captain, and had heard the roar of battle, as one of his legs testified,
having had the calf blown away by a cannon-shot.   Worthy old man, in
our anger we called him Tommy Codger, and forgot the Pomfret cakes
which he always carried in his waistcoat-pocket, to bestow if he heard
a cough—and heaven knows he heard many a one—as he went his evening
rounds through the bed-chambers when on duty.   At the bottom of our
souls, however, we loved him; and he was more worthy of our love than
we knew, for he had abandoned bright prospects in his profession and
encountered, knowingly and undauntedly, scorn and poverty, from his
conviction of the anti-christianity of war.   He had suffered much; and
had we been aware of this, we might have borne with him more patiently
when he grew old, and kept a great fire in the school-room all the summer,
and sat close to it; and still feeling himself chill, could not imagine but
that we must be so too, and therefore broiled us, and kept close door and
window, and made us button up our waistcoats to the throats till we were
ready to melt away.   Many a time did we wish him a thousand miles off;
yet when he sunk under age and infirmities, and was obliged to vacate his
office, he wept, and we wept too.

"I must pass over Boxall, the chanter of Homer and Ossian; and
Stackhouse, the satirist and engraver on wood; and Sams, who has
since trod the deserts of Egypt, and explored Jerusalem for ancient
MSS." *

* 'Boy's Country Book,' page 258.

Joseph Sams has been elsewhere described as a dignified person, "who wore a three-cornered looped hat, called a three-decker, buckles to his knee breeches, and also to his shoes." He left Ackworth, and began a private school in Darlington, mentioned in a former chapter of this book. He finally "abandoned the profession of teacher for that of vendor of Antiquities, Books, MSS. and curiosities, for which purpose he had a shop in Darlington, and another in Great Queen Street, London. He travelled in Egypt and Palestine in search of MSS., and was generally regarded as a remarkable and eccentric character."[*]

Another master, William Singleton, is not mentioned by William Howitt. He succeeded the old naval captain as reading master, and was an enthusiast in his subject, teaching the boys to read and recite Cowper's ballads with energy and fervour. "Like Master Joseph," it has been said, "he was a fine looking man, erect and dignified, and like him with hair combed straight back, and cut at the neck like a girl's."[†] William Singleton would not use the cane on any occasion whatever. He asked, like another Friend :—

> "If, with Solomon, I whip,
> Why not, with Moses, stone ? "

It is said that his pupils were exceptionally obedient and attached to him, and he afterwards became a successful private schoolmaster.

The Superintendent figures in only one of William Howitt's stories. During one of the long walks, a boy, who was the happy possessor of a bow and arrow, took successful aim at a dead goose which he saw lying in a farm-yard. The next day a farmer came to the school, carrying the goose with the arrow still sticking in it, and demanded compensation from the Superintendent. In vain did the boy declare that although he had shot the goose he did not kill it; the innocent Superintendent paid the farmer five shillings, and the boy was left under the imputation of falsehood. Very speedily, however, he was told that he was completely exonerated from blame, and it soon transpired that his character had been cleared by the cook, who, on the goose being brought to her, indignantly cast it forth from

---

[*] 'History of Ackworth School,' page 116.
[†] 'From the Lune to the Neva,' by J. Benson, page 48.

her domain, declaring "that it had been dead a month!" William Howitt's school life must have been at the end of the reign of Dr. Binns, and the beginning of that of Robert Whittaker. We need not here decide which of these good men, by neglecting to use all the faculties with which nature had endowed him, fell such an easy prey to the wily Yorkshire farmer.

Robert Whittaker's thirty years of office was on the whole a peaceful and prosperous time at Ackworth, and many boys spoke with gratitude of his fatherly care. Their testimony has been confirmed from a somewhat unexpected quarter. A Friend during a tour on the Continent was thrown into companionship with a well-known actor of one of the principal London theatres. In the pleasant intimacy of travel, the actor confided to his companion that he too was born a Friend, and had been educated at Ackworth! He traced his success in his profession to the admirable way in which reading and elocution were taught at the school, and said, "I love the memory of Robert Whittaker as I do that of my own father!"* Truly the seed of good teaching and of good example is not always lost, although it may sometimes bear fruit in a way little anticipated by the sower!

As in ancient and venerable seats of learning some young men have been known as "the Saints," so at Ackworth early in this century, there was a group of lads commonly called the "serious boys," who held a sort of Bible class amongst themselves. During Robert Whittaker's term of office, a chapter of the New Testament was read every morning, and selections from the Bible were used in the school routine. Great reserve has always characterised Friends in speaking of the most solemn of all subjects, and their principle of directing every person to attend to the dictates of a Monitor and Guide in his own heart, caused them, perhaps, somewhat to neglect the teaching of the outward facts of Revealed Religion. They must be judged, not by the standard of our day, but by that of seventy years ago. It would not be correct to say of any Friend's school early in this century as has been said of the greatest school in England, "At that time there was no religious instruction whatever,"† but it may

---

* 'History of Ackworth School,' by Henry Thompson, page 133.
† 'Reminiscences of the Rev. William Rogers.'

2 c

be granted that there was but little given at Ackworth as compared with what is thought requisite in modern times. Joseph John Gurney, examining the children in the Scriptures in 1816, found their Biblical knowledge very small. He wrote afterwards to the Superintendent:—"I am of opinion that the minds of the boys are not properly cultivated on the subject of religion. They are remarkably sheltered from evil, but do not appear to me to be positively led to good." He proposed that instead of a Bible being given to a child on leaving the school, it should be given on entering it, and that a copy should be at once supplied to every child then at Ackworth. Then, proposing to examine them at the next General Meeting, he offered to give prizes to those who should have made the greatest progress during the year. The children studied their Bibles early and late, not only for the sake of the prizes, but for the love of him who promised them. One of a family of brothers and sisters remarkable for their gifts of mind and of person,—cultured, prosperous, and generous,—Joseph John Gurney was a man of great influence in his generation. His sweetness of nature expressed itself in a manner full of the most winning courtesy, in a consideration for the feelings of the humblest and youngest person, and in a remembrance of individuals—qualities which are supposed to belong in an especial manner to "exalted personages." Such did that handsome, gracious, large-hearted man seem to the Ackworth children when he appeared upon their green, "the focus to which every hurrying foot sped, and upon which every smiling face concentrated." "He walked about the garden like a Prince surrounded by his loyal subjects," said one who remembered those visits,—red-letter days indeed at Ackworth, and of which the holiday he begged for the school, and the shilling he gave to every child in it, were but secondary pleasures. The girls, too, came under his influence. A lady who was at Ackworth in 1825, and who has described how the girls expected their friends at the General Meeting, goes on to say:—"But there was one arrival anticipated in which all appeared to share with almost equal interest, and when it was announced that Joseph John Gurney had reached the school, the girls gathered with one accord upon the green, clustering round him like a swarm of bees. To this day I have not lost the impression of delight with which we received his courteous and most kindly greetings . . . . The Scriptural Examination he was to conduct was looked forward to as among the chief interests of the

General Meeting."* This Scriptural Examination, so popular with the children, was looked upon by many Friends as " an experiment of doubtful tendency," and by others as a "dangerous innovation," but in time it was generally approved.

The curriculum of the school was gradually widened. Geography had been well taught by the aid of good maps early in the century. 1820, the year which saw the abolition of the leather breeches, saw also the introduction of English History as a regular study, and Latin was added in 1824. A group of clever young masters and apprentices, to whom a neighbouring clergyman was engaged to teach the classics, established for themselves and the boys an "Association for the Improvement of the Mind." A room was set apart in the evenings for boys who wished to draw, to write, or to read, and another for those who preferred mechanical pursuits. The "Association" started more than one periodical. The 'Censor,' the 'Ackworth Gazette,' the 'Budget,' and the 'Camera Obscura,' each flourished for a time. One of the writers in the last of these serials was William Allen Miller, afterwards Professor in King's College (London), whose 'Elements of Chemistry' is still a standard work on the subject. Another of the group was John Hattersley, the first Ackworth scholar who was entered at Cambridge, where, in 1847, he was Eighth Wrangler. He, like Howitt's friend, Jeremiah Wiffen, was a remarkable linguist. Another Ackworth scholar was James Wilson of Hawick, afterwards founder of the 'Economist' newspaper, and a successful financial administrator in Government departments both at home and in India. One number of the 'Ackworth Gazette' had a Royal visit to chronicle. The Duke of Gloucester and his suite visited the school in 1823, leaving with gracious and complimentary expressions. Still more memorable was the 1st of August, 1834, when Slavery was abolished in all British Colonies. The day was kept as a holiday at Ackworth, and visitors and children held a "grand meeting,' at which Luke Howard presided, and Joseph John Gurney was present. Speeches were made alike by boys and by visitors. The following Resolution was proposed :—

" That this meeting unites in the feeling of humble gratitude to the Author of all Good, who has condescended so to bless the efforts of all

* 'History of Ackworth School,' page 177.

Christians of every denomination in this country, that the curse of Slavery throughout the British Empire is this day ended, and that all the slaves are free."*

The resolution was seconded by an old Ackworth boy, then a young man of three and twenty—John Bright.

But in spite of this one day of rejoicing, 1834 was a dark year at Ackworth. Heavy calamities had fallen upon the school during this time of intellectual activity. Repeated outbreaks of fever had alarmed parents, diminished the numbers of the school, and impaired its discipline. During the fever of 1824, a master, John Donbavand, died. He was the son of the accomplished penman who, bent with age, had just retired to a cottage on a pension. During the still more serious fever of 1828, several deaths occurred, one being that of Henry Brady, a young master of great promise. Of these sad days, memories have been preserved by persons who were pupils at the time. The school had at all times a truly kind friend and neighbour in Luke Howard, who lived with his kind and hospitable wife at the "Villa" in Ackworth. To this charming abode, where the walls were painted in fresco by an Italian artist, and beautiful and curious things were scattered about in abundant profusion, boys and girls accustomed to the bare stone walls of Ackworth were invited to tea. Those were happy afternoons, and in adverse times Luke Howard and his wife were friends indeed. The same lady who described Joseph John Gurney at a General Meeting, writes :—

"As one after another sickened, the nurseries became filled to overflowing, and one of the boys' chambers, and one also of the girls' bed-rooms were filled with the prostrated ones. As I was spared in comparative health through most of the time of greatest trial, I was in and out as office-bearer, both in the Wing and Centre. As ' Superintendent's Waiter,' I remember witnessing the distress of Robert Whittaker as his overwhelming cares and responsibilities pressed heavily upon him, and upon his true-hearted, competent wife. The strength of the latter at length gave way, and for a little while she was confined to her chamber. There were doctors and nurses from Leeds, and Luke Howard most kindly rendered assistance in the "Apothecary's shop' in dispensing medicine, acquiring thereby, from one

* ' History of Ackworth School,' page 206.

of the Leeds nurses, the designation of 'the old Potecary.' Maria Bella Howard's cook was continually busy preparing delicacies suited for the invalids, which were sent from the ' Villa ' morning by morning."[*]

Luke Howard had been a London chemist, partner at Plough Court with William Allen, so well known as a philanthropist and a man of science. Both were Fellows of the Royal Society. Luke Howard was chiefly known as a meteorologist, and from his classification and nomenclature of the clouds. He wrote a work on the climate of London, which was considered to be the best on the subject in that day. He was a very popular person at Ackworth, but his popularity probably reached its height one day during the epidemic, when he broke up the week-day meeting at the end of half an hour, saying, " under present circumstances, I think the children ought to have shorter meetings and more generous diet ! "[†] The last part of this pleasant recommendation was carried out, for great improvements in the domestic arrangements of the school were made after the fevers, but the establishment had been unsettled and disorganised. In 1828, during a rebellious scene amongst the boys, Robert Whittaker entered the room and said, " Boys, if this ever occurs again, I believe I shall take my leave of Ackworth School ! " We are told that " rebellion vanished at these words,"[‡] for the old man was generally beloved. In 1834, bowed down by failing health and the loss of his wife, he resigned his post.

A " convinced Friend," Robert Whittaker had probably much of the proverbial zeal of the convert and his name is with some persons, synonymous with old-fashioned Quakerism, but his kindness of heart and his self-denying devotion to the interests of the school are acknowledged by all. He never accepted additions to his salary, and would hardly be persuaded to take needful change and rest. His employments were of a very varied character. At stated times, he went round the estate with the carpenter, to decide what trees should be pruned or felled, and what fences needed repair. He went to Pontefract market to buy wheat, which was ground at a mill at High Ackworth for the use of the school ; and for the supply of beef for the table, he bought small Scotch cattle out of the droves which passed

* 'History of Ackworth School,' page 190.
† 'History of Ackworth School,' by Henry Thompson, page 195.
‡ J. H. Barber's Speech at Ackworth Centenary.

along the Great North Road to London.   He met the drovers at Went Bridge, Ackworth's point of contact with the world, at which place there was a good hostelry where stage coaches stopped to change horses, and for their passengers to dine, while the poor little scholars, alighting stiff and tired after the long coach journeys of early days, were transferred to a cart, which took them and their luggage to Ackworth, and was drawn by the school bull.

It is to be feared that Ackworth pupils who had no money to spend in tips, were not very popular fares.   A tale is told of a serious-looking woman Friend who was taking three little boys to school, and happened to overhear the coachman speak of her little charges in somewhat con-temptuous terms.   When the coach arrived at Went Bridge, and its jolly driver presented himself for remembrance, the lady, after giving him her own modest gratuity, gravely laid three sixpences into his hand.   "This," said she, "is from Rag, this is from Tag, and this is from Bobtail! "

Upon the retirement of Robert Whittaker, the Committee wisely resolved that the new Superintendent should not be burdened by the care of a large farm.   It was decided to let the land, except what would be required for the pasture of the cows which supplied the school with milk, and instead of cattle being fed and slaughtered upon the farm, to contract with butchers for the meat. It may be interesting to know that eighty acres of the land was let on lease at £1 16s. 0d. an acre; that milk stood in the school accounts at sevenpence a gallon; and that in 1835, two contracts were entered into for meat "of prime quality," at five shillings and five and sixpence per stone.*

Thomas Pumphrey of Worcester was the new Superintendent, and although the outdoor labours belonging to the post might be lessened, its difficulties were sufficiently great.   Brought up to the management of a manufacturing business, and entirely unused to the ways of school-boys, he had, as the historian of the school says, " to feel his way inch by inch along a thorny path.   But possessed of a settled conviction that he was in his right place, he pressed on with no little courage and patience.   The way was long and weary, and taxed his every energy heavily."† His wife,

* ' History of Ackworth School,' page 200.
† Ibid. page 208.

a daughter of George Richardson of Newcastle, was like minded with himself, and they both gave themselves up without reserve to the service of the
school. Its fortunes had never been at so low an ebb as when they came
to preside over it. These years have been called the "Dark Ages" of
Ackworth. The views of its enlightened founders fifty years before had
been in advance of their age, but succeeding generations had rather
narrowed than widened the spirit in which their laws were administered.
The system by which boys or girls who showed an aptitude for teaching
became articled pupils, and in time masters and mistresses, produced some
admirable men and women, but they were necessarily ignorant of any world
but that of Ackworth, and accustomed to judge everything by the standard
of that place, which they only quitted for a fortnight's holiday every year.
When a period of rapid change set in throughout England, the authorities
of Ackworth were slow to perceive it, and loath to yield to it. When old
restrictions became intolerable, there was only one method—repression.

To people who know Friends, it is needless to say that the discipline
at Ackworth was never cruel. The cane, in the use of which Joseph
Donbavand was so discriminating, and which William Singleton would
never touch, was reserved for very serious offences. Many old boys never
saw it used. In cases of flagrant disobedience, punishment was to be
inflicted "by a master who was not offended." During Thomas Pumphrey's first week at Ackworth, he spoke of the "demoralising effect of too
many rules," and made the following entry in his Diary:—"Examined the
records of caning, a very humiliating volume, it carries its own refutation
with it, as to the good effects of such kinds of punishment,—235 inflictions
in a year, of which half the number have been upon eight boys, varying
from three to twenty-four times in the year. My mind is greatly pained by
the perusal."* It was many years before Thomas Pumphrey felt himself
strong enough to remodel the system of Ackworth, and to start the school
upon that course of improvement and of adaptation to modern requirements
in which it has since made such rapid progress.

The girls' school at Ackworth seems to have been like the "happy

* J. S. Rowntree's 'Historical Sketch of Ackworth School.' Centenary Volume,
page 152.

nation whose annals were vacant." "In good order, and very agreeably conducted" is the report given of it in varying words for many years. Pleasing figures pass across the peaceful scenes of the history. The widow lady who, "allowed to bring her youngest child as a pupil," was the first mistress, and who, feeling her health to be unequal to that post, offered "to serve the school in any capacity," and came back to nurse the sick and to mend the linen ; the young mistress, whose beautiful reading every one crowded to hear, and whose "gentle and graceful life" was a power for good ; and the lady minister, Charlotte Dudley, who felt it her duty to come on a visit to the school for many months to live amongst the children, and whose example and companionship had in them as much of teaching as the sweet counsel delivered in her winning Irish tones. Nor must the foundling, Elizabeth Rolfe, be forgotten, who left all her savings to the school, where she had for forty years been a faithful servant. The records of the girls' industry, especially in knitting and plain sewing, is marvellous. Fine work was taken in that the girls might be instructed in the art, and by its sale they gained for the funds of the Institution twenty-four pounds in one year. In 1807, Geography with the use of maps was introduced ; and a new material, cotton, was made a cautious trial of, "for mending purposes only." Spinning, an important occupation in the first days of the school, gradually declined, and was abandoned in 1817. About that time a girl named Sarah Stickney was a pupil. As Mrs. Ellis, she was the author of many works, which had a very wide circulation, but none of them were more charming than her early sketches, 'Pictures of Private Life,' a book which found its way into some houses from which fiction was generally excluded, because its author was not only a Friend, but a cousin.

Upon one occasion the whole girls' school seems to have misconducted itself, and was "forbidden to go upon the green." As to the nature of the offence committed, or the duration of the punishment, we know nothing, but when the mistresses appeared in solitary state upon the favourite spot, the boys gathered upon their own green in large numbers, and made an "uproarious demonstration" against them. Fifteen ringleaders in this riot were singled out and brought before the masters, who are suspected of some sympathy with the boys' feelings. At any rate, the punishment under the circumstances was not severe, for the offenders were simply in their turn "forbidden to go upon the green."* Let us hope the two sentences expired on the same day!

The same lady whose Reminiscences have been quoted, describes the dress of the girls at the General Meeting of 1825. "They were dressed in their usual dark stuff frocks, with white muslin caps and tippets, the short sleeves of the frocks being supplemented by long mittens, as covering for the arms and hands." These short sleeves and mittens, long discarded by the rest of the world, were still worn by very plain Friends in the Twenties of this century. Of Ackworth indoor dress, the same writer says, "In 1825, one fourth of the girls, those sitting at the first table in the dining room, wore small, thick muslin caps. All had their hair cut short and just parted on the forehead. Before I left in 1829, the caps had almost disappeared . . . . They were still retained for going to meeting in during the summer, I believe, while 'Friends' bonnets,' and long cloth cloaks formed the winter costume on these occasions. A variety of beaver and straw bonnets, &c., did service when we all went out together for our monthly walk in procession."† The caps disappeared altogether in 1837. Muslin tuckers, drawn rather high round the neck, were worn within doors.

The "Friends' bonnets" mentioned by this lady, were, of course, the close silk ones which we still call by that name in common conversation. Considered in their day to be a mark of orthodox Quakerism it was forgotten that they were really of modern date. Yet, when at the close of the last century these bonnets (which probably bore some resemblance to those worn at the time by all English ladies) began to supersede the large beaver hats, the change was thought to be a serious one. It is said that in a Meeting in one of the Yorkshire dales, the question was referred to the Friends of another Meeting, "Whether it may be lawful for our Women Friends to wear silk bonnets?" and that the answer returned was, "It may be lawful, but it is not expedient."

The girls' school participated in the unsettled condition of the whole establishment after the fevers. Instead of the great satisfaction always expressed with the girls' department, the Examiner's report in 1830, speaks of their conduct as "pretty orderly with some exceptions," and of

* 'History of Ackworth School,' by Henry Thompson, page 154.
† Ibid. page 178.

2 D

the improvements in their studies as "rather less than heretofore."*
Three mistresses left in consequence of this report, changes were made,
and the monitorial system was introduced, but both schools were declining
in numbers and efficiency when Thomas Pumphrey came to the head of
affairs in 1834.

During that year, the death of the aged widow of Lindley Murray terminated Hannah Richardson's long residence at Holdgate, and that home
being broken up, she was staying amongst her friends at York when she
heard of the difficulties at Ackworth. She had never had the charge of a
large establishment, nor had she any experience of school life, and it is
probable that she had never even seen Ackworth ; but the spirit in which
the new Superintendent was entering upon his difficult post appealed to
her sympathies, and his wife was her near relative. It has been said that
Hannah Richardson offered her "poor services" until some one more
competent could be found to fill the vacant post of "Governess." That
appointment involved no teaching duties, but the oversight of the whole of the
girls' department, nearly resembling that of "Principal" in a modern school.
Hannah Richardson was a person who, to use a homely phrase, "never did
anything by halves." We have seen how she brought into the seclusion of
Holdgate the same spirit and energy with which she had entered into the
pursuits and pleasures of youth ; and now when her aged charges were
laid at rest, and she herself was no longer young, she carried the same
enthusiasm into a widely different sphere of action, and threw herself heart
and soul into her new duties. The historian of the school says :—

"The health of Priscilla Kincey, the Governess, which had never been
very strong, broke down in 1835, and it became necessary for her to leave
her post. Early in 1836, Hannah Richardson, of York, undertook to
supply her place temporarily. Once in the office for which she was so
admirably fitted, it would have been difficult for her to withdraw from it
under any circumstances, but as no one offered to release her from it, she
retained it for upwards of ten years. Her kindness and gentleness combined with great force of character, her suavity and urbanity associated
with much native dignity, united to give her a large place in the esteem and
affection of the whole community, whilst her large heart and quick

* 'History of Ackworth School,' page 191.

maternal instincts enabled every parent to feel that in her, her girl had a true mother. The extraordinary popularity of the girls' school during her presidency, in marked contrast, as we shall see, to public feeling towards the boys' side during the same period, is itself the best evidence of the admirable management of Hannah Richardson and the teachers who worked so harmoniously under her leadership."*

The above is a very accurate description of Hannah Richardson during the ten years when she was Governess of Ackworth School. The historian has touched upon many salient points in her character. Her dignity, her urbanity, even her entire forgetfulness of self, would have been of little avail without her large-heartedness. A very sociable woman, and a true lover of humanity, she took a great interest in personality, and her varied life had given her considerable insight into character. A strict observer and enforcer of the rules of the school, and with no indulgence for self-willed fancies, she held firm sway; yet every girl felt that she took note of her as an individual, took interest in her peculiar feelings and tendencies, in her home ties, and her school friendships, and that in sickness or sorrow she had a friend in "Governess." "She mothers them up," said a homely woman whose daughters were at the school. The writer well remembers, when herself at school at York, how the girls who had been old Ackworth scholars and felt a little strange in their new surroundings, longed for the Quarterly Meeting when "Governess" would come and ask for them. The time came, and with it the much expected cheerful visitor, forgetting no one in the long list of those whom she wished to see. Every girl was greeted with kisses, and most affectionate enquiries as to her happiness and well-doing in her new school, and assurances of remembrance and love in her old one. And in age, when Hannah Richardson lived with her sisters at North Shields, with what delight did she welcome the visits of those blooming young women whom she had known as children! "Why, Lilias, thou art almost as tall as I am," she said to one of these visitors. A suggestion was made of "measurement," but the young girl started away. "For me to be measured with Governess! It would be desecration!" she exclaimed.

The historian of the school says:—"During the three or four years

* 'History of Ackworth School,' by Henry Thompson, page 317.

immediately preceding 1836, when Hannah Richardson took the post of Governess, there was no heavy run on the girls' school, the number on the list for admission being usually very low, and at one time, none. But after Hannah Richardson's worth had been recognised, which it was speedily, and during the years of depression on the boys' side, the girls' school was always full, and the numbers on the list heavy. For five years (1810 to 1814) the number of girls in the school and on the list combined exceeded that of the boys similarly treated; although the complement of the girls was only two-thirds that of the boys."* During Hannah Richardson's early years at Ackworth, a girl of fifteen came to be apprenticed to the school. The ordeal of appearing before so many girls as one who was to have authority over them was a very formidable one, and she never forgot how Hannah Richardson at once took her under her care and helped her through it; presenting her to the girls as a native of the same town as herself, and saying, "I knew Mary's grand-parents and her mother, and I remember Mary herself as a baby in a pretty white frock,"—trivial matters to record, but very cheering to the timid spirits of the young apprentice. This girl remained many years at Ackworth, and became a valuable mistress. She thus writes of Hannah Richardson :—" She had a way of making every one at home with her, and knew exactly what would please individuals. I could always talk to her and feel that she had leisure and interest at command. She was the most unselfish, disinterested character I ever knew. She is before me now with her kindly smiling face, in her ' Friendly ' attire, with her erect form and somewhat measured step, as though pondering the fitting words for each girl, looking in their faces as they stood in the play room at seven o'clock in the morning. If any one did not look so lively as usual, away she was to go to the apothecary's shop, or to the nurse. Ackworth School never had and never will have one who more successfully occupied her trust, and won the hearts of all around her. Wherever we were, going out to dinner at a Quarterly Meeting to houses where footmen stood behind our chairs, (so different from our school life) we were sheltered behind our pioneer, to whom we looked up with unmixed confidence and respect, mingled with deep love. She put her heart into all she did; and ' if the

* ' History of Ackworth School,' page 236.

office did not give her dignity, she gave dignity to the office,' as was said of the old Athenian. The memory of her straightforward speech, of her cheerful, buoyant, indomitable spirit, and of her self-denying, energetic Christian life, is ever with me as a healthful stimulus and example. She once told me that if she could have only two books they must be the Bible and 'Thomas à Kempis;' and I always connect with her, Addison's Hymn, 'When all thy mercies,' &c. It was her great favourite."

The same correspondent recalls many proofs of the Governess' watchful care over her. "Now dear, do not sit up too late to study, and hurt thy sight;" useful little presents; and when a bag was lost containing little feminine niceties of dress, an offer to help to replace them, with the kind words, "Now do not let it trouble thee, dear."

Like her sister Elizabeth, Hannah Richardson carried independence to a fault. Ready to give, whether of her time, her labour, or her slender means, she was unwilling to receive. Her birthday was kept a strict secret. At Ackworth the chairs were of plain heavy wood, and nervous persons yet remember with a shudder the grating noise they made as they were drawn to table over the sanded floor. Hannah Richardson, however, made light of such trifles as discordant sounds and hard seats; and when some of the young mistresses and apprentices worked what was considered to be a most beautiful cushion for her chair, their disappointment was great indeed when she would not use it, and gave as a reason that "it was too great an indulgence for her to give way to!" It is probable that a dislike to be distinguished in any way from those around her influenced her in refusing the loving gift.

To the sorely tried Superintendent in his early years at Ackworth, the coming of an elder woman like Hannah Richardson was a great boon. His sister-in-law writes:—

"Of our dear cousin Hannah Richardson, when Governess at Ackworth, I saw a good deal. I was frequently there as helper to my dear sister Rachel Pumphrey, and so was something of an on-looker, though a most interested one in the affairs of the school. I well remember Cousin Hannah's consultations with my brother Thomas Pumphrey; and the deep interest she took in the best welfare of the Institution. In this way she shared with him in the heavy responsibilities devolving upon him as Superintendent; and thus materially lightened his load. She was a most vigilant official in every respect. She was firm and decided in her manner, there was no appeal from her conclusions, so that to obey became easy as a habit. At the same time she was very sympathizing and affectionate, and self-sacrificing in doing good to others in various ways. Her sympathies were acute and widely extended, and she found full scope for their exercise at Ackworth. She gained the love of both teachers and scholars, and filled her position there most usefully for many years. Having, from conviction, learned the value of the principles of Friends, she was a valuable member of the Meeting to which she belonged."

The " consultations " held between the Heads of the two schools at Ackworth were probably often upon general subjects, but there were individual cases in which the Governess invoked the aid of the Superintendent. A tale is told of a girl whose character seems to have excited interest, but who was little amenable to rules. She was brought before the Superintendent and Governess to be reasoned with and admonished. Thomas Pumphrey was not only Head of the school, but an earnest minister, and it is probable that his reproof was both tender and touching. Troublesome girls are often emotional, and this girl sought for wherewithal to dry her tears, forgetful of the contents of her pocket. As she drew forth her handkerchief, a living mouse leaped from its folds, and delighted to escape from confinement, ran about the room, regardless of August Presences. Alas for the gravity of the Superintendent and of the Governess! Very human and humorous persons, they, like Charles Lamb on a memorable occasion, " had no more muscles that day." The delinquent (let us hope in company with her mouse) was dismissed with scant solemnity.

The wild girl had a chequered history. She had her own bread to earn, and found the accepted ways of doing so rather dull. On one occasion she engaged herself to the proprietors of a travelling exhibition of wax works to help in their show. The Friends of the town where she was then living, hearing of this rash proceeding, at once intervened and paid money to free their young member from this " most unsuitable " engagement. After other adventures, she wished to go to Australia, and the anxious, long-suffering Friends provided her with a good outfit and paid her passage money, one kind lady visiting her in her cabin as the vessel set sail. When this lady returned in the pilot boat, the first objects which met her sight upon the quay were the trunks of the young emigrant containing all her wardrobe. The stewardess had no pity for her forlorn condition, but other persons, especially the doctor of the ship, were more sympathetic, and the girl again found friends. She soon married after her arrival in Australia. Left a widow in a few years, she proposed to return to England with her children. The ship by which she was expected to arrive was lost, and although her name was not found in the list of passengers, her friends mourned her as dead. Some years afterwards they received a letter from her written in a remote part of Australia, where she had long been married and settled with a second husband and with two groups of children around her. Such was the career of one Ackworth girl.

Again, detailing the difficulties on the boys' side, the historian says :— "The girls' school was, at this time, highly popular. In 1835, the number in the school was but 113, and there were not more than two or three 'on the list.' Since Hannah Richardson's advent, the numbers seeking admission had greatly increased, until in 1841, there were seventy-six 'on the list.' The Committee began seriously to think of enlarging the girls' department." This was done on a liberal scale. A new dining-room, a large dormitory, and other additions were made to the building, and the work was completed in 1842.

Very light and spare in figure, Hannah Richardson's activity was noted. "I will just step over to Pontefract" she was wont to say, as an easy method of solving the difficulty when something was wanted which could only be obtained at the old town four miles away, where the bridge was broken so very long ago, and where the "guilty closure" of the grim castle's walls frowned over peaceful fields of liquorice, grown by a Friend to manufacture into his "Pomfret Cakes." During the last years of her life at Ackworth she had some serious accidents. In one instance, while going round the long passages in the evening to see that all was safe, she tripped over a saucer of a disinfectant (containing oil of vitriol) placed on the floor. Her foot and ankle were severely burned, and she was for some time confined to her bed. This was very irksome to her, and long before such an effort was prudent she came downstairs on crutches. Although surrounded by the kind young mistresses, she rejected all their offers of help, and her crutches slipping on the stone steps as she returned, she fell and broke her right arm. Rest became imperative after this second accident, and her constitution being a very healthy one, both injuries were soon cured. About a year later she was walking out with the school in frosty weather, and "stepped on first" to see if some steep descent was fit for the girls to go down. She slipped and fell, but made no remark until the walk was over, and the girls safe at home. Then she went to the Doctor, and he told her that she had broken her arm—this time the left one. We need hardly wonder that one of the mistresses writes, that she "never knew any one with so much self-control, and so entirely independent of circumstances."

When Hannah Richardson came to Ackworth on what was supposed to be a visit, there was no question of remuneration. When, however, she proved so well fitted for the post which she temporarily occupied, the authorities were only too glad to secure her services, and the usual salary was offered to her. This she decidedly refused, and the firmness of her family, which in some cases amounted to obstinacy, came into play. She, however, had a wise friend on the Committee, Samuel Tuke, who during her long residence at York had acted as her banker. Knowing the modest proportions of the sum which was in his hands in her name, he could judge what was fitting for Hannah Richardson herself, as well as what was just and right to those who should succeed her in the post of Governess. He therefore quietly accepted the salary for her, and placed it to her credit in his books. When this act of kindly despotism came to her ears she submitted, but the tradition at Ackworth was that she returned the amount in a subscription. The belief shows the estimate formed of her character, and she probably did subscribe liberally; but the exact amounts of the salary and of the subscription are quite unknown to the writer.

Ackworth General Meeting was always a sort of Quaker Festival. Held in the month of July, the weather was usually brilliant, and the spacious gardens and playgrounds gave ample space for the many visitors. These filled to overflowing the School Inn in the village, and every lodging which the place afforded. Wealthy benefactors to the school had the unwonted experience of rustic life amid homely surroundings, and parents came with delight to visit their children. The Meeting lasted for nearly a week, and it was said that acquaintances formed between youths and maidens during those days of freedom and open air enjoyment often resulted in the formation of closer ties. Within-doors there was sufficient interest both for the old and for the young. There were the solemn "Meetings for Worship," and the examinations into every department of the school, for which purpose committees were appointed. Early in the Forties, the Friends formed an Educational Society, and its meeting was one of the most interesting features of the Ackworth week.

The present writer, a stranger to Ackworth, was present at the General Meeting of 1846. The girls were then a healthy, happy-looking group of plainly dressed children, with their short hair neatly parted on the forehead, and white pinafores over their stuff frocks. The mistresses were dressed in the fashion then passing away amongst other young Friends, and their high-crowned, transparent caps encircled some sweet young faces. Happy groups of parents and children, meeting after years of separation, were to be seen at every turn. Amongst the visitors on the green there were many striking figures :—the Treasurer of the school, the great banker, Samuel Gurney, and his fair-haired daughters; John Pease, the eloquent preacher, and his brother Joseph, the first Quaker M.P., gracious and genial; Christine Majolier, then new to that English society where she was to make so many friends from Royalty downwards, scattering comfits amongst the younger girls with her short French arms ; and John Bright, moving about the place with the assured step of an old pupil who knew it well, finding very free fault with the past, and suggesting great improvements for the future. The presence of John Bright at gatherings of Friends in those days was not always a source of unmingled gratification. What had they done ?—those gentle, soft-voiced people, who never imputed a motive, passed a hasty judgment, or made a rash promise, who wrapped up even their censure in elaborate sentences of long Latinized words, who were above all things peacemakers,—that from their midst should come a young man whose short words smote like sledge-hammers ; who never " believed," nor " hoped," nor " trusted," but was always quite sure that he was in the right ; who set himself in opposition to the prejudices of whole classes of English people; who treated some leading Friends with no more reverence than he would have treated a Bishop ; and who spoke of some Quaker institutions with little more respect than of the House of Lords ! John Bright's personal appearance was conspicuous in an assembly of Friends in the North of England, where the prevailing type is tall, thin, long-faced, and regular featured. The young "Tribune's" physique, his resolute carriage, the head thrown defiantly back, the sensitive mouth set as firmly as if he were facing a howling mob, or standing at the bar of a hostile court, may have resembled some of the Friends of the seventeenth century, but not those of the nineteenth. His "strength of chest and limb" suggested other leaders of men.

> "So sturdy Cromwell pushed broad-shouldered on,
> So burly Luther breasted Babylon."*

The 'Epistle' issued annually to members of the Society of Friends by the Yearly Meeting, is drawn up by a Committee appointed for the purpose, and is then read over sentence by sentence to the whole assembly. The year 1843 was a time of Repeal Agitation in Ireland, of distress in England; the Chartist disturbances were then recent, and the Anti-Corn Law League was in the height of its career. One sentence in the 'Yearly Meeting's Epistle' ended with the words, "We trust Friends may always be found amongst those who are quiet in the land." John Bright sprung to his feet to express a hope that this sentence was not intended to condemn those who were striving to effect the repeal of unjust laws! The Clerk rose to call the speaker to order, but before the reproof could be uttered, the young man went on, "Now the Clerk need not fear that I will introduce politics into this assembly," and proceeded to make an effective speech, in which the word "corn" did not occur, but which was in effect a defence of the action of himself and his friends. Applause is unknown in the Yearly Meeting, but a slight tapping noise was heard as John Bright resumed his seat.

As time went on, and the vexed questions of free trade in corn and in sugar (upon which even Friends were not unanimous) were settled, John Bright became more in unison with his fellow-members. When, in 1854, amidst the almost universal enthusiasm for the war with Russia, John Bright stood up against the passions of the people as he had done against the power of the aristocracy, and risked his popularity and his seat in Parliament unflinchingly; and when in later years he pleaded for the sympathy of England with the great American people in the crisis of their history, it is probable that most of his fellow-members could have

* 'The New Timon,' by the late Lord Lytton.

said, in the words used by Sir Robert Peel of another great Englishman,
" We are all proud of him." *

There were more Reformers than John Bright at the Ackworth General
Meeting of 1846. Change was in the air. A young Friend, James Hack
Tuke (whom the Irish famine of the autumn was to enlist in another
cause, with which his name is still linked), had been travelling in America,
and read a paper at the meeting of the Educational Society on the
" Common Schools " of that country. The paper described how boys and
girls were taught together ; how classes of boys were taught by young
women ; and above all, described a new method of examination of pupils
by requiring them to answer papers of questions in writing. This plan he
recommended for use at Ackworth. It was a great innovation, and he, of
course, met with opposition, but the great-grandson of William Tuke had
a hereditary right to be heard at Ackworth, and, having the Superintendent
on his side, the change was made.

At the same General Meeting, the experiment of a vacation was
decided upon, and in 1847, the school broke up for the first time in
its history.

The introduction of railways had made travelling so easy that parents
began to ask for visits from their children, and these optional holidays had
become so frequent that it was seen that the time had arrived for a general
vacation. Parents had always been at liberty to visit their children, and
merry parties of boys and girls were gathered together at the School Inn
when these visits occurred. But there were many to whom such pleasures
were impossible. The historian of Ackworth tells us of a tender mother
upon whom sorrow and misfortune had fallen heavily while her son was at
school. Her husband had died during the time, and she had opened a
baby-linen shop to support her family. She knew the day her boy was to
leave the school, and expected him hourly; yet when a tall youth entered
her shop, he was so entirely a stranger to her that she bent over the
counter to enquire his business. When the boy, in a voice husky with
emotion, said " Mother! " the sensitive woman felt as though she had
committed a crime in submitting to so long a separation that she could not
recognise her son.† Another tale is of a poor Friend in Cornwall who sent

* Written before the death of John Bright.
† 'History of Ackworth School,' by Henry Thompson, page 34.

one child after another to Ackworth in its early days.   As his children left school, places were found for them in the busy and prosperous North of England, and the parting with their father was for life.

Hannah Richardson left Ackworth at the end of the year 1846. Since that date changes have been rapid in that Institution. The buildings have been enormously enlarged, and boarded floors, tepid baths, warmed and well-ventilated rooms, have succeeded the old "Spartan" regimen. The system of graduated charges has been introduced, and the fees now range from £15 to £40. The course of study has been greatly enlarged, and probably the minds of most persons of mature years received a shock when they first read an advertisement in the 'Friend' for a music mistress for Ackworth. Prose has failed to describe the transformation of the school, and verse has been pressed into the service.*   Yet, in spite of change of forms, it may be said of Ackworth School—

"The spirit of her early days is with her even now."

This sketch cannot conclude better than with the words of Mr. J. G. Fitch, who visited Ackworth in 1866, on behalf of the School Enquiry Commission. After describing the very thorough and intelligent manner in which the various subjects are taught, and dwelling upon "the beauty and finish of the girls' reading," Mr. Fitch concludes his report by saying :—

"I cannot sufficiently express my admiration of the order, seriousness and repose of this great Institution; nor my sense of the advantage which the pupils enjoy in the watchful supervision of the Society to which they belong." †

Upon a hill overlooking Ackworth School there now stands a stone building called the "Flounders' Institute." It is a college for training young men of the Society of Friends as schoolmasters, and was opened in 1848. A dear and honoured relative of the writer has most kindly contributed an account of the chain of events, dating far back into the last century, which led to the foundation of the college. With the present and future of Flounders' College, and of the modern Ackworth School, this history has no concern. It is a record of the past.

* See Appendix.

† J. S. Rowntree's 'Sketch of Ackworth School,' Centenary Volume. "Mr. Fitch —than whom there is no more excellent authority on Educational Matters" (speech of Mr. John Morley in the House of Commons, on Friday, May 11th, 1888).

CHAPTER XVII.

𝕿𝖍𝖊 𝕺𝖗𝖎𝖌𝖎𝖓 𝖔𝖋 𝖙𝖍𝖊 𝕱𝖑𝖔𝖚𝖓𝖉𝖊𝖗𝖘' 𝕴𝖓𝖘𝖙𝖎𝖙𝖚𝖙𝖊.

(COMMUNICATED BY J. R. PROCTER).

In the middle ages of the Society of Friends, the rules respecting "mixed marriages," as they were called, were so strictly enforced that it led very many persons to be cut off from membership who might otherwise have proved a strength to the body, but it probably had the effect of more widely spreading a knowledge of the religious principles of the Society amongst the general population. In many a retired valley where once Friends abounded, they have, as a community, now ceased to exist, but the tradition of them still exists, and when opportunity offers, their descendants flock to hear the exposition of the views which their ancestors held dear. But this is not the result with which we have to do, but rather with the effect produced on those who adhered to the rules of the Society, which occasioned almost continual inter-marriages. We have seen something of this between the Priestmans and the Procters, and still more strikingly between the Procters and the Richardsons.

There is a quaint old book called ' Besse's Sufferings,' which gives an account of the extraordinary sufferings which this conscientious body of sincere Christians had to endure. One of these was a Yorkshire yeoman, Thomas Procter, who after having served in Oliver Cromwell's army, was filling the office of constable at Clifford or Newton, where he was ordered to take a Friend to prison. This he boldly refused to do, saying, " he would rather be a sufferer than a persecutor," and was sent to prison with the Friend. Some time after this, he was again in prison, having joined the Society whose follower he had refused to persecute. He was committed to York Castle for non-payment of tithes.*

In the early part of the next century we find his grandson, Emanuel, living in the quiet little town of Yarm on the right bank of the Tees,

* See *ante*, chapter IX, page 73.

across which one of the first cast-iron bridges in England was afterwards erected. Unfortunately, the inhabitants had not long rejoiced in the opening of this bridge, when they awoke one morning to find that it had disappeared beneath the waters. Its place is now occupied by a substantial stone bridge, and near to that is a lofty railway viaduct. I have often heard from the heroines of this book of the great sensation caused in the neighbouring town of Stockton by this catastrophe.

Two of Emanuel Procter's daughters were married to Priestmans, brothers of the mother of the heroines,—Sarah to Thomas Priestman of York, and Barbara to John Priestman of Thornton. Joseph (Emanuel Procter's eldest son, who lived to maturity) married Jane, the daughter of Benjamin and Barbara Flounders of Yarm. This Benjamin Flounders had a son John, who was educated at David Hall's school at Skipton, and as a boy became attached to David Hall's daughter. Faithful to this early affection, when of age to marry he went over to Skipton, hoping to be favourably received, but he had not sufficiently considered that some time should have been allowed for the renewal of acquaintance before the lady of his choice could reasonably be expected to accept his proposals. On his arrival at Skipton, late in the evening, these were made in due form to the father. It may be that the young lady resented that they were not made first to her, but the result, unfortunately, was that after breakfast next morning she said to her suitor, "John Flounders, thy horse is at the door!" After this summary dismissal, much as he was mortified, he does not appear to have been heartbroken, for he rode off to consult some of his old acquaintances as to the probability of his finding any other suitable young Friend to whom he might offer his hand and (shall we say it?) his heart. In this he was unsuccessful, so nothing was left him but to wend his way home down the beautiful valley of Wensleydale. Being too far for one day's ride, he stopped the night at Leybourne, the scene of Mary Queen of Scots' capture, some say through the loss of her "shawl." In the morning he found the innkeeper could not give him change, so that he was at a loss how to pay his bill, till his host said that there was a Quaker gentleman lived in the town, who, though he did not think he would give *him* (the innkeeper) change, yet if his guest, who was a Friend, would go, he would be almost sure to accommodate him with it. John Flounders then went to the house of Friend Bickerdike, who was a wealthy linen bleacher.

The door was opened by a young lady with a red flannel round her throat. The traveller soon got what he wanted, and found the visit so pleasant that ere long it was repeated, and the acquaintance ended in a wedding. Before this took place, he received a private intimation that a renewal of his visit to Skipton would not be unpleasant, but it was then too late, and we have reason to believe that the issue of the hasty conduct of these two young people was much unhappiness in two families. I do not wish to imply more than that my great-uncle John Flounders, and his wife, were not so congenial to each other as he and his first love would probably have been, and she, I believe, afterwards married unhappily. I remember being taken to see Aunt Flounders about sixty years ago, when she was a venerable old lady, and she had a beautiful cat with a ribbon round its neck sitting by her side, which I am afraid made a deeper impression on my childish mind than did its mistress. She lived nearly next door to her only son, Benjamin, of whom I must now proceed to speak. He was my father's first-cousin, and living in the same town, and both being serious-minded Friends, they became very intimate companions, until after my father settled in North Shields in the drapery business, where he became acquainted with my mother, Elizabeth Richardson, and they were married in 5th mo., 1799.* My mother's most intimate companion before her marriage was Mary Walker, one of the daughters of John Walker of Dockwray Square, a wealthy shipowner, and a native of Whitby. She was a young woman of good education, and of very superior endowments, sanctified by Divine Grace. Benjamin Flounders had previously paid his addresses to Elizabeth Backhouse of Darlington, but had been refused, and I suppose when visiting my parents he became acquainted with Mary Walker, to whom he was ultimately married. It was rather a curious coincidence that the late Thomas Richardson of Sunderland had previously offered to Mary Walker and been refused, and now paying his addresses to Elizabeth Backhouse was accepted. I have been told that when each was travelling on horseback to visit their respective friends, they met on the road between Sunderland and Stockton, and finding what their errands were, they parted cordially, wishing each other success in their respective missions. A life-long blessing attended Thomas and Elizabeth Richardson's union, but Benjamin Flounders was soon deprived of his lovely wife by

* See chapter IX, "The Low Lights."

death. She left him with an only daughter, who married an officer (a Colonel Lowe, I think), who proved a very unkind husband, and she died, it was said, of a broken heart. Her father was desirous of reserving a piece of ground in Eglescliff churchyard to be buried by her, but her husband (it was said) out of spite had her buried close to the wall in such a position as to leave no room for him. Not to be deprived of this last satisfaction, the father bought the adjoining land, and had it added to the churchyard. Long before this, however, in fact soon after the death of his wife, Benjamin Flounders had left Friends, and had indulged more in the gaieties of the world than was at all consistent with his previous profession. This change so annoyed his Uncle Bickerdike, whose wealth he expected to inherit, that he threatened entirely to disinherit his nephew. Some Friends, however, interceded to prevent this extreme course, and Bickerdike ultimately left Benjamin Flounders, I believe, £40,000, on condition that if he left no children it was to be devoted to the use of the Society of Friends. Benjamin Flounders had long ceased to have any intercourse with his relatives, or with any members of the Society, but in his old age he seems so far to have softened towards them that he consulted the late Jonathan Backhouse and Joseph Pease how best to apply the money left by his uncle, and I believe that it was under their advice that the " Flounders' Institute " was established for the training of Friends as teachers. He left, I believe, nearly as much more in the hands of the three trustees out of which to pay several annuities, and afterwards to be devoted to the promotion of education of an un-sectarian character. With the consent of the Charity Commission, the trustees have united with a previously existing Church Establishment at Barnard Castle in founding a school for the education of the sons of farmers and other middle-class people in these Northern Counties; the Boards of Guardians, through their chairmen, elect one of the Governors, but it is likely to be mainly a Church Establishment, though with a strict conscience clause. I believe the fees are expected to be about £30 per annum. Long ago the last of our relatives left the snug little town of Yarm, and the Society of Friends, too, is extinct there. Long since, too, have the large droves of donkeys laden with coal ceased to pass through its quaint old street. Whether the sound of the curfew bell, which sounded so pleasantly in my childhood, still continues I know not.

CHAPTER XVIII.

The Sisters in Age.

1839—1869.

> " Not bed time yet ! We long to know
> What wonders time has yet to show,
>   What unborn years shall bring ;
> What ship the Arctic pole shall reach,
> What lessons Science waits to teach,
> What sermons there are left to preach,
>   What poems yet to sing.
>
> Not bed time yet ! The full-blown flower
> Of all the year—this evening hour—
>   With friendship's flame is bright ;
> Life still is sweet, the heavens are fair,
> Though fields are brown, and woods are bare,
> And many a joy is left to share
>   Before we say " Good Night ! "
>
> Dr. O. W. Holmes.

> " Oh let me still from self my feelings bear,
>   To sympathise with sorrow's starting tear :
>   Nor sadden at the smile which joy bestows,
>   Though far from me her beam ethereal glows.
>   Let me remember, in the gloom of age,
>   To smile at follies happier youth engage ;
>   See them fallacious, but indulgent spare
>   The fairy dreams experience cannot share ;
>   Nor view the rising morn with jaundic'd eye
>   Because, for me, no more the sparkling moments fly."
>
> Mrs. John Hunter.

ELIZABETH RICHARDSON gave up her school in North Shields at the
Christmas of 1839. For the next eight years she led a somewhat
wandering life. Although more than sixty years old, she could still enjoy
seeing the world, and she paid visits to London, to her old friends at

2 F

Derby, and to her many relatives in Yorkshire. In these different families the young people found their elderly cousin a cheerful companion, who entered with spirit into their pursuits, who was ready to help them with their drawing and painting, and who was eager to learn from them the last new pattern in the fancy knitting, netting, and crochet work, upon which they were all then engaged. At one time a mania prevailed for the manufacture of cushions, which were to be stuffed with thistle-down, and Elizabeth astonished the thrifty Yorkshire farmers by enquiring for spots where thistles grew! She was a good correspondent, and her graphic letters were welcome to her friends at Shields. At that time it was remarked that you could generally judge by the handwriting of a letter whether or no your correspondent was a Friend. At fashionable boarding-schools, ladies were taught to write in the manner so laboriously imitated by the disguised Prince in Lord Tennyson's poem :—

> " In such a hand as when a field of corn
> Bows all its ears before the roaring east."

Few Friends wrote in that pointed, sloping style, and their hand-writing often showed marked individuality. Elizabeth's strong, square, legible writing resembled that of some ladies of the present day. It was rapid and careless, and some surprise was excited when a letter was received from her written so beautifully that it might have been mistaken for copper plate. A postscript revealed the reason of this unusual care. " The Americans often said to sister Isabel, ' What bad writers English people are!' Let us all try to do better!" She must have been nearly seventy years old when her spirit of patriotism was thus roused; and she often quoted the saying of one of her favourite authors, that " it is a man's own fault if he does not improve, mentally and spiritually, until he is seventy." At one time Elizabeth resided in a cottage at Ayton, reviving old friendships, and enjoying the beautiful country familiar to her in her childhood; and she afterwards spent some time at different places in the still more beautiful Lake Country.

People whose memory carries them back easily to the Forties, vividly remember the sensation caused in English society by the publi-cation of the ' Life of Dr. Arnold,' and nowhere was that sensation more profound than in the quiet circles of Quakerism. Arnold's intense truthfulness and force of character, his daily life as depicted by his biographer, his letters and his sermons awakened intense sympathy and admiration in the minds of many Friends, and especially of those who had been engaged in educational work. Five and twenty years ago, a Committee appointed by the Yearly Meeting to visit the Meetings of Friends in different parts of England arrived in due course in Surrey. The Committee counted some North Country schoolmasters amongst its numbers, and these turned out of their way to make a reverent pilgrimage to Laleham, where in those days the large, old, red brick house where Dr. Arnold had lived was still standing. It was then used as the National School, but the cedar trees round it gave some idea of what the garden had been in Arnold's time. The Church where he had preached and prayed was fraught with interest to the visitors. The churchyard was, even then, linked with the name which has made the Thames-side village famous wherever the English tongue is spoken. Elizabeth Richardson was one of Dr. Arnold's warm admirers. His biography was one of her treasured books, and during her tarriance in the Lake Country she was one of the earliest pilgrims to Fox How.

Her zeal in another cause than that of hero worship led her into more dangerous pilgrimages. The study of the different varieties of ferns first became general in England during the Forties, and Elizabeth, forgetting her age and infirmities, entered with all the enthusiasm of youth upon this new pursuit. Searching for a fern which was said to grow upon Latter Barrow, she attempted to climb one of the walls, which on those hills are formed by piling stones roughly together without any mortar or cement. The loose stones gave way in her grasp, and falling upon her feet and ankles crushed them terribly. Her hands being unhurt, she was able to remove the stones and to draw herself backwards the way she had come until she reached a gate. Here she lay for some hours, until a boy passed on an adjoining road with a horse and cart. He brought some help, and she was taken home to her lodgings, and such medical aid as the neighbourhood afforded was procured. Having, as we have seen, the use of her hands, she was able to write to her friends, slightly mentioning that she had hurt her foot, and months elapsed before intelligence reached them through other sources of the serious character of the accident. Her sister and niece visited her at a cottage at Skelwith-fold, near Brathay, and found that although her position had to them seemed lonely, there were Friends in the neighbourhood who had been anxious to offer help and sympathy, but Elizabeth's old independence of character rendered her somewhat difficult to approach with such offers. She recovered in time from the effects of the accident, but it was as an infirm old woman that she finally returned to Shields in 1847.

At that date her sister Mary, although only two years younger, was still a vigorous person. Her life of forty-five years at the Low Lights had been a varied one. The early days, when she was allowed full liberty to indulge her taste in the re-modelling of the garden and the beautifying of the house, must have been busy and bright; the coming of her sisters to North Shields in 1811 made her feel that place to be indeed her home: and when, in 1820, she received under her loving care the three orphan children whose mother had been her intimate friend, the charge filled every hour with interest and with happiness. In 1834 came the great sorrow of her life, the death of her cousin, Henry Richardson, soon followed by that of one of her adopted children, Sarah Procter, who is still remembered as a lovely girl of great gentleness and refinement.

Hannah, the elder daughter of Joseph and Elizabeth Procter, who inherited the bright, dark eyes and brilliant complexion of her mother, possessed great intelligence and vivacity, and was a cheerful presence in her home, and an active worker in the charities of the town. She married, in 1839, a Friend from the South of England, who had come to reside at Darlington—Isaac Sharp, who is still amongst us, having, in his vigorous old age visited nearly every part of the world as a preacher. Isaac Sharp's married life with his sweet wife was short, for after the birth of her second child she returned to her old home at the Low Lights to die. Her two little girls were frequent visitors to that place, looking upon it as a second home, and upon their cousin Mary in the light of an indulgent grandmother.

Except for such visitors, Mary Richardson and her adopted son, John Richardson Procter, lived alone for eight years at the Low Lights. The life was a quiet one for the young man, but it did not seem to depress him, for a more even-tempered, cheerful person it was impossible to imagine.

Mary, although she was growing old and deaf, was too original in character and too ready and racy in speech ever to be a dull companion, and never did a real mother and her son more completely understand each other.   Their garden, with its steep grassy slopes, its fine trees and its carefully tended flowers, afforded occupation and pleasure to both of them. With the Friends' Book Society, the Subscription Library, and their own good collection of books, they were well supplied with literature ; and in those quiet evenings the young man had ample time to read, to think out questions for himself, and to form decided opinions, which, although time might soften, it did not change. Already his name was on every committee formed to promote the good of the town, and he has been known to take the long, exposed field walk through rain or snow to some meeting, and then to find himself the only person present. Secluded as was the home at the Low Lights, many visitors found their way to it. There, as has been said, came Robert Murray, of New York, and his son, fresh from their travels in Greece and Italy ; and there came Paschal Morris, of Philadelphia, and his fair sister, whose house had been the home of Isabel Casson during her travels in America. There came Frederick Douglas, that fine specimen of the African race, and other anti-slavery workers ; and there, too, came at times during his early vigorous manhood, one for whom all England is now mourning—John Bright.

It was at the Meeting of the British Association at Newcastle in 1838, that the name of John Bright was first heard in the North of England. Earlier in the same summer, he had taken his sisters to Ackworth General Meeting, and had there seen a fair face, the remembrance of which drew him to Newcastle in September. A certain touch of gentleness and of poetic feeling, which in John Bright softened the sturdiness of the democrat, showed itself thus early in his choice of a wife. The eldest daughter of the friend and correspondent of our heroines, and of his wife Rachel Bragg, Elizabeth Priestman was reared in a home where intellectual activity existed side by side with a strict form of Quakerism ; where the utmost refinement of manner was combined with the warmest popular sympathies, and where the strongest opinions were urged in the gentlest tones. When brought into contact with such a family, John Bright's bluntness and directness of speech stood out in marked contrast, but his manly honesty and uprightness were at once recognised, and it soon became evident that he would win the prize which he had come to seek. The manufacturing districts were a little-known part of England :

it then seemed a long way from Newcastle to Rochdale, and North Country Friends felt that a precious possession was about to be carried away. "Who is this young man Bright whom Elizabeth Priestman is going to marry?" one of them asked in anxious tones of a Lancashire Friend. "A very popular young man, very much thought of by our working people," are the only words of the answer now remembered.

Simple as was the marriage ceremony of the Society, it was yet fenced round by many formalities, dating from the time when Friends were first allowed by the Legislature to solemnize matrimony in their own meeting houses. Nearly two months before a marriage, the parties concerned attended a Monthly Meeting, and when, after the solemn gathering for worship was over, Men and Women Friends separated into their respective meeting houses, the intending bride and bridegroom, accompanied by the parents of both when possible, entered the Women's Meeting. There they took seats facing the assembly, forming an interesting spectacle to its younger members, and gave notice of their intention of taking each other in marriage. Then the parents of both gave consent, verbally when present, in writing when absent. The transaction was recorded by the clerk, and the parties were then at liberty to proceed to the Men's Meeting, where the same ceremony (a sufficiently formidable one for the lady) was gone through. Two Friends were appointed in each Meeting to enquire whether the betrothed persons were clear from other marriage engagements. The result of these enquiries was brought before the next Monthly Meeting, and if the report was favourable, the wedding followed in due course. It was at a Monthly Meeting at North Shields that John Bright and Elizabeth Priestman "presented their marriage." Although fifty years have passed since that day, the writer well remembers the frank, bold tones in which the young man said, "Friends, I intend to take Elizabeth Priestman to be my wife, if the Lord permit!" and the soft, clear accents which followed, "Friends, I intend to take John Bright to be my husband, if the Lord permit!" The fair girl was surrounded by her relatives, her grandmother and uncle being with her, as well as her parents. Jacob Bright's consent to his son's marriage was given in writing. It did not escape remark that the usual "My friend" before the proper names was omitted by these two young people. It is probable that John Bright, who, though he dearly loved the principles and the manner of life of those whom he so tenderly called his "own people," never scrupled to smile at their phraseology, thought the words entirely needless. He wished to make another innovation in Quaker usage, and to take his betrothed bride, after the severe ordeal she had passed through, at once back to her home. On this point he had to give way. After the meetings were over, the young couple dined, in company with many other persons, at the Low Lights. About thirty years ago, a notice in writing was allowed to be substituted for the personal declaration of an intention of marriage, and other changes have occurred. Persons not in membership are now allowed to be married in Friends' Meeting-houses, but the simple marriage ceremony has undergone very little change.

There are people in Newcastle who still remember the November day when Pilgrim Street was crowded with people who came to see the marriage of Elizabeth Priestman. The dingy old Meeting-house was filled, chiefly with young men and maidens, many of the latter, whether of Lancashire or Northumbrian birth, very fair to look upon, and their lustrous garments brightened the dull place.

It is possible that this book may be read by some one who never saw a Quaker wedding, where there is no priest to conduct the ceremony, and for such a reader the scene shall be described. The bride and bridegroom, surrounded by their friends, sat facing the assembly, and after a time of silence, they rose, and the bridegroom said, " Friends, I take Elizabeth Priestman to be my wife, promising, through Divine assistance, to be unto her a loving and faithful husband, until it shall please the Lord by death to separate us." The bride then uttered the same promise, in which, of course, the words "husband" and "wife" changed places. Solemn prayers were offered for the young couple, and every blessing craved for them that loving hearts could desire. Legal documents were signed, and the marriage ceremony was over. We all know how brief was the happiness it brought, how soon came the time of parting when, in John Bright's own touching words, he " was left alone in the world with a motherless child." Of the events in his after life, amongst which not the least remarkable is the change in public feeling towards him, we may now read in every newspaper.

In this book, where some of his characteristics of manner have been before noted, it may suffice to say, that those who knew him best loved him best. His earliest followers, the Lancashire working people, trusted him through evil report and good report. When, during the American Civil War, the Cotton Famine brought starvation into their homes, they stood with John Bright firmly on the side of the North and of freedom. As true friends to him all his life long were the members of that quiet household which yielded him its choicest treasure on that November day. To the one lovely child of the marriage, the Newcastle home was all but as dear as the one at Rochdale. Through his arduous conflicts, through prosperity as through adversity, and even after he had formed new ties, John Bright turned for sympathy to the family of his early love. Nothing ever broke the bond which bound him to it, and even in old age his eyes brightened and his voice softened when he heard its name.

His sympathisers and admirers are very numerous now. Let us not enquire too curiously into the cause, but rather be thankful that at last honesty and uprightness are acknowledged and honoured; that all English-speaking people are at one to-day, whilst party cries are hushed and party weapons are sheathed over the grave of a true man.

During the spring of 1847 Mary Richardson was busily engaged in preparing the old home at the Low Lights for the reception of a new mistress. In July of that year, John Procter was married to his second cousin, Lydia, the daughter of William Richardson, of Cherry Hill, York, and his wife, Martha Mildred.* With this branch of the Richardson family all the heroines of this book had long been on terms of peculiar intimacy and affection; and although Mary's long life at the Low Lights was now ended, the marriage filled her heart with joy. To no one could she have yielded her place in that household with so much pleasure as to the wife whom her adopted son had chosen; and now, when her last labours of love for the comfort of the two persons who were almost equally dear to her were ended, Mary removed to one of the large, old-fashioned houses in Dockwray Square, and there her two sisters, Elizabeth, after her lonely sojourns in beautiful but remote places, and Hannah, after her active life at Ackworth, came at her invitation. Seldom, probably, have

* See ante, Chapter VIII.

three sisters come to reside together in age, whose lives had run such different courses since the same roof sheltered them all in childhood.

The three old ladies formed a cheerful household, and so many people came to see them that a neighbour said, " Miss Richardson keeps our side of the Square quite gay." Yet that side of the Square could never have been a dull one, for its west aspect, while it debarred it from the sea view commanded by the windows of the opposite houses, left it open to the afternoon sunshine, and made its broad dry flags a favourite promenade, where, probably from the earliest days of the Square, ladies and gentlemen walked on Sundays after church, talking of the lighter topics of the day; shipping and politics being reserved for the walk by the railings on the bank top which overlooked the harbour. If our heroines did not join the cheerful groups which passed and re-passed their windows, they yet looked upon them with kindly interest, and were, in their turn, regarded with respect by their neighbours, especially by those who had known Elizabeth in the days of her school. Each sister had to yield a little to the other in the matter of visitors. The large circle of acquaintance which Elizabeth had in the town was very different from the seclusion in which Mary had lived at the Low Lights, into which few persons except Friends ever penetrated; whilst as to Hannah, when she in her turn received guests, her sisters occasionally remarked with wonder, how inexhaustible were all subjects of conversation connected in any way with Ackworth School! It was probably these varied experiences of life, added to a certain frankness of speech common alike to all the sisters, which made their society interesting and amusing to young people, and prevented their house from ever coming under the reproach of dulness. The impression made by the sisters upon some of these young relatives is well described in the following letter. It is from a younger daughter of Jonathan Priestman, who has been so often referred to in this book as the cousin and life-long friend of the heroines. The letter may, perhaps, afford some excuse for the book having been written.

Letter from Miss Priestman.

"9, Durdham Park, Novr. 4th, 1884.

" Only a few days before your last letter reached me, I had been talking to F. about our cousins Richardson and wishing I could make them live for her—as they do for me—with the brightness and charm special to each, and the strength and nobleness common to all. So it delighted me to find you were preparing a little sketch of figures so original and attractive and so worthy to be remembered. We were accustomed to hear our parents speak of your aunts with affectionate esteem ever since I can remember. When my father was a young man, lonely in lodgings in Newcastle, your aunts' house was thrown open to him with the utmost cordiality. He was always grateful for their kindness and for the privilege of such association, and used often to speak warmly of the benefit he felt it had been to him to visit at a house where the standard was so high, and the tone so broad and intellectual and cultivated. Your aunts must have thought and judged for themselves from their earliest days. Coleridge's 'Friend' was not a book likely to be met with, then, in Quaker families, but we have a copy amongst my father's books, bearing date at that period, which, with other volumes of a similar or varying character, show the sort of subjects which came under the notice of your aunts' free and independent thought. Your Aunt Elizabeth was wont to complain in her cheerful way sometimes that she had been born too soon, and to wish she had lived fifty years later. She had a fine skill in painting; we have a beautiful group of flowers painted by her on an old-fashioned screen that now adorns our drawing-room, as it did that of our parents long ago, when to sit beside those beautiful flowers often helped to beguile the dulness of having to be quiet and proper while Friends were calling ; but she had to cultivate her powers under difficulties and opposition that would have thwarted a less resolute character. In later life she gave lessons in the art they had condemned to the grandchildren of those under whose ban she had worked. A quick sense of beauty must have belonged to all your aunts ; when we were quite little and were often taken to dine at Low Lights, I remember the wonder and pleasure it was to me to see the flowers on each little custard-glass, and on the tart-dishes and the fruit. Your Aunt Mary had anticipated by many a year the floral decorations that are so common on tables now ; and her taste in arranging the drawing-room flowers used to give ideality to the somewhat sober character of the furnishing, throwing over all a grace and brightness. Long afterwards, when failing strength made such little dainty touches troublesome, there was still the same love of nature and of beauty, shown pathetically in the few bright evergreens with rosy berries 'to last through the winter,' in the drawing-room in Dockwray Square. If Cousin Hannah's many years at Ackworth had somewhat checked the active development of her artistic feeling, still it was there. Do you not recollect the kindly amusement with which her sisters would tell about her accident at the lakes, when she leant forward to admire the moon so rapturously, that with clasped hands she over-balanced herself at the low window-sill and fell forward on the grass, involving sundry pots of flowers in her sudden fall? I can almost hear the laughter with which this little incident was told, for your aunts had abundant sense of humour. It gave great zest to their conversation. Many a good saying of Cousin Mary's passed current in our circle. And what charming tales Cousin Elizabeth used to tell us when we were little! I used to think the stories in our children's books of cross old school-mistresses must be all made up, when the only one I knew was so kind and entertaining. But with her strong character, of course, there would be occasions when her pupils might find her stern. None of your aunts would consent for a moment to any failure in duty, and with principles so strong, perception of character so keen, and language so racy and to the point, they would have been formidable neighbours if they had not been at the same time truly generous-hearted and always sensible of that respect which is due from one human being to another.

"I do not know whether your sketch is only of your Aunts Richardson, or whether it is to include some records of your Aunt Isabel Casson, whose face of motherly beauty seemed to carry comfort wherever it went; and of your own beloved mother, who united to those sterling qualities that distinguished her sisters a sweetness of disposition which surely never was surpassed, for its gentleness never failed, however deeply her sensitive nature might have been moved.

"I would give you the warmest encouragement in your work.

"A. M. P."

The writer of this book is indebted for many details of the early life of its heroines to a dear friend who, the devoted daughter of Isabel Casson and her constant companion for thirty years, treasured up her mother's stories of old times. Closely united by ties of affection to all the sisters, Hannah Casson, like the kind writer of the foregoing letter, includes them all in her loving memory.   She writes :—"How I loved and revered those five sisters, and how I lament that there are so few in the present day to be compared with them in originality, truth, warm-hearted sincerity and unselfishness.   Not one of them was capable of falsehood or of meanness."

The five sisters, of whom these perhaps too-partial portraits have been drawn by such loving hands, had been long the only survivors of their father's large family.   The youngest, with her genial husband, lived in Dockwray Square, opposite to her sisters; the eldest was often their guest. Isabel, the quietest and most retiring of the sisters, had been by far the greatest traveller.   Early in the Forties she had visited Ireland as a minister, and something in her character must have attracted, in no common degree, the warm-hearted Friends of that country, amongst whom she was long held in tender remembrance.   Many and delightful were the letters she would read to her relatives, from charming Irish women whose vivacity and brightness of spirit no strictness of the Quaker rule could ever subdue, amongst whom the names of Newsom, Gough, and Clibborn are still remembered.

In 1848, Isabel Casson sailed for America, in company with a dear friend, the wife of her cousin Jonathan Priestman.   The eloquent preacher, John Pease, was their fellow voyager, but his service in America laid in a different direction to that of the two Women Friends, who travelled together in very loving companionship.   At the end of a year Rachel Priestman felt that her work in America was accomplished; she therefore returned to her home and family, and Isabel Casson was, in her somewhat pathetic phrase, "left alone in America."   The timid woman, who in her youth had feared to trust herself in a boat on the placid waters of the Yorkshire Ouse, now, in her age, had to cross the St. Lawrence within sight and sound of Niagara!   In some journeys she had more than a glimpse of the privations of settlers in the woods, and was once the guest of a Friend whose wife had narrowly escaped from wolves, the savage beasts pursuing her to the very door of her home.   Isabel saw also the brighter side of American life.   In Philadelphia she had a charming home in the house of Catherine Morris and her sisters, to which from time to time she returned, and to which her letters were always addressed.   Of these ladies the eldest sister was the life-long friend of Isabel Casson; the youngest is still the friend and correspondent of her daughter.   There were many other American homes where the English stranger found a kind welcome, but here one name can alone be mentioned, that of the aged minister, Stephen Grellet.

All who have read any record of the life of this good man must have taken note of the way in which he and his message of love found access to persons of widely differing character and pursuits, alike to the famous Tom Paine ("rebellious needleman "), whose last days were soothed by his kindness, to Jews in their separate life, to nuns in the seclusion of their convents, to kings and emperors in their palaces. In England we read how he addressed meetings of the nobility, of military and naval officers, of the poor weavers of Spitalfields, and of the very thieves and outcasts of London, whom he gathered into solemn assemblies; and how, after his visits to the prisons, he was the first to direct the attention of Elizabeth Fry to the state of the women in Newgate. All these things, and many more, may be read of in Benjamin Seebohm's Biography, but this book is an attempt to preserve family traditions; and we must all remember how the voices of our mothers and grandmothers softened into tender tones when they spoke of Stephen Grellet. In many a Friend of that day, a spirit as loving, feelings as sensitive, and sympathies as wide, struggled beneath the weight of English reserve and Quaker formality, but in the old French exile these qualities had free play, and found fitting expression in a manner of the most winning courtesy, which had a peculiar charm for those who came under its spell in youth. A citizen of the American Republic, a minister of the most democratic sect, Stephen Grellet, whose father was a courtier of the unfortunate Louis XVI., retained the manner and deportment that distinguished the old French nobility. We have little sympathy with the rigid Friend who felt it his duty to remonstrate with the gentle minister upon some of his peculiarities, and to ask him, " Why dost thou bend thy body when thou greetest thy friends?" It is even said that Stephen Grellet tried to correct some of these habits, but the attempt failed signally, and those who loved him best rejoiced when he abandoned it in despair. " You may grind a Frenchman to powder, and his very ashes will still be French," he was wont cheerfully to say, and to the last the manner natural to Etienne de Grellet du Mabillier, the French noble, survived in Stephen Grellet, the humble-minded Quaker preacher.

Isabel Casson, who spoke of her last visit to him as "heavenly," did not love him the less for his old-world courtesy.

Of the five sisters, Isabel alone wore the real Friends' dress, as shown in her portrait, the clear muslin cap encircling the smooth hair and the placid face, the kerchief in its many folds crossing the bosom, the gown of dark silk or poplin, with the skirt plain and of moderate width, and the silk shawl over the shoulders, completing the costume. This dress, which well became the calm serenity of Isabel Casson, would have been ill suited to the active habits and quick movements of her sister Mary. She and Hannah wore little capes, closed at the throat and then sloping away, in a bygone fashion lately revived. These capes were of the same material as their dresses; but while Mary indulged her fancy by choosing handsome, bright-coloured silks, Hannah's dress was of black poplin, relieved only by her neat white muslin cap and tie. Alone of all the sisters, she had a touch of asceticism. Scrupulously neat in her dress, she avoided the little dainty touches that brightened the Quaker garb. If silk or satin was used, it was but to line the grave poplin. Looking upon her smiling face, with its still fresh complexion, and listening to her animated conversation, you forgot the sombreness of her garments; and the money she grudged to spend on them brightened many a sad home.

Sometimes the sisters, when they all met together, talked of their own childhood, and younger people listened, alas! too carelessly. In these days, when old customs are taken note of, it may be recorded that one night in the year, at Stockton (could it have been Shrove Tuesday?), was given up to a sort of rough play, which they watched from their windows with delight, a leading feature being that even the gravest persons, if they should appear in the street, were liable to be chalked on the back. But when the conversation turned upon such topics, Mary sat apart. She was no lover of old memories nor praiser of past times. A great reader of history, she had no reverence for antiquities; and when she visited Holyrood with a party, resolutely turned her back upon grim portraits and blood-stained floors, and gazed out of the window at the landscape. Proverbially a "clannish" person, she had no respect for family relics. In these days, when we seem in danger of returning to the "worship of ancestors," her biographer records with a blush that she sold the silver tankards of her great grandfather, Henry Vasie, and bought new-fashioned

silver articles with the money.   When people talked to her of the past, she
would say exultingly, " I am so glad that I live in these days, when there
are such great improvements."   The days in which she thus gloried to
live were those of the middle of this century, when the cobble-stones
disappeared from the streets to be replaced by good pavement, when the
slow coaches and canal-boats gave way to railways and steamships, when
the window-seats and the dados were taken away out of our old houses and
the brass handles off our old furniture, and when gorgeous flowers bloomed
upon our walls and our floors.   She lived to see the romantic revival, and
to marvel at it.   It was as wonderful to her that her younger relatives
should call their children by such old-fashioned names as " Mabel " and
" Ruth," as that they should allow them to read the fairy tales so entirely
despised and discarded when she was young.

Nothing more delighted the sisters than to gather their friends around
them.   At the Monthly Meetings held at Shields four times in the year,
Mary would have thought her dinner-table scantily filled had she not had
twenty guests around it, and great was the preparation for such times of
festivity.   These companies consisted chiefly of Friends from Newcastle
and Sunderland, amongst whom those bearing the name of Richardson
largely predominated; but visitors from more distant places, and especially
ministers travelling in the North of England, often made their home with the
sisters.   At other times, large parties assembled to tea at five o'clock, when
the Friends of Shields met to arrange the affairs of their Book Society, or
for purely social purposes, and trays of tea and coffee, and of every
possible variety of cake which Mary's ingenuity could devise or her skilful
hands concoct, were handed round.   It pleased the sisters when young
people filled their rooms, for they all loved to see young faces.   When they
settled in Dockwray Square, the somewhat elegant indoor dress which had
distinguished young Friends was beginning to disappear.   We, who were
children in the Thirties, had looked upon this dress with admiration and
wonder.   The transparent cap showed the neat hair, which was parted on
the forehead and arranged in the way familiar to us in the pictures of the
Madonna, and still more familiar to us in the early representations of the
young Queen of England.   Sometimes the hair was confined by a band of
narrow black velvet, and raised high at the back of the head with a comb.
The dress was cut round by the shoulders, and underneath it was worn

some thin material which veiled the fair neck (surely in those days young
Friends were always fair ?).   This net was closed at the throat by a dainty
gold pin, or tiny brooch, and over the shoulders was thrown a scarf of
white crape or silk.   Change came gradually.   As the high combs
vanished and the hair was dressed lower on the head, the caps altered in
form and soon disappeared altogether, except for married women.   When,
in 1845, dresses began to be made high to the throat, the wise fashion was
at once adopted by young Friends, and diaphanous draperies became
needless.   As to out-door head-gear, the custom of ladies wearing large straw
hats, which first became general in England at the time of the Crimean
War, recommended itself to young Friends by its simplicity and usefulness, and its adoption still further assimilated their appearance to that
of the rest of the world.   About thirty years ago, the Society made some
change in the wording of its Queries, making it evident that, although
simplicity and moderation were still recommended, singularity of dress and
speech was no longer considered necessary for its members.   The opinion
amongst Friends must have been fully ripe for the change, for, except in
the survivors of the generation for whose sake the quaint dress is still so
dear to us, the Society has ceased to be, in externals, " a peculiar people."
The " drab bonnets," of which Bernard Barton sang so sweetly, will soon
become valuable as relics of old English costumes.   It is now somewhat
difficult to procure one.   Quaker milliners, if we may apply so worldly a
term to those gentle widows and spinsters who made a modest livelihood in
their secluded rooms by their neat handiwork, were never a numerous
class.   They were, of course, always members of the Society (who else
could have been trusted to make articles of such nicety ?), and one or two
of them might be found in such towns as Leeds or Newcastle ; but many
Friends acted like those of Whitby, who had their bonnets sent down by
sea from London.   The best makers lived in the metropolis, and they had
the newest shapes, for even in Friends' bonnets the fashions changed.   A
lady of our day, who joined the Society, wished to make the fact known in
her circle of acquaintance by her change of dress, and went to one of these
London establishments to order a bonnet.   The convert was a fine-looking
woman, dressed like other English ladies, and the Friend in charge of the
business thought that such a customer could only require a Friend's
bonnet to wear as part of a fancy costume, and therefore refused to
supply it.

But the heroines of our narrative saw only the beginning of these changes. Mary would probably soon have accepted them as improvements. She might have disliked to see change in the appearance of those near to herself in age, but she had always great tolerance for the fancies of the young. William Richardson, of Sunderland, often told his children that when, as a little motherless boy, he spent his holidays at the Low Lights, his cousin Mary always took out of his shoes certain leather fastenings which he disliked and replaced them by ribbon shoe-strings. She had some strong antipathies, one being to the wearing of black garments by any member of her household, in marked contrast to the taste of many ladies of the present day; and when, during the prevalence of the crinoline mania, the distended dress of a young visitor swept down a little table with its vase of flowers, Mary exclaimed, "I will die protesting against crinoline!" But she lived to triumph over the extinction of the hated fashion.

Of all the sisters, Hannah would have sorrowed the most deeply over the changes which have passed over Friends. We have seen that when, in her youth, she left the Society and threw off its peculiarities of dress and speech, she entered eagerly into the gaieties of the world. Only by the light of her changed life can we read the history of her changed ideals, and understand how complete had been the revolution in her views, how entirely she had felt herself to be in the wrong path, or how severe was the judgment which she had passed upon her own conduct. She never referred to that period of her life, and anything which recalled it to her, or which made her fear that some young relative might embark upon a similar course, seemed, for the moment, to cloud her cheerful temper, and to narrow her catholic spirit. One summer evening, when a party of young people were assembled at the sisters' house, the conversation turned on photography, and Elizabeth denounced in no measured terms the unflattering character of the presentments which that art, then in its infancy, had made of some of her relatives. "Do you call this thing a likeness of that nice-looking woman? why it is some ugly old witch!" was her unsparing criticism of one portrait. Her old artistic fervour revived as she talked of the art of miniature painting, and of the beautiful miniatures she had seen. She was too much carried away by her enthusiasm to heed Hannah's warning glances, and disappearing from the room she returned with two miniatures in her hand, which were eagerly seized upon by the visitors. To their eyes, the miniatures seemed to be most beautifully executed, and that of Elizabeth, quietly dressed and wearing the muslin fichu of the period, was duly admired, but the vivid portrait of Hannah in her youth, with her light brown hair raised over cushions on her forehead, her brilliant colour, and her countenance beaming with animation, called forth exclamations of delight from the simply-dressed young Friends who saw it. It was but for a moment they had that pleasure. Elizabeth, who at first said brightly, " Hannah was just like that picture when it was painted," soon saw that she was giving pain to her sister and took away the portraits. Hannah only said of hers, " It was never like me," meaning, it was supposed, that the artist had flattered her, although, even as she sat there, in her sombre dress, with an unwonted cloud upon her pleasant face, the likeness could still be traced. A relative, who was not present that evening, afterwards asked Hannah Richardson to show her the portraits of which all the young people were talking. The answer was kindly but gravely spoken,—" Thou must never speak of them again, my dear." Alas! the miniatures were never seen after that day.

But such episodes were rare in Hannah's cheerful old age, when every day brought its occupation. On her first coming to North Shields she entered at once into the interests of the place, and worked upon committees, whether for charitable or educational purposes, with much of her old energy: while at home her warm affection for both her sisters united them all in a happy household, to which her vivacity gave its chief charm. Her many correspondents kept her in touch with a wide circle, so that visitors to the house in Dockwray Square always heard what was passing in the little world of Quakerism, while the latest newspapers, the newest quarterlies and the best books of the day lay upon the table. Their love of reading was a great source of happiness to all the sisters, and age did not narrow their choice of books. They did not put aside Macaulay's History because of his onslaught upon William Penn, nor refuse to read ' Uncle Tom's Cabin ' because it was a fiction. Elizabeth had always been near-sighted, and when intent upon pursuits which required close application she had never spared her eyes, and they now began to fail her. As her blindness increased, Hannah devoted herself to reading aloud to her,

considered her taste in the books she read, and deferred in every way to
Elizabeth's wishes as the elder sister, without ever seeming to remember
that she herself had ever filled a post of authority. Nor should it be
forgotten that Mary, who had for so many years been a very absolute
monarch in her own domain, now often gave way to what she considered to
be Hannah's superior judgment upon some points. " Sister Hannah knows
best about that," she would often say, generally referring to important
matters of the Society, into which she thought her younger sister's wider
experience had given her more insight than she had obtained in her useful
but more bounded life. Perhaps from having lived in this somewhat
narrow circle, Mary was a person of strong likings and dislikings, which
were not always confined to inanimate objects. Some of her prejudices
were observed to soften as she advanced in age, but others were
insurmountable, and those in her household had simply to submit to them.
When, on the other hand, Elizabeth occasionally showed that the old spirit
of independence and self-will was not dead within her, Hannah would
gently say to the youngest sister, " Thou knowest, dear, we cannot make
her over again."

Except for financial troubles which fell upon every Friend's family in
North Shields from the failure of the Union Bank in 1847, the first six
years of the sisters' life together were unclouded by any especial calamity.
After that time their circle began to narrow. In 1853 their youngest
sister, Sarah, the beloved wife of William Brown, was taken from her
family, and in 1858 Isabel Casson died at the age of eighty. These two
sisters were both, like their grandmother Isabel Vasie, eminently peaceful
women, and full of love to those around them. The happy nature of the
youngest had made her an especial favourite in her youth, when her sweet
voice in singing, her cheerful optimism, and her dislike of anything dismal
and dreary were noted facts in the family. In later life she still looked on
the bright side of things, and never anticipated troubles, but when
calamity came, the courage to meet it was not wanting. Of Isabel Casson
a sketch chiefly of her ministerial work is given in the 'Annual Monitor'
for 1859, and the same volume contains a Biography of another
great-grandchild of William and Elizabeth Richardson of Ayton, Edward
Pease, who having like so many of his mother's family attained the ripe
age of ninety-one, died at his home at Darlington in 1858. A genuine

North-countryman, long-headed and far-sighted, simple in personal habits, kindly, clannish, keen of wit and sharp of tongue, Edward Pease is a person to be remembered. But for his sagacity and insight the genius of George Stephenson might have been long unrecognised, and the making of railways in England have been delayed for years.

The three heroines of this narrative were now left alone, the last survivors of their family. Age was now with them, and sorrows had left their mark. Elizabeth felt her powers failing, and often wished to join those who had gone before. "I am willing to wait, my dear, but longing to go," was often her answer to an enquiry after her health. A scrap of paper was found after her death, on which she had written, " I feel deeply that my life has run a perilous course ; precipices on every hand ; but, thanks to a merciful Providence, I have never been utterly cast down."

She now applied to be reinstated in the membership of that Society from which she had severed herself half a century before. Although rarely able to join with her friends in their public worship, she felt comfort in being again united in fellowship with them at the close of her life. At this time a gleam of brightness was shed upon the little community of Friends in Shields by the frequent presence of two ministers at its meetings. One of these, Dr. Thomas Hodgkin, has since made his mark in the literary world, and has earned the gratitude of all lovers of history by his valuable works, which treat of those stormy years when the nations of modern Europe were being formed out of the ruins of Roman civilization. Thomas Hodgkin was a young man in 1860, and had recently come to the North of England, where his individuality was very marked, and his brief addresses, full of thought and of culture, were an intellectual treat to the younger Friends. He was then newly married, and had come to live at Tynemouth with his young bride, Lucy Fox, one of that Cornish family so well known for the many charming women which it has produced, and for the delightful ' Memorials ' associated with the name of one of them. Thomas Hodgkin and his wife were members of Newcastle Meeting, but they often preferred the little gathering at Shields, where the young man's voice was so welcome, and where he, in his turn, loved to listen to that of another minister. Of Charles Brown, the dear brother of the author of this book, it is especially difficult for her to write, yet as one of the sons of William Brown and Mary Richardson of Langbarugh, he has an undoubted right to a place in this Record.

In early youth Charles Brown was chiefly remarkable for his good abilities, his utter fearlessness, his ready speech, and his love of fun. These qualities made him a very popular companion; but it was observed that he had a high standard of right and wrong, and that in his most humorous sallies he never forgot the reverence due to sacred things. The calamities which fell upon him in his early manhood were heavy enough to quell the brightest spirits. His sweet young wife died at the birth of her first child, and in the following year he lost all his property by the failure of a joint-stock bank, and became a heavily-burdened man. The years which followed these misfortunes were clouded, yet he did his utmost to perform the duties of a good citizen, and took the warmest interest in the welfare of those around him. His love of reading was a source of happiness which no worldly calamity could take away, and his choice of books was varied. His knowledge of the Bible was remarkable, and he was a student of the old English writers, Milton, Bacon, and Jeremy Taylor. He had personal friends amongst the evangelical clergy, of whom he spoke with affection to the end of his life, and he was well versed in the writers of that school, Newton, Venn, Cecil, Legh Richmond, and the elder Wilberforce. In later life he never travelled without his tiny copy of the 'Christian Year,' as well as his small Testament, and often a volume of Shakespeare or of Molière. With all this varied culture, all this experience of the joys and griefs of life, with keen sympathies and quick perceptions, he was becoming fitted, during these sorrowful and somewhat lonely years, to minister to his fellows. When, after his happy second marriage, and with young children growing up around him, he first opened his lips as a minister, it seemed as though he spoke from the fulness of heart and mind the thoughts which had been maturing for years. His prayers were like collects,—brief, terse, undoubting,—the very essence of earnest reverent devotion. His preaching was neither emotional nor dogmatic, neither sensational nor coldly in-tellectual, but the fervent pleading of one human creature with his fellows, that all might strive for the better way; and the motive urged for the struggle was never fear, but always gratitude and love. His expositions of Scripture were full of interest, and his sermons were remarkable as compositions, from his great command of language, and from his habit of expressing himself, even in common conversation, with a certain brief emphasis, which gave almost an epigrammatic point to what he said.

This forcible mode of expression, enhanced by the deep tones of his voice, rivetted the attention even of the most careless persons, while the marked absence of conventional phrases added to the impression of originality. Although more than forty years old, he had preserved a certain youthfulness of heart, and a cheerfulness and contentedness of mind, in spite of his heavy cares, which made him very attractive to young people, who found with delight a sympathising friend and a genial companion in the minister they so highly honoured. For four years the Friends of Shields hardly once met together, on Sundays or week-days, without hearing his voice in prayer and teaching. What his services were to them it is impossible to describe, and they were also valued and accepted by the Friends of the Monthly Meeting, who, knowing Charles Brown's high character and consistent life, very soon acknowledged him as one of their ministers. "He is a preacher for these times on the old Foundation," said one of the heroines of this book. "He will be one of our greatest ministers," said another Friend. But this was not to be. Although a healthy and fairly vigorous man, Charles Brown had, to use his own words to a doctor, "lived too intense a life for some years." A partner in a large flour-mill, he and his brother were fighting against adverse circumstances under heavy burdens; the father of many young children, their welcome and tender claims on his time were never repulsed; and a good citizen to the best of his ability, he now added ministerial work to these many duties. His spirit never flagged, but his bodily strength was overwrought, and when acute illness came, he sank at once. One Sunday, late in December, 1863, he spoke with great solemnity upon earthly idols, hoping that none would trust too much to earthly help and guidance, and dwelling upon the different idols man is prone to set up and worship. In the prayer which followed he petitioned, "with even more than his wonted fervour, that nothing might be allowed to come between those present and their God; that if such were the case with any, if they were leaning on any other arm than His, that He would take away that vain support, even should it be their dearest earthly treasure, rather than that it should be allowed to separate them from Him."* It was but a fortnight after that prayer, so awful in its earnestness, that the sorrow-stricken Friends of Shields met with the

* 'Annual Monitor,' 1865.

knowledge that they would hear no more the voice of their beloved minister; that if they had made him their idol he was, indeed, taken away.*

Before this heavy calamity came, Elizabeth and Hannah Richardson had been gathered to their rest. Hannah's health began to fail in 1860, and her decline was gradual. Her intellect was bright, and her spirits cheerful to the last. The independent habits of the sisters made it difficult for them to fall into the ways of invalids, and fires in bed-rooms, even in the severe climate and with the abundant coal of Northumberland, were not submitted to without protest. Hannah had many alleviations in her illness. Loving letters came from her many friends, and loving hands tended her. When assisted into the room she occupied in the daytime, and settled upon her sofa, she would say, " Now, wilt thou give me my nice book ? " This volume, whose perusal thus cheered her last days, was the ' Life and Letters of Samuel Tuke,' printed for his family, but which Hannah Richardson, as an old and familiar friend, was allowed the privilege of reading. She died in March, 1861. It was sad to see the two older sisters when her bright presence was gone from their home, but Elizabeth did not long survive the sister she so sorely missed, for she passed away in August of the same year.

Mary Richardson was now left alone, the last of her family and nearly the last of her generation. In 1860 her eightieth birthday had found her in vigorous health, and she spent the day in Newcastle, paying visits to her many relatives, whose homes lay in different parts of the town. But the loss of her sisters made her an old woman. Her age was not without its pleasures. She preserved her keen sight to the last, and her love of reading cheered her lonely hours. Relaxing the rules of former days, she, like so many old people, found interest in fiction, and enjoyed the pleasant pages of Mrs. Craik and Mrs. Oliphant. She was a constant reader of the daily papers, and when a visitor, thinking she lived out of the world, solemnly broke to her the news of some great battle in the American Civil War, she quickly told him that his was not the latest news, and that she had read of another battle, in a later edition of the paper, which had materially altered the aspect of affairs.

* See Appendix.

The chief happiness of Mary Richardson's last days was derived from the affection of that large circle of relatives to whom she was still the "cousin Mary of the Low Lights," who had made that place so pleasant to the children of two generations. Nearest to her in affection, after the family of John Richardson Procter, were the two daughters of his sister Hannah Sharp, who, by their care over the age of the cousin whom they regarded as a grandmother, repaid the love which she had lavished on their childhood. They and other relatives were less with her as years went on, but her adopted son was near her to the last, cheering and comforting her by his daily visits, and by his almost more than filial affection; while his family were a constant pleasure in her old age. Mary Richardson died on July 31st, 1869, in her ninetieth year. Warm and gentle of heart, if somewhat blunt and plain of speech, ungrudging of labour for those she loved, incapable of falsehood or of flattery, the last of a generation of strong men and women, not exempt from the faults which accompany strength, passed away with her. It has been said that she and her sisters had little of the formality which marked other Friends of that day. There were households where every word seemed to be weighed, every expression carefully chosen; and where youthful vehemence was gently repressed. "Hate: but thou shouldst never hate any one, my dear," and "Surely we should call none of God's creatures ugly" are well-remembered reproofs; and it may be that learning to avoid the use of the harsh word tended to subdue the harsh feeling. Caution in making an assertion, or in giving a promise, was carried to an extreme in such families, and so well was this known that "I intend to do so," was considered on Newcastle Corn Market to be equivalent to a promise from a Friend. In some cases this caution produced an uncertainty of manner, but this was not so with all Friends, and their known exactitude had its weight. "Why, I would stake my life upon that man's word!" the writer, as a little child, overheard a working-man say of her father. He and the heroines of this book were more frank and less cautious in speech than some of their brethren, but they always endeavoured to judge charitably of others, and in the well-known words of one of the 'Queries,' were "careful to avoid and discourage tale-bearing and detraction." Caution and charity were carried beyond ordinary limits by the Friend who spoke (in meeting) of "one who, we are told, was a liar from the beginning, and who, there is reason to fear, may not have been improved by age."

JOHN RICHARDSON PROCTER,

Born at North Shields, September 16th, 1812;
Married at York, June 16th, 1847, to Lydia Richardson;
Died at Clementhorpe, North Shields,
October 11th, 1888.

These records would probably never have appeared in their present form, had it not been for the constant sympathy and assistance of one who had carefully preserved many of the traditions of the family, John Richardson Procter. The labour of collecting the materials has been lightened by the thought of the pleasure it would give him to see them gathered together, and the end of the work is saddened by the knowledge that he has not lived to see it completed. It has been recorded in former chapters * that Joseph Procter, great-grandson of the old Cromwellian soldier, came to North Shields from the town of Yarm, and it was in the old garden at the Low Lights that he wooed and won his wife Elizabeth, the youngest daughter of John Richardson of that place, in 1799. There were two sons of this marriage, between whom there was twelve years difference of age and considerable difference in mental constitution. The eldest son, Joseph Procter, was for some time under the tuition of the Presbyterian minister at North Shields, and so highly did the boy's intellectual powers impress his instructor that he remarked, "Surely, Mr. Procter, you will bring up this son to the ministry?" The enquiry provoked a smile from parents who considered preparation to be of no avail for that office, but the Scotch minister had a true discernment of the qualities which in his own land would have marked a boy for the service of the Kirk. Joseph Procter was a man who delighted in theological studies and in abstruse speculations, and who, in spite of his constitutional diffidence, did not fear to differ from his fellows upon many points. In the intense spirituality of his devotion, in his amiable disposition, and in his blameless life, he was a true Friend. His mind was one in which the imaginative and contemplative faculties predominated, while that of his younger brother was eminently practical. John Procter was but eight years old when he came to live at the Low Lights on the death of his parents, and little more than twenty-one when he became a partner in the tannery with his uncles. He was thus brought up in a very secluded circle, and in the strictest form of Quakerism. Yet, as we have seen, his willingness to work for public objects, and his punctual discharge of any duty which he undertook, gradually became known, and his unbending integrity and calm judgment marked him as a man to be trusted. In the Forties, parties were sharply

* See *ante*, Chapters VII. and XVII.

2 I

divided in the Church of England ; and it was singular that certain warm adherents, whether of the "Puseyite" or "Evangelical" section, alike poured their grievances against each other into the ears of the young Friend, confiding to him differences on points of ornament and of ritual, which had as little meaning to his mind as his straight collar and plain speech had to theirs. As years went on, any little formality in his manner, inherited from the rigid school in which he had grown up, seemed to pass away, while his unruffled serenity of temper, and the modest dignity appertaining to a man who respected the convictions of others while holding firmly to his own, made him generally esteemed and beloved. When, after the incorporation of the town, many public bodies were formed, the remark was often heard, after the names of different persons had been mentioned as desirable, "but Mr. Procter we cannot do without." His services as a Poor Law Guardian, as a Town Councillor, as a member of the School Board, and as one of the River Tyne Commissioners, are fresh in the memory of all who live near the Tyne. As age came on him he began to withdraw from these offices, and had said that he would retain longest that of Guardian, because he thought in that post he could do the most good. But a lengthened life was not to be his, and he died, as may be said, in harness, being taken ill as he returned from a meeting of which he had been the chairman, at some miles distance from his home. Not long before his death he was asked who were now his fellow-workers in some public body, it may have been the School Board. He said, " Well, I think I am most in sympathy with one of the curates, with the Scotch minister, and with the Catholic priest." All these and many more of those who had worked with him, met around his grave in the Preston Cemetery, which had never before seen such a gathering. To some of us it seems as though the past of his family, almost the past of Quakerism in the North of England, was buried with him, and as though we were left face to face with a new generation and with a new order of things.

The Richardsons of the present day, as we have seen in a former chapter, are still middle-class English people, most of them members of the Society of Friends. Few of them live in the old homes of their ancestors. Within the last six years, the estate of Langbarugh, with the dear old house, as well as the newer mansion, has passed from the family.

Except the eldest son, who has a manufacturing business in the town of Darlington, all the sons and sons-in-law of the last John Richardson, of Langbarugh, are engaged in farming, and are scattered over England from the fair hills of Tweedside to the level lands of Northamptonshire and Essex. Some of the younger generation have made homes for themselves in Canada.

The Stickneys have long ceased to be farmers, and have left that pleasant home of Ridgmont, over which the poetry of Mrs. Ellis cast such a charm for her young readers fifty years ago.* Of the many great-grandsons of William Stickney, one is a Government Inspector of Mines in New Zealand, another a young painter already known to fame.

For the last thirty years none of the Richardson family have lived at the Low Lights, and the Tannery, founded by John Richardson in 1765, is now being dismantled. His descendants are very numerous in the counties of Northumberland and Durham. In Newcastle, his great-grandsons, James and David Richardson, have a leather manufactory at Elswick, thus continuing, amidst very different surroundings, and by very different methods, the business which seems to be hereditary in their branch of the family, having been transmitted from father to son for six generations and for a period of two hundred years. Their cousin, Wigham Richardson, is a well-known shipbuilder. In the county of Durham, other great-grandsons of John Richardson of the Low Lights are prominent figures in the commercial world—millers, paper-manufacturers, and ship-builders. The cousins in both counties are active and useful men, willing to serve their neighbours on School Boards and Local Boards, and other posts involving hard work. Edwin Richardson has recently been Mayor of Sunderland; Henry Richardson, of Backworth, has succeeded his cousin,

* William Stickney, the father of Mrs. Ellis, was wont to relate a circumstance curious enough to be recorded in this history of past times. We must remember that it happened nearly a hundred years ago. Every autumn, Irish reapers came to work at the harvest at Ridgmont, and some of the same men came year after year. At the end of one harvest, a reaper was profuse in his thanks to William Stickney for having employed him for so many years, and offered to do anything to prove his gratitude. He was told that he could do nothing better than to come again another year and work as hard as he had always done before. Still the grateful Irishman was not satisfied, but pressing close to the Friend he persisted, "Is there nothing that I can do to oblige your honour? Is there not anybody that your honour would like to have put out of the way?"

John Procter, as Chairman of the Tynemouth Board of Guardians, and has been chosen a member of the Northumberland County Council.

At York, the house built at Cherry Hill by Isaac Richardson, a hundred years ago, is still inhabited by his grandson. The memory of the sweet women who have lived there, of Martha Mildred, the wife of William Richardson, and of her lovely daughter Sarah, is still cherished in their old home, where their place is well and worthily filled.

The Fossicks, long ago, left Welbury in North Yorkshire, and settled in London, where the sons of the kindly physician, Dr. Bevan, are well known; while his daughter has found a home in the north as the wife of the cultured man who presides over Flounders College. Of the two sons of the eccentric man of genius, William Bennett, the elder is earnest in many causes; editor of a Temperance paper, and Secretary to the Society of Psychical Research. The younger is Botanical Lecturer at St. Thomas's Hospital, and the author and translator of many valuable scientific works.

All the sons of Isaac Richardson, of Whitby, left that town during the last century. The descendants of his daughter Elizabeth, who married Ingram Chapman, have already been recorded. They, like the numerous descendants of Richard and Lydia Richardson, are conspicuous in many walks of English life.

Turning back over these records of two hundred years to the simple, upright, God-fearing man and woman with whom this history began, we may hazard the enquiry, what would they think of the changed circumstances of English life, and of the part which their descendants take in it? It might not seem unfitting to William Richardson, the tanner, of Ayton, that one of his descendants should be considered the highest authority in England upon the "Chemistry of Tanning," and should be chosen to lecture upon that subject to technical classes founded by the City and Guilds of London. It would probably surprise him more to know that another descendant has filled the office of High Sheriff of a county; that a third has provided a bishop with a residence befitting his office; and that a fourth has accepted a baronetcy. And even the young daughters of the house are to be found in varied paths of life. One is a student and teacher of Advanced Mathematics; another is a musical composer; a third has received the Red Cross from the Queen, for nursing wounded soldiers in Egypt; and a fourth has married into the Peerage.

All these are amongst the workers of the world, all are attached to, if not all in membership with, the Society of Friends. The Society seems to have a stronger hold upon descendants of the Richardsons than upon those of more conspicuous families. It often happens that in the contemporary annals of English philanthropy we meet with names which are very familiar to the ears of Friends, and observe with pleasure that those who bear them, clergymen and members of the Church of England as they may be, are true to the traditions of their Quaker descent, and have a hearty hatred of wrong and oppression all over the world. These men are an honour to the sect to which their ancestors belonged; nor do they need to blush for their origin, for the Society of Friends has a fair record.

Alone of all the sects which had their birth in the stormy seventeenth century, it can be said of Quakerism that her hands are clean from the guilt of persecution, and that upon her sober garments there is no stain of blood. Those who have left her fellowship for that of older communities, whose chequered records extend over many centuries, and whose beautiful liturgies and solemn rites command their reverence, may yet wish that they may be as true Christians as some of those whose brows were never marked by the sign of the cross, whose lips touched no outward sacrament. Many Friends of a past day, reserved and reticent as they were in speaking of sacred things, yet, in the words of Lawrence Oliphant, "lived the life." They showed by their forbearance, tenderness, and care for others, how closely they strove to follow in the footsteps of the Master Whose name was so reverently, yet so rarely, taken upon their lips. And those who, in our day, own no worship but that of Humanity, can hardly hope to be more self-sacrificing in the Service of Man than were some of these humble Christians.

Of late years a great change has been observable in the attitude of cultivated English people towards the Society of Friends. Once the object of persecution and afterwards of ridicule, Quakerism now excites the interest and commands the respect of many thoughtful persons. It is said that a lady, who inherits a very honourable name, was often engaged in discussions upon the grounds of religious belief. Her opponents were very able men, and she found one outwork of her faith after another crumble away beneath their attacks, until the citadel alone was left to her. Retiring into this unshaken fortress of her faith, she found it to be identical with the simple belief of the Society of Friends. It may be well in these days, when to so many minds creeds have become a bondage and symbols meaningless, to point out the strong position of a sect which has always held, without the aid of creed or symbol, what must surely be the essence of all religion—a belief in a communion with the Father of Spirits, who influences, aids, and directs those who trust in Him. They who firmly believe in this communion, whether through the medium of an outward rite or only in the secret chambers of the heart, stand indeed upon a foundation, and hold a citadel which cannot be taken.

> The old order changeth, giving place to new,
> And God fulfils himself in many ways.

APPENDIX A.

An abridged copy of a Letter from John Richardson of Langbarugh, to his nephew John Richardson, who was a son of the second William Richardson of Ayton, and who lived in the house in which his grandparents had lived.

Langbarugh, 4th Month 7th, 1750.

Lo. Nephew,

I have often had cause to remember my young years, which I spent in the place where thou art settled, I hope agreeably to the will of God, who I hope will show favour to thee and thine, if you obey Him.

Many things have appeared in the view of my mind, since I heard that thy little daughter has the same name that thy grandmother bore during that part of her time that she lived in the same place, which was from her marriage to her death. I think it my duty to remind thee of her, though I may say little but what thou hast heard before. My father and mother were married in 1684, at Lythe Parish Church, they being brought up in that way; but some things in practice among them,* which they thought disagreeable to the will of God, made known in their hearts, obliged them either to forsake the friendship they had with them of the same way (which were of the more sober sort), or lose the favour of Him who said, "If any man will come after Me, let him deny himself, and take up his cross daily, and follow Me," which they did, and joined with the Quakers, which at that time was a name of much scorn and derision, and their principles not to be followed without being willing to part with all for Christ's sake. As the little finger is of some use to the body, they were a help, through the mercy of God, to the Society they joined, in bringing about the favour which we now enjoy, which the Almighty put into the hearts of the King and of those in authority under him, to grant unto them and unto us.

Being married and settled with a small stock,† my father employed it and himself in the tanning trade, in such a way that we always had plenty; and as we followed the same trade after him, we met with many who expressed a wish to deal

---

* *I.e.*, the members of the Church of England.—Ed.
† Of money?—Ed.

with us, having been well done to by him. I think the little stock he had was managed to as much advantage for himself and those he dealt with, as by any at that time ' and considering our numbers, I think Providence favoured him and us, so that he saw us all in a likely way to do well. But now to say something how it was with us when very young. I must say most on my mother's account, being the most under her care in the house while my father was caring for us out of doors. I cannot understand that they meddled much with each other's business, for they well knew that they need not bid one another do their best, though I know they used to advise one with another in things of moment; for I have heard my father say, if ever he did anything that my mother advised him not to do, it proved not well.

My mother had us all to teach most of the reading and writing that we got, though we were twelve in number—Mary, Elizabeth, Rachel, Ann, Rebecca, Sarah, John, William, Martha, Hannah, Isaac, and Lydia. Ann died when I was so young I cannot remember her. Martha died in the small-pox when she was nearly nine. She was much to be remembered, for her qualifications were more than common for her age. Her look was very pleasant, though innocent; and I think I never saw any one quicker, if so quick, at work or learning. Her words and behaviour in her illness are not to be forgot. When she had borne her affliction for many days with patience, she was for some time, to all appearance, so near death that none thought to hear her speak more, when, on a sudden, she revived, and spoke with such pleasure and clearness that, although she told us she was going to part from us and leave this world and go to a place of peace and rest, we yet thought her likely to recover; but her understanding, as well as her words, was so clear, that nothing that was said to her seemed to alter her mind, and the event proved her words true. I seeing nothing but that she was likely now to recover, went into the Garth, where I think I had not been eight minutes before my father came to let me know that, according to her word, she was gone.

The other ten lived to be men and women. If I should say all that my mother did for us, would anyone trust my report? There are many yet alive that have often seen her, and they may say they never saw her like, being in haste neither in words nor works. If any neighbour was not well, she was one of the first in going to visit them, and seldom seemed as if she had need to go away so long as she could do them good. I think she hardly ever left the house to us, except to visit and assist the sick and those in want, or on some religious account; and whatever led her out, I think I may say that, as soon as she thought she had done her duty, she was sure to return to where there was always something for her to do. As to her never seeming to be in haste, I have often thought, as there is a difference in natural tempers, what passions she was naturally inclinable to. She was often saying, " All by nature were children of wrath." She must certainly have been born again, for I cannot understand that I ever saw, or heard, anything done, or said, by her that any way looked like a child of wrath; for in all her behaviour she seemed to love righteousness and hate iniquity. I have often seen, as I may say, her footsteps; and whenever I tread in them, I have been sure to step safe; but there is no hitting them without taking up this daily cross, which, for want of, I have at times missed my way.

It often affects me very much when I think what was done for us in our young years; how we had one favour after another as to the things of this world. I question whether some of us, now, may not have ten times as much as our father ever had, yet we and ours can be in no better situation, on that account, than he and his were. He and his had plenty, and were likely as content as any that may have a hundred times as much as we have now. I say *have*, but should say, are made stewards of, and know not how soon the Lord may call. I see little difference whether we have a greater farm or a lesser, since our Lord never fails every tenant of His who waits on Him to know His will, and is careful to obey Him; and He lets us all know that, though He has given us all life, breath and being, and made us lords over, some a greater, some a lesser farm, it is only for a few days, for a purpose of His own glory, and for our own good if we obey Him. Then He will take it from us or us from it, and give as it may please Him, and who shall say to Him, " What doest Thou ?"

My mother often had to say how God in His love had invited all. Her heart was filled with His love, and she longed to have us all filled with the same love to Him and to one another. Now as her mind was then longing for the good of all, the Established Church of England was in her view, and she would express at times her regard for them, and her hope for them, though they performed some ceremonies in a way she durst not. She knew well that the first step in worship ought to be in silence before Him, that though Heaven is His throne, and the earth is His footstool, yet to that man will He look who is of a broken heart and of a contrite spirit, and who trembles at His word. As she thus waited, she knew she was not to speak or act without faith to believe that what was to be done or said was agreeable to His will, being assured if it was done without faith it was sin. What, she said, gave her the greatest stroke was their manner of sprinkling little children, which she could have dispensed more easily with, had they not, after pretending a child was born in sin and conceived in iniquity, made it a child of Christ, and then had some persons to promise and vow that it should renounce the devil and all his works, with all the sinful lusts of the flesh, and keep God's holy will and commandments all the days of its life. * * * * * * What added to her sorrow was, that after the child was made a Christian, and all the vows made, then the vowers affirm there is no living a day without sin, making the Almighty, who is a God of order, like a God of confusion. * * * * * * But though she thus laboured to promote the spiritual worship, and the laying aside of outward performances, which too many were in the practice of without coming to the life of true religion, yet she had a great regard for all who were in the way she had been brought up in, who were careful to walk agreeably to what they professed. They who believed it their duty to take the bread and wine in remembrance of Christ, she was very careful not to discourage in performing what they believed was their duty; but would endeavour to persuade them to prove all things and hold fast that which is good, and be sure not to act in matters of worship of the Almighty without faith to believe that what was to be done was agreeable to His will. She had sorrow of heart that the priests made it appear to many as though they had power to make the bread and wine more holy than other bread and wine. * * * * * * She reminded us how it was said, " Whether you eat or drink, or whatsoever you do, do all to the glory of God;" and as we thus remember Him when we have bread to break, whether at morning, noon, or evening, for the nourishment of the outward man, He at such times strengtheneth our faith in Him, so that our hearts are thankful for His favours every way, although all silent as to the outward ear. She said some have run into confusion about outward performances until the meek and quiet spirit of love has been so far lost that envy and hatred have got into the heart; and numbers have been killed under pretence of acting for Christ; which all must see is as contrary to Him, and to the Scriptures, as black is to white. * * * * * * Speaking of the Lord's call to us to leave this world, she often cried out, "Put not off making ready for it until a sick bed, for many are taken away, and scarce have time to say, ' Lord, have mercy upon me,' if it was on their mind; and on a sick bed there is enough to do to struggle with the afflictions of the body."

Now, as I say, many things come fresh in my mind, like as if I was with her, and heard her speak, and while I thus see her, I think I never see her laugh. She would say that she never read that Christ was seen to laugh, but often to weep, and that after laughter comes sadness. She was cheerful beyond what could be expected, her situation considered. She advised not to perplex ourselves about the day of judgment as many do; how it may please the Almighty who made us to order us then, but to be content to hear the Preacher in the heart, whose voice is loud to the humble, although the proud and covetous will not hear it. Be content to follow its directions; it is the Lord who made and upholds us, and it is His right to reign and rule in us here, and to do with us as He thinks best hereafter. It is our duty and our interest to entirely cast our care upon Him. If we do, He will take care of us now and for ever.

She had much care over us lest we should do wrong, yet she behaved to us, when we did amiss, as she advised us to do one to another and to all; not to give one bad word for another, but to overcome evil with good. Railing did but add fuel to the fire, she often said, but "a soft answer turneth away wrath." If one said "it is" and another "it is not," that was a fault, because one must be wrong. To say "I will" or "I will not," was not to be in practice, because of the uncertainty of all things here. She oftener talked of the rod than used it. If it had to be used, there was much endeavour to make sensible of the necessity for it, which often had the effect desired without stripes, in giving hope, by submission, of being better for the time to come.

Much endeavour was used that we might take delight in our books, and in doing any little turn, if but innocent, though of little service. While very young, to play a little was allowed, but not on the First-day of the week, which Christians have set apart for worship. And to play for anything, were it but for a pin or a cherry-stone, is better let alone. Childer have pride enough in overdoing one another, without playing for anything (I remember when I would have fought for a cherry-stone), and to play for anything of value, so as to covet what we have not laboured for, was not to be allowed at any rate. Endeavour was used that we might learn to work with as much pleasure as to play, even when we were so young that our work was not worth one farthing, yet thy father and I received many pennies for it. We were to learn to labour justly and truly with our hands to get a living, and to keep them from picking and stealing, and our tongues from evil speaking, and using bad words, that are hard to be rooted out. She often, with sorrow, viewed the wickedness that was committed at the time called Christmas, and other pretended holy days, and said, "What a sad thing it is people should pretend to set days apart to keep holy, and be more wicked then than at other times."

Now I must mention one thing that may, I expect, be called a piece of folly. Before I can remember, my father had built a malt-kiln near to his little tan-house. There was a good pump which supplied his lead-cisterns for steeping his corn, as well as his cisterns for tanning, and all things, to appearance, went on with good success. Although he had no great stock, he could get what money he thought proper to venture in trade. Things looked as though the advance of the income might answer the outlies of an increasing family. But this malt trade was soon overturned, for my mother, as it was her daily care to wait to know what to do and what to leave undone, thought it her duty to advise to let go that profit, though it seemed considerable, and need of it to bring up so great a family. I can remember, although thy father and I were so young that we were not fit to go anywhere with a horse, her saying to our father, "If these lads live, and if this malt-kiln be kept on, they may, likely, be sent to ale-houses with malt; and if they should get a habit of drinking, what will all we can get signify? Let us part with it. I have no fear but Providence will provide for us and them if we do as we ought. Let us be content with the tanning trade." Now much might have been said, and with reason, as, "besides the loss, what will all our well-wishers say when all this cost and labour must be wasted? and, so far as we have tried, things have proved to more advantage than might have been expected; and the conveyance and management of the business have been much commended. They may say, 'There is no regard to the family,' if we undo what we have done." But my mother said, "Need we mind what the world will say? It can say no more of us than it did of Christ; I think it is His will for us to leave it off; and we can but do His will, none can make us afraid; we need not fear what the world can say or do; if He is on our side the world cannot hurt us; if He is against us, the world cannot help us." Now, as I said before, my father believed that what my mother advised had to be done if he intended to do well. So as nothing less than making all things useless for malt-making would do, the drying-place was put into a little dwelling-house; the chamber where the barley was, made a bark-chamber; the lead-cistern was taken to tan leather in; the malt-chamber to lay corn in. Chambers were not then so plentiful among the farmers as they now are, and a very plentiful crop of wheat, and very cheap, the farmers pressed upon my father to take their wheat, as they knew he had a great family, and good lying for it. He bought as much as his chambers would hold, at (or near) two shillings a bushel, exceeding good. This proved well, for, harvest coming on, the weather was so wet that much of the wheat was wasted; and what was got into the barns was so bad it was not fit to use, if better could be had; and, bad as it was, it was sold for seven shillings a bushel. This looked like a favour, for had the chamber not been cleared we should likely have been obliged to live upon very ordinary wheat, as our neighbours did, and pay very dear for it. As it was, we had as good, if not the best I ever knew, and the cheapest; but I cannot understand that things looking like the world's favouring any more lifted up, than its seeming to frown cast down.

Now things took a very sudden turn for the tanning trade, the only visible means for a livelihood for the family. A duty was laid upon leather, and an oath or affirmation obliged to the "entering" of all leather taken out of the pit to dry. The Government (before this) had granted an affirmation, which my father took once or twice, but the more he considered it the worse he liked it. This soon became a close trial. Either the command of Christ must be broken, or they must leave off the tanning trade, or in a little time have all the stock they had taken away by fines for not submitting to the law. What made things seem much harder, the justices and officers seemed to upbraid much that the Government had granted an affirmation at our own request, and for any to refuse deserved no pity. I cannot forget one officer, what a great look and words he had when he came to take away leather to raise money to answer the fines for not swearing. My mother being not far off, and I near her, he in an upbraiding manner directed his speech to her, in a manner as though we would neither obey magistrates nor Christ. "What," says he, "there be but two sacraments, and you deny them both." But a very few words, calmly spoken, with a very innocent look, made him silent, then and for ever, from ever speaking in that way to her. Covetous of gain, he and the then superior, I believe, endeavoured to get what they could, though they seemed to talk fair, and pretended they were obliged by law to do as they did.

Now, being carried before justices time after time, things appeared more and more that it was only for fear of offending the Almighty that they suffered; for the officers several times said before the justices that they believed my father did not all offer to wrong the King, and they did believe some who did swear did wrong the King. Now the case began to affect most of the thinking part, for my father was well thought of both with rich and poor, though many of the justices seemed to talk somewhat rough as though the refusing could be nothing but conceit. Yet Christ, when He gives the command not to swear at all, leaves no room for it in any case: He tells them swearing *had* been lawful and the vow to be performed, but He was come to put an end to the law of outward ceremonies to all that believe on Him; but if He did not put an end to all oaths, He made no alteration on that account, for vain and needless oaths were always contrary to the law; so to argue, "He did not forbid all swearing," is to argue that what He said stands for nothing, and it is true it stands for nothing with all that will not obey Him, for He is only an end of the law for righteousness to them that do obey Him. Now, see, by the officers' confession they did not believe people for swearing; and, as my mother said, "Dare we call the Almighty to be a witness to every worldly concern?"

He will not hold us guiltless if we take His name in vain, and all swearing is in vain, for in this that they will not believe a man though he swears. If to be a false witness was by law as great a fault without an oath as with an oath, there might be a hope of fewer false witnesses ; but as long as Christ's command be broken in swearing, many may say, "Why may we not break it in another thing ?" for this command, "Swear not at all," is as positive as any other command ; and instead of an oath, He bids, "Let your yea be yea, and your nay, nay ; " and if we say more than this "it cometh of evil." Now things set in a clear light, and a subject of the King, careful to pay him his due, willing to obey every ordinance of his for the Lord's sake, that had been careful to maintain his own family and had been helpful to many others, was likely to have all his property taken away by fines. Now the thinking part left persuading him to take the affirmation, as there was in it taking the name of the Almighty in vain ; and many of them used endeavours in speaking and writing to men in power ; and the case and some others similar was represented to some of the greatest men in the nation, while my father and mother were putting their trust in the Almighty, who, they believed, could make a way for deliverance when they could see no way, by the working of His mighty power in the King and in those in authority under him to grant a favour. But before it was brought about there were many things that looked so hard, that had there not been an entire giving up of all, and casting their care upon the Lord alone, who never fails those who trust in Him, they could not have held out the trial. As I said before, things favoured so that there was always enough, yet having had at the beginning but little stock, money was borrowed, which was paid interest for at the rate of six per cent., which was as common as three and a half is now, and as the little they began the world with increased the trade had increased also, so that they still remained in debt ; so that although none, as I can understand, had any fear of losing by them, yet there was something in it which added to the trial. Time after time they continued to fine, and take leather away to answer the fines, till I think there might be one-third of what they might call their own taken from them. This caused some thought of leaving off the trade, while they had something, lest they should come short of paying their just debts : but my mother, having strong confidence in Him who never failed, could not give way to that, so long as they had anything to call their own, because she thought it was not being willing to part with *all* for His sake. Now this trial being over, things answered to satisfaction, I think I may say, in every respect ; and in a few years they had more of the world's wealth than before ; it looked as though there was a confirming of what had often been said, that "All things work together for good to those who love God."

Many opportunities we had wherein we were made sensible of the favours we enjoyed many ways. I may not forget how thankful my mother always was that we all of us had the use of all our members ; and were in a likely way to work for our livings, which she thought the safest situation in this life ; only to have something to be rather helpful than needful.

Now in a few years she found her natural strength begin to fail, but I think I may say her strength in Christ increased, and her voice as strong as ever, and she had a sight that her time would not be long here. She laboured with all her might, time after time, that we might wait on Him who never failed her in time of need, assuring us by what she learned of Him that His strength and His love was such that though He might suffer us for the trial of our faith to go through the fire, the flames should not hurt us; through the water, the waves should not overwhelm us, nor should any be able to pluck us out of His hand, for He never did and never would fail them who put their trust in Him. Now the things come as fresh into my mind as if I had heard her voice; what I can say may not be worth notice to others; but if what I say looks like folly in me, if all who see that folly be filled with that love that filled her heart, they will pity me, and endeavour to help me in what I may be wrong in. * * * *

Thus having hinted how things were with us before thy time, I need not say much how it has been with us since, as thou mayest by looking back see pretty well how it has been with us. I think I may say she was a favourite of Heaven, and to the end of her days she was careful to make good use of the interest she had there for our good, and not for our's only, but many times for all the children of men to the ends of the earth. Now I may say for my own part, Providence has so far answered her request that wherein I have been amiss it has been my own fault.

One thing I may say I have come short of my duty in is this, my not going to week-day meetings when I have let little things hinder. I cannot say that I condemn myself when anything hinders that could not well be helped; but when, upon examination (as I find daily need to examine myself), and to let things have a fair trial, I find that by rising a little sooner, or by being a little later in retiring at night, I might have got to meeting. I should have done this for a very small worldly affair, and therefore cannot help placing judgment upon myself because I have been putting a greater value upon a few worldly things than upon that Power that has made me from the dust of the earth, and upholds this earthly tabernacle of clay by the same Power.

Several copies of John Richardson's letter seem to have been taken, and to have been carefully preserved in different households. The copy preserved at the Low Lights was believed to be a literal one, (although it is probable that the spelling was modernized), and of it, the foregoing abridgement has been made. Nothing has been omitted except some lengthy religious disquisitions, and although some of the sentences have been divided, the language of the writer is always given. The letter seems to have been left unfinished. Another abridgement of it is to be found in the 'Annals of the Cleveland Richardsons,' by George Richardson.

APPENDIX B.

It is stated in the narrative, page 10, that the families of the four elder daughters of Wm. and Elizabeth Richardson,—Mary, Rachel, Rebecca, and Sarah,—appear to be extinct. This is certainly the case with regard to Rachel, whose only grandson was drowned; and to Sarah, whose two daughters died single. It is believed that there are no living descendants of the Pickerings, grand-children of Mary; while as to the descendants of Rebecca there has been a difference of opinion. She was first married to Timothy Chadwick, and of that marriage Elizabeth Waller was the sole surviving child. Rebecca Chadwick was afterwards married to Joseph Gaskin, of Whitby, and there were no children of that marriage—the Ann Gaskin, named in the Annals, being a daughter of Joseph Gaskin's first wife, Ann Chapman, of Whitby, as Joseph Foster has ascertained.

The following abstracts of the respective Wills of Elizabeth Waller and of her mother Rebecca Gaskin, were given to the Author by John Richardson Procter. They both point to there being no descendants, and to the probability that Joan Waller died before her grandmother, and unmarried.

Abstract of the Will of Elizabeth Waller.

Elizabeth Waller, of Whitby, widow, made her Will, 6th month 7th, 1751, leaving all her property to her daughter Joan; in case of Joan's death, to her mother Rebecca, wife of Joseph Gaskin, for her life; and after her death, as follows:—

	£	s.	d.
To the Poor of Quaker's Meeting at Whitby	5	0	0
" " " Stockton	5	0	0
To Ann Lotherington, of Whitby......................	5	0	0
To Newark Hart	5	0	0

The residue to her Executors or the survivors, to be disposed of in such a manner as they think fit. She appointed her said mother, her uncles and aunt,—John Richardson, Wm. Richardson, Isaac Richardson, and Lydia, the wife of Richard Richardson,—to be her Executors.

Abstract of the Will of Rebecca Gaskin.

The Will is dated the 4th day of Sept., 1762, and leaves all her property to be equally divided amongst her three brothers,—John, William, and Isaac Richardson; and her two sisters,—Hannah Fossick, widow, and Lydia, the wife of Richard Richardson.

APPENDIX C.

COPY OF A SAMPLER WORKED BY ISABEL VASIE, AT WHITBY, IN HER
ELEVENTH YEAR. (See page 11.)

Henry Vasie and Mary Mackridge were married the 4th of 2nd month, 1688.
Children :—

Thomas.	Born, 2nd of 2nd month,	1689.
Christfer.	,, 12th ,, 2nd ,,	1691.
Sarah.	,, 10th ,, 2nd ,,	1693.
Mary.	,, 28th ,, 2nd ,,	1695.
Lydia.	,, 28th ,, 2nd ,,	1697.
Henry.	,, 11th ,, 1st ,,	1699.
Margery.	,, 18th ,, 6th ,,	1700.
Richard.	,, 21st ,, 6th ,,	1702.
Isbell.	,, 28th ,, 5th ,,	1704.

Worked by Isbell Vasie, 2nd month, 1715.

Mary, the wife of Henry Vasie, was buried at Whitby, the 8th of 6th month, 1704.

CHILDREN OF HENRY VASIE LIVING, WHEN, ON THE 15TH DAY OF MAY, 1726, BEING
SICK AND INFIRM OF BODY, HE MADE HIS WILL :—

Thomas Vasie.	Mary Vasie.
Ann Campion, widow.	Lydia Vasie.
Sarah Cockerill, widow.	Margery Vasie.
Richard Vasie, Master of his father's ship, " Henry."	Isabel Vasie.

S. Cockerill, and Mary and Lydia Vasie were the Executrices; and John Walker,
Jarvas Coates, and William Wilson, Trustees.

APPENDIX D.

✦

Isabel Richardson to ——————.

> "Whitby, 12th mo. 18th, 174—.
> (The last figure is wanting in the manuscript.)

"Dear Friend,

"I am very sorry for thy disorder, and shall be glad to do thee all the good that is in my power; but I hope thou knows that all power, both in heaven and upon earth, is committed unto Him that saith, 'Look unto me, all ye ends of the earth, and be ye saved.' Therefore, as I am made sensible of those things, I do dearly entreat thee to endeavour, as much as in thee lieth, to be still: for God will ever give a blessing to such, which maketh truly rich, and adds no sorrow; for as men and women come to labour truly for this stillness, they please God, and are made in a good degree co-workers with the Spirit of Truth, which shall lead into all truth, and so by this thou shalt know the voice of Him that sayeth, 'Be still, and know that I am God,' from all other voices; and thou shalt know him to manifest his great power so in thee, that it shall be above every power that may be presented, if thou do but keep in obedience to this light, life, and call, that is in thee. For he doeth not only call from the ends of the earth, but out of every thing that is reproveable, or that would in any measure separate us from him: for his children are made to know, many times, he delights to have them near him; and not only to pray for his kingdom to come, and his will to be done, but he is answering their petitions and requests, so that at times they are ready to say, like some of old, that their sitting is certainly in heavenly places in Christ Jesus, and their fellowship is with the Father, Son, and Holy Ghost. So here is great encouragement, not only to look unto the Lord, but to have our whole dependence upon him. For he never required any thing of either man or woman, if they were but obedient thereto, but he gave power to perform it.

"So now, dear friend, I shall conclude with a persuasion that thou still hath a little hope, which, if rightly minded, it will be as an anchor to thy soul. But I entreat thee be very watchful, lest the enemy, which envies all our happiness, should transform himself in any visible object, and so cause thee to lose thy hope. For there is no true nor saving hope which is visible, and therefore did the servant of the Lord Jesus declare, saying, 'Therefore do we, with patience, wait for it.' And so, by patient

2 L

continuance in well-doing, the new man, Christ Jesus, will become to thee thy 'hope of glory,' which will cause thee to triumph over all—both his and thy enemies.

"And now, being drawn much farther than I expected, I dearly bid thee farewell in the unchangeable truth.

"ISABEL RICHARDSON.

"My husband desires his love to thee, and I request a few lines from thee the first opportunity, and hope shall remain thy faithful friend."

'*Annals of the Richardsons*, p. 88.

"New Tan House, 4th mo. 2nd, 1764.

"LOVING SON AND DAUGHTER,

"These may inform you we are all well, through mercy. I received a letter from thy father last Third-day, and he was well, and designed to be at Tottenham last Fourth-day, and so proceed homeward. Sister Rebekah is well. I desire to know how you do, and how the little one (Margaret) grows. I think to send the lead bowls the first opportunity. So conclude with love to you, and brother and sister Stead and family.

"From your loving and affectionate mother,

"ISABEL RICHARDSON.

"All your brothers and sisters have their love to you. I sent you a bottle of wine, which I hope came safe."

Addressed to John Richardson, at Seghill, East New Houses, to be left at Thomas Atley's, Newcastle.

'*Annals of the Richardsons*,' p. 84.

"20th of 9th month, 1761.

"The day when King George the Third was crowned, expecting greater suffering for not complying with (the practice) of my neighbours in illuminating windows and rejoicing, as they called it, than I had ever done before; which was by having my windows broken three times. The first time was the worst—the second time was less than the first—and this time less than the second. But as the cry was, ' They will break and tear all to pieces where they will not light candles,' I was brought very low in my mind, and for some time did not know what to do; and temptations crowded in apace; and it was as if it had been said to me, ' They, it may be, will set the houses on fire,' which (thought) took great hold, because my son Henry's flax-shops and heckling-chamber joined the street, where the rude creatures used to run with squibs and burning tar-barrels. But help then began to arise in my mind, and led me to remember who gave me those houses (in the town of Whitby), and that if he pleased to take or suffer them to be taken from me in that way, it was his right. Then came in another closer trial than this last, which was, whether I should be there at that time or not. It rose in my mind that (our Lord) said, ' If the good man of the house had known what time the thief would come, he would have watched and not suffer his house to be broken.' So then I thought I might go and make my appearance. Then another temptation arose, which was, that likely they would throw stones at me, and do me much damage, or kill me. This temptation was hardest of all. Then I looked at the testimony I had borne, and I was comforted, and my heart was deeply engaged in inward supplication to the Lord, mentally praying that He would be pleased to strengthen my love to him, that I might be worthy of his providence, which I believed to be sufficient in every state and condition. I was ready to say, ' Now I am willing to suffer, or to be as thou wouldst have me to be, only be thou with me.' In a little more time of waiting and stillness, which was pleasant, my heart was filled with love inexpressible, and it was as if One with great authority had said,—' They shall not hurt thee.'

"It was verified: the rulers of the town took more care to keep the rabble in subjection than they ever had done before; and my neighbours, who aforetime had been ready to laugh at me, and count light of my suffering, showed me kindness, and assisted in dispersing the rude people; so, through the goodness of Providence, I suffered little or no damage: hard things were made easy to me, and therefore I earnestly desire that all who read these few lines may mind the heavenly gift in themselves, which, if truly waited for, will arise in the brightness of its own glory, in its own dwelling-place, to the scattering and dispersing all enemies, and in the room thereof will fill with joy and comfort, to the praise of Him that is worthy now and for ever.   I. R."

' Annals of the Richardsons,' p. 85.

Isaac Richardson, of Whitby, to John Richardson, of the Low Lights.

" New Tan House, 2 mo. 15th, 1778.

"Dear son and daughter,

        " It is in my mind to give you some account of our dear child and daughter Elizabeth (Chapman), who departed this life on the 14th inst., in the evening, near nine o'clock. We were favoured with her company seven weeks and some days at our house, where she innocently left her body. When she came to our house, she had strength to walk and ride a little; but as she found herself grow weaker, she was more desirous to have her mind fastened on the Lord; and she said she thought she was come here to have her mind from her family. There were many friends and neighbours came to visit her; some of them were deeply concerned for her, and spoke to her about mending, and she told me she thought it hurt her; for when she had the fever, she was very desirous to mend; but it was not so now, for she had rather die. * * * * I could not well forbear saying to her mother, ' What a wonder is this! that she, being so filled with tender love to her family, should be so weaned from outward things; and that the whole employment of her mind was so much inward, I thought as much so as any I had ever known.'

"She one time said, 'Pride! it must come down, it must come down.' At another time, she inclined to say something to her eldest daughter, when none else were present; and she told me afterwards, that she had advised her to plainness, and never to dress herself like some who (indulged) in superfluous dress.

"When she was a little free from pain, she was very lovingly concerned for the good of all that came into her mind. * * * *

"On the morning of the sixth-day of the week, her nurse came to our bedside, and said she was grown worse, and that she desired her father would get up. We quickly rose, and went to her bedside, and found her (to appearance) just going. She put out both her hands, and I kept one of them upon my knee some hours; and a very hard and painful day it was to her; but her patience was remarkable in that day of great trial, which was the hardest day she ever had. Next day, she was pretty easy and pleasant, and had a favourable night.

"On First-day morning, on her mother asking how she did, she enquired how her father was, knowing that he was unwell the night before. On her mother saying, 'He is better,' she said, 'I shall be better too.' About noon she grew worse, but was sensible to the last. She once said, 'The pains of death are hard to bear; if I had been one of the worst, I think it could not have been harder.' I said, 'I would not have thee to say so; I think the best of people are tried the most.' And the words of afflicted Job came quickly into my mind, when he said, 'Behold, I go forward, and he is not there; and backward, and I cannot perceive him: on the left hand, where he doth work; but I cannot behold him—he hideth himself on the right hand, that I cannot see him; but he knoweth the way that I take, and when he hath tried me, I shall come forth as gold.' I asked her if she heard? she said, 'Yes, father;' and I think, from that time, to the last words she spoke, there appeared a good degree of faith and patience.

"When she was near to draw her last breath, her sister Mary asked her what they could do for her. She lovingly answered, 'Nothing, but pray for me.' She quickly added, being the last words she spoke, 'The Lord can do all.'

"She died on the evening of First-day, and was buried on the Fourth-day following. Her remains were accompanied to the grave by many friends and neighbours. It was a fine day, and, I believe, many were awfully affected, and waited in abundance of love and patience. There was not much said by way of testimony; but I believe the opportunity will be remembered for good. * * * *

"I now conclude in dear love, thy mother, and son, and thy brother Ingram, to you and yours.

"P.S. Please give our love to Samuel Campion and wife."

'Annals of the Richardsons,' p. 80.

ISAAC AND ISABEL RICHARDSON, OF WHITBY, TO JOHN AND MARGARET RICHARDSON
OF THE LOW LIGHTS,

"20th of 4th mo., 1774.

"DEAR SON AND DAUGHTER (John and Margaret Richardson),

"Just now we have heard that yours and our dear child, Isabel, was buried last First-day, the sorrow for which did deeply affect our minds; and I unwarily struck my hand upon my knee, and said in my mind, 'Lord, hold thy hand,' looking directly at the removal of so many of our dear offspring of late, and having spared us for so many years. This I soon saw to be too rash of me. But oh! how ready is He (the Father of Mercies) to pass by and accept our innocency, if it is but there; and it was as if spoken by a voice good to hear, 'May not I take to myself the most pleasant flowers which I have planted?' Then was my spirit revived and sweetened, and ready to say, 'Thy will be done. Amen. Amen.' We were just come from meeting when we were told the sorrowful news; and for great part of the time we were at the meeting, my mind was deepened with a sorrow unknown: but from the sense I had, my desire was strong to be preserved from repining, by a living hope to be as an anchor to the mind, the attainment of which is not to be found but by patiently waiting upon an ever mindful Giver to them who prefer His presence before their chiefest joy, and who do not turn from him out of the silent before he scatters his and our enemies. We all know that if our obedience be but enough in the motion of His power, they must flee away. * * *

"Though I do not write to you often, (yet) you and yours are near our lives, with desires for your preservation and good every way.

"From your affectionate father and mother,

"ISAAC AND ISABEL RICHARDSON."

'Annals of the Richardsons,' p. 88.

[In John Richardson's answer to this letter, which is full of touching details of the long illness of this child, he says:—"Although her race was short, I believe she answered the end of her having a being here. I think I may safely say she lived in innocency, died in love, and her memorial is sweet in the minds of those who best knew her." The full letter is given in the 'Annals of the Richardsons,' p. 75.]

ISABEL RICHARDSON'S TESTIMONY CONCERNING HER DEAR HUSBAND ISAAC RICHARDSON.

(Copied from a manuscript lent to the Author by J. R. PROCTER.)

It is in my mind to give some account of my dear deceased husband, the fore part of which I have had chiefly from his own mouth. He was born at Ayton, near Stokesley, in Yorkshire, in the year 1707; his parents were reputable Friends, whose names were Wm. and Elizabeth Richardson. His father, being a tanner, had distress made upon his goods, until he was much reduced, because, for conscience sake, he could not swear to his entries.   His mother was a worthy religious Friend, and was called into the work of the ministry, and her testimony was living and of good service, her life and conversation recommending what she preached; and though they never had much of this world, yet Providence blessed their endeavours, so that they were enabled to bring up a large family, and entertain public Friends who travelled in the Truth's service.   As to their children, they were careful to educate them in a Godly conversation, in frequent reading the Holy Scriptures, as also in plainness of speech, behaviour, and apparel; and their labour was not in vain, although my dear husband was but about eleven years of age when his mother died, and he of a lively disposition, yet the good advice which he had received from her remained with him, often springing up in his mind (a Divine visitation attending it) to the softening of his heart, which preserved him, in a good degree, from evil. While he was an apprentice at Stockton, when his mind was drawn into retirement, he had many openings into Divine mysteries, and, as he gave up to what the Almighty made manifest, they have been fulfilled in their season. While he continued at the above place, he associated himself with some young men of the same profession with himself, and, so long as their lives and conversation were innocent, he liked their company; but as they grew up, some of them began to incline to go to public-houses, which became a great trouble to him, and a concern came upon his mind to speak to them; so he took an opportunity when they were all together, and, in a childlike manner, addressed them to the following purport:—"Lads, we are betwixt lads and men, and betwixt winning and losing; if we continue in this course of life, it will be our own ruin;" which words had so much reach over them, at that time they made no reply; but they, not forsaking their course of life, he refrained their company (the above young men, most of them, proved dishonourable).   About the twenty-fourth year of his age he and I joined in marriage, and settled near Whitby.   About the twenty-eighth year of his age he was called to the work of the ministry, but, being of a backward disposition, it became a great cross to him to give up to what the Lord required of him, but, as he kept under the baptizing power, he was made willing to yield to the Divine requirings; his testimony, as I well remember, was living, and well received by sensible Friends; and, as he persevered in the way of his duty, he grew in the knowledge of Divine mysteries.   He visited, at sundry times, the meetings of Friends in some of the southern, northern, and western counties, as also our own county, always being careful to have the concurrence and certificate of his own Monthly Meeting: all which journeys, I believe, he was enabled to perform, in a good degree, to the satisfaction of Friends and the peace of his own mind.   To return a little to his conduct in the world, he was, most of his time since we were joined together, of a weakly constitution, but careful and industrious according to his ability; and very careful to keep all his concerns within the bounds and limits of truth, denying himself all unrighteous gain; and Providence blessed his honest endeavours, so that we were enabled to raise a large family, whom he was careful to instruct in the principles of Christianity, and inure them in industry and necessary care; and, while under our immediate direction, in exemplary plainness in every respect; he enforcing his advice by his example, so that I think I can justly say of him, he was a man fearing God, and hating covetousness. He was very exemplary in attending meetings for worship and discipline, both on First-days and other days of the week, and honestly concerned therein, having experienced a walking in the straight and narrow way. He was often favoured with a clear discerning of the various states of the people; where he found honesty, sincerity, and simplicity, he had a fatherly care for such, but where he discovered unsoundness of principle (though under a high profession) or undue liberty in practice, he found it his duty to deal in great plainness with such.

It pleased the Almighty to remove him by a short illness, but, through mercy, his understanding was clear so long as he had strength to speak. One day, his daughter Mary being by him, he expressed himself to the following purport:—"As to life or death, I know not, but I find my mind quite easy as to my own state, and am resigned; I desire nothing more but patience, and an easy passage." He expressed something of the heavy exercise he had had, on account of some of the members of our particular Monthly Meeting; he said his tongue was not able to express it, and desired her and her husband might be careful while they lived not to strengthen the hands of those that were against the Truth. Now though his removal be my inexpressible loss, I desire to be resigned to the Divine will, as I firmly believe he is now centred in that mansion of rest and peace, "where the wicked cease from troubling, and the weary are at rest." He departed this life, the 10th; and was decently interred in Friends' Burial-ground, near Whitby, the 13th of the 9th month, 1780. A large company of Friends and neighbours attending his funeral, I thought it was a solemn opportunity, which I hope will not be soon forgot by some. He died in the seventy-third year of his age; a minister forty-four years.

The six older children of Isaac and Isabel Richardson were born at Bog Hall. Probably on account of this increasing family they removed about 1774 to a place called "New Tan House." Whether Isaac Richardson built this house, where it was situated, or whether it still exists, are matters quite unknown to the Author.

APPENDIX E.

———◆———

From an article in Burke's ' Landed Gentry,' we learn that the registers and rolls of Whitby Abbey prove this family to have lived at Yburn Dale, near Whitby, in very early times. In 1381, Roger and John Chapman were "prosecuted and imprisoned by the Abbot of Whitby for maintaining their just rights and privileges, but were soon set at liberty by the Abbot, without paying any fees." Many of the descendants of these independent persons were to be found in the ranks of the Parliamentary Army during the Civil War, as we learn from the authority just quoted; and we know from other sources that about the same period of time many of them joined the Society of Friends. Of the complicated genealogy of the Chapmans, a portion (kindly copied for the author by Mrs. Chapman, of Weymouth) is given below. The Solomon Chapman, there mentioned, was, by his marriage with Ann Linskill, the father of Ingram Chapman, who married Elizabeth Richardson; and Ingram, the only son of the last-mentioned marriage, became the husband of Jane, the twelfth child of John Chapman and Jane Mellor. Solomon Chapman's brother Abel was three times married: first, to Susanna, daughter of George Lotherington; secondly, to Elizabeth, daughter of John Walker, and, thirdly, to Hannah, daughter of William Gaskin:—all these being well-known Whitby people, bearing names met with from time to time in these Records. The descendants of Abel Chapman have intermarried with more important Quaker families,—the Reynolds, Gurneys, and Barclays. The ' Monthly Chronicle of North Country Lore and Legend' (Walter Scott) contains in its September number an interesting article on "William Chapman, Engineer and Inventor," a member of the Whitby family, who settled in Newcastle at the end of the last century, and whose memory well deserves to be revived in that town, so famous for its great engineers.

Robert Chapman, d. 1607: (his son) John Chapman, d. 1614; (his son) Robert Chapman, d. 1685; (his sons)—(1) John, (2) James, (3) Robert, (4) Ingram, (5) *William*.

William Chapman's sons were (1) Ingram, (2) *Solomon*, (3) Isaiah, (4) *Abel*, (5) Aaron, (6) Benjamin.

Abel Chapman, b. 1694, d. 1777. His sons were *John* and Abel.

John Chapman, b. May 27th, 1732; m. January 9th, 1755, Jane Mellor. Their children were—(1) Abel, (2) John, (3) William, (4) Robert [d. aged 103 years], (5) Henry, (6) Thomas, (7) Jonathan, (8) Edward, (9) Aaron [M.P. for Whitby many years], (10) Benjamin, (11) Elizabeth, (12) *Jane*.

APPENDIX F.

THE PRIESTMANS OF THORNTON, NEAR PICKERING.

OF this family, first mentioned on page 21, the following particulars have been most kindly furnished to the Author. They are copied from a Family Tree:—

"John Priestman, born at Thornton, 1647. He married Elizabeth Smithson, who died in 1708, leaving no children. In 1707 he married Anna Story; she left a son, named John.

"John Priestman, born 27th of 11th mo., 1707,8. He was apprenticed to William Richardson of Ayton, in Cleveland, where he learned the tanning business. He planted the tan-yard at Thornton, where it now is (1844), and continued to live in his father's house. He married Ann Marshall of Aisleby, 1733, by whom he had seven sons and one daughter. She died after the birth of her youngest son, 29th of 7th mo., 1759. Children:— 1. John died, an infant. 2. Thomas, born, 1736. Settled in York as a tanner. Married Sarah Procter of Clifford, near Tadcaster. John Woolman died at his house, 1772. He died in 1811. 3. John, born, 24th of 2nd mo., 1739. Succeeded his father at Thornton. He married Barbara Procter, 1764. He died at Thornton. His widow removed to Pontefract, where she died. 4. Hannah, born, 1741. Married Henry Richardson of Whitby. 5. Henry died, aged six years. 6. David, born, 16th of 3rd mo., 1749. Married Elizabeth Taylor, who was an approved minister, and the mother of his children. After her decease he married Elizabeth Rowntree. 7. Henry. Married Ann Dale. 8. Jonathan, born, 11th of 7th mo. Died, unmarried, in America."

The "William Richardson of Ayton, in Cleveland," from whom the second John Priestman acquired his knowledge of tanning, is the person described in the second chapter. His grandson, Henry, we see by this extract from the Priestman Family Tree, and in our Fourth Chapter, married Hannah, the only daughter of the same John Priestman, and of that marriage the heroines of this book were the children. The marriage of John Priestman's two elder sons—of Thomas, who lived at Marygate, York, and of John, who succeeded his father at Thornton, to the two daughters of Emmanuel Procter of Clifford—have been mentioned at pages 73 and 214. The descendants of these marriages, especially of that of John Priestman and Barbara Procter are very numerous, and some of them are influential people in the neighbourhood of Hull and of Bradford. The sons and daughters of the younger brother, David Priestman, who settled at Malton, are often mentioned in this narrative. They were the life-long friends of the heroines, and to one of the sons, Jonathan Priestman of Newcastle (whose portrait is in the book), the letters in Chapter XII. were addressed,

APPENDIX G.

———◆———

A Whitby Household.

On page 28 it is stated, that in 1784 some women Friends met together to raise funds for the establishment of a Girl's Boarding School at York. These proprietors, far from expecting dividends, seem generally to have made up amongst themselves the deficiency which the balance-sheet at the end of the year too often showed. The nine shareholders were Esther Tuke, Mary Proud, Tabitha Middleton, Ann North, Sarah Grubb, Sarah Priestman, Martha Routh, Sarah Swanwick, and Elizabeth Hoyland. All these names should be held in honour, and many are well known to us; but the second name on the list has an especial charm for lovers of Whitby, and draws us back to an old house by the harbour in the middle of the eighteenth century. Can this be the same Mary Proud, who, when acting as housekeeper to the good Whitby shipowners, John and Henry Walker (see page 65), was wont to place a candle on a table in a quiet corner for their young apprentice James Cook, " that he might read and write by himself, while the other apprentices were engaged in idle talk or trifling amusements"? (Miss Linskill's "Pictures from Whitby," ' Good Words,' 1885). We can almost see the gentle Friend in her neat dress, caring for the quiet of the studious boy in the long winter evenings, with a watchful kindness which he never forgot; and it is a pleasant thought that in her later years she still took interest in young people, and was able to promote the education of the girls of her own Society, both at York and at Ackworth.

John Walker was one of the trustees appointed under Henry Vasie's will (p. 256). He was the intimate friend of Isaac Richardson, and his daughter was married to Abel Chapman (p. 264). His son, John Walker, settled in North Shields, acquired property in the place, and was one of the earliest inhabitants of Dockwray Square (p. 115). The Low Lights House and Tannery, Walker Place, and other parts of North Shields, were built upon his land. His daughter Mary, whose unusual mental endowments have been described (p. 215), became the wife of Benjamin Flounders.

APPENDIX II.

The Richardsons and Maysons of Hull.

The Richardsons of Hull (p. 47) are proved to have lived in that town since the time of Queen Elizabeth. The Rev. Valentine Mayson came from Warwickshire to Yorkshire in the succeeding reign. The two families seem to have been connected by repeated intermarriages, and to have produced some remarkable persons. The sharp contrast presented by the lives of those who became Friends, and endured persecution and imprisonment, and of others who, as clergymen of the Church of England, obtained high preferment, might well tempt a biographer. The fame of the author of 'Elfrida' sheds a certain distinction on the Mayson family, although that fame may have waned in our day. In another walk of life was the Hull merchant, Robert Mayson, of Welton, who, expelled from the office of Alderman by James the Second, reinstated by popular acclamation on that monarch's fall, once Sheriff of the town, and three times chosen to be its Mayor, must have been a man of mark. The Richardsons were in less public positions. The Thomas Richardson who joined Friends is generally said to have been, like his predecessors, a Merchant and Master Mariner, who carved the figure-heads of his ships, and painted family coats of arms for amusement; but another account says:—
"Thomas Richardson was by trade a carver and escutcheon painter: when convinced of Friends' principles, he had a new employment to seek, and commenced Maltster" (!) His son, the fifth Thomas Richardson of Hull, left that town for Whitby. He was first married to Mary Peacock of the county of Durham, and afterwards to Elizabeth Dickenson of Whitby, whose father, Roger Dickenson, had been in business at Robin Hood's Bay, and issued his own tokens. One still existing is described as being of brass, and heart-shaped, "its obverse bears in the field two archers, one of whom is in the act of fitting an arrow to his bow, the circumscription being 'ROGER DICKENSON'; reverse, 'OF ROBIN HOOD BAY'; and in the field, 'HIS HALFPENNY—1669.' "

Soon after his second marriage Thomas Richardson died at Whitby, and his children were brought up in that town by his brother Richard (p. 47). The son, Thomas, settled in Sunderland and married Frances Haswell, whose connection with Tinkler's Hill and Benfield Side, a part of Durham to which some of her descendants returned, must not tempt us further. The daughter married John Dearman, a London merchant. The descendants of both marriages are very numerous. See 'Smith of Doncaster and connected Families.' From that book the description of the token and other details are taken.

APPENDIX I.

***

The Peases of Fishlake, Yorkshire.

This family is traced back to the time of King Henry the Eighth, when Edward Pease who was "seized of lands" in the parish of Fishlake on the Don, near Doncaster, died intestate. His great-great-grandson, Joseph Pease, lived at Shafton, in the parish of Felkirk, a village between Barnsley and Pontefract, where he died in 1719. By his marriage with Ann Coldwell he was the father of Edward Pease, who, in spite of the opposition of his family, joined the Society of Friends, and who, coming as a stranger to Darlington, so soon won the esteem of his neighbours (see p. 48). The son of this good man married Mary Richardson, whose father was one of the Hull family spoken of in Appendix H, and whose mother was the youngest daughter of William and Elizabeth Richardson of Ayton. The subsequent history of the Pease family is too well known to need to be dwelt upon here.

In our own day, the grandsons and great-grandsons of the second Edward Pease, of Darlington, the "Father of Railways," have shown that they, like their ancestors, have the courage of their opinions, and follow, unflinchingly, the course of conduct which they have conscientiously adopted, whether that course may lead them to stand on the popular or on the unpopular side. Of Joseph, the younger son of Joseph Pease and Mary Richardson, it has been said (p. 49) that his extended sympathies and philanthropic work have been too much forgotten. His descendants, if they occupy less prominent positions in life than those of his elder brother, have yet done their share in the work of the world. His son, John Beaumont Pease, was for many years the honoured Chairman of the Darlington Board of Guardians, a post in which he was succeeded by his son Edwin Lucas Pease, whose sudden death while his fellow-townsmen were voting for him as their County Councillor, cut short a career of great usefulness and promise. Elizabeth, the only daughter of Joseph Pease, is happily still with us. The widow of a man of varied and brilliant gifts, Professor Nichol, of Glasgow Observatory, Mrs. Nichol has been true during her long life to the causes for which her father laboured.

APPENDIX J.

———◆———

Richardson, Overend and Gurney (p. 49).

In the materials collected by Joseph Foster for the Richardson Pedigree (never printed) the following paragraph occurs:—

The Origin of Overend, Gurney & Co.

"It was in Norwich that arose the world-famous firm of Overend & Co. The firm was a direct offshoot of the Norwich Bank established by Mr. Henry Gurney in 1770. One evening, whilst discussing the interesting subject of bill broking, Mr. John Overend, an enterprising young man, clerk to Mr. Joseph Smith, of Norwich, said, 'Why not establish a house solely devoted to the trade in bills?' The suggestion was favourably entertained on all sides, and the matter led to negotiations between the proprietors of the Norwich Bank and the leading merchants of the place. Mr. Joseph Smith declined to connect himself with the proposed business, but offered to give his advice and assistance; and it was ultimately determined to put forward three young men as founders of the firm—*viz.*, Mr. John Overend, Mr. Samuel Gurney, and Mr. Thomas Richardson, a clerk in the banking house of Messrs. Smith, Wright & Gray, afterwards Esdaile & Co. These three young men, all clerks at the time, laid the basis of one of the most gigantic financial establishments of modern days. The firm was brought forward under the title of Richardson, Overend & Co., but as Mr. Richardson soon retired, the house commenced trading as Overend & Co., which name it retained, although Mr. Overend died not long after, leaving Mr. Samuel Gurney sole representative of the firm."

There are, unfortunately, no dates in this paragraph, but as John Overend was born in 1769, and Thomas Richardson in 1771, and they are spoken of as young men, we may infer that the firm was started in the last century. Overend (a Yorkshireman like Thomas Richardson) was married at Ayton to his partner's sister Martha in 1809, but she survived her marriage for little more than a year. Overend himself died in 1832. Thomas Richardson had retired from the business before that time. The following account of the commencement of the firm differs but slightly from Joseph Foster's. It is from a great-nephew of Thomas Richardson:—

"John Overend was the inventor of the plan of charging one commission on bills. He told John Gurney of his new idea, who approved of it, and Overend left the banking house of Smith and Holt, and began business as a 'Discount and Bill Broker' on this one commission system, John Gurney supporting him. Overend induced Thomas Richardson, who was then a clerk in Smith, Wright & Gray's Bank, to join him in this enterprise, and the rapid success which followed induced John Gurney to send his young son Samuel to enter the concern. Thomas Richardson retired from business when not much past middle life."

APPENDIX K.

JOHN RICHARDSON'S FARM (p. 63).

THE name of the farm taken by John Richardson in 1760 was Seghill East New Houses. The house where he lived is still standing, but is now used as a stable. The boundary of the district of the Cramlington Local Board, of which John Richardson's great-grandson, Henry Richardson of Backworth, is Chairman, skirts the farm. Henry Richardson has recently been chosen to represent the Backworth Division of Northumberland on the County Council, and also as Chairman of the Tynemouth Board of Guardians (see p. 244).

THE LOW LIGHTS TANNERY (p. 65).

THE details in Chapter IX. respecting John Richardson's removal from Seghill to the Pew Dene, of his arrangements made with John Walker for the land, and of the surroundings of the place when he first built his house and planted his tan-yard were dictated to the author by John Richardson Procter. For details of the after-life of the family, and for George Richardson's interesting sketch of the daily life and character of his father, the 'Annals of the Cleveland Richardsons' may be referred to. One paragraph, which brings before us the simplicity of country life in England a hundred years ago, shall here be given:—

"Having for many years endeavoured to walk in the ordinances and commandments of the Lord with much innocency, and being often deeply concerned for the spiritual improvement of those around him, he received larger measures of divine grace, and of the gifts of the Spirit, and was called to the work of the ministry of the gospel of life and salvation through our Lord Jesus Christ. He had long taken much delight in reading the Holy Scriptures; often when sitting in the kitchen amongst his children and servants, would he turn to his Bible, and read audibly for a considerable time together in the precious volume—and I do believe the effect was very salutary on the minds of his household."

'Annals of the Richardsons,' p. 51.

In Isaac Richardson's letter to an uncle, dated "Newcastle, 4 mo. 5, 1800," after speaking of the death of his father, and of the large company who attended the funeral (p. 70), he says, "We of his family shall feel, at times, the loss of his advice and of his fatherly care over us, but the change is doubtless a blessing to him. He looked forward to it with cheerfulness and earnest desire."

The following paragraph appeared in a newspaper, the 'Newcastle Advertiser,' of 4 mo. 5, 1800:—

"Died on Saturday last, advanced in years, at the Pew Dean Tannery, Low Lights, near North Shields, Mr. John Richardson, tanner. He was one of the people called Quakers, and maintained through life the strictest integrity, which, combined with true meekness and industry, gained him the esteem of all who knew him."

The following minute, by way of testimony, was issued by the Monthly Meeting of Newcastle:—

"John Richardson, of the Low Lights, near North Shields, in the county of Northumberland, departed this life on the 29th of the 3rd month, 1800, and his remains were interred on the 2nd of the 4th month, aged near 67 years: a minister upwards of 14 years.

"The memory of this our dear deceased friend feels precious to the minds of many of his survivors. His humble, upright, and exemplary conduct endeared him to all ranks.

"In ministry, his communications were acceptable, being often delivered in great tenderness, and accompanied with the savour of truth. In the discipline of the Church, he promoted the exercise of the rules established amongst us with firmness and impartiality, yet with much Christian tenderness.

"In his last illness, with which he was confined for several weeks, the expressions which dropped from him evidenced a mind resigned to the Divine disposal, and prepared for a final change; yet fully sensible that it was not for any good works of his, but through Divine mercy and redeeming love, that he felt his mind sweetly replenished with the living presence and love of God, so as to remove all fear of death."

'Annals of the Richardsons,' p. 59.

APPENDIX L.

The Procters of Clifford, near Tadcaster (pp. 72–213).

To the future biographer of this family must be left the task of tracing its connection with the "Mr. Procter, of Shipley," to whose son Sir Walter Calverley stood godfather in 1708, and who is mentioned in that gentleman's "Note Book" as dining with him in company with the Fairfaxes and Vavasours of that part of Yorkshire; with the Prebend of Ripon, who was Charles the First's Chaplain; and with Sir Stephen Procter, of Fountains Hall. There is a curious description of this mansion in the Harleian MSS. (No. 6853, folio 451), quoted in an old Guide to Ripon. Not a word is said of the beautiful Abbey, whose "Scite" is offered for sale, but much of the "very beautyful House newely built, the like whereof for bewty and good contrivinge is not in the North," of "Fishe Ponds inclosed in a wall," of orchards "well furnyshed with deinty fruits," and of "ripe and goodly grapes hanging and growing upon a high rock," of "Granges and farms," and of "Milnes and Garners, Royalties and Libertyes," formerly belonging to the Abbey. The whole is offered for sale for speedy payment, and the "Incombrances with which the owner hath clogged it" are mentioned. There is no date to the paper, but as the property had changed hands in 1627, it must have been written before that date. From the fact of the names of Thomas and of Stephen occurring in both families, it would appear probable that there was a connection between the Procters of Clifford and of Fountains Hall. But such matters are only the curiosities of genealogy. No family could have a more worthy ancestor than the old soldier of the Commonwealth, who deliberately chose to be a sufferer, rather than to take any part in persecution.

Willington Mill on the Tyne (pp. 72–185).

The original firm was Brown, Unthank and Procter. The order in which the names stand is surprising, as William Brown was much the younger man of the three; but it is supposed that he alone of the partners had any practical knowledge of milling. Of the other partners, Joseph Unthank brought his greater age and business experience, and Joseph Procter is supposed to have provided the greater part of the capital. Soon after William Brown's marriage with Mary Richardson, of

Lanbarugh, in 1807, he obtained a mill of his own in Shields, and left the firm at Willington. When Joseph Proctor died, in 1813, at the age of forty-one, no provision had been made for such an event, so far as regarded his capital which was embarked in the firm at Willington, and it was in the power of Joseph Unthank and his son George to have claimed the mill as their own. This, however, they were too honest and honourable men to do, and in course of time Joseph Procter's eldest son, born in 1800 (see page 241), succeeded to his father's place in the firm. Upon George Unthank's death, in 1842, Joseph Procter was left as the only partner. About the year 1864 a debt was paid to him which was due to the long defunct firm of Brown, Unthank and Procter. He scrupulously divided it between the representatives of all the partners, some of whom were much surprised to receive money which had been owed to a firm of whose very existence they had never heard.

With regard to the alleged spiritual manifestations in the dwelling-house adjoining the mill at Willington, upon the nature of which the author offers no opinion, those curious in such matters may consult Mrs. Crowe's 'Night Side of Nature,' William Howitt's 'Journal,' 'Visits to Remarkable Places' and 'Local Historians' Table Book,' Tomlinson's 'Guide to Northumberland,' and Part IV. (June, 1887) of the 'Monthly Chronicle' (Walter Scott). This list of authorities might be greatly extended.

THE LATE MR. GEORGE RICHARDSON, BY THE REV. JOHN COLLINGWOOD BRUCE, LL.D.

Reprinted from the 'Northern Daily Express,' Monday, August 11th, 1862.

A PATRIARCH has passed away. Mr. George Richardson, one of the oldest and most respected of the inhabitants of Newcastle, died at his residence in Albion Street, a little before midnight on Saturday last. Mr. Richardson was born at the Low Lights, North Shields, in the year 1773, and was consequently at the time of his decease nearly ninety years of age. He came to Newcastle in the year 1792, when he was apprenticed to the business (that of a grocer and leather-dealer), which he carried on until his sixtieth year. Having succeeded in establishing himself in a shop in the Flesh Market (now called the Cloth Market), he was in 1800 married to Miss Eleanor Watson, who was for nearly half a century the sharer of his joys and sorrows. It is now several years since Mr. Richardson retired from business, and he has devoted the whole of his time and energies ever since to the promotion of plans of public usefulness and private benevolence. Probably a more unselfish man never existed, nor one who was more untiring in his efforts to do good. Benevolence beamed in his countenance, and we have known school-girls look in at his shop-window to enjoy the sight of his happy face. The spring of all his actions was love to that Master of whom that holy book which he made his constant companion told him so much. As was most fitting, the religious body—the Society of Friends—to whom he was attached, obtained the first place in his affections, and his best services. So early had he become imbued with religious feeling, and so early had he come to a decision upon the most momentous of all questions, that he was not more than twenty years of age when he was acknowledged as a minister by the Society. He exercised his office till the close of life. All his utterances were characterised by power and heavenly unction. In prayer he seemed to get within the veil. He was an ardent friend of the Bible Society. So thoroughly did he throw himself into the work of the Newcastle Society that he might with truth be said to be *the* Society. During his long connection with it as depository, upwards of 250,000 copies of the Scriptures passed through his hands. Even this fact gives but a feeble idea of his labours in connection with this great cause. The ordering of the books, their unpacking and re-issuing; the keeping of the complicated accounts, the arrangement of the business of committees, and the formation and visiting of branch associations, are some of the items of duty to which for many years he diligently and cheerfully applied himself. So excellent was his method of business, and so delightful was the spirit which he uniformly breathed, that the members of the Bible Committee always felt it to be a privilege to attend its meetings. He laboured most zealously and most successfully in the cause of Negro Emancipation. The cause of Education early attracted his attention. Before British or National Schools were dreamed of, he was in the habit of spending his evenings in teaching classes of adults to read and write. When in October, 1809, it was resolved, instead of a public illumination in Newcastle on the occasion of King George the Third's entering his jubilee year, to found a school for the purpose of teaching the children of the poor to read the Bible, the scheme had his cordial sympathy and support. For many years he was upon the Committee of the Royal Jubilee Schools, and gave his best efforts to promote their usefulness and efficiency. The fishing village of Cullercoats was the scene of his latest efforts in the cause of education. Here, previously, very little provision was made for the instruction of the young. Mr. Richardson, by dint of great perseverance, patience, and good nature, succeeded in establishing an infant school in the place, and in rearing, by great personal exertion, a fitting building for it. The good results of these efforts have already appeared. The last public speech he ever delivered, was made at the anniversary meeting of this school nearly three years ago. The sympathies of the audience were powerfully drawn forth by the earnest expressions of the venerable speaker, whom they even then feared they would not hear again. To the poor at large he was a constant friend. He was emphatically a friend to those that had no helper. The door of his office was frequently and for hours at a time literally besieged by necessitous persons seeking his help. His bounty was not indiscriminately given. He spared no pains in visiting the poor in their own houses, to ascertain their real state, and to give them that counsel, as well as relief, which they needed. After advancing age rendered such a task positively unsafe, he might be seen clambering the dark and dirty stairs leading to the tenements of the poor —unwilling to forego the luxury of personally doing good. Mr. Richardson was a true friend. He did not fail in kindness and humility to tell his friends of their faults—and seldom, it may be supposed without effect. One of the last labours in which he engaged was the work of exciting the Society of Friends to take more active measures than they had hitherto done in disseminating the Gospel at home and abroad. Very many letters, breathing an earnest missionary spirit, he wrote to such members of the Society as he thought could help forward his object. His efforts have already borne fruit, and his death will probably speak even more powerfully and successfully than his pen did.

For nearly two years and a half Mr. Richardson has been confined to a sick-bed. An attack of bronchitis, brought on by exposure when paying a visit of kindness and charity to a dying youth, was the immediate cause of his long confinement and final illness. During the whole of that time he resigned himself passively into the hands of his Master. Not the slightest symptom of impatience ever escaped him. He wished to be as his Master wished him to be, to do, to suffer whatever was his will. He was too humble a man to speak much of himself; when the subject of the great future was referred to, he briefly but with decision spoke of the strong hope which he enjoyed. His whole life was a testimony to the reality of his faith—the heavenliness of his disposition —and his untiring and complete devotedness to the highest and holiest of all causes. His latter end was peace. "Blessed are the dead which die in the Lord." * * * *

What a changed world this is since Mr. Richardson entered it! And what a different place Newcastle then was! It had probably not twenty thousand inhabitants. Dean Street, Collingwood Street, and Mosley Street, to say nothing of Mr. Grainger's erections, had no existence. Its walls and gates were nearly intact, and there were few houses outside the walls. Fields of corn might be seen waving within the walls. In the Flesh Market, during the whole of the winter, nothing but salted meat was exposed for sale— turnip husbandry not being then sufficiently advanced to supply fat stock all the year round. With few exceptions, none of our numerous literary and religious institutions had any existence. Let the men of the present day emulate and if possible excel their forefathers, for assuredly they have greater advantages and greater responsibilities.

Memorial of the late George Richardson.

Extracted from the Minutes of the Newcastle Bible Society.

The Committee of the Newcastle Bible Society, especially summoned on account of the demise of their venerable and much-revered Vice-President, Mr. George Richardson, desire to state the sense which they entertain of the loss which they and the Society have sustained. They do so, not so much in obedience to the inspired injunction,—"Render, therefore, honour to whom honour is due,"—as from regard to the direction of the Apostle, "Be ye followers of them who, through faith and patience, inherit the promises."

Our late Vice-President was an Israelite indeed, in whom was no guile. He had a simplicity of aim which few of the disciples of the Lord Jesus attain unto. Of most of the world's great ones the saying is true, that they are great only at a distance; of our deceased friend, it may be said, that they who knew him most intimately esteemed him most highly. Few men bore so strongly as he, the impress of the Master's likeness. He seemed not to know what it was to be weary in well-doing. Personal interests were not suffered to intervene between him and the well-being of his fellow-creatures, or the glory of his Divine Master.

From early youth he was a lover of the Bible. Not only were his leisure hours devoted to its study, but such fragments of time as could be, by singular watchfulness, culled even from the busiest period of the day, were spent in the perusal of it, or in meditating upon its contents.

He was one of the originators of this Society, and, to within the last two years, one of its most active promoters. For nearly fifty years he acted as its depository. In the course of this time, about two hundred and fifty thousand copies of the Scriptures passed through his hands. He ordered the books, he unpacked them, and placed them in the depôt. He attended to their sale, and distributed them amongst the branch associations. He kept the accounts of the Society, and carried on its business correspondence. He arranged the annual meetings of many of the district associations, and, whilst health and strength lasted, was never backward in attending them; in truth, during the whole fifty-two years of the existence of the Society, he has been the mainspring of its energy, the chief agent, under God, of its success. It need scarcely be added, that his only reward was the luxury of doing good, and that recompence which he has now gone to receive.

Next to his Saviour, his family, and that religious Society to which he was consciously attached, he loved the Bible Society, and to it, accordingly, he devoted that large measure of interest and effort which it has received from him. As increasing infirmities stole upon him, it was with manifest regret that he retired from the management of its affairs. He did not do so all at once, but only retreated a step at a time as necessity compelled him. At length, when laid upon that sick-bed from which he was not to rise again, he saw that his task was done, and he then calmly and cheerfully resigned his much-loved Bible Society into the hands of his Lord and Master.

The Committee, in contemplating the graces and labours of their departed friend, would adore the goodness of that Saviour, who so graciously imparted to him of His own fulness, and, by His Spirit, enabled him to bring forth so much good fruit.

They would wish also to convey to his bereaved family their warmest sympathies, praying that that void, which has been occasioned by his removal, may be made up by the manifested presence of the Lord himself.

APPENDIX M.

COLERIDGE'S 'FRIEND.'

THE story of this short-lived periodical (see pages 100 and 226) may not be known to all who read this book. The poet Coleridge was constantly urged by his friends to give to the world some of the materials which, from his observation, reading and reflection, he was always storing up, and with which his note-books overflowed. He conceived the idea that it would be best for him to do this by a weekly essay in the form of a newspaper, to be sold for a shilling, and to be published by himself at Grasmere. Coleridge had warm admirers and generous friends; a Member of Parliament franked the first issue, and a newspaper editor inserted advertisements without charge. But a weekly periodical, written at Grasmere and printed at Penrith, places so remote from the world and divided from each other by high mountain passes, was predoomed to failure, and we need not marvel that it expired with its twenty-seventh number, in March, 1810. The list of original subscribers to Coleridge's 'Friend,' which forms the Appendix to a volume of 'Letters of the Lake Poets,' recently printed for private circulation, has an interest in our day. Among the many Bishops and Peers, some (like the Earl of Lonsdale) were personal friends of the Poet. There are some illustrious names— Canning and Romilly, Scott and Jeffrey, Savage Landor, Roscoe of Liverpool, and Strutt of Derby. Edinburgh, Derby, Bristol and the Lake District are well represented on the list, and North Country eyes rest on the names of Sir J. E. Swinburne of Capheaton, "J. Losh, Esq., Jesmond, Newcastle," and "Mr. Maude, Sunnyside, Sunderland." But especially interesting is it to note the number of Friends who wished to have the opportunity of reading weekly the opinions of Coleridge on literature, philosophy and public affairs. There are Braithwaites of Kendal, Lloyds of Birmingham, Backhouses of Darlington, Hulls of Uxbridge, and many names of less note. In London there are David and Robert Barclay, Richard Reynolds, Luke Howard, William Allen, John Corbyn and others, of whom it may safely be asserted that they were not found in the number of those who failed the Poet in his hour of need.

The interest felt in Coleridge by many members of that Society whose literary organ now bears the name of his short-lived periodical, did not cease with his death. His gifted son, the "lile Hartley," of the true-hearted Westmoreland peasants, found gentle sympathy and forbearing love amongst the Friends who lived in that part of

England.   Nor did their welcome fail for the other son of blameless life, Derwent Coleridge, called by Dean Stanley " the greatest master of language in England," when, in the brief holidays of his arduous life as a clergyman and schoolmaster, he returned to look on the hills he loved so well.

APPENDIX N.

NORTH SHIELDS AND SUNDERLAND (PAGE 112).

THE rough sketch of the early history of Tynemouth and of North Shields, given in this chapter, is gathered from local histories and traditions.   By a printer's error, Saint Cuthbert has been made to live in the eleventh instead of the seventh century.   It is only just to say, that although the ruins of Tynemouth Priory were encroached upon by barracks early in the century, and are shaken by ordnance practice in our own day (pp. 113—118, 122), yet it was chiefly by the efforts of the officer in command of the Castle forty years ago that the little oratory was cleansed from gunpowder and restored.

The chapter has been written for the pleasure of recalling and preserving the old Shields and Sunderland stories, which the writer's father and uncle loved to tell.

CHARACTER OF THE LATE SOLOMON CHAPMAN ESQ., WHO DIED AT HIS RESIDENCE, BISHOPWEARMOUTH, AFTER A SHORT ILLNESS, ON WEDNESDAY, 30TH MAY, 1838, AT THE PATRIARCHAL AGE OF EIGHTY-EIGHT YEARS.

" He that believeth in me, though he were dead, yet shall he live! and whosoever liveth and believeth in me shall never die."—*St. John*, xi. 25, 26.

THIS exemplary individual was a member of the Society of Friends, and a true and faithful representative of the ancient gentlemen of that most excellent class of Christians; and though firm and undeviating in his adherence to the principles and usages of that section of the Church of Christ, to which he was attached, yet were his kindness and hospitality extended to all whom he esteemed without reference to their creed.

With a sound judgment and reflecting mind, he united much patience and industry of investigation, so that, to the last, on matters of shipping and trade, in which he had been long and extensively engaged, his opinion was much sought for, and relied on, by those who had the honour of his acquaintance. He was a firm and uncompromising advocate for protection to native productions and native industry—in opposition to the anti-English system, through which so much injury has been inflicted on both. In works of private and public charity, and well-doing, he never wearied; he retained his bodily and mental faculties, as well as his kind and affectionate feelings, to the latest period of his long, honourable, and useful life; and died in peace with the world—beloved and respected by a widely-extended circle of relatives and friends.

The death of this most excellent gentleman has naturally produced a mournful feeling amongst the inhabitants of Sunderland—as his respectable and unobtrusive manners and appearance, combined with his well-known ability, are indelibly associated with the earliest recollections, of every age and degree in the town, where his remembrance will be long cherished, for of him might be truly said—"all his ways were the ways of pleasantness, and all his paths were peace."

"Reader, whoe'er thou art, go thou and do likewise; and may thy latter end be like his."

The above eulogium, printed in Sunderland at the time of Solomon Chapman's death, is preserved here as characteristic, both in language and sentiment, of society in that town fifty years ago. An extract from the 'Annual Monitor' of 1835, respecting Jane Chapman, is here added. "More in reality than in display," describes well the religion of many Friends of that day.

"Jane Chapman, Bishop Wearmouth, Sunderland. 90. 6, 3 mo., 1834. Wife of Solomon Chapman. They had been united above sixty-one years. 'Given to hospitality,' it might be said she was a succourer of many, evincing peculiar satisfaction in promoting the comfort of those who were engaged to travel in the Lord's service; yet her liberality was not confined within narrow limits, being ever ready, though often in secret, to extend itself to all who claimed her assistance. * * * * As to religion, there is reason to believe she was more in reality than in display: and as the close of her long life drew nigh, her mind, in deep humility, appeared to be sustained by faith and resignation, and she often uttered the language of filial prayer, as 'Merciful Father! be pleased to look down upon me, now on the verge of time. God of Mercy and Love, have compassion upon me!'"—*Annual Monitor*, No. 23, p. 18.

DR. JOSEPH BROWN (p. 128).

THIS well-known inhabitant of Sunderland, although bearing no trace of Quakerism in manner or deportment, was by birth a Friend. His father, George Brown, called "the poet" in Chapter XIII., was born at Bishop Auckland, about the middle of the last century, and educated at the Grammar School of that town, then under the sway of an accomplished scholar and lover of classical literature, who found a pupil after his own heart in the Quaker boy. Intercourse was maintained through life between master and pupil, and when the latter had children of his own, and sent them to Bishop Auckland to visit their grandparents, one little boy remembered a hand being laid kindly upon his head, and an old clergyman saying, "And so this is one of George's boys!" George Brown settled in North Shields, and married Ann Ogden of Sunderland, whose sister Jane was was the wife of Solomon Chapman. Jane was childless; Ann was the mother of eight sons. Both sisters were fair women, with yellow hair.

George Brown and his wife lived at first in the Low Street of North Shields, and afterwards at No. 5, Dockwray Square. He was a man of many callings, possessing ships, a brewery and a draper's shop, and had for some years his share of worldly prosperity. His lively conversation and ready rhymes made him a favourite with his neighbours, although some of them shook their heads with a pitying smile when they spoke of his political opinions, for, as has been said, he was a staunch Whig. A man of extensive reading and of broad religious views, there was considerable difference, both in speculation and in practice, between him and strict Friends, yet he was for many years Clerk to Shields Meeting. His elder sons were sent to a Friends' Boarding School, where Bernard Dickenson, of Coalbrookdale, was their school-fellow and companion.

These elder sons, sorrowfully spoken of by Friends as "wild lads," grew up men of spirit and ability, but wanting in principle; and most of them had short and stormy lives. One seems to have possessed, amongst other attractive qualities, an unusually fine voice in singing, which caused him to be sought after in society of varied kinds. This youth died of typhus fever in Ireland, and another died of yellow fever in New Orleans. Of two other sons, one of whom, when last heard of, held the office of Purser in the Navy, the ultimate fate was never known. These two sons brought their father to poverty in his old age. Entrusted by him with the management of a warehouse in Newcastle, they failed in their undertaking, and involved him in their ruin.

Their disappearance, leaving their father to bear the brunt of their wrong-doing, and their mother full of anxiety as to their fate, filled up the measure of misfortunes. In this emergency a younger son, William Brown, became the comfort of the family. He was just entering upon life as a partner in Willington Mill, and not without hopes of his own; but he seems to have laid aside all personal views, and devoted himself to the support of his aged parents and the care of his two younger brothers. His journey to Edinburgh in 1805 (p. 50) seems to have happened before the family troubles, and public events fix the date of his next journey, which was to London. In 1806 the Ministry of "All the Talents" was in power, and Sir Charles (afterwards Earl) Grey was at the Admiralty.

The runaway sons of George Brown were believed to have taken refuge on board ships of war, and it was to obtain some clue to their fate that the old man sent his young son with a letter to the statesman to whom all Northumbrian Liberals looked as their leader. In what way the fugitive sons were traced and assisted in their new career is unknown now, but that Earl Grey's sympathy and remembrance did not fail his old follower in time of need was a fact never forgotten by the family which had passed through such troubled days.

William Brown sometimes told his children of the incidents of this visit to London, of the long coach-journey, and the halting-places on the road; of the mutton he had to carve at midnight, and of the lady who asked for four ribs in succession, so that he himself went supperless; of his first sight of the great city; of his interview with the First Lord of the Admiralty, at his simple breakfast of tea and toast; of the statesman's neat and formal dress; and of his grave courtesy and kindness. This journey was almost the only circumstance, connected with that time, of which William Brown ever spoke. His children vaguely knew that their father had had heavy troubles to bear in his youth, but they did not realise until after his death how noble was the part he had played. Some details came to them through old friends of their father in humble life, but more were gathered from the letters, full of passionate affection, written to him from the Continent by his brother Joseph, which fell into their hands with old family papers.

Joseph was the seventh son of George Brown and Anne Ogden, and was born at North Shields in 1784. He and his brother William went together to the school of Miss Weir (p. 117), and to that of the Unitarian minister of Shields. At the latter school, Joseph, like his father, took kindly to the study of the classics. He was apprenticed to Dr. Greenhow, the first of that family of whom three generations practised in North Shields. Young Brown went to Edinburgh for his hospital training, took his Surgeon's Degree at the University of that city, passed some time at Manchester as assistant to a Friend, Dr. Dockwray, and then went to London for further improvement. The misfortunes of his family, which occurred about this time, decided him to go abroad. He obtained the post of Surgeon in the 57th Regiment of Foot, and joined it in Jersey, leaving England with a sad heart. He saw the last of London in a keen frost, and it was on the ice in St. James's Park that he parted from a friend who had been his fellow-student at Edinburgh, and who was afterwards known as Sir Henry Holland. The 57th Regiment was, in 1808, ordered to Portugal, to join Sir Arthur Wellesley's army, in which Brown was afterwards attached to the Staff Corps Cavalry. He passed through the terrible scenes of the Peninsular War, being present at the battles of Busaco, Albuera, Vittoria, the Pyrenees and the Nevelle, his silver medal having five clasps, commemorating his presence at these engagements.

Dr. Brown lived to see the Crimean War in 1854, and when the English people, long inured to peace, were angry and indignant at the sufferings of their troops he marvelled at the simplicity which could expect war to be carried on without suffering. His military life obliterated all traces of Quakerism and left him a thorough soldier; but he was a tender-hearted man, and he never forgot the horrors he had witnessed. As to privations, he recalled different periods when to undress, to bathe, or to sleep under a roof were luxuries unattainable for many weeks. Dr. Brown entered France with the British Army, was present at the taking of Toulouse, and saw the entry of Louis XVIII. into Paris. After the peace, he returned to England under changed circumstances. His father was dead, but in the home of his brother William at North Shields, and from many old friends he found a warm welcome. He went to Edinburgh to obtain his degree of Physician, but was summoned to rejoin the Army on Napoleon's return from Elba.

After the final peace, he remained some time in France with the Army of Occupation, and then married a beautiful woman, whose husband, Lieutenant John Raleigh Elwes, of the 71st Light Highland Infantry, had been killed at Waterloo. The young widow was left with a little daughter, born a few days after the battle. This child grew up, and was married to the Rev. John Linskill, son of the old squire of North Shields, and descended, like so many persons named in this book, from a Quaker family of Whitby. In 1819 Dr. Brown brought his wife and stepdaughter to Shields, and afterwards to Edinburgh, where he took his degree of M.D., and then settled in Sunderland as a physician. To that town he had many ties of affection. It was his mother's native place, where her children had a second home at the house of her sister, Jane Chapman, and where many other members of the Ogden family resided. The Society of Friends has long been of importance in the County of Durham, and amongst its members Dr. Brown's Quaker descent was not forgotten, while his intellectual power and professional skill were soon recognised by a wider circle, and his advice was sought for in difficult cases by surgeons, in places which then seemed far distant from Sunderland,—Darlington, Barnard Castle, and York. His whole heart was in his work, and to do his utmost for the cure of disease, or for the alleviation of suffering, was the greatest pleasure of his life. He gave as much attention to each of the poor patients who crowded his consulting-rooms and even the yard of his house on certain mornings of the week, as he did to the owners of the great mansions to which he was occasionally summoned. His special faculty lay in the diagnosis of disease, in which he was rarely known to fail; and he once told the writer of this book that it was his custom, on first seeing a patient, to look intently into his face to discover the probable cause of suffering, and that, in a very large majority of cases, subsequent examination confirmed the opinion which he formed from his study of the countenance. A similar remark has been made by police magistrates, to whom long experience in the observation of human faces has given the same faculty in the diagnosis of moral, as a skilled physician has in that of physical disease. Dr. Brown was one of the Physicians to the Sunderland Infirmary, and visited that institution from his appointment in 1822 until the week before his death in 1868. He attended at a similar institution in South Shields every Friday, for many years, generally crossing the Tyne afterwards to visit the northern town, his native place, where his presence was often required in consultation, and where, at the house of his brother, invalids in humble circumstances, workmen and domestic servants, were sometimes gathered to seek his aid. Dr. Brown was on the staff of the 'British and Foreign Quarterly Medical Review,' and a coadjutor with Sir John Forbes in that gentleman's 'Cyclopædia of Practical Medecine.' In both these works Dr. Brown's articles were highly esteemed by his professional brethren, and his book entitled, 'Medical Essays on Fever, Inflammation, Diseases of the Heart, &c,' which was published by Longmans in 1828, was considered an authority in its day on the subjects of which it treated. Dr. Brown took part in the controversy which was carried on in the columns of the 'Athenæum,' during Miss Martineau's residence at Tynemouth, on the subject of Mesmerism and Clairvoyance. So far as the writer's memory serves her, after the lapse of forty years, his letters had less reference to Miss Martineau's recovery from illness by aid of mesmerism than to the credibility of her servant. This young girl, when under the influence of mesmerism, was supposed to be clairvoyant, and to have described a shipwreck of which she had never heard. Dr. Brown and Dr. Headlam Greenhow, who was then Miss Martineau's medical attendant and who now, in 1889, has only recently gone from amongst us, investigated the case, and satisfied themselves that the girl had, before her trance, been into North Shields, where the news of the shipwreck was in everyone's mouth.

Dr. Brown thoroughly identified himself with the town of Sunderland, and gave his time ungrudgingly to its service. One of the first borough magistrates appointed in the town, he discharged the duties of the office with diligence and ability. He served on the Town Council for many years, was chosen as Mayor in 1839, and was afterwards elected Alderman. As Chairman of the Sanitary Committee of the Town Council, he urged upon his colleagues the necessity for sanitary improvements in the dwellings of the poor, a subject upon which he was qualified to speak with authority; but finding himself powerless to carry out what he knew to be needful, he resigned his office. He lived, however, to see other men able to make some progress in the right direction, and to give them his sympathy and help. Like his father, Dr. Brown was a staunch Whig. Although all his life a poor man, no consideration of personal advantage ever weighed with him for a moment, when what he conceived to be for the public good was in question, and in the early years of Sunderland's existence as a parliamentary borough he was one of the leading Liberals of the place.

Amidst all these varied employments, Dr. Brown found time, even in his busiest days, to indulge his love of books, and he turned to them for the solace of his old age. A man of very general culture, he was as familiar with our English classics as with those of Greece and of Rome, and quotations from them came as readily to his lips. Addicted, as a boy, to chaunting lines from Pope's 'Homer' while running upstairs in his old home in Dockwray Square, he was somewhat of a heretic with regard to poets later than Scott and Byron, until, by listening to an impassioned rendering of 'Locksley Hall,' he was converted into an admirer of Tennyson. Quick at acquiring languages, he obtained a knowledge of Spanish and Portuguese during the Peninsular War, while in French he was proficient. He often translated articles from 'Le Revue des Deux Mondes' for the local papers, and one of his French correspondents, Dr. Majendie, visited him in Sunderland in 1831, when that town became a focus of interest to the medical profession, on account of the outbreak of Asiatic cholera.

In his later years Dr. Brown published 'A Defence of Revealed Religion,' 'Memories and Thoughts,' and an essay on 'The Food of the People.' Waking early in the mornings, he amused himself until breakfast-time with his books. In this way he read the Greek Testament through after he was eighty years old, and had commenced the study of the Fathers in the original. When he was on his deathbed, his intimate friend and medical attendant, Dr. Morgan, spoke some words of Latin in his ear. The old man's face lighted up, and with weak voice but perfect recollection he finished the paragraph. Surrounded by those he loved, his last words to them were full of affection, and of the quiet humour natural to him. Dr. Brown died in 1868. His brother William had died at North Shields six years before. Both were eminently cheerful, companionable men, with strong family affections, and to recall their memory is a pleasure.

Sunderland was not unmindful of the services of Dr. Brown. A few years before his death a testimonial of £1000 was presented to him; and a medallion likeness in profile on white marble in bas-relief is now in the Subscription Library, an institution of which Dr. Brown was an ardent supporter, and of which, for many years, he was President.

Dr. Brown's father, George Brown, who came from Bishop Auckland to North Shields in the Sixties or Seventies of the last century, had a sister Mary who married a Friend from the South of England, John Beaumont, who lived at Battersea Rise, not then a part of London, but a country place. John Beaumont and his wife died in middle life, and their children were left under the guardianship of Dr. Pope, of Staines, whose name is not forgotten in the Thames Valley. Member of a firm of country apothecaries, Pope, Tothill, and Chandler, who kept open shop according to the custom in the last century, and who were all Quakers, Dr. Pope was brought under the notice of King George the Third and his family. He became the trusted friend and physician of the Princess Amelia, attending her during her long illness, especially during her somewhat lonely sojourns at Weymouth. Dr. Pope's daughter lived to a great age at Staines, and amongst her treasures were many royal gifts. A silver tea-kettle, perfectly plain except for the narrow beading admired then as now, and bearing the simple inscription, "The Princess Amelia to Dr. Pope," was one of these heir-looms. Royal favour brought Dr. Pope many patients, and tradition tells us how, on returning from his daily rounds in the neighbourhood of Windsor Park and Englefield Green, he would take up the pockets of his long drab overcoat and shake the guineas into his wife's lap! He was a plain Friend in dress and speech, and an old patient remembered his cheerful greeting, "Well, neighbour Northcroft!" The quaint words had a kindly sound in her ears. Of the five children of John and Mary Beaumont, who were brought up at Staines under the guardianship of Dr. Pope, the eldest son, Abraham Beaumont, was long a resident of Stamford Hill, and another son, John, also lived in the South of England. The youngest son, William Beaumont, an agreeable and courteous man, was for many years a familiar figure in Newcastle. Of the two daughters, the eldest, Elizabeth, married Joseph Pease, of Feethams, Darlington (p. 49), and died in 1824, leaving two children, the late John Beaumont Pease and Mrs. Nichol (p. 268). The youngest daughter, Sarah Beaumont, a charming woman, died unmarried.

Two excellent articles by Mr. William Brockie, which appeared in the ' Sunderland Weekly Echo,' May 4th, 1888, have been of use in this sketch of Dr. Brown's life.

Jane Chapman's father, John Ogden (page 125), had a brother Bernard, who lived at Darlington. Their father, John Ogden, lived in Wensleydale. All those persons, like the earlier John Ogden, of Sunderland, were clockmakers. Hence the remark in the text that "the art of the horologer seems to have been hereditary in the Ogden family."

APPENDIX O.

————◆————

LINDLEY MURRAY'S PUBLICATIONS (p. 148).

Power of Religion on the Mind	Pub. 1787.
The English Grammar	„ 1795.
Abridgment of the English Grammar	„ 1797.
English Exercises and Key	„ 1797.
A First Book for Children.	
English Reader	„ 1799.
Sequel to the English Reader	„ 1800.
Introduction to the English Reader	„ 1801.
Lecteur François	„ 1802.
English Spelling Book.	„ 1804.
Introduction au Lecteur François	„ 1807.
The Duty and Benefit of a Daily Perusal of the Holy Scriptures in Families.	
A Selection from Bishop Horne's Commentary on the Psalms	„ 1812.
A Compendium of Scriptural Teaching.	

————————

APPENDIX P.

————◆————

ACKWORTH SCHOOL AND THE JUBILEE YEAR OF QUEEN VICTORIA (p. 212).

I had left the school for fifty years,
  And wandered o'er sea and land;
And now had returned from my far-off
    home,
    To revisit the dear old land.

Once more I had seen, at the Ackworth
    Inn,
  An English tea-table spread;
And once again I had fallen to sleep
    In white sheets and a four-post bed.

It was twelve o'clock, and I heard a knock,
  And a voice which startled me most,—
"Please open the door and let me in,
  I'm Robert Whittaker's ghost!

"I heard thou hadst come, and wert staying
    here,
  And I thought I should like to call;
There are many things they are doing now,
  Which I cannot approve at all.

"The way the children chatter and laugh
  Is most distressing to see;
And the Superintendent plays at games
  And is not, in the least, like me.

"The boys go walking, to drag out snails
  From their homes in the ponds and
    bogs;
And they've got a room with bottles in
    rows,
  Where they cut up rabbits and frogs.

"The little girls are curling their hair,
  And calling their teachers 'Miss';

In dear old Hannah Richardson's time,
  They didn't behave like this.

"Instead of their learning to darn and sew,
  They teach them to paint and sing;
It never was so in those good old days,
  When William the Fourth was King.

"The Scriptural names,—where have they
    gone?
  And Echo answers, ' Where?'
Mary and Sarah and Ruth give place
  To Beatrice, Ethel and Clare.

"Friends are not farmers and grocers now,
  For they quit every useful trade;
They must all be Doctors, or Engineers,
  Or Members of Parliament made.

"I cannot stand the Penny Post;
  I hate an Excursion Train;
You may keep the Jubillee Year who like,
  I think I'll go back again."

AN OLD ACKWORTH BOY.

LAMENT OF THE OLD CLOCK FACE AT THE ACKWORTH CENTENARY:
RECITED BY GEO. F. ARMITAGE.

Here I have gazed from year to year
On happy childhood playing near,
And scenes familiar grown so dear,
    I loved them well.

How oft I've watched with rare delight
The cricket-ball in rapid flight,
And football played in friendly fight,
    I fail to tell.

The girls' gay laughter too I've heard,
Buoyant and blithe as any bird,
Its mirth my old heart oft has stirred,
    And kept it young.

What changes I have lived to see!
Will Quakerism cease to be,
All good old ways along with me
    Away be flung?

True broad-brimmed hats, they are no
    more,
The modest bonnets I deplore;
The old plain language used of yore
    Is scarcely heard.

Where now are all those corduroys,
That erst did clothe those manly boys?
I hear no more their creaking noise
    Now cloth's preferred.

And more than this, the girls' short
    hair,
Which showed the shape of heads so fair,
Is now replaced—I will not spare—
    By pigtails long.

A soothing sound I used to hear,
Of hymn repeated loud and clear;
But now I fain would shut my ear,
    To drown the song.

And must my work be past and done,
The hundred years so nearly run?
And shall I miss the joyous fun
    Of celebration?

But in this world 'tis ever so,
The old for young must always go;
I am too proud to let tears flow
    From this high station.

What matters it, I'm doomed to fall,
I too must change as changed have all;
I make this plaint from turret tall,
    My requiem sad.

They will not let me die in peace,
The thumps and blows they never cease,
The burnished lamb with gaudy fleece
    At heart is glad.

'Tis said, " that silence gives consent,"
That lamb then to a lie is lent,
The midnight hour was never spent
    Upon the green.

They'll praise the new, forget the old,
I faithfully the time have told,
My figures once were fair and bold,
    And plainly seen.

And think, dear friends, when gazing high
At new clock face 'gainst autumn sky,
How could I leave without a sigh,
    The dear loved spot?

But as grown old, I may not stay,
My life, well-spent, has had its day;
There is one boon of you I pray
    Forget-me-not.

F. A. M. A., AND M. W.

APPENDIX Q.

CHARLES BROWN (p. 286).

From ' THE FRIEND *' for Second Month, 1864.*

THE death of our late dear friend, Charles Brown, of North Shields, is an event full of such deep. though melancholy interest, that we can hardly pass it by with no further notice than the accustomed line in our obituary column. It is, we believe, not quite four years since he first opened his mouth among us as a Minister of the Gospel, and little more than three since he was recognised by his brethren in this capacity. Nor has he during that period been engaged in any extensive service at a distance from home, and we do not remember his taking, on any occasion, a prominent part in the proceedings of the Yearly Meeting. It is very possible, therefore, that to many of our readers his name may be almost unknown; but Friends of his own immediate neighbourhood will be at no loss to understand our reasons for calling attention to the great—we had almost said the irreparable—loss which our little church has sustained by his removal. For the gift which he had received from his Divine Master for the benefit of his brethren, was one of such rare fulness, and variety and power, that into the few years of his ministration a lifetime of Christian teaching seems to have been condensed; and yet there was about him such an appearance of unbroken strength, so much of almost youthful freshness of spirit, that standing as he did, still on the morning side of the noon of life, he naturally suggested to the minds of his friends the idea of many years of future service in the cause of Christ, perhaps sometimes of conspicuous and widely-extended labours for His sake.

He was a man of most loving and genial nature, and, if we may be allowed the expression, of great spiritual modesty. The entire absence of assumption on his part, and a certain vein of humour in his character, which he did not think it necessary utterly to repress, made him decidedly popular with his younger friends. To young men he was especially useful: he understood their difficulties, sympathised with their temptations, and often, by sharing, solved their doubts. It should be added that he was, to use the Scripture phrase, "well reputed of by them that are without." A business acquaintance, one who would be rather repelled than attracted by his religious profession, said not long ago, "There is not a more honest man in Newcastle Corn Market than Charles Brown."

The most striking feature in the ministry of our dear brother was his intense conviction of the greatness of the love of God towards us as manifested in the face of Jesus Christ. As before hinted, there was great richness and variety in his discourses, but on whatever subject they treated, they always seemed to revolve round this one central idea, "Behold what manner of love the Father has bestowed upon us, and how can we refuse to open wide our little stores of love to Him in return?"

The Epistle to the Ephesians was a very favourite portion of Scripture with him, and often did that rich treasury of Christian doctrine supply the text for his discourses. His prayers, which were characterised by great earnestness and fervour, often contained a very marked allusion to the sermon which had preceded them: supplicating for deliverance from the temptation, or bestowal of the grace, upon which in his previous discourse he had been especially led to dilate. It was in entire accordance with the trustful, childlike love which was the prevailing attitude of his spirit, that the words "Gracious Father!" were his usual form of speech in addressing the Most High.

On the First-day immediately preceding his death, he attended meeting apparently in his usual health, and spoke at some length in the afternoon. On his return home, or shortly after, he was seized with severe cold, which soon turned to pleurisy. He was a good deal reduced in strength by the illness early in the week; but till Sixth-day evening no idea of immediate danger was entertained. On Seventh-day he was evidently worse: he seemed somewhat relieved towards evening, but it was only the case of approaching dissolution. A rapid change took place between 9 and 10 o'clock, and before the latter hour he had quietly "fallen asleep."

It was not a death-bed which would have afforded any time for preparation, had he not been already prepared to meet his Judge. His mind wandered a good deal; and there was not even, we believe, any conscious leave-taking of the wife and children, eight in number, most of them still very young, whom he loved so tenderly. Once, when his thoughts were wandering, he seemed to imagine himself preaching in Sunderland meeting. "Let not," he said, "the young say to the old, 'We have no need of you;' nor again the old to the young, 'We have no need of you;' but let each, whether young or old, seek to know for themselves an interest in Christ." These words, though spoken with dying lips and clouded consciousness, expressed the burden of his whole life during these later years. He was himself a most powerful link between two generations, and longed to bind them together yet more closely, but always "in Christ."

We will not attempt to describe all the sad musings of our hearts at the most mysterious dispensation of Divine Providence, which has thus suddenly, in the midst of his days, removed one of our most loved and honoured teachers from amongst us. The Psalmist's words, " I was dumb, I opened not my mouth because thou didst it," express, we believe, the feeling which reigned in many hearts when they heard the sorrowful and unlooked-for tidings. Only the help of the Comforter Himself can enable us, even when contemplating *this* loss, with bowed heads and submissive hearts to say, " He doeth *all things* well."

The following lines, which have been sent us by one who, though not a member of the same meeting, had seen and prized the rare graces of his Christian character, will, better than any further words of ours, express our own feelings in pondering over our loss and his unquestioned gain :—

LINES ON THE DEATH OF CHARLES BROWN.

We see by faith thy glorious kingly crown,
   Lit with the radiance of the Eternal Throne,
Where saints, triumphant, low are bending down,
   Ascribing glory to their Lord alone.

We know thy golden harp is tuned to praise ;
   For, ere thy spirit winged its flight above,
We heard thee speak of God's all-righteous ways,
   And dwell with fervour on His wondrous love.

That love to tell to sinners here below,
   Ambassador of Christ ! thy blest employ ;
That love, where ransomed hosts with rapture glow,
   Shall be thy theme in everlasting joy.

But we who stand beside the river's brink,
   With weeping eyes upon this desert strand,
Feel that our aching hearts must almost sink,
   While thou art treading on the promised land.

We miss thy spirit's strength upon the way,
   Can hardly bear to think thy race is run,
But only bow our heads and humbly pray,
   " Teach us, O Lord, to say, ' Thy will be done.' "

Oh, no ! not thus, our comrade once in fight ;
   If rests the victor's crown upon thy brow,
Shall we not gather courage at the sight,
   And press to join thee where thou dwellest now ?

If from the harvest-field the Master calls
   Another reaper to a brighter land,
Shall we not take the sickle as it falls
   E'en from the grasp of thy unwearied hand ?

With the Forerunner in the Holy Place,
   Thine eyes, with mists of earth no longer dim,
Shall see our God for ever face to face !
   With thee in glory may we gaze on Him.

The above sympathetic and truthful portrait of Charles Brown in his later years, is from the pen of Dr. Thomas Hodgkin. The touching lines were sent, it is believed, by

Jane Gurney Pease. A short biography of Charles Brown, written by his brother William, who was his close companion from boyhood, appeared in the 'Annual Monitor' for 1865. William Brown was a very lovable character, a great student, and a deep thinker on matters of spiritual religion.

APPENDIX R.

DEATH OF MR. J. R. PROCTER, OF NORTH SHIELDS.
'NEWCASTLE DAILY LEADER,' *October 12th*, 1888.

IT is with deep regret that we record the death of Mr. John Richardson Procter, of Clementhorpe, North Shields, which took place at his residence rather suddenly and unexpectedly last evening. Mr. Procter was in his usual health up till Tuesday evening last, and even yesterday the sad event was not looked for. In the fulfilment of his duties as chairman of the Harbour and Ferries Committee of the River Tyne Commission, Mr. Procter attended a meeting of the committee at the docks on Tuesday afternoon, and in the company of his colleagues visited the various places there. On concluding the business of the meeting, Mr. Procter hurried off to the railway-station, and it is supposed that he over-exerted himself, for on arriving home he felt faint and ill. Next day the symptoms continued, and Dr. Bramwell was called in. After a while, however, he rallied, and it was thought that he would get over his illness. He had another relapse, however, and was again very ill, but, recovering, appeared to be more like himself. The recovery was only temporary, however, for he was seized with illness yesterday, and, although he rallied somewhat in the course of the day, died quietly about five o'clock, the cause of death being an affection of the heart.

Mr. Procter was one of the best known and most highly respected men in North Shields, and, it might be said, on Tyneside. He was in his 77th year. He was the son of Joseph Procter, of North Shields, who carried on business near the foot of the Wooden Bridge Bank, in the Low Town, and afterwards in premises which stood on the site now occupied by the drapery establishment of Messrs. Joseph and John Foster Spence. The father of the brothers Spence served his apprenticeship with the father of Mr. J. R. Procter. While a young man, Mr. Procter was sent to the works of his uncles, William and Henry Richardson, of the Low Lights Tannery, where he learnt the business, and ultimately succeeded his uncles as proprietor of the business, which he successfully carried on, latterly with the assistance of his son.

He was a member of the Society of Friends, and married a lady of the family of the Richardsons, of York. He was a man of few words, but no one was listened to with more respect. He was, with the exception of Mr. J. C. Stevenson, M.P., the oldest member of the River Tyne Commission, in the work of which he took the deepest interest, giving ungrudgingly his time and talents to the very last.

With the town of Shields, his native place, his life was inseparably bound up. There was no movement for the good of the people or the prosperity of the borough in which he did not manifest the liveliest interest, and there were few movements having the same objects in view in which he did not take an active part. Very early in life he showed an interest in the Bible Society, which he continued to support throughout his long life. He was for many years a member of the committee of the Royal Jubilee Schools, and for a time acted as secretary. He was also a member of the old Literary and Philosophical Society, which institution was ultimately merged in the Free Library, of the committee of which he was a member. He was also a member of the Kettlewell School Committee, which he joined in 1845, and at one time acted as corresponding secretary and chairman. He was chairman of the Dispensary Committee, and he also took a deep interest in the Tyne Sailors' Home, of which he was one of the directors. Of the public bodies of the borough he served as a member of the Tyne Commission, as above stated, of the Town Council, the School Board, and the Board of Guardians. He was elected a member of the River Tyne Commission in 1863, and at the time of his death was Chairman of the Harbour and Ferries Committee. He was elected a member of the Town Council in 1852, and retired in 1867, he then being chairman of the Sanitary Authority. He was elected a member of the School Board at the second election after its formation, and when he retired he was chairman. Of the Board of Guardians he was a member for about forty years, and at the time of his death was chairman. Among the other institutions with which he was connected was the University Extension Society, in which he took great interest up to the last. Indeed, Mr. Procter continued his connection with every one of the numerous movements in which he was interested up to the day of his death. He was a loyal and consistent Liberal, and during the visit of Mr. Harris, the Liberal candidate, attended two or three of the meetings, taking part at the last one held in the Oddfellows' Hall, where he was enthusiastically received. Mr. Procter leaves a widow and two sons, with whom the greatest sympathy is felt.

From the 'NEWCASTLE DAILY LEADER,' *October 12th*, 1888.

A LARGE public on Tyneside will regret to hear of the death of Mr. J. R. Procter, of North Shields. Through a long life, reaching considerably over the three score years and ten, Mr. Procter has always had at heart the welfare of the community among whom he lived. In most charitable objects he was a leading spirit, and was, besides, an unostentatious and cheerful giver in private ways. He was an advanced Liberal, and a sound adviser. Being a member of the Society of Friends, he objected to take an oath or to administer one. This conviction kept him from accepting the office of chief magistrate of his native borough, and ultimately practically drove him from the Council in order to get rid of the pressure to take a high position. He was a model citizen.

JOHN RICHARDSON PROCTER.
From the 'SHIELDS DAILY NEWS,' *October 12th,* 1888.

RARELY in our public annals has the sudden stroke of death kindled a deeper sense of loss in the community, than that which yesterday followed the announcement of the death of Mr. J. R. Procter. For so many years in the front of all that was estimable, energetic and helpful in our public service, and, up to the very last, apparently in the fulness of his honours and his activities, there was no slackening of the grasp or diminishing of the ardour with which he devoted himself to the manifold interests and duties, to which, for a lifetime, he had given so much of his time and talents. Winning an almost unique position of respect and honour, frankly accorded to him, in sincere esteem of his character and conscientious guidance of so many good causes, he carried the modest dignity and the inward kindliness of the Society of Friends into all the varied relations of this life. Not for the titles or the public honours of the service were his labours given, but out of strong sympathy with all men, and a yearning to be ever in the front when anything was to be done or said on behalf of freedom and liberty of conscience, or help to be given to the downcast or the outcast, or more light to be given to those who sat in darkness and the shadow of ignorance. His services to education alone, as one of the oldest and most able directors of Kettlewell's School, have been of great value to the community, given with such fervent zeal and judgment at the period of greatest need, and maintained to the very last. There is scarcely an effort or an occasion when the onward and upward movement of our social and political life bring us together, where his familiar presence and his generous help will not be missed.

SERMON BY THE REV. D. TASKER, PRESBYTERIAN MINISTER, NORTH SHIELDS, ON THE DEATH OF J. R. PROCTER.
'SHIELDS DAILY NEWS,' *October 15th,* 1888.

IF the history of a nation be the history of its great men, the same truth holds on a more limited scale. Upright and honourable men, who serve their fellow-citizens in the conduct of public affairs, should be held in high esteem, not merely, or even chiefly, for the service they render, the time and care they devote to public matters without fee or reward, but for the healthy influence they exert by their weight of character, of Christian character, on the community at large. This healthy influence is always in inverse proportion to the love of notoriety, or that hankering after a cheap popularity which characterises weak and ignorant minds. It is our proud boast that no nation on earth is better served in this respect than our own. In our halls of legislature, at our council boards, there are men of sterling integrity, of high Christian principle, proud to serve their country for their country's sake.

The grave will close to-morrow over one who for many years faithfully served this community, and sought in every way to advance its highest interests, socially, morally, and religiously. On the marble block in the quiet nook in Preston Cemetery, where more than a twelvemonth ago we saw him sorrowfully turn away from a newly-filled-in grave, I would inscribe these words :—"Having served his generation by the will of God, he fell on sleep." If ever any man endeavoured faithfully and conscientiously, according to his light, to carry out the will of God, that man was John Richardson Procter. I speak thus with the less reserve, not only because he belonged to another Christian communion, but because, on many subjects, political and ecclesiastical, we held very different and widely divergent opinions. This was only to be expected, for we were trained in very different schools — he a member of the Society of Friends, I a Presbyterian. But these differences never interfered with personal friendship, nor did they prevent us from discussing them in a quiet way, as opportunity offered. On the vexed question of the connection between Church and State we held diametrically opposite views. I can vividly recall the quiet smile and shake of the head with which he greeted some of my favourite heresies on that subject. We differed also on many religious questions, but when we left the circumference of the circle and travelled inwards towards the centre, —salvation through the atoning work of Christ, and sanctification through the indwelling and inworking of the Holy Spirit — ah! there we found ourselves lovingly at one. I felt for him then the affection of a son for a father. I felt the better for being in the good old man's company. Servant of God, well done! The Master has called thee from diligent service on earth to the companionship of the First-born in Heaven. May we be followers of them who through faith and patience now inherit the promises.

ERRATA.

Page 47, ninth line from top, *for* "fifteenth and sixteenth centuries" *read* "sixteenth and seventeenth."

Page 113, seventeenth line from top, *for* " eleventh century " *read* " seventh."

Page 115, top line, *for* " John " *read* " Robert."

INDEX.

A

Ackworth School, 28, 172—212, 224, 225, 285, 287
Actor educated at Ackworth, 193
Addison, Joseph, 76, 92, 205
Affirmation Bill, 8, 9, 107, 252, 253
Aikin, Dr., 37, 175, 179
Allen, William, 197, 277
American Civil War, 224, 239
———— Friends, 22, 61, 138 —154, 170, 176, 221, 228—230
———— War of Independence, 170, 171
Anstey, 'Bath Guide,' 43
Armstrong, Family of, 15
Arthington, Robert, 172

B

Backhouse, James, of York, 48, 147, 152
Baker, Dr. Robert, 49
———— John Gilbert, F.R.S., 10, 49, 285
Barbauld, Mrs., 37, 179
Barber, J. H., 197
Barclay, David, 171, 277
Barnes, Sarah Mayleigh (wife of Isaac Richardson of Cherry Hill), 58
Beckwith, Miss Anne (Mrs. Towse), 33
'Bee,' The, 43
Bennett, Family of, 244
———— of Derby, Family of, 83
Benson, Mrs., 'From the Lune to the Neva,' 186, 192
Bevan, Family of, 244
Bewick, Thomas, 35, 36
Bible Society, Newcastle, 93, 274, 275, 276
Bickerdike property, 214, 216
Binns, Dr. Jonathan, 179, 193

Books for children at Ackworth, 178, 179, 185
Books in a Friend's household, 35—45, 231, 239
Boxall, Richard, 185, 191
Bradshaw, Thomas, 191
Brady, Henry, 196
Breeches, Leather, 158, 177, 195
Bright, John, 196, 209—211, 221—224
Brockie, Mr. W 284
Brown, Captain (Conchologist), 103
———— Charles, 135, 136, 236—239, 287—289
———— Dr. Joseph, 40, 116—120, 123—128, 278—284
———— Family of, 46, 56, 57, 74, 116—120, 123—128, 135, 136, 227, 228, 235, 236—239, 278—284, 287—289
Bruce, John Collingwood, LL.D., 89, 273—275
Burke, Edmund, 31, 55
Burns, Robert, 44

C

Casson, Family of, 54, 55, 61, 227—230, 235
Chapman, Family of, 11, 18, 19, 126—128, 135, 264
———— Solomon, 126—128, 135, 278, 280
Chipchase, Hannah, 33
———— John, 28, 33, 85
Citizens, Friends as, 10, 11, 49, 70, 122, 146, 169, 209, 221, 240—244, 290—293
Clear-starching and ironing, 32, 100, 101
Coleridge, Samuel Taylor, 43, 44, 95, 99, 100, 277
Collingwood, Mr., Secretary to the Foundling Hospital, 162
Committees, Ackworth School, 172, 177—180, 198, 208

Committees to visit Friends, 136, 219
Convincement, 179, 197
Cook, Captain James (the discoverer), 2, 36, 65, 266
Cotton introduced at Ackworth, 200
Cowper, William, 40, 192

D

Dale, Mary (wife of Wm. Richardson, of Whitby), 63
Darwin, Dr. Erasmus, 43, 82
Day, Thomas, 36, 83
Delaval, Lords of, 114
Disownment, 23, 52, 105, 106, 109
Dockwray Square, 21, 65, 67, 106, 107, 115—118, 120, 121, 122, 129—132, 135, 136, 224 —240, 280—284, 287—289
Donbavand, Joseph, 191, 192, 196, 199
Douglas, Frederick, 221
Dreams, 12, 13, 64
Dress, Friends', 32, 33, 46, 81, 83—85, 101, 105, 129, 151, 167—169, 177, 201, 209, 210, 231
Dudley, Charlotte, 200
———— Mary & Elizabeth, 60

E

Eclectic Review, 99, 100
Edgeworth, Maria, 37, 38, 45, 149
Enfield, Dr., 'The Speaker,' 39, 148

F

Flounders, Family of, 73, 213—216, 265
———— Institute, 212, 213—216

Foreign Missions, Friends', 15,
92, 107
Fossick, Family of, 10, 54, 244
Foster, Robt., of Hebblethwaite
Hall, 24
———— " William and Ann,
1719," over door of Bog Hall,
15
Fothergill, Dr. John, 161—175,
180
Foundling School, Ackworth,
156—162
———————————— London,
155
Foundling Hospital, 155—162,
200
Fox, George, 5, 163, 171
Franklin, Dr. Benjamin, 171,
175
Friend,' The, 287
———— Coleridge's, 99, 100,
226, 277, 278
Friends of Cotherstone, 33,
34
———— of Ireland, 42, 60,
61, 200, 228
———— of North Shields,
103
———— of Philadelphia, 61,
138, 141, 221, 228
———— of York, 10, 146,
147, 149
———— testimony against
oaths, 8, 9, 252, 262, 292
———— against paying
tithes, 31, 47, 73, 213
———— against war, 17 —
18, 52, 118, 119, 181, 191

G

' Gentleman's Magazine,' 169
Gilpin, Rev. —, ' Lives of the
Reformers,' 100
Gladstone, Rt. Hon. W. E.,
offer of clerkship, 124
Goldsmith, Oliver, 38, 40, 43,
179
Grace, Silent, 6, 250
Green bag, The, 121
Grellet, Stephen, 229—230
Grey, Rt. Hon. Earl, 118, 121,
280
Griscom, John, Prof. of Chem-
istry, New York, 150
Guisborough, 2, 3, 159
Gurney, Elizabeth (Mrs. Fry),
168
———— Joseph John, 194, 195
———— Samuel 10, 49, 166,
209, 269, 270

H

Hack, Maria, 44
Harpur Street, 169, 174
Heckling Chamber, 17
Hesleton, Family of, 15
Hild or Hilda, Saint, 1, 51
Hill, John, 172, 173, 177, 178
Hipsley, John, Superintendent
of Ackworth School, 178
Hodgkin, Thomas, LL.D., 236,
287—290
Hogarth, William, 155, 175
Hollingsworth, Mary, 152
Howard, Luke, 195, 196, 197,
271
Howitt, William, Extracts from
' Boy's Country Book,' 181—
193

J

Jay, John Esq., Governor New
York State, 143
Jeffrey, Lord, 44
Jones, Ann, 61
Joysey, Mary, of Sunderland,
56
Jubilee Schools, 92, 93, 120, 291

K

Keble, The Rev. John, 237
Kinnersley, Ebenezer, of Phila-
delphia, 138
Kissam, Benjamin, Esq., of
New York, 143
Klopstock, F. and Meta, 41, 42,
43

L

Lamb, Charles, 46, 80, 81, 178,
184, 206
Language, Guarded, 6, 64, 240,
250
———— The plain, 25, 55,
56, 129, 181, 232, 284, 286
Leadbeater, Mary, of Ballitore,
42
Lee, Dr. Timothy, Rector of
Ackworth, 156, 157, 160, 161
Leslie, Sir John, of Edinburgh
University, 56, 57
Letters, Family, 4—9, 18, 68,
70, 247—254, 257—268
———— from an Ackworth
Mistress, 204, 205, 207, 208
———— from Ann Fothergill,
166, 167, 172, 173, 174, 175

Letters from Dr. Fothergill,
164, 165, 168, 169, 173, 174,
———— from A. M. Priestman,
225, 227
———— from Ellen Richard-
son, 205, 206
———— of the sisters to J.
Priestman, 97—110
Lilburn, Colonel Robert, 115
Linskill, Family of, 11, 18, 264,
282
———— Mary, 52, 266
Linton, George, 115
Lotherington, Family of, 11,
264
Low Lights, 65—74, 89, 96, 97,
104, 116, 132, 135, 153, 215,
220, 226, 233, 241—244, 254,
259—261, 266, 270, 271, 290
Lowther, Sir James, 160
Loy, Family of, 56

M

Mackridge, Mary (wife of Henry
Vasie), 11, 256
Majolier, Christine (Mrs. R.
Alsop), 209
Malt-kiln, The, 7, 8, 251, 252
Malton, 21, 50, 52, 78, 88, 108,
265
Martin, Family of, 15
Mayson, Family of, 47, 267
Meetings, Ackworth General,
172, 194, 201, 208, 211, 221,
———— Essay, 104
———— Monthly, 29, 53,
106, 107, 120, 222, 231, 238,
262, 271
———— Quarterly, 29, 53,
204
———— Yearly, 29, 46, 53—
56, 106, 126, 162, 172, 210
Mildred, Family of, 59, 60, 224,
244
Miller, William Allen, 195
Ministers, 5, 16, 22, 47, 54, 59
—61, 69, 89—94, 144, 152,
168, 190, 194, 200, 209, 220,
228—230, 235—239
' Miseries of Human Life,'
39
Missions, Foreign. See Foreign
Missions.
Montagu, Mrs. Elizabeth, 102
Montgomery, James, 31, 87
Monthly Magazine, 102
More, Mrs. Hannah, 39
Morris, Family of (Philadel-
phia), 221, 228

Murray, John, of New York, 153
——— Lindley, 31, 138—154, 179, 180
——— Robert, of New York, 153, 221
——— Robert Lindley, 153, 221
Muskett, Mary (wife of Wm. Richardson, of Langbarugh), 14, 46
Myles, George, 13

N

'Newcastle Advertiser,' 271
——— Chronicle,' 88, 151, 264, 273
——— 'Daily Leader,' 290, 291
New York, 138 — 144, 149 — 153, 221, 229, 230
Nichol, Elizabeth Pease, 49, 268, 284
'Nicholson's Journal,' 101
'Northern Daily Express,' 273
North Shields, Traditions of, 113—120

O

Ogden, Family of, 125 — 128, 135, 278, 283
Oliphant, Lawrence, 245
——— Mrs., 239
Opie, Amelia, 43
Oswi, Founder of Whitby Abbey, 1, 113
Overend (Richardson, Overend and Gurney), 10, 49, 269, 270

P

Pease, Edward, 48, 49, 78, 235, 236, 268
——— Family of, 10, 48, 49, 209, 216, 235, 236, 268, 284
——— Joseph, of Feethams, 48, 49, 54, 268, 284
Pillion Seat, 16, 50, 51, 53, 66, 169
Pontefract, 181, 207
Pope, Alexander, 'The Iliad,' 40, 41, 185, 186, 191
——— Dr., of Staines, 284
Portraits, 21, 78, 82, 83, 148, 155, 175, 231, 233, 243
Priestman, Family of, 20, 21,

50, 52, 60, 73, 76, 78, 80, 88, 96—110, 176, 214, 221—227, 228, 265
Priestman, Jonathan, 88, 96—110, 221—227, 265
——— Joseph, of Thornton, 60, 61
——— Thomas, of Hull, 60, 61
Priestley, Dr., 173
Procter, Family of, 72—74, 101, 102, 135, 213, 216, 220, 221, 224, 241, 242
——— John Richardson, 73, 74, 122, 135, 220, 221, 224, 240—244, 261, 270, 290
Pumphrey, Thomas, 177, 198, 199, 202, 205, 206

Q

Queries, The, 29, 232, 240

R

Reinstatement in Membership, 23, 136, 236
Representatives, 29
Retreat, Friends', York, 28, 29, 49, 147, 175, 176
Richardson, Elizabeth, 21—28, 32, 43, 50, 76 — 84, 88, 93, 96—111, 129—133, 205, 217 —220, 224—239
——— Hannah, 22 — 24, 28, 35—48, 50—52, 76—89, 93, 94, 95—104, 107 — 111, 136, 137, 151 — 154, 202 — 209, 212, 214, 224—239
——— Isabel (wife of Henry Casson), 22—25, 28 —33, 35—48, 50—55, 58— 62, 76, 77, 84, 228—230, 235
——— Mary, 22—24, 28, 32, 35—48, 50—52, 71, 72, 74, 76, 77, 84, 89, 94, 96, 97 —102, 132—136, 153, 214, 220—240
——— of Holderness, Family of, 47, 267
Richardsons of Ayton, 2, 4—13, 15, 24, 47, 49, 244, 247— 255, 265
——— of Cherry Hill, York, 55, 59, 61, 63, 70, 224, 240, 244
——— of Langbarugh, 4, 12—15, 46, 134, 135, 138, 236, 242, 243

Richardsons of Lynn, 64, 70
——— of Newcastle, 70, 89—94, 106, 107, 132, 133, 199, 202, 205, 231, 239, 243, 273—276
——— of North Shields, 97, 98, 101, 104—107
——— of Sheffield, 63, 71
——— of South Wales 70
——— of Sunderland, 70, 231, 233, 243, 244
——— of the Low Lights, 64—74, 97, 98, 116, 132, 133, 220, 243, 270, 271
——— of Whitby, 13, 15 —19, 21—23, 51—52, 58, 63, 64, 65, 71, 136, 257—264
——— of York, 63, 71
Robinson, Mary, wife of Wm. Richardson, of Ayton, 15
Rowntrees of York, 10, 180, 199, 212

S

Sampler, Isabel Vasie's, 11, 256
Sams, Joseph, 14, 191, 192
Saturday Review, 36, 38
School, Ackworth. See Ackworth School
——— York Girls', 28, 32, 59, 147, 148, 266
Schools, American, 27, 138, 140, 211
——— Grammar, 163, 279
——— Jubilee. See Jubilee Schools
——— of North Shields, 117, 129—132, 281
——— Private, conducted by Friends, 14, 28, 70, 129 — 132, 171, 280
——— Sunday. See Sunday Schools.
Scott, Sir Walter, 40, 44, 45, 51, 112
Seward, Anna, 43, 99, 102
Sewell, Joseph Stickney, Missionary, 15
'Shields Daily News,' 292, 293
Silliman, Professor, of Yale College, 150
Singleton, William, 192, 199
Smales, Family of, 19
Smith, Elizabeth, 41, 42, 43
Southey, Robert, 21, 44
Spencer, of York, Family of, 63, 64, 71
Spinning, 16, 64, 66, 76, 77, 176, 200

Staines, 59, 284
Stead, John, 64, 68
———— Margaret (wife of John Richardson, of the Low Lights), 64—74
Stickney, Family of, 10, 200, 243
———— Sarah (Mrs. Ellis), 10, 200, 243
Sunday Schools, Friends, 107
Sunderland, Traditions of, 123—128
———————— 'Weekly Echo,' 284
Sutton, George, Esq., of Stockton, 25.

T

Tag, Rag and Bobtail, 198
Tankards, Silver, Henry Vasie's, 11, 230
Tatham, Joseph, 14
Taylor, Dr. Jeremy, 237
Taylors of Ongar, Family of, 44
Tea, Five o'clock, 97, 103, 231, 233
Thelwall, John, 77
Thornton, 21, 50, 60, 61, 76, 86, 265
Tuke, Ann, 29, 31, 147, 148
——— Esther (wife of Thomas Priestman), 54, 69, 60
——— Esther (née Maud), 28, 29, 51, 266
——— Henry, 59
——— James Hack, 161—175, 180, 211
——— Mabel (wife of John Hipsley), 59, 60, 147, 148
——— Samuel, 208, 239

Tuke, Sarah (wife of R. Grubb), 176—177
——— William, 28, 29, 59, 147, 175
Turner, Rev. Wm., 104

U

Umbrella, The, a new invention, 24
Unthank, Family of, 74, 272, 273

V

Vasie, Family of, 11—20, 71, 235, 256
——— Henry, 11, 12, 13, 230, 256, 266
——— Isabel (wife of Isaac Richardson) 11—20, 63, 66, 71, 235, 256—264
——— Lydia (wife of John Richardson), 12, 14, 256
——— Margery, her dreams, 12, 13, 256
Vesey, Family of, 19

W

Wakefield, Family of, 11
Walker, John, of North Shields, 21, 65, 266, 270
——— of Whitby, 65, 256, 264, 266
Watson, of Staindrop, Family of, 19, 103
Wheat, Price of, 8, 65, 118, 180, 181, 247, 251, 252
Whitby, 1—2, 4, 11—23, 36,

51, 52, 58, 63, 64, 65, 69, 70, 71, 74, 116, 118, 126, 128, 136, 232, 255—264, 266, 282
White, Dr. Taylor, 157, 162
——— Rachel, of Ayton, 85, 86
Whittaker, Robert, 179, 193, 197, 198
Whitworth, Sir Charles, 160, 162
———————— the Doctors, 25
Wiffen, Jeremiah, 185, 187, 195
Wilberforce, Bishop Samuel, 92
———————— William, 237
Wilkinson, Thomas, of Yanwath, 30, 31, 55
Willington Mill, 74, 135, 272, 273, 280
Wills, 12, 14, 71, 255, 256
Wilson, Elizabeth (wife of William Richardson), 4, 10, 13, 15, 20, 47, 54, 244, 247—255, 262, 265, 268
———James, 195
———Joshua, of Sunderland, 46, 135
Winn, Sir Rowland, of Nostel Priory, 162
Wordsworth, William, 31, 44, 63, 79, 80, 138
Wormall, Henry, 31
Woolman, John, 21, 176, 178, 265

Y

York Girls' School. See Schools

Z

Zouch, The Rev. Henry, Vicar of Sandal, 171

Alphabetical List of the Marriages

RECORDED IN THE TABLES OR NAMED IN THE BOOK.

TABLE

ADAMS, M. JAMES, Sanitary Engineer, Manchester, b. at Eastbourne, Sept. 17, 1856, son of James and Anna Adams; m. at Isleworth, Oct. 23, 1883, Anne Eliza, dau. of Charles Brown and his 2nd wife Emily Spence 2

ADAMS, S. HENRY, Sanitary Engineer, London, b. at Eastbourne, Sept. 17, 1856, son of James and Anna Adams; m. at Isleworth, Aug. 7, 1884, Emily, younger dau. of Charles and Emily Brown 2

ANDREW, CHARLES, son of Charles and Eliz. Andrew; m. at Birstwith, Yorks., Nov. 12, 1870, Deborah Richardson, dau. of John Fox Oxley and his wife Deborah Richardson 8

ARMISTEAD, WM., son of Joseph Armistead, of Leeds; m. at Ayton, July 13, 1854, Caroline, dau. of Richard Richardson and his wife Sarah Buxell . . . 9

ARMSTRONG, ALBERT, b. at Dorset, Vermont, U.S.A., Dec. 1, 1842, son of John and Mary Armstrong; m. at Clark Co., Missouri, April 18, 1864, Mary Ellen, dau. of Stephen and Lydia Halladay 8

ARMSTRONG, JOHN, b. in London, Dec. 23, 1816; m. 1838, Mary, dau. of Julius and Lucy Robolee 8

ARMSTRONG, THOS. FARRER SLINGER, b. at Glasgow, June 17, 1826, son of Wm. Armstrong and his wife Hannah Martin; m. at Ayton, June 10, 1846, Jane, dau. of John Martin and his wife Sarah Raisbeck 8

ARMSTRONG, WM., of Glasgow; m. in London, Hannah, dau. of Isaac Martin and his wife Rachel Richardson 8

ARMSTRONG, WM. WALLACE, b. at Dorset, Vermont, Jan. 25, 1840, son of John and Mary Armstrong; m. at Gage Co., Nebraska, April 4, 1868, Lydia, dau. of Thos. and Susan Blakely 8

BACKHOUSE, FREDERICK, b. at Darlington, April 29, 1808, son of Wm. and Mary Backhouse; m. at Wandsworth, Sept. 5, 1833, Eliza, dau. of Samuel Fossick and his wife Anne Lucas 5

BACKHOUSE, JAS. EDWARD, b. at Sunderland, May 18, 1845, son of Thos. Jas. Backhouse and his wife Margt. Richardson; m. at Wanstead, Eliz. Barclay, dau. of Hy. Fowler of Woodford, Essex, and his wife Ann Ford Barclay . . 6

BACKHOUSE, THOS., b. at York, June 15, 1792, son of Jas. Backhouse and his wife Mary Dearman; m. at Oustwick, April 27, 1826, Hannah, dau. of Wm. Stickney and his wife Esther Richardson 4

TABLE

BACKHOUSE, THOS. JAMES, b. at Sunderland, 1810, son of Edward Backhouse and his wife Mary, dau. of Edwd. and Eliz. Robson; m. at North Shields, Aug. 18, 1841, Margt., dau. of Wm. Richardson and his 2nd wife Margt. Robson . . 6

BAKER, GEORGE R., b. at Thirsk, Jan. 19, 1838, 2nd son of John and Mary Baker; m. at North Shields, April 28, 1868, Margt., younger dau. of Geo. and Mary Unthank 6, 9

BAKER, JOHN, b. April 5, 1806, son of Geo. and Sarah Baker of Danby Bridge; m. at Ayton, Feb. 28, 1833, Mary, dau. of John Gilbert and his wife Jane Richardson 9

BAKER, JOHN GILBERT, F.R.S., F.L.S., &c., Sub-Curator of the Royal Herbarium, Kew, eldest son of John and Mary Baker, b. at Guisboro', Jan. 13, 1834; m. at North Shields, July 19, 1860, Hannah, dau. of Geo. Unthank and his wife Mary Baker 6, 9

BAKER, ROBERT, M.D., Superintendent of Friends' Retreat, York, b. at Thirsk, 1843, 3rd son of John and Mary Baker; m. Oct. 14, 1864, Jane Martha Packer . 9

BAKER, THOS., 4th son of John and Mary Baker, b. at Thirsk, April 10, 1835; m. Eliz. Welsh 9

BARKER, JOS. HIGGINS, son of Wm. and Isabella Barker; m. at Whitby, Oct. 7, 1863, Rebecca Mary, dau. of Gideon Smales and his wife Maria Robinson Wakefield . 7

BARRETT, C. R. B., M.A., Carshalton House, Surrey; m. Alice Lydia, dau. of Major-General Ingram Francis Chapman and his first wife Louisa, dau. of Gen. Aplin 7

BAUMGARTRIER, JOHN RICHARD, M.R.C.S.; m. Aug. 3, 1887, Augusta Mary, dau. of Jas. Richardson and his wife Augusta Ann Dixon 6

BENNETT, ALFD. WM., M.A., b. in London, June 24, 1833, son of Wm. Bennett and his wife Eliz. Trusted; m. at St. Ives, Hunts, April 2, 1858, Katharine, dau. of Wm. Richardson of Sunderland and his wife Eliza Brown . . 5, 6

BENNETT, EDWD. TRUSTED, b. in London, July 1, 1831, eldest son of Wm. and Eliz. Bennett: m. at Olveston, Gloucestershire, Aug. 25, 1858, Sarah Ann, dau. of Josiah and Eliza Hunt 5

BENNETT, WM., son of Rd. and Mary Bennett of Donnington, Salop; m. in London, Feb. 15, 1797, Hannah, dau. of Samuel Fossick and his wife Hannah Marishall 5

BENNETT, WM., b. in London, Feb. 29, 1804, son of Wm. and Hannah Bennett; m. at Ross, Oct. 31, 1828, Eliz., dau. of John and Mary Trusted . . 5

BEVAN, CHAS. HY., b. in London, Jan. 27, 1832, 2nd son of Dr. Bevan and his wife Hannah M. Bennett; m. at Rotherham, Dec. 16, 1858, Hannah Maria, dau. of Joseph Davy of Sheffield 5

BEVAN, ROBERT EATON, b. April 25, 1835, 3rd son of Dr. Bevan and his wife H. M. Bennett; m. at Wellington, Dec. 1, 1859, Charlotte, dau. of Gray and Sarah Hester 5

BEVAN, THOS., M.D., b. at Swansea, son of Rees and Grace Bevan; m. in London, Aug. 15, 1827, Hannah Marishall, dau. of Wm. Bennett and his wife Hannah Fossick 5

BEVAN, THOS., J.P. for Kent, b. in London, Nov. 26, 1829, eldest son of Dr. Bevan and his wife Hannah M. Bennett; m. Emma, dau. of Thos. and Mary Ann Bayes 5

BINNS, CHAS., b. at Lancaster, Oct. 23, 1813, son of Jonathan Binns and his wife Rachel Stickney; m. (1st) at Liverpool, Aug. 6, 1839, Eliz., dau. of Sir Joshua and Lady Walmsley; (2ndly) at Dulwich, May 17, 1871, Julia Parker, dau. of the Rev. Thos. Hartcup and granddaughter of General Hartcup . . 4

TABLE

BINNS, JONATHAN, b. at Lancaster, May 13, 1785, son of Jonathan and Mary Binns; m. at Oustwick, Yorks., Feb. 17, 1809, Rachel, dau. of Wm. Stickney and his wife Esther Richardson 4

BINNS, JONATHAN GEO., b. at Lancaster, Sept. 23, 1816; m. at Liverpool, Sept. 1, 1846, Fanny, dau. of Charles and Sarah Harker 4

BINNS, JONATHAN GEO., Government Inspector of Mines, Dunedin, New Zealand, b. at Stoneleigh, Lancashire, July 31, 1855, son of Jonathan Geo. Binns and his wife Fanny Harker; m. Constance Mary Smith 4

BOTTOME, Rev. WM. MACDONALD, Vicar of Over Stowey, Somerset, b. at Merridew, Connecticut, U.S.A., son of the Rev. Frank Bottome, D.D., and his wife Margt. Macdonald; m. at Darlington, Oct. 27, 1875, Margaret, dau. of Charles Albert Leatham and his wife Rachel, dau. of Joseph Pease and his wife Emma Gurney 9

BOYCE, GEORGE, Member for the Chertsey division of the Surrey County Council, b. at Egham, June 12, 1832, son of John Pierce Boyce and his wife Ann, dau. of Wm. and Ann Northcroft; m. at Tynemouth Church, June 17, 1862, Anne Ogden, dau. of Wm. Brown of North Shields and his 2nd wife Sarah Richardson 8

BRAYSHAW, ALFRED, son of Benjamin and Annie Brayshaw of Leeds; m. at Manchester, Jan. 3. 1861, Jane Eliza, dau. of Shipley Neave and his wife Elizabeth Stephenson 5

BROWN, ALFRED HENRY, of Luton, Beds., b. at North Shields, March 3, 1860, son of Charles and Emily Brown; m. at York, 1885, Ursula Isabel Macdonnell . 2

BROWN, CHARLES, b. at North Shields, Oct. 15, 1816, 3rd son of Wm. Brown and his 1st wife Mary Richardson; m. (1st) at North Shields, Feb. 9, 1843, Jane, dau. of Robert Spence and his wife Mary Foster; (2ndly), at Wakefield, May 20, 1852, Emily, dau. of John Spence and his wife Deborah Smith . . 2

BROWN, CHARLES, son of Charles and Emily Brown, b. at North Shields, Oct. 19, 1854; m. 1880, at Stockton, Eleanor, dau. of Samuel and Agnes Tennent . 2

BROWN, FREDERICK, b. at North Shields, Oct. 15, 1840, son of Richardson Brown and his wife Frances Gilmour; m. at Staindrop, Sarah Ann, dau. of John Hills and his wife Isabella Davy 2

BROWN, HENRY, b. at North Shields, June 29, 1818, eldest son of Wm. and Mary Brown; m. Aug. 17, 1837, Eliz. Foster, dau. of Robert Spence and his wife Mary Foster 2

BROWN, ISAAC, of the Isle of Ely; m. Sarah, dau. of Wm. Richardson and his wife Eliz. Wilson 1

BROWN, ISAAC, b. at Thirsk, July 31, 1801; m. at Stoke Newington, Priscilla, dau. of John and Mary Brown 4

BROWN, JOHN SPENCE, b. at North Shields, April 19, 1853, eldest son of Charles and Emily Brown; m. Martha A. Blanchard 2

BROWN, WILLIAM, b. at Thirsk, April 11. 1764; m. at Ayton, May 28, 1800, Hannah, dau. of Nicholas Richardson and his wife Esther Kilden . . . 4

BROWN, WILLIAM, b. at North Shields, July 5, 1788, son of Geo. Brown of that place, and his wife Anne Ogden of Sunderland; m. (1st) at Sunderland, April 16, 1807, Mary, widow of Joshua Wilson, and dau. of Wm. Richardson of Langbarugh and his wife Mary Muskett; and (2ndly) Sarah, dau. of Henry Richardson of of Stockton and his wife Hannah Priestman of Thornton . . 2, 8

TABLE

Brown, William, son of Wm. and Mary Brown, b. at North Shields, Sept. 5, 1815; m. at Ayton, Aug. 19, 1847, Mary, dau. of John Wheatley and his wife Hannah Barron 2

Brown, William, b. at North Shields, Sept. 2, 1861, son of Charles and Emily Brown; m. at Bodmin, Emily, dau. of Samuel and Thomasine Stripp . . 2

Brown, Wm. Henry, b. at North Shields, Jan. 8, 1839, only son of Henry Brown and his wife Eliz. Foster Spence; m. May, 1863, Margt., dau. of Joseph Ogilvie and his wife Margt. Smith 2

Brown, Richardson, b. at North Shields, March 12, 1818, youngest son of Wm. and Mary Brown; m. Frances Gilmour 2

Brown, Richardson, b. at North Shields, April, 1844, son of Richardson and Frances Brown; m. in London Emma Rowley 2

Butler, John Theobald; m. Rachel Mary, dau. of Charles Albert Leatham of Wakefield and his wife Rachel, dau. of Joseph Pease and his wife Emma Gurney . 9

Carrington, Arthur, Ankerbold, Chesterfield; m. Florence, dau. of Charles Binns of Clay Cross Hall, Derbyshire, and his wife Eliz., dau. of Sir Joshua Walmsley 4

Casson, Benjamin, b. at Hull, Jan. 12, 1798, son of Henry and Eliz. Casson; m. (3rd wife) Hannah, dau. of Aaron Richardson of Stockton and his wife Deborah Proctor of Selby 8

Casson, Henry, son of Mordecai and Sarah Casson of Thorne; m. (2nd wife) at Pickering, Jan. 14, 1824, Isabel, dau. of Henry Richardson and his wife Hannah Priestman 8

Casson, Henry, b. at Hull, Feb. 27, 1802, son of Henry and Eliz. Casson; m. at North Shields, Jan. 19, 1832, Henrietta, dau. of Wm. and Mary Brown . 2

Chadwick, Timothy; m. at Ayton, March 7, 1719, Rebecca, dau. of Wm. Richardson and his wife Eliz. Wilson 1

Chapman, Abel, b. at Low Barnes, Sunderland, Aug. 15, 1869, son of Wm. Chapman and his 1st wife Hannah Bayner; m. at Whitby, Aug. 29, 1816, Eliz., dau. of Gideon Smales and his wife Hannah, dau. of Ingram and Eliz. Chapman . 7

Chapman, Ingram, shipowner, b. at Whitby, April 18, 1725, eighth son of Solomon Chapman and his 1st wife Ann Linskill; m. at Stainton Dale, Feb. 12, 1759, Eliz. dau. of Isaac Richardson and his wife Isabel Vasie . . . 7

Chapman, Ingram, b. at Whitby, Oct. 5, 1764, only son of Ingram and Eliz. Chapman; m. at Whitby, April 16, 1794, Jane, dau. of John Chapman and his wife Jane Mellor 7

Chapman, Ingram, b. at Whitby, March 28, 1798, only son of Ingram and Jane Chapman; m. at Bombay, Oct. 20, 1827, Agnes Stamms, dau. of General Willis . 7

Chapman, Ingram Francis, Major-General of the Bombay Army, b. March 1, 1831, only son of Ingram and Agnes Chapman; m. (1st) at Poonah, India, Sept. 15, 1853, Louisa, dau. of General Aplin; (2ndly), Feb. 17, 1874, Frances Mortimer, dau. of Major-General J. G. Scott, Bombay Army 7

Chapman, Thomas Edward, b. at Sunderland, Jan. 24, 1820, son of Abel Chapman and his wife Eliz., dau. of Gideon Smales and his wife Hannah Chapman; m. at Newcastle-upon-Tyne, Oct. 3, 1848, Jane Anne, dau. of Jos. and Margt. Crawhall of St. Ann's, Newcastle, and Stagshaw Close House . . . 7

TABLE

CHAPMAN, WM., artist, b. at Sunderland, Sept. 16, 1817; m. at York, May 17, 1847, Harriet Wright 7

CLARK, HENRY ECROYD, missionary to Madagascar, b. at Doncaster, June 28, 1836, son of Joseph and Ann Clark; m. July 18, 1866, Rachel Maria, dau. of Wm. Rowntree and his wife Ann, dau. of John and Mary Cooke of Millbank, West Derby 4

CLARK, JOHN, son of Joseph and Ann Clark of Doncaster; m. at Hull, Oct. 4, 1855, Mary Eliz., dau. of Henry Casson and his wife Henrietta Brown . . 2

CLARK, JOSEPH HENRY, b. at Balby, Sept. 10, 1856, son of John and M. E. Clark; m. 1886, Janet, dau. of John Taylor of London 2

COOPER, ALFRED WM., Artist, b. in London, Oct. 23, 1830, son of Abraham Cooper, R.A., and his wife Maria Gomm; m. at Brighton, Dec. 10, 1870, Eliz., dau. of Henry Brown of North Shields and his wife Eliz. Foster Spence . . 2

CURRY, HY. JOHN; m. April 22, 1875, Mary, only child of Wm. Augustus Loy, M.R.C.S., and his wife Hannah, dau. of Geo. Jackson, Tanton Hall . . 2

DINGLE, the Rev. JAMES, Vicar of Ruswarp, Whitby; m. at Whitby, June 16, 1859, Eliz. Dent, dau. of Gideon Smales and his wife Maria Robinson Wakefield . 7

DODDS, JOHN, of Bishop Auckland; m. Isabel, dau. of Michael Watson and his wife Ann Chapman 7

DODSHON, WM.; m. Susanna, dau. of John Irving and his wife Hannah Masterman . 5

DRAWBRIDGE, the Rev. WM. BARKER, Chaplain in the Indian Army, son of Wm. Drawbridge, M.D., of Rochester, and his wife Maria; m. at Kirby Moorside, July 7, 1860, Alice, dau. of John Fox Oxley and his wife Deborah Richardson . 8

ECROYD, WM. FARRER, J.P., b. at Lomeshaye, July 14, 1827, son of Wm. Ecroyd and his wife Margaret Farrer; m. at York, Oct. 1, 1851, Mary, dau. of Thomas Backhouse and his wife Hannah Stickney 4

ELLIOTT, JAMES; m. Mary, dau. of Joseph Richardson and his wife Mary Ann Perkins 9

ELLIS, the Rev. WM., missionary to the South Sea Islands; m. May 28, 1838, Sarah, dau. of Wm. Stickney and his wife Esther Richardson 4

EVANS, EDMUND, of Witley, Surrey, colour-printer, b. in London, Feb. 23, 1826, son of Henry and Mary Evans; m. at Godalming, Aug. 23, 1864, Mary, dau. of Henry Brown and his wife Eliz. Foster Spence 2

FAIRBRIDGE, JOSEPH; m. at Sunderland, Nov. 16, 1845, Eleanor, dau. of John Gilbert Holmes and his wife Margaret Richardson 6

FAY, MUNROE M., of Lynville, Tennessee, U.S.A.; m. Dec. 25, 1870, Mary Ann, widow of Albert M. Hooke, and dau. of Thos. Richardson and his wife Ellen Hagood 9

FAUSSETT, JOHN, M.D.; m. Anne Mary, dau. of Richardson Hesleton Gilbert of Thornton-le-Street and his wife Eliz. Packer 8, 9

FISHER, PETER MOOR, b. at Youghal, Nov. 15, 1809, son of Abraham and Jane Fisher; m. at Wicklow, Sept. 13, 1860, Rachel, dau. of Isaac Rowntree and his wife Sarah Smithson 4

TABLE

FLETCHER, CALEB, b. at Kirby Moorside, April 2, 1751, son of Caleb and Lydia
    Fletcher; m. at Richmond, Yorks., Jan. 22, 1764, Eliz., dau. of Jas. Masterman
    and his wife Hannah Fossick   5

FLETCHER, CALEB, b. at Kirby Moorside, June 16, 1784, son of Caleb and Eliz.
    Fletcher; m. at Leeds, Sept. 23, 1811, Mary, dau. of Geo. and Susanna Eddison 5

FOSSICK, DANIEL, of Welbury, near Northallerton; m. at Ayton, March 5, 1725,
    Hannah, dau. of Wm. Richardson and his wife Eliz. Wilson   .   .   1, 5

FOSSICK, GEORGE, b. March 23, 1810, in London; m. at Stockton, June 9, 1859,
    Jane, dau. of Alf. and Ann Brady   5

FOSSICK, SAMUEL, b. in London, Feb. 25, 1726; m. at Devonshire House, Bishopsgate,
    May 1, 1759, Sarah, dau. of Samuel and Hannah Marishall   .   .   . 5

FOSSICK, SAMUEL, b. in London, Sept. 17, 1760; m. at Westminster, Sept. 25, 1800,
    Anne, dau. of Benjamin and Eliz. Lucas   5

FOSSICK, SAMUEL, b. in London, July 31, 1806; m. at Rushen, Isle of Man, April 15,
    1835, Ellen Gawne   5

FOSSICK, WILLIAM, b. at Wandsworth, Oct. 13, 1812, son of Samuel Fossick and his
    wife Anne Lucas; m. at Darlington, July 22, 1858, Amelia, dau. of Alfred and
    Mary Birchall of Leeds   5

FOSTER, ROBERT, b. at North Shields, Jan. 27, 1812, eldest son of Myles Birket
    Foster and his wife Ann King; m. at Newcastle-on-Tyne, July 7, 1858, Ann,
    dau. of Isaac Richardson and his wife Deborah Sutton of Newcastle   .   . 6

FOSTER, Rev. WILLIAM, son of Jonathan Foster and his wife Mary, dau. of Rear-
    Admiral Storr; m. at Edinburgh, Sept. 18, 1860, Hannah, dau. of Joseph
    Stickney and his wife Eliza Mennell   4

FOWLER, JOHN, of Melksham, Wilts; m. Eliz. Lucy, dau. of Joseph Pease and his
    wife Emma Gurney   9

FOWLER, WM., son of John and Rebecca Fowler of Melksham; m. Rachel, widow
    of Charles Albert Leatham and dau. of Joseph Pease and his wife Emma
    Gurney   9

FRY, RICHARD, of Bristol; m. Rachel, dau. of Edwd. Pease and his wife Rachel
    Whitwell   9

FRY, THEODORE, of Bristol, M.P. for Darlington, 1888; m. Sophia, dau. of John Pease
    and his wife Sophia Jowitt   9

GALLILEE, GEORGE, Shipowner, Whitby; m. Mary, dau. of Isaac Richardson and
    his wife Isabel Vasie   8

GALLILEE, ISAAC, b. at Whitby, July 30, 1776, son of Geo. Gallilee and his wife
    Mary Richardson; m. at York, May 14, 1807, Hannah, dau. of John and
    Eliz. Thurnham   8

GALLILEE, THOMAS, b. at Whitby, March 11, 1772; m. at New Malton, Sept. 27,
    1799, Eliz., dau. of Joseph and Eliz. Clark of Whitby   .   .   . 8

GASKIN, JOSEPH; m. Rebecca, widow of Timothy Chadwick and dau. of Wm.
    Richardson and his wife Eliz. Wilson   1

GATTY, Rev. R. A., of Bradfield Rectory, Yorks.; m. Florence Emily, dau. of Arthur
    David Vesey and his wife Emily Persis Allix of Willoughby Hall, Lincoln-
    shire   7

TABLE

GAYNER, ROBERT HAYDON, b. at Felton, Gloucestershire, Jan. 5, 1831, son of John and Martha Sturge Gayner; m. at Sunderland, Dec. 27, 1866, Emily, dau. of Caleb Richardson and his wife Mary Driver 6

GELDARD, JOHN; m. Laura Eliz., dau. of John Fowler and his wife Eliz. Lucy Pease 9

GIBSON, FRANCIS, of Saffron Walden; m. at Darlington, May 7, 1829, Eliz., dau. of Edwd. Pease and his wife Rachel Whitwell 9

GILBERT, JOHN, of Newcastle; m. at Ayton, Dec. 31, 1807, Jane, dau. of Robert Richardson and his wife Caroline Garth 9

GILBERT, RICHARDSON HESLETON, b. at Gt. Ayton, Feb. 2, 1838; m. at Redcar, Sept. 8, 1860, Eliz. Packer of Thirsk 8, 9

GILBERT, ROBERT, b. at Newcastle, Sept. 28, 1808, son of John and Jane Gilbert; m. June 16, 1836, Mary, dau. of Philip Hesleton and his wife Mary Richardson 8, 9

GILL, Rev. WILLIAM, son of John and Mary Gill of Kirby Moorside; m. at Malton, June 20, 1841, Mary, dau. of Gideon Smales and his wife Hannah Chapman . 7

GILLETT, GEORGE, son of Joseph Ashby Gillett of Banbury; m. at York, Oct. 16, 1867, Hannah Eliz., dau. of Joseph Rowntree and his wife Sarah Stephenson . 4

GINGELL, ——; m. Martha, dau. of John Irving and his wife Hannah Masterman 5

GOODMAN, ALBERT, b. at Wilton, Hunts., June 25, 1840, son of Joseph and Rose Goodman; m. at Sunderland, Dec. 28, 1864, Olivia, dau. of Wm. and Eliz. Richardson 6

GRACE, HENRY, born at Clifton, Bristol, Sept. 29, 1837, son of James Grace and his wife Ellen Thirnbeck; m. at Manchester, May 6, 1869, Hannah Mary, dau. of Shipley Neave and his wife Eliz. Stephenson 5

GRACE, JOHN THIRNBECK; m. Hannah Maria, widow of George Pumphrey and dau. of Abraham Sewell and his wife Hannah Stickney 4

GRAHAM, Rev. HENRY JOHN, Rector of Pudsey, near Leeds, b. at York, Sept. 29, 1819, son of Hewley Graham and his wife Mary Dyson; m. at Whitby, July 1, 1845, Ann, dau. of Gideon Smales and his wife Maria Robinson Wakefield . . 7

GRAVELY, ARTHUR F., of Wellingboro'; m. 1884, Margt., dau. of Henry Hutchinson of Selby and his wife Eliz. Richardson of Langbarugh 2

GREER, ROBERT JOHN; m. Anna Rachel, dau. of Thomas Pumphrey and his wife Rachel Richardson 6

GWATKIN, OWEN, M.R.C.S., b. at Brighton; m. at York, 1878, Jane Spence, dau. of Chas. Brown and his first wife Jane Spence 2

HAMLYN, VINCENT CALMADY, Barrister-at-Law, of Lea Wood and Paschoe, Devon; m. Emma Josephine, dau. of Sir Joseph Whitwell and Lady Pease . . 9

HARRIS, HENRY, b. at Tottenham, Feb. 28, 1833, son of Anthony Harris and his wife Sarah Capper; m. at Malton, June 9, 1859, Eliz., dau. of Abraham Sewell and his wife Dorothy Stickney 4

HENDERSON, JEREMIAH, b. at Scarboro', Feb. 24, 1718; m. at Stockton, Aug. 16, 1759 (2nd wife), Catherine, dau. of Francis Husband and his wife Rachel Richardson 1

HESLETON, PHILIP, b. at Moorsome, Sept. 18, 1764, son of Rd. and Mary Hesleton; m. at Ayton, Nov. 30, 1786, Mary, dau. of John Richardson and his wife Rachel Snowdon 8

TABLE

HJERLEID, SIVERT, b. at Doore, Norway, Dec. 8, 1836, son of Ole and Marit
Hjerleid; m. at Middlesboro', Sept. 12, 1857, Eliz., dau. of Isaac Sharp and his
wife Hannah Procter 6

HODGKIN, JONATHAN BACKHOUSE, b. Dec. 27, 1848, son of John Hodgkin and his wife
Ann Backhouse; m. April 24, 1873, Mary Anna, dau. of John Pease and his
wife Sophia Jowitt 9

HOLMES, ALFRED, b. at Newcastle, Oct. 18, 1858: m. Amelia Constance, dau. of
Jas. Richardson and his wife Augusta Ann Dixon 6

HOLMES, HENRY, b. at Sunderland, Nov. 8, 1829, son of John Gilbert Holmes and
his wife Margaret Richardson; m. at Hornchurch, Essex, Oct. 20, 1863, Emilie
Helena Mary, dau. of John and Helena Mary Wagener 6

HOLMES, JOHN GILBERT, b. at Sunderland, April 25, 1798, son of Benj. and Eleanor
Holmes; m. May 5, 1822, Margaret, dau. of John Richardson of Sunderland
and his first wife Hannah, dau. of Caleb and Judith Wilson . . . 6

HOLMES, WM., b. at Sunderland, Jan. 15, 1792, son of Thomas and Hannah Holmes;
m. at Whitby, Dec. 11, 1822, Ann, dau. of Gideon Smales and his wife Hannah
Chapman 7

HOLMES, WM. HENRY, b. at Newcastle-on-Tyne, March 29, 1824, son of Wm. and
Ann Holmes; m. at Manchester, May 15, 1851, Mary Jane, dau. of John Beeby
and his wife Eliz. Brockbank 7

HOOKE, ALBERT M.; m. at Chattanooya, Tennessee, U.S.A., Mary Ann, dau. of
Thos. Richardson and his wife Ellen Hagood 9

HUDSON, WM.; m. at Whitby, June 10, 1792, Isabel, dau. of Isaac Richardson and
his wife Isabel Vasie 8

HUSBAND, FRANCIS, b. at Guisborough, May 19, 1688, son of Christopher and
Eliz. Husband; m. at Ayton, 1718, Rachel, dau. of Wm. Richardson and his
wife Eliz. Wilson 1

HUSTLER, JOHN, b. at Bradford, June 4, 1777, son of Jeremiah and Sarah Hustler;
m. at Darlington, Oct. 18, 1798, Eliz. dau. of Joseph Pease and his wife Mary
Richardson 9

HUTCHINSON, ALFRED, b. at Selby, July 27, 1860, son of Henry Hutchinson and his
wife Eliz. Richardson of Langbarugh; m. at Ontario, 1884, Margaret Allen . 2

HUTCHINSON, ERNEST, b. at Selby, Jan. 3, 1862, son of Henry and Eliz. Hutchinson;
m. at Westminster, 1885, Louisa M. Cash 2

HUTCHINSON, HENRY, b. at Selby, son of Jonathan Hutchinson and his wife Eliz.
Massey of Spalding; m. at Ayton, Sept. 22, 1859, Eliz. dau. of John Richardson
of Langbarugh and his wife Jane Procter 2

IRVING, JOHN; m. Hannah, dau. of James Masterman of Welbury and his wife
Lydia Fossick 5

IRVING, JOHN, son of John and Hannah Irving; m. Belle Anne Barnard . . 5

KAYE, WALTER JENKINSON, Principal of Ilkley College; m. at North Shields, July 27,
1869, Ann Isabel, dau. of Ingram Chapman Watson and his wife Jane Spence . 7

KING, HENRY, b. at York, Oct. 23, 1821, son of Joseph King and his wife Sarah
Awmack; m. (1st) at Malton, Feb. 21, 1850, Esther Richardson, dau. of Abraham

TABLE

Sewell and his wife Dorothy Stickney; (2ndly), at York, Sarah, dau. of Henry
    Casson and his wife Henrietta Brown 2, 4

KING, WM. SEWELL, b. at York, July 25, 1852, son of Henry King and his first wife
    Esther Richardson Sewell; m. in 1878, Kate Harris Hudswell .   .   . 4

KUHLMANN, ARTHUR, Engineer; m. Dec. 11, 1879, Ellen Ann, youngest dau. of
    Edward Richardson of Newcastle and his wife Jane Wigham of Edinburgh . 6

LEADBEATER, THOMAS, of Lurgan, Ireland, b. June 10, 1823; m. Mary, widow of
    Enoch Oldfield Tindall of Scarborough, and dau. of Isaac Rowntree and his
    wife Sarah Smithson 4

LEAN, WILLIAM SCARNELL, M.A., Principal of Flounder's College, b. at Birmingham,
    June 8, 1833; m. at Rochester, Sept. 15, 1864, to Marianna, dau. of Thos.
    Bevan, M.D., and his wife Hannah Marishall Bennett .   .   . 5

LEATHAM, CHAS. ALBERT, son of Wm. and Margaret Leatham, of Heath, Wakefield;
    m. Rachel, dau. of Joseph Pease and his wife Emma Gurney .   . 9

LITTLEBOY, THOMAS GRAHAM, of Crowmarsh, near Wallingford; m. at Sunderland,
    Sept. 5, 1855, Sophia, dau. of Caleb Richardson and his wife Mary Driver . 6

LOY, THOS., M.R.C.S., son of the Rev. Richard Loy and his wife Jane Glover Knaggs;
    m. at Edinburgh, Eliz., dau. of Wm. Richardson of Laugbarugh and his wife
    Mary Muskett 2

LOY, THOS., M.A. Cantab., M.R.C.S., b. at Ayton, April 1, 1816, son of Thomas and
    Elizabeth Loy; m. at Stokesley, June 26, 1848, Eliz., dau. of Geo. Jackson of
    Tanton Hall 2

LOY, WM. AUGUSTUS, M.R.C.S., b. at Ayton, Feb. 26, 1819, son of Thos. Loy and his
    wife Eliz. Richardson; m. in Scotland, June, 1843, Hannah, dau. of Geo.
    Jackson of Tanton Hall 2

MARRIOTT, WILSON, b. at Reedyford, May 22, 1796, son of John Marriott and his
    wife Ann Wilson; m. at Bradford, April 20, 1825, Margaret, dau. of Wm. Maude,
    M.D., and his wife Margaret Richardson 3

MARTIN, ISAAC, b. at York, May 17, 1753, son of Wm. and Eliz. Martin; m. at Ayton,
    Rachel, dau. of John Richardson and his wife Rachel Snowden .   . 3

MARTIN, ISAAC, b. at Ayton, April 1, 1783, son of Isaac Martin and his wife Rachel
    Richardson; m. at Darlington, Sept. 1812, Eliz., dau. of Michael and Sarah
    Pease 3

MARTIN, ISAAC RAISBECK, b. at Newcastle, Jan. 24, 1813, eldest son of John Martin
    and his wife Sarah Raisbeck; m. (1st) at North Shields, Feb. 1844, Jane, dau.
    of James and Phyllis Anderson; (2ndly), in Illinois, U.S.A., 1852 (name of 2nd
    wife unknown) 3

MARTIN, JOHN, b. at Ayton, Dec. 26, 1789, son of Isaac Martin and his wife Rachel
    Richardson; m. at Newcastle, Sarah, dau. of Wm. and Mary Raisbeck .   . 3

MARTIN, WM., b. at Ayton, Feb. 18, 1783, eldest son of Isaac and Rachel Martin;
    m. at Ayton, Nov. 18, 1815, Ann, dau. of Joseph and Ann Lenaker .   . 3

MARTIN, WM., b. at Newcastle, April 6, 1825, son of John Martin and his wife Sarah
    Raisbeck; m. at Jarrow Church, May 29, 1846, Phœbe, dau. of Joseph and
    Phœbe Hargrave 3

TABLE

MARTINDALE, SENHOUSE, Lloyd's Surveyor, London, son of Senhouse Martindale,
Cumberland; m. at Durham, Jan. 20, 1853, Mary, widow of Isaac Richardson,
and dau. of Joseph and Margaret Unthank 6, 8

MASTERMAN, JAMES, of Richmond, Yorks.; m. Hannah, dau. of Daniel Fossick and
his wife Hannah Richardson   5

MASTERMAN, JAMES, of Welbury; m. Lydia, dau. of Daniel Fossick and his wife
Hannah Richardson   5

MAUDE, WM., M.D., b. at Bradford, Feb. 18, 1765, son of Timothy and Ann Maude;
m. at Ayton, Feb. 22, 1792, Margaret, only child of Wm. Richardson of that
place and his first wife Ann Hill   8

MAYSON, RICHARD, Merchant, of Hull, son of Valentine Mayson, Rector of Driffield;
m. Mary Richardson. (See Richard Richardson.)   .   .   . Chap. VII.

MERZ, JOHN THEODORE; m. at Newcastle, Dec. 17, 1873, Alice Mary, dau. of Edward
Richardson and his wife Jane Wigham   6

METFORD, JOSEPH, b. at Eastonbury, Somerset, June 3, 1805, son of Joseph and
Eliz. Metford; m. at Pickering, April 25, 1832, Esther, dau. of Wm. Rowntree
of Riseborough and his wife Rachel, dau. of Nicholas Richardson and his wife
Dorothy Kilden   4

MYERS, JOHN; m. Eliz., dau. of Daniel Fossick of Welbury and his wife Hannah,
dau. of Wm. Richardson of Ayton and his wife Eliz. Wilson   .   .   5

NEAVE, JOHN HENRY, b. at Manchester, April 18, 1842, son of Shipley and Eliz.
Neave; m. Aug. 17, 1870, Annie, dau. of Josiah Newman of Leominster   .   5

NEAVE, SHIPLEY, b. at Longham, Dorsets., Sept. 14, 1798, son of John and Hannah
Neave; m. at Manchester, Aug. 18, 1836, Eliz., dau. of Isaac Stephenson and
his wife Hannah Masterman   5

NEWMAN, JOSIAH, of Leominster; m. at York, March 21, 1860 (2nd wife), Mary
Priscilla, dau. of Caleb Fletcher and his wife Mary Eddison   .   .   5

NEWMARCH, JOHN, son of Rev. Henry Newmarch, Vicar of Hessle, near Hull;
m. at Whitby, Feb. 16, 1861, Julia, fifth dau. of Gideon Smales and his wife
Maria Robinson Wakefield   7

NICHOL, JAMES PRINGLE, LL.D., Professor at Glasgow University, Author of 'Archi-
tecture of the Heavens,' and other works on Astronomy; m. at Darlington,
1853, Eliz., dau. of Joseph Pease and his wife Eliz. Beaumont   .   .   9

OVEREND, JOHN, one of the founders of the firm of Richardson, Overend and Gurney,
b. at Settle, Yorks., June 2, 1769, son of John and Isabel Overend; m. at Ayton,
Jan. 26, 1809, Martha, dau. of Robert Richardson and his wife Caroline Garth .   9

OXLEY, ALFRED HARDCASTLE, b. at Askerne, April 26, 1846, son of John Fox Oxley
and his wife Deborah Richardson; m. at Selby, April 26, 1871, Sophia, dau. of
John and Amy Fothergill   8

OXLEY, JOHN FOX, M.R.C.S., son of Samuel and Susanna Oxley of Pontefract;
m. at Selby, Feb. 9, 1836, Deborah, dau. of Aaron Richardson and his wife
Deborah Procter   8

PACKER, JAMES JOHN; m. at Thirsk, 1858, Sarah Jane, dau. of John Baker and his
wife Mary Gilbert   9

TABLE

PEASE, ALFRED EDWARD (M.P. for York, J.P. and C.C.), b. at Darlington, June 23, 1857, son of Sir J. W. Pease and his wife Mary Fox; m. Helen Anne, dau. of Sir R. N. Fowler and his wife Sarah Charlotte Fox 9

PEASE, ARTHUR (M.P. for Whitby, 1880), b. at Darlington, 1837, son of Joseph Pease and his wife Emma Gurney; m. 1864, Mary Lecky Pike of Bessborough, Co. Cork 9

PEASE, CHARLES, b. at Darlington, 1848, son of Joseph and Emma Pease; m. 1871, Sarah Eliz. Bewley of Dublin 9

PEASE, EDWARD, b. at Shafton (parish of Felkirk, Yorks.), Sept. 26, bap. Oct. 25, 1711, son of Joseph Pease and his wife Ann Coldwell; m. at Darlington, Oct. 2, 1735, Eliz., dau. of Michael Coates of Caselee and his wife Ann Hunter . Chap. VII.

PEASE, EDWARD (founder of first passenger railway in England), b. at Darlington, July 31, 1767, eldest son of Joseph Pease and his wife Mary Richardson; m. at Kendal, Nov. 3, 1796, Rachel, dau. of John Whitwell and his wife Dorothy Wilson 9

PEASE, EDWARD, b. at South End, Darlington, June 24, 1834, second son of Joseph and Emma Pease; m. at Birmingham, Feb. 26, 1862, Sarah, dau. of Charles Sturge and his wife Mary Darby, dau. of Barnard Dickenson and his wife Ann Darby 9

PEASE, EDWIN LUCAS (Mayor of Darlington, Chairman of Board of Guardians, &c.), b. at North Lodge, Darlington, Oct. 27, 1838, son of John Beaumont Pease and his wife Sarah Fossick; m. at Ross, Oct. 1, 1862, Frances Helen, dau. of Wm. Peter Edwards and his wife Marianne Headwell 9

PEASE, GURNEY, b. at South End, Darlington, 1839, son of Joseph and Emma Pease; m. 1865, Katharine Wilson 9

PEASE, HENRY (M.P. 1857), b. at Darlington, May 4, 1807, son of Edward Pease and his wife Rachel Whitwell; m. (1st) at Uxbridge, Feb. 25, 1835, Anna, dau. of Richard and Mary Fell; (2ndly), at Birmingham, Jan. 19, 1859, Mary, dau. of Samuel Lloyd 9

PEASE, HENRY FELL, of Brinkburn (M.P. for Cleveland), b. at Darlington, April 28, 1838, son of Henry Pease and his wife Anna Fell; m. 1862, Eliz., dau. of John Beaumont Pease and his wife Sarah Fossick 9

PEASE, HOWARD, b. at Newcastle, July 12, 1863, eldest son of John Wm. Pease, of Pendower, and his wife Helen Maria Fox; m. at Cheltenham, Oct. 27, 1887, Margaret, dau. of the Rev. Herbert Kynaston, D.D., Principal of Cheltenham College . 9

PEASE, JOHN, Minister of the Society of Friends, b. at Darlington, Sept. 30, 1797, eldest son of Edward Pease and his wife Rachel Whitwell; m. at Leeds, Nov. 26, 1823, Sophia, dau. of Joseph Jowitt and his wife Grace Firth . . 9

PEASE, JOHN BEAUMONT (Chairman of Board of Guardians, &c.), b. at Darlington, July 27, 1803, only son of Joseph Pease and his wife Eliz. Beaumont; m. at Wandsworth, Aug. 18, 1825, Sarah, dau. of Samuel Fossick and his wife Anne Lucas 5, 9

PEASE, JOHN WILLIAM, Banker, of Pendower, Newcastle, b. at North Lodge, Darlington, Aug. 13, 1836, 2nd son of John Beaumont Pease and his wife Sarah Fossick; m. at Falmouth, Sept. 13, 1860, Helen Maria, dau. of Alfred Fox and his wife Sarah Lloyd 9

TABLE

PEASE, JOSEPH, Woollen Manufacturer, b. at Darlington, March 25, 1737, son of Edward Pease and his wife Eliz. Coates; m. at Darlington, Oct. 13, 1763, Mary, dau. of Richard Richardson of Hull and his wife Lydia, dau. of William Richardson of Ayton and his wife Eliz. Wilson 9

PEASE, JOSEPH, b. at Darlington, Jan. 28, 1772, 2nd son of Joseph Pease and his wife Mary Richardson; m. 1st, at Westminster, July 23, 1801, Eliz., dau. of John Beaumont of Battersea Rise, Surrey, and his wife Mary Brown; 2ndly, at Grace-church St., London, March 16, 1831, Anna, dau. of Thos. and Sarah Bradshaw . 9

PEASE, JOSEPH (first Quaker M.P.), b. at Darlington, June 22, 1799, son of Edward Pease and his wife Rachel Whitwell; m. at Norwich, March 20, 1826, Emma, dau. of Joseph Gurney 9

PEASE, JOSEPH ALBERT, b. Jan. 17, 1860, son of Sir Joseph W. and Lady Pease; m. Elsie, dau. of Sir H. Havelock Allan . . . .

PEASE, JOSEPH BEAUMONT, b. at Darlington, Dec. 27, 1833, eldest son of John Beaumont Pease and his wife Sarah Fossick; m. (1st) at Staines, Sept. 15, 1859, Louisa, dau. of Frederick Ashby and his wife, Susanna Lucas; (2ndly) Mary, dau. of Isaac Wilson of Nunthorpe Hall, Yorks., and his wife Anna Benson of Kendal 9

PEASE, Sir JOSEPH WHITWELL, Baronet, of Hutton Hall, Guisborough (M.P. for South Durham, 1865—1889, J.P. and C.C.), b. at South End, Darlington, June 23, 1828, son of Joseph Pease and his wife Emma Gurney; m. at Falmouth, Aug. 23, 1854, Mary, dau. of Alfred Fox and his wife Sarah Lloyd .

PELLY, EDMUND; m. Emma Mary, dau. of John Fowler and his wife Eliz. Lucy, dau. of Joseph and Emma Pease 9

PELLY, JOHN GURNEY; m. Jane Gurney, dau. of Charles Albert Leatham and his wife Rachel, dau. of Joseph and Emma Pease 9

PICKERING, NATHAN, b. at Whitby, 1713, son of Wm. and Grace Pickering; m. at Stainton Dale, Dec. 6, 1740, Jael, dau. of John Ward and his wife Mary Richardson 1

PRICE, CHARLES STRUVE, son of Henry Habberley Price, of the Rhydding, Swansea; m. at Neath, Aug. 7, 1856, Hannah Isabella, dau. of Joshua Richardson and his wife Hannah Burt 6

PRICE, HENRY H., son of Henry H. Price; m. at Neath, March 10, 1864, Mary Eliz., daughter of Joshua Richardson and his wife Hannah Burt . . 6

PRIESTMAN, SAMUEL, b. at Thornton, Feb. 21, 1800, son of Joshua and Hannah Priestman; m. at Pickering, July 2, 1823, Rachel, dau. of William Rowntree of Riseborough and his wife Rachel, dau. of Nicholas and Dorothy Richardson . 4

PRIESTMAN, THOMAS, son of Samuel Priestman of Hull and his 2nd wife Mary Ann Dent; m. Aug. 25, 1870, Caroline, dau. of Joseph Stickney and his wife Eliza Mennell 4

PROCTER, EDMUND, b. at Willington-on-Tyne, Dec. 21, 1839, son of Joseph Procter and his wife Eliz. Carr; m. at Newcastle, July 28, 1869, Alice, dau. of James Watson of Hawick, N.B., and his wife Mary Spence of North Shields . . 6

PROCTER, EMMANUEL, of Clifford, Tadcaster, and afterwards of Yarm, b. Dec. 20, 1679, son of Stephen Procter of Cowton, afterwards of Pallathorpe Hall, near Tadcaster; m. (1st) at Selby, Feb. 28, 1709, Rebecca Collier; (2ndly) at York, Barbara, dau. of Thomas Conyers of Heworth, York . . . Chap. IX.

TABLE

PROCTER, HENRY RICHARDSON, F.C.S., Author of 'Text-Book on Tanning,' &c., b. at the Low Lights, May 6, 1848, son of John R. Procter and his wife Lydia Richardson; m. Oct. 20, 1874, Emma Lindsay, youngest dau. of James Watson and his wife Mary Spence 6

PROCTER, JOHN, b. at Willington, March 22, 1845, son of Joseph and Eliz. Procter; m. at Basingstoke, Eliz., dau. of Jas. Stevens and his wife Sarah Hewitt Gregory 6

PROCTER, JOHN R. (River Tyne Commissioner, &c)., b. at North Shields, Sept. 26, 1812, son of Joseph Procter and his wife Eliz. Richardson; m. at York, June 16, 1847, Lydia, dau. of Wm. Richardson, of Cherry Hill, and his wife Martha, dau. of Daniel and Lydia Mildred of London 6

PROCTER, JOHN WM., of York, b. at the Low Lights, Sept. 28, 1849, son of John R. and Lydia Procter; m. July 11, 1877, Eliz. Dymond 6

PROCTER, JOSEPH, b. at Clifford, Jan. 27, 1730, son of Emmanuel Procter and his wife Barbara Conyers; m. (1st) at Scarborough, 1755, Eliz. Milner; (2ndly) at Yarm, May 16, 1760, Jane, widow of Andrew Wheldon and dau. of Benjamin and Barbara Flounders of Crathorne, near Yarm . . . Chap. IX.

PROCTER, JOSEPH, b. at Yarm, May 3, 1772, son of Joseph and Jane Procter; m. at North Shields, May 15, 1799, Eliz., dau. of John Richardson of the Low Lights, and his 1st wife Margaret Stead 6

PROCTER, JOSEPH, b. at North Shields, Feb. 25, 1800, son of Joseph Procter and his wife Eliz. Richardson; m. at Kendal, Aug. 9, 1831, Eliz. dau. of Jonathan and Jane Carr 6

PROCTER, STEPHEN, b. at Clifford, near Tadcaster, about 1658, son of Thomas Procter, Yeoman, of Clifford; m. at York, March 1, 1679, Sarah Whitten of York . . . . Chap. IX.

PUMPHREY, GEORGE R., b. at Worcester, June 30, 1830, son of Thos. Pumphrey and his wife Rachel Richardson; m. at Malton, Aug. 1, 1861, Hannah Maria, dau. of Abraham Sewell and his wife Dorothy Stickney . . . 4, 6

PUMPHREY, THOS., Superintendent of Ackworth School, b. at Worcester, June 10, 1802, son of Stanley and Ann Pumphrey; m. (1st) at Newcastle, Nov. 10, 1826, Rachel, dau. of George Richardson and his wife Eleanor Watson; (2ndly) at North Shields, Dec. 11, 1845, to Isabel, dau. of Joseph Unthank and his wife Margaret Richardson 6

PUMPHREY, THOS., b. at Worcester, Sept. 9, 1832, son of Thos. and Rachel Pumphrey; m. at Newcastle, Aug. 24, 1858, Emma, dau. of John Richardson and his wife Sarah Balkwill 6

RAMSBOTHAM, HERWALD; m. Ethel Margaret, dau. of Thos. Bevan and his wife Emma Bayes 5

RHEAM, HENRY CASSON, b. at Hull, Dec. 13, 1836, son of Edward Rheam and his wife Eliz. Casson; m. at Hull, Jan. 21, 1857, Mary, dau. of Joseph and Eliza Stickney 4

RHEAM, WM., b. at Hull, July 27, 1831, son of Edward and Eliz. Rheam; m. Oct. 28, 1858, Lucy, dau. of Joseph and Eliza Stickney 4

RHUDAL, —, Wine Merchant of London; m. about 1810, Rachel Isabel, dau. of Aaron Richardson of Whitby and afterwards of Lynn, Norfolk, and his wife Mary Postglove of Lynn 8

TABLE

RICHARDSON, AARON, b. at Whitby, Nov. 20, 1747, youngest son of Isaac Richardson and his wife Isabel Vasie; m. Mary, dau. of Robert and Rachel Postglove of Lynn 8

RICHARDSON, AARON, b. at Stockton, Dec. 7, 1775, son of Henry Richardson and his wife Hannah Priestman; m. Aug. 2, 1804, Deborah, dau. of Thos. and Alice Procter . 8

RICHARDSON, the Rev. ALFRED, b. in the North of Ireland; m. Emma, dau. of Chas. Albert and Rachel Leatham 9

RICHARDSON, ARTHUR, b. at Langbarugh, Sept. 18, 1841, son of John R. and his wife Jane Procter; m. at Islington, Nov. 24, 1870, Ellen Sophia, dau. of Daniel Messent of Bardfield, Essex 2

RICHARDSON, CALEB, Miller, b. at Sunderland, March 14, 1796, son of John R. and his first wife Hannah Wilson; m. at Leeds, April 26, 1827, Mary, dau. of John and Frances Driver 6

RICHARDSON, CHAS. STANSFIELD, b. at Sunderland, June 11, 1836, son of Wm. R. and his wife Eliza Brown; m. at Bayford Hall, near Hertford, May 1, 1861, Florence Sophia Hensley 6

RICHARDSON, DAVID, Leather Manufacturer (V.-P.U.K. Alliance), b. at Newcastle, March 3, 1835, son of John R. and his wife Sarah Balkwill; m. at Culmstock, Devon, July 10, 1861, Catherine, dau. of Robert and Jane Fry . . 6

RICHARDSON, EDWARD, Tanner, b. Jan. 12, 1806, son of Isaac R. and his wife Deborah Sutton; m. at Edinburgh, April 28, 1830, Jane, dau. of John and Ann Wigham 6

RICHARDSON, EDWIN (Mayor of Sunderland, 1888), b. at Sunderland, Aug. 29, 1834, son of Caleb and Mary Richardson; m. Emma P. Walker, dau. of John Walker of West Brixton 6

RICHARDSON, FREDERICK, b. at Sunderland, Feb. 22, 1837, son of Caleb and Mary Richardson; m. at Cockermouth, Jan. 8, 1861, Sarah Maria, dau. of John Harris 6

RICHARDSON, GEORGE, Author of 'Annals' of Cleveland Richardsons, b. at the Low Lights, Dec. 18, 1773, fourth son of John R. and his wife Margaret Stead; m. at Newcastle, July 17, 1800, Eleanor, dau. of Joshua and Rachel Watson . 6

RICHARDSON, GEORGE, b. at Selby, June, 1845, son of Thos. and Eliz. Richardson; m. at New York, Nov. 14, 1869, Mary, dau. of Thos. and Mary Thistlethwaite of Ackworth 8

RICHARDSON, HENRY, Flax and Iron Merchant, b. at Bog Hall, Whitby, Sept. 10, 1740, son of Isaac R. and his wife Isabel Vasie; m. at Pickering, Aug. 11, 1768, Hannah, only dau. of John and Ann Priestman of Thornton . . 8

RICHARDSON, HENRY, b. at Langbarugh, April 15, 1741, son of John R. and his wife Lydia Vasie; m. at Stockton, Feb. 20, 1772, Eliz., dau. of Joseph and Mary Thornhill 2

RICHARDSON, HENRY (Ed. of 'Peace Advocate'), b. at Newcastle, Sept. 18, 1806, son of Geo. and Eleanor Richardson; m. at Chipping Norton, July 4, 1833, Anna, dau. of Samuel and Esther Atkins 6

RICHARDSON, HENRY, b. at Cherry Hill, Jan. 13, 1814, son of Wm. R. and his wife Martha Mildred; m. at Byham, Jan. 20, 1858, Maria, dau. of John and Eliz. Heath 8

TABLE

RICHARDSON, HENRY. b. at Langbarugh, Sept. 28, 1840, son of John R. and his wife
    Jane Procter: m. Oct. 6, 1864, Emma Maria Crummey   2
RICHARDSON, HENRY (C.C. for Backworth Division of Northumberland and Chair-
    man of Tynemouth Board of Guardians), b. at Newcastle, Aug. 10, 1841, son of
    John R. and his wife Sarah Balkwill; m. Aug. 10, 1865, Emily, dau. of Joseph
    Watson and his wife, Sarah Spence   6
RICHARDSON, ISAAC, Tanner, of Whitby, b. at Ayton, Oct. 18, 1707, youngest son of
    Wm. R. and his wife Eliz. Wilson; m. Feb. 18, 1732, Isabel, dau. of Henry
    Vasie and his wife Mary Mackridge 1, 6, 7, 8
RICHARDSON, ISAAC, of Cherry Hill, York, b. at Bog Hall, Whitby, Dec. 4, 1738,
    2nd son of Isaac R. and his wife Isabel Vasie; m. in London, Jan. 5, 1779,
    Sarah Mayleigh, dau. of Samuel and Sarah Barnes of Clapton .   .   8
RICHARDSON, ISAAC, Tanner, of Newcastle, b. at Seghill, Feb. 11, 1761, eldest son of
    John R. and his wife Margt. Stead; m. Aug. 20, 1795, Deborah, dau. of David
    and Rebecca Sutton   6
RICHARDSON, ISAAC, b. at Stockton, Feb. 5, 1784, son of Henry R. and his wife
    Hannah Priestman; m. at North Shields, Nov. 16, 1837, Mary, dau. of Jos.
    Unthank and his wife Margt. Richardson   8
RICHARDSON, JAMES, Leather Manuf., b. at Newcastle, Sept. 26, 1831, son of
    John R. and his wife Sarah Balkwill; m. June 17, 1857, Augusta Ann,
    dau. of Jeremiah Dixon   6
RICHARDSON, JOHN, of Langbarugh, b. at Ayton, Oct. 8, 1698, eldest son of Wm. R.
    and his wife Eliz. Wilson; m. at Whitby, April 8, 1727, Lydia, dau. of Henry
    Vasie and his wife Mary Mackridge   1
RICHARDSON, JOHN, b. at Ayton, June 27, 1723, son of Wm. R. and his wife Mary
    dau. of Nicholas and Mary Robinson; m. at Ayton, Aug. 2, 1752, Rachel, dau.
    of John and Rachel Snowdon   3
RICHARDSON, JOHN, Tanner and Farmer, of the Low Lights, b. at Bog Hall, Whitby,
    April 1, 1733, eldest son of Isaac R. and his wife Isabel Vasie; m. (1st) at New-
    castle, Jan. 24, 1760, Margt. dau. of John Stead and his wife Margt. Raper;
    (2ndly), June 15, 1785, Jane Nichol, of Longtown, Cumberland .   .   6
RICHARDSON, JOHN, Tanner, of Sunderland, b. at Seghill, March 13, 1765, son of John
    R. and his wife Margaret Stead; m. (1st) at Sunderland, May 8, 1794, Hannah,
    dau. of Caleb and Judith Wilson; (2ndly), at Darlington, Sept. 26, 1804, Mary,
    dau. of John Harrison and his wife Agnes Backhouse, and widow of Joseph
    King of Newcastle; and (3rdly), at Stockton, Oct. 21, 1808, Sarah, widow of
    George Blaxland of Hitchin   6
RICHARDSON, JOHN, b. at Sunderland, March 16, 1795, eldest son of John R. and his
    wife Hannah Wilson; m. at Staindrop, Sept. 27, 1821, Sarah, dau. of George
    and Rachel Dixon of Cockfield   6
RICHARDSON, JOHN, b. at Langbarugh, Sept. 27, 1795; m. (1st) at North Shields,
    Feb. 13, 1833, Jane, dau. of Jos. Procter and his wife Eliz. Richardson; (2ndly),
    at Selby, Feb. 20, 1845, Hannah, dau. of James Procter of Selby   .   2
RICHARDSON, JOHN, Tanner, b. at Newcastle, April 20, 1799, son of Isaac R. and his
    wife Deborah Sutton; m. at Plymouth, Oct. 5, 1825, Sarah, dau. of Benjamin
    and Eliz. Balkwill   6

TABLE

RICHARDSON, JOHN GEORGE, Chemical Manuf., of Monkton, b. at Sunderland,
Jan. 20, 1841, son of Wm. R. and his wife Eliza Brown; m. at Sherston, Wilts,
Oct. 31, 1866, Eliz. Ann, dau. of Edmund and Mary Rich   .   .   . 6

RICHARDSON, JOHN WIGHAM, Ship-builder on the Tyne, b. at Torquay, Jan. 7, 1837,
son of Edward R. and his wife Jane Wigham; m. at Brixton, April 12,
1864,Marianne Henrietta, dau. of John Philip Thöl and his wife Agnes Augusta
Popert   6

RICHARDSON, JOHN WINN, b. at Sunderland, April 9, 1828, eldest son of Caleb R. and
his wife Mary Driver; m. at Warborough, Oxon, Sept. 26, 1860, Mary, dau. of
James Green of Shillington   6

RICHARDSON, JOSEPH, of New York, b. at Darlington, Nov. 18, 1783, son of Robert R.
and his wife Caroline Garth; m. at Stockton, Mary Ann Perkins   .   . 9

RICHARDSON, JOSEPH, of Potto Hall, Northallerton (J.P. for Co. York, High Sheriff
of Durham, 1887), b. at Sunderland, Jan. 15, 1830, son of Caleb R. and his wife
Mary Driver; m. at Stockton, Dec. 18, 1856, Ann Eliza, dau. of Frederick
Backhouse and his wife Eliza Fossick 5, 6

RICHARDSON, JOSEPH HANCOCK, Chemist, b. at Newcastle, Feb. 8, 1844, son of John
Richardson and his wife Sarah Balkwill; m. at Plymouth, May 5, 1868, Anna
Mary, dau. of Joseph Hancock and Ann Balkwill   6

RICHARDSON, JOSHUA, Civil Engineer, of Neath, b. at Sunderland, Feb. 10, 1799, son
of John R. and his 1st wife Hannah Wilson; m. Hannah, dau. of Thos. and
Isabella Burt of Newcastle   6

RICHARDSON, NICHOLAS, b. at Ayton, July 25, 1730, son of William R. and his 1st
wife Mary, dau. of Nicholas and Mary Robinson of Rounton in Cleveland;
m. at Masham, April 15, 1760, Dorothy, dau. of John and Esther Kilden   . 4

RICHARDSON, RICHARD, b. at Hull, April 21, 1686, bap. May 1, 1686, son of Thos. R.
(4th of that name in Hull) and his wife Mary, dau. of Richard Mayson and
Mary Richardson; m. at Whitby, April 11, 1735, Lydia, youngest dau. of Wm. R.
of Ayton and his wife Eliz. Wilson   9

RICHARDSON, RICHARD, b. at Darlington, Feb. 26, 1769, son of Robert R. and his wife
Caroline Garth; m. in the Isle of Thanet, Jan. 1, 1799, Sarah Buxell   .   . 9

RICHARDSON, ROBERT, b. at Darlington, Oct. 15, 1741, son of Richard and Lydia
Richardson; m. Caroline Garth   9

RICHARDSON, SAMUEL, b. in London, Oct. 30, 1779, son of Isaac R. and his wife
Sarah Mayleigh, dau. of Samuel and Sarah Barnes of Clapton; m. at Fordingbridge, Hants, Eliz. Robinson   8

RICHARDSON, STANSFIELD, b. at Sunderland, Dec. 25, 1840, son of Caleb and Mary R.;
m. at Bray, Co. Wicklow, Anita Mary, dau. of James Pim, jun., Killarney
Wood, Bray   6

RICHARDSON, THOS., one of the founders of the firm of Richardson, Overend & Gurney,
b. at Darlington, Sept. 15, 1771, son of Robert R. and his wife Caroline Garth;
m. in London, Oct. 15, 1799, Martha, dau. of John and Martha Beeby, of Allonby,
Cumberland 9

RICHARDSON, THOS., b. at Stockton, Dec. 7, 1775, son of Aaron R. and his wife
Deborah Procter; m. at Selby, June 14, 1842, Eliz., dau. of Jacob and Hannah
Jones   9

TABLE

RICHARDSON, THOS., b. in London, Oct. 17, 1816, son of Joseph R. and his wife
Mary Ann Perkins; m. (1st) at Everton, Lanc., May 3, 1843, Susan Annette,
dau. of Gamaliel and Susan Skidmore; (2ndly), at Chattanooga, Tennessee,
Nov. 11, 1866, Josephine M. dau. of Wm. H. and Eliza A. Oakman of Bain ell
District, South Carolina 9

RICHARDSON, THOS., b. at Market-town, Ulster Co., New York, July 18, 1846, son of
Thos. R. and his wife Susan Annette Skidmore; m. at Chattanooga, Dec 25,
1869, Ellen M., dau. of Wm. and Rachel Hagood of Bainwell, S. C. . . 9

RICHARDSON, WM., Tanner, of Ayton; m. at Lythe Church, Whitby, July 31, 1684,
to Eliz. Wilson 1

RICHARDSON, WM., b, at Ayton, 1700, 2nd son of Wm. R. and his wife Eliz. Wilson;
m. (1st) at Yarm, Sept. 13, 1722, Mary, dau. of Nicholas and Mary Robinson of
Rounton, in Cleveland; and (2ndly) at Ayton, April 7, 1772, Mary, widow of
Joseph Thornhill 1, 3

RICHARDSON, WM., b. at Ayton, Sept. 20, 1724, son of Wm. R. and his wife Mary
Robinson; m. (1st) at Whitby, Jan. 4, 1764, Ann, dau. of John and Margaret
Hill; (2ndly) at Ayton, Jan. 17, 1777, Ann, dau. of John Bellerby . . 3

RICHARDSON, WM., b. at Langbarugh, Nov. 21, 1736, son of John R. and his wife
Lydia Vasie; m. at Ayton, Nov. 21, 1774, Mary, dau. of Mary Hart and her
former husband, John Muskett of Newton, Norfolk 2

RICHARDSON, WM., b. at Bog Hall, Whitby, March 7, 1742, fourth son of Isaac R.
and his wife Isabel Vasie; m. (1st) at Scarboro', May 8, 1771, Mary, dau. of
Robert and Ann Dale; (2ndly), Eliz. Reay of Alston 8

RICHARDSON, WM., b. at Whitby, May 24, 1772, son of Wm. R. and his wife Mary
Dale; m. at York, Oct. 31, 1793, Ann Mercy, dau. of Nathaniel and Judith Bell . 8

RICHARDSON, WM., b. at Low Lights, Sept. 13, 1771, third son of John R. and his
wife Margaret Stead; m. (1st) at York, May 9, 1804, Sarah, dau. of Thos. and
Sarah Priestman of Mary Gate; and (2ndly) at Sunderland, June 18, 1817,
Margaret, dau. of Thos. Robson and his wife Margaret, dau. of Edward and
Eliz. Pease 6

RICHARDSON, WM., b. in London, June 11, 1781, son of Isaac R. and his wife Sarah
Mayleigh Barnes; m. at Tottenham, Oct. 17, 1811, Martha, dau. of Daniel and
Lydia Mildred 8

RICHARDSON, WM., Miller and Tanner, b. at Sunderland, June 3, 1801, son of John R.
and his 1st wife Hannah Wilson; m. at St. Ives, Hunts., May 7, 1828, Eliza,
dau. of Wm. and Eliz. Brown of Houghton 6

RICHARDSON, WM., of Darlington, b. at (New) Langbarugh, June 6, 1836, eldest son
of John R. and his wife Jane Procter; m. at Staines, May 19, 1859, Mary Anne,
dau. of Edward Ashby and his wife Mary Anne Dudley 2

RICHARDSON, WM. DUDLEY, b. at Darlington, Jan. 15, 1862, eldest son of Wm. R. and
his wife Mary Anne Ashby; m. in 1887, Harriet Hern of Ashburton, Devon . 2

RICHARDSON, WM. HENRY, Paper Manuf., of Monkton (J.P., and Chairman of Jarrow
School Board), b. at Sunderland, April 30, 1829, son of Wm. R. and his wife
Eliza Brown; m. (1st) at Ross, Herefords., June 16, 1852, Lucy Smart, dau. of
Thos. and Hannah Trusted; (2ndly) Anne, dau. of Joseph Foster and his wife
Eliz. Taylor 6

RICKMAN, SAMUEL, b. at Liverpool, Jan. 3, 1846, eldest son of Samuel Rickman; m. April 17, 1873, Emily Rachel, dau. of Charles Binns, of Clay Cross Hall, Lancashire, and his first wife Eliz. Walmsley 4

RIDDELL, WM., of Glasgow; m. at Ayton, April, 1841, Rachel, dau. of Wm. Armstrong and his wife Hannah Martin 3

ROBSON, WALTER, b. at North Shields, son of Edward and Mary Robson; m. 1873, Jane Elizabeth, dau. of Ingram Chapman Watson and his wife Jane Spence 7

ROSS, CHAS.; m. Gertrude Maud, dau. of Thomas Bevan and his wife Emma Bayes 5

ROWNTREE, CHAS. JOHN, b. Dec. 23, 1846, son of Wm. Rowntree and his wife Ann Cooke; m. at Scarborough, June 20, 1871, Mary de Horne, dau. of Chas. Brightwen of Newcastle 4

ROWNTREE, HENRY, b. at Calverley, June 28, 1835, son of Isaac and Sarah Rowntree; m. at Youghal, Ireland, Charlotte, dau. of Peter Moore and his wife Margaret Ann Fisher 4

ROWNTREE, HENRY ISAAC, b. at York, Feb. 11, 1838, 3rd son of Joseph and Sarah Rowntree; m. at Scarborough, Feb. 25, 1868, Harriet Selina, dau. of Wm. Osborne of York 5

ROWNTREE, ISAAC, b. at Riseborough, Dec. 20, 1796, son of Wm. Rowntree and his wife Rachel Richardson; m. at Malton, Aug. 4, 1823, Sarah, dau. of Richard and Sarah Smithson 4

ROWNTREE, JOHN SMITHSON, b. at Calverley, Jan. 3, 1827, son of Isaac and Sarah Rowntree; m. at York, Aug. 23, 1858, Lavinia Emily, dau. of Matthew and Isoline Todd 4

ROWNTREE, JOHN STEPHENSON (Lord Mayor of York, 1880), b. at York, May, 1834, eldest son of Joseph and Sarah Rowntree; m. (1st) at Leeds, Aug. 25, 1858, Elizabeth, dau. of James and Sarah Hotham; (2ndly), at Sheffield, April 10, 1878, Helen, dau. of Daniel and Maria Doncaster 5

ROWNTREE, JOSEPH, b. at Scarborough, June 10, 1801, son of John Rowntree and his wife Elizabeth Lotherington; m. at Manchester, May 3, 1832, Sarah, dau. of Isaac Stephenson and his wife Hannah Masterman 5

ROWNTREE, JOSEPH, b. at York, May 4, 1836, son of Joseph and Sarah Rowntree; m. (1st) at Luton, Aug. 15, 1862, Julia Elizabeth, dau. of Benjamin and Esther Seebohm; (2ndly) at Hitchin, Nov. 14, 1867, Emma Antoinette, dau. of Wilhelm Seebohm of Hamburg 5

ROWNTREE, RICHARDSON, b. at Riseborough, Dec. 4, 1801, son of Wm. Rowntree and his wife Rachel Richardson; m. at Pickering, Oct. 1, 1834, Rachel, dau. of Joshua and Hannah Priestman of Thornton 4

ROWNTREE, WM., b. at Riseborough, April 27, 1768, son of Wm. and Hannah Rowntree; m. at Ayton, July 23, 1794, Rachel, dau. of Nicholas Richardson and his wife Dorothy Kilden 4

ROWNTREE, WM., b. at Riseborough, April 3, 1798, son of Wm. Rowntree and his wife Rachel Richardson; m. at Liverpool, April 5, 1838, Ann, dau. of John and Mary Cooke, of Millbank, West Derby 4

TABLE

SCARR, JOHN, b. at Yarescott, Sept. 14, 1786, son of George and Patience Scarr; m. at Kirby Moorside, June 5, 1812, Hannah, dau. of Caleb Fletcher and his wife Elizabeth Masterman 5

SEWELL, ABRAHAM, b. at Great Yarmouth, Aug. 22, 1789, son of Wm. and Hannah Maria Sewell of Ipswich; m. at Oustwick, Yorks., March 22, 1814, Dorothy, dau. of Wm. Stickney and his wife Esther Richardson 4

SEWELL, EDWARD FULLER, b. at Yarmouth, Aug. 10, 1822, son of Abraham Sewell and his wife Dorothy Stickney; m. at Malton, May 10, 1855, Sarah Jane, dau of Joseph and Sarah Taylor 4

SEWELL, JOSEPH STICKNEY, Missionary in Madagascar, b. at Yarmouth, Dec. 30, 1819, son of Abraham Sewell and his wife Dorothy Stickney; m. at Pickering, Nov. 1, 1843, Mary Ann, dau. of James and Mary Ellis of Thornton . . . 4

SEWELL, JOSEPH TAYLOR, b. at Whitby, Jan. 1, 1857, son of Edward Fuller Sewell and his wife Sarah Jane Taylor; m. at York, 1885, Agnes Harrison, dau. of Henry King and his wife Sarah Casson 2, 4

SHARP, ISAAC, b. at Brighton, July 4, 1806, son of Isaac and Mary Sharp; m. at North Shields, Feb. 6, 1839, Hannah, dau. of Joseph Procter and his wife Elizabeth Richardson 6

SIDDALL, JOSEPH BOWER, b. at Matlock, March 4, 1840, son of George and Mary Siddall; m. at Yokohama, Japan, Feb. 5, 1870, Mary Eliz. dau. of Charles Binns and his 1st wife Eliz., dau. of Sir Joshua and Lady Walmsley . . . 4

SIMPSON, BENJAMIN; m. at New York, June 8, 1850, Isabella, dau. of Joseph Richardson and his wife Mary Ann Perkins of Stockton 9

SIMPSON, THOS., b. at Pinchinthorpe Hall, 1834, son of Wm. Simpson and his wife Mary Loy; m. Lena Jodin 2

SIMPSON, WM., of Pinchinthorpe Hall, Cleveland; m. Mary, dau. of Thos. Loy, M.D., of Ayton, and his wife Eliz. Richardson of Langbarugh 2

SIMPSON, WM., b. at Pinchinthorpe Hall, 1836, son of Wm. Simpson and his wife Mary Loy; m. Margt. Brown 2

SKINNER, Rev. JAMES, son of Wm. and Mary Skinner of Stockton-on-Tees; m. at Whitby, April 18, 1855, Georgiana Duesbury, dau. of Gideon Smales and his wife Maria Robinson Wakefield of Tynemouth 7

SMALES, CHARLES, b. at Whitby, May 14, 1838, son of Gideon Smales and his wife Maria Robinson Wakefield; m. at Hartlepool, July 29, 1869, Alice, dau. of Jonathan Garbutt 7

SMALES, EDWARD HENRY, b. at Whitby, Sept. 6, 1843, son of Gideon Smales and his wife Maria Robinson Wakefield; m. at Whitby, Sept. 9, 1869, Annie, dau. of Wm. Frankland 7

SMALES, GEORGE WAKEFIELD, b. at Whitby, April 7, 1833, son of Gideon Smales and his wife Maria Robinson Wakefield; m. at Whitby, June 5, 1861, Sarah Margaret, dau. of Geo. and Dorothy M'Lellan 7

SMALES, GIDEON, b. at Whitby, son of Thos. Smales and his wife Mary, dau. of Gideon Dent and his wife Elizabeth Vaughan; m. at Whitby, Dec. 19, 1792, Hannah, dau. of Ingram Chapman and his wife Elizabeth Richardson . 7

SMALES, GIDEON, b. at Whitby, Aug. 22, 1796, son of Gideon Smales and his wife Hannah Chapman; m. at Tynemouth, April 6, 1820, Maria Robinson, dau. of George Wakefield and his wife Ann Wright 7

TABLE

SMALES, GIDEON, b. at Whitby, April 30, 1821, son of Gideon Smales and his wife
Maria Robinson Wakefield; m. at Whitby, June 29, 1854, Emily, dau. of John
and Ann Campion 7

SMALES, THOMAS CHAPMAN, b. at Whitby, June 17, 1824, son of Gideon Smales and
his wife Maria Robinson Wakefield; m. at Newcastle, Oct. 2, 1849, Mary, dau.
of Wm. Swanston 7

SMALES, WAKEFIELD ROBINSON, b. at Whitby, July 14, 1822, son of Gideon Smales
and his wife M. R. Wakefield; m. at Hartlepool, Jan. 6, 1858, Jane Botcherby of
Darlington 7

SOUTHALL, SAMUEL, son of Thomas and Elizabeth Southall of Leominster; m. Oct.
18, 1785, Sarah, dau. of Samuel Fossick and his wife Sarah Marishall . . 5

SPENCER, ISAAC (twice Lord Mayor of York), b. at York, Dec. 2, 1770, son of Isaac and
Phœbe Spencer; m. Anne, dau. of Wm. Richardson and his wife Mary Dale . 8

SPENCER, REV. ISAAC, M.A., Vicar of Acomb, Yorks., b. at York, Nov. 29, 1795, son
of Isaac Spencer and his wife Ann Richardson; m. at Clontarf Church, Dublin,
Dec. 5, 1824, Martha Harriet, dau. of Wm. Phipps of Clontarf . . . 8

SPENCER, WM. HENRY, Capt. in 6th West York Militia, b. at York, June 11, 1832, son
of Rev. Isaac Spencer and his wife M. H. Phipps; m. at Graham's Town
Cathedral, Oct. 21, 1856, Mary Lamont, dau. of Fred. Lucas, of Graham's Town,
Cape Colony 8

STEAD, JOHN, b. at Ampleforth, in the North Riding of Yorkshire, 1710, son of John
Stead of Craike, and afterwards of Whitby, and his wife Sarah; m. at Stockton-
upon-Tees, May 10, 1738, Margaret, dau. of Geo. Raper of Stockton . Chap. IX.

STEPHENSON, ISAAC, b. at Bridlington Quay, Nov. 15, 1765, son of Isaac and Eliz.
Stephenson; m. at Kirby Moorside, June 7, 1798, Hannah, dau. of James
Masterman and his wife Haunah Fossick 5

STICKNEY, JOSEPH, b. at Ridgmont, Hull, April 6, 1792, son of Wm. Stickney and
his wife Esther Richardson; m. at Scarborough, July 6, 1825, Eliza, dau. of
Isaac Mennell and his wife Martha Dearman of Thorne 4

STICKNEY, WALTER MENNELL, b. at Ridgmont, Dec. 1, 1846, son of Joseph and Eliza
Stickney; m. at Hull, Sophia Helena, dau. of Alfred H. West and his wife
Sarah Ann Petchell . . . .

STICKNEY, WILLIAM, b. Sept. 20, 1764, son of Ambrose Stickney and his wife
Rachel Turner, and grandson of Ambrose Stickney and his wife Rachel, dau. of
John Richardson of Hutton-in-the-Hole; m. at Ayton, Sept. 22, 1788, Esther,
dau. of Nicholas Richardson and his wife Dorothy Kilden . . . 4

STURGE, JOHN EDMUND, of Montserrat, b. at Charlbury, son of Edmund and Lydia
Sturge; m. at Newcastle, 1873, Jane, youngest dau. of John Richardson and his
wife Sarah Balkwill 6

SWANSON, GEORGE ISLES, M.D.; m. at Thirsk, Ellen, dau. of John Baker and his
wife Mary Gilbert 9

SWIFT, FREDRICK; m. Ann, dau. of John Irving and his wife Anna Masterman . 5

TAYLOR, HENRY, b. at New Malton, Feb. 17, 1829, son of Joseph and Sarah Taylor;
m. Jan. 21, 1858, at Malton, Eliz., dau. of Richardson Rowntree and his wife
Rachel Priestman of Thornton 4

TABLE

TINDALL, ENOCH OLDFIELD, b. at Scarborough, son of John and Alice Tindall; m. at
    Bradford, May 21, 1861, Mary, dau. of Isaac Rowntree and his wife Sarah Smithson   4
TRISTON, JOHN HORRELL; m. Lydia, dau. of John Irving and his wife Anna
    Masterman   5
TUKE, DANIEL HACK, M.D., Author of 'Hist. of the Insane in England,' &c., b. at
    York, April 19, 1827, son of Samuel Tuke and his wife Priscilla Hack; m. at
    Pickering, Aug. 10, 1853, Esther Maria, dau. of Joseph and Eliza Stickney   .   4
TUKE, JOHN, b. at Bishop Auckland, Nov. 22, 1848; m. at Salford, Dec. 1, 1868, Eliz.,
    dau. of Isaac Raisbeck Martin and his wife Jane Anderson of North Shields   .   3

UNTHANK, GEORGE, b. at Whitby, June 22, 1792, son of Joseph Unthank and his wife
    Margaret Richardson; m. at Castleton, in Danby Dale, July 25, 1832, Mary,
    dau. of John and Mary Baker   6
UNTHANK, JOSEPH, b. at Castleton, Oct. 17, 1762, son of George and Eliz. Unthank;
    m. at Newcastle-on-Tyne, Aug. 10, 1791, Margaret, dau. of John Richardson
    and his wife Margaret Stead   6
UNTHANK, JOSEPH, b. at Willington-on-Tyne, March 18, 1834, son of George and
    Mary Unthank; m. in London, 1888, Eliz. Parley   6

VASIE, HENRY; m. at Whitby, Feb. 4, 1688, Mary Mackridge   .   .   Chap. III.
VESEY, ARTHUR DAVID, b. at Huntingdon, Jan. 14, 1825, son of David Vesey and
    his wife Eliz. Chapman; m. at Ancaster, Sept. 11, 1851, Emily Persis Allix of
    Willoughby Hall   7
VESEY, DAVID, b. at Huntingdon, Dec. 11, 1791, son of David and Anna Vesey;
    m. at Whitby, Oct. 10, 1817, Eliz., dau. of Ingram Chapman and his wife Jane,
    dau. of John Chapman and his wife Jane Mellor   7
VESEY, FRANCIS GERALD, LL.D., Honorary Canon of Ely, Archdeacon of Huntingdon,
    b. at Huntingdon, July 15, 1832, son of David Vesey and his wife Elizabeth
    Chapman; m. at Sullington, Sussex, Aug, 26, 1868, Annie, dau. of Rev. G.
    Palmer, Rector of Sullington   7

WALLER, —, of London; m. Eliz., dau. of Timothy Chadwick and his wife Rebecca
    Richardson   1
WALLOP, ISAAC NEWTON, Viscount LYMINGTON, eldest son of the Earl and Countess
    of Portsmouth; m. Beatrice Mary, only child of Edward Pease and his wife
    Sarah Sturge   9
WARD, JOHN, b. at Whitby, Jan. 9, 1680, son of John and Sarah Ward; m. at
    Broughton, Yorks., Jan. 5, 1707, Mary, eldest dau. of William Richardson and
    his wife Eliz. Wilson   1
WATSON, HUGH, b. at Staindrop, May 3, 1783, eldest son of Michael and Ann
    Watson; m. Martha Evans   7
WATSON, INGRAM CHAPMAN, b. at North Shields, Sept. 19, 1794, son of Michael and
    Ann Watson; m. Sept. 17, 1842, Jane, dau. of Robert Spence   .   .   7
WATSON, MICHAEL, b. at Staindrop, Sept. 29, 1749, son of Hugh and Anna Watson,
    of Raby; m. at Whitby, June 5, 1782, Ann, dau. of Ingram Chapman and his
    wife Elizabeth Richardson   7

TABLE

WATSON, MICHAEL, b. at Whitby, May 21, 1788, son of Michael and Ann Watson; m. at Thirsk, Sept. 10, 1833, Eliz., dau. of Wm. Richardson and his 2nd wife Elizabeth Reay 7

WATSON, ROBERT SPENCE, LL.D., b. at Gateshead, June 8, 1837, eldest son of Joseph Watson and his wife Sarah Spence; m. June 9, 1863, Eliz., dau. of Edward Richardson and his wife Jane Wigham 6

WEBSTER, CALEB, son of Caleb and Mary Webster; m. at Ayton, April 23, 1736, Mary, dau. of William Richardson and his wife Mary Robinson . . . 4

WEBSTER, THOMAS W., b. at Whitby, Feb. 4, 1768, son of Caleb Webster and his wife Mary Richardson; m. Ann — ? 4

WHITE, ISAAC, of Ayton; m. Jane, dau. of Robert Richardson and his wife Caroline Garth, and widow of John Gilbert of Newcastle 9

WHITE, JOHN GREGORY, M.D., of Bournemouth, b. at Apsley Guise, Beds., Jan. 23, 1838, son of Richard Edward and Mary White; m. at Newcastle, Aug. 22, 1866, Jane Emily, dau. of Edward and Jane Richardson 6

WILCOX, FRED. HUME, son of Wm. Wilcox and his wife Mary Ann Marwood, of Busby Hall, Cleveland; m. June 22, 1872, Annie, dau. of Thos. Loy, M.A., and his wife Eliz. Jackson 2

WILFORD, JOSEPH, b. at Brompton, Northallerton, Dec. 19, 1812, son of John Wilford; m. at Newcastle, Feb. 2, 1846, Mary, dau. of John Martin and his wife Sarah Raisbeck 3

WILSON, HENRY L.; m. at Glasgow, Hannah, dau. of William Armstrong and his wife Hannah Martin 3

WILSON, JOSHUA, b. at Sunderland, Sept. 2, 1769, son of Caleb and Judith Wilson; m. at Ayton, Sept. 30, 1802, Mary, eldest dau. of William Richardson of Langbarugh, and his wife Mary Muskett 2

WILSON, WM. JOHN, b. at Kendal, Dec. 29, 1834, son of Isaac and Fanny Wilson; m. at Clay Cross, Aug. 13, 1863, Adeline, dau. of Charles Binns and his wife Eliz. Walmsley 4

WOOD, WILLIAM, b. at Berwick, Dec. 26, 1827, son of Andrew Wood; m. at Ayton, July 7, 1870, Sarah Jane, dau. of John Richardson of Langbarugh and his wife Jane Procter 2

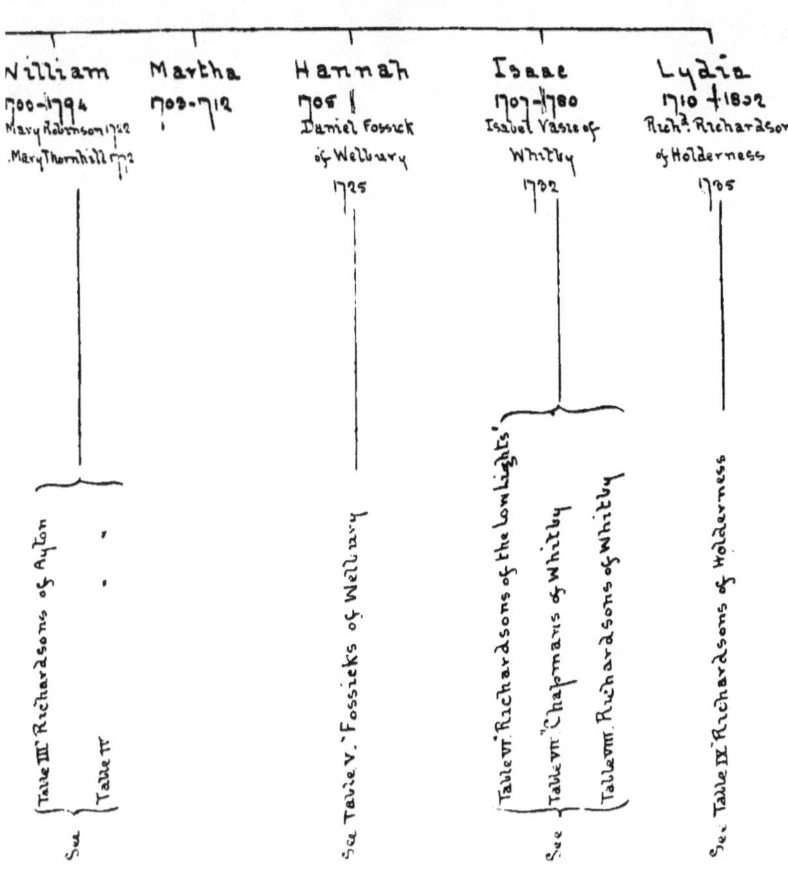
ilson

William
1700-1794
Mary Robinson 1742
Mary Thornhill 1752

Martha
1703-1712

Hannah
1705
Daniel Fossick
of Welbury
1725

Isaac
1707-1780
Isabel Vasie of
Whitby
1732

Lydia
1710 +1832
Richd. Richardson
of Holderness
1735

See { Table III Richardsons of Ayton
      Table IV

See Table V. Fossicks of Welbury

See { Table VI. Richardsons of the Lowlights
      Table VII. Chapmans of Whitby
      Table VIII. Richardsons of Whitby

See Table IX Richardsons of Holderness

RICHARDSONS of CLEVELAND

William Richardson of Great Ayton, married, at ... Church, ...

Elizabeth	Rachel		Ann	Rebecca	Sarah	John	William	Martha	Hannah	Isaac	Lydia

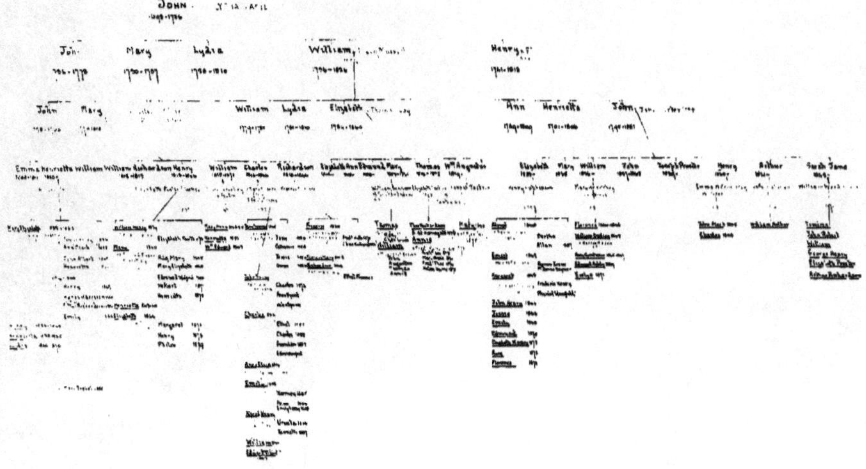

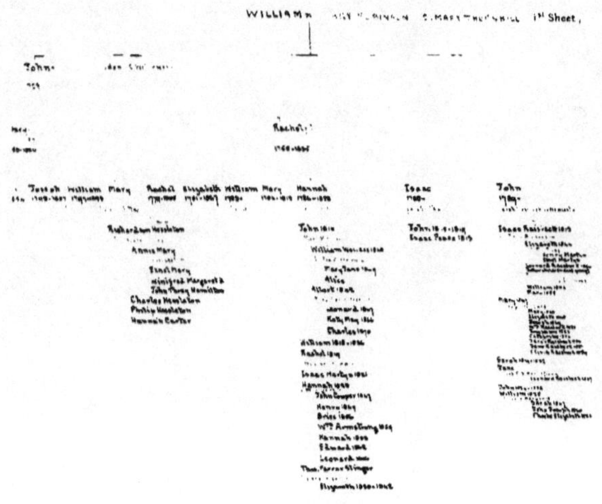
RICHARDSONS of AYTON
WILLIAM R.   1st Sheet,
John
Rachel
1766-1845
Joseph   William   Mary   Rachel   Elizabeth   William   Mary   Hannah
Richardson Middleton
Annie Mary
John 1810
William
Isaac
John

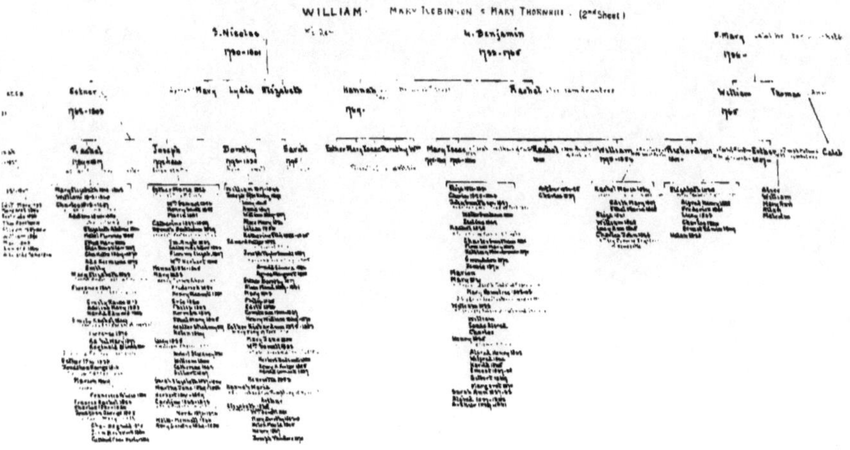

WILLIAM · MARY ROBINSON & MARY THORNHILL . (2nd Sheet)

3. Nicolas
1750-1801

4. Benjamin
1752-1765

5. Mary
1756-

Esther
1758-1805

Mary   Lydia   Elizabeth

Hannah
1749-

Rachel

William   Thomas   Ann
1755-

FOSSICKS OF WETBURY

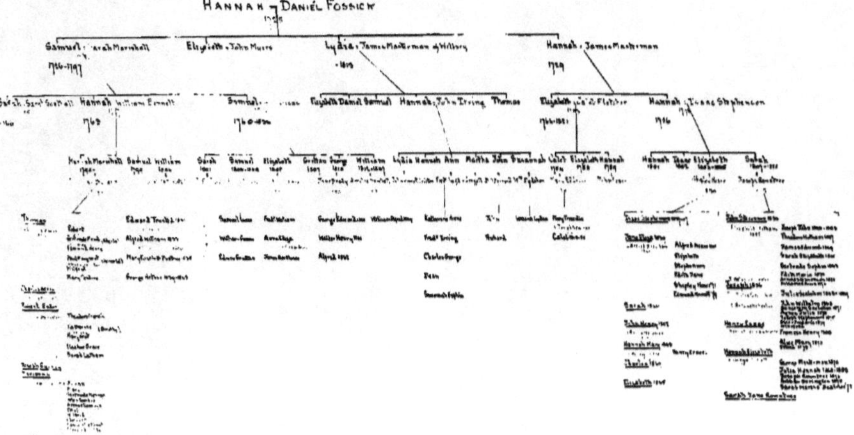

RICHARDSONS of THE LOW LIGHTS

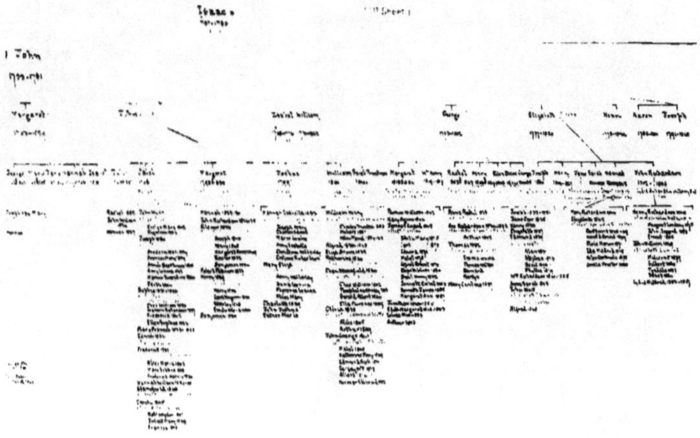

CHAPMANS of WHITBY

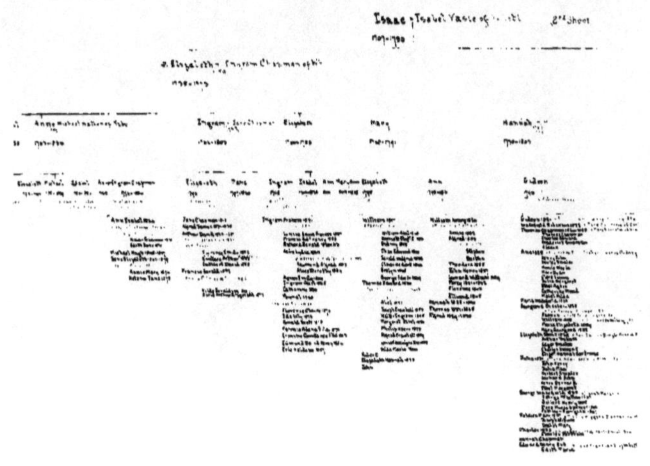

RICHARDSONS of WHITBY

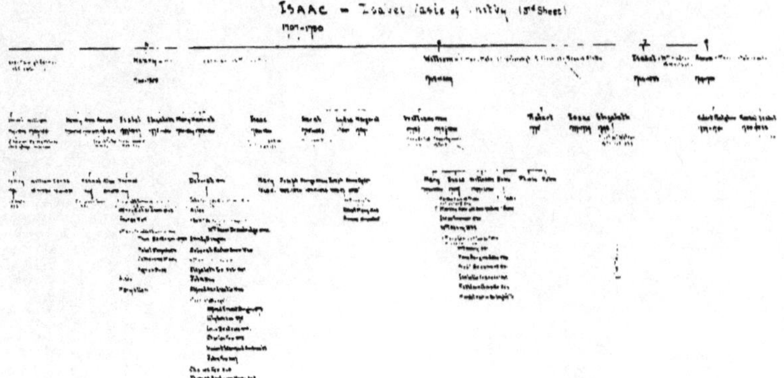

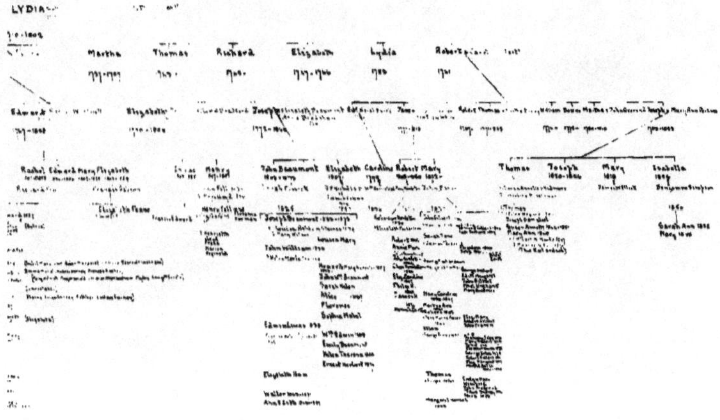
LYDIA
Martha
Thomas
Richard
Elizabeth
Lydia
Robert
Edward
Elizabeth
Joseph
John Beaumont
Elizabeth
Caroline
Robert
Mary
Thomas
Joseph
Mary
Isabella